LEGAL METHOD AND THE RULE OF LAW

Law and Philosophy Library

VOLUME 59

The titles published in this series are listed at the end of this volume.

LEGAL METHOD AND THE RULE OF LAW

by
SEBASTIAN URBINA
*Professor titular de Filosofia del Derecho Universidad Illes Balears,
Palma de Mallorca*

KLUWER LAW INTERNATIONAL
THE HAGUE / LONDON / NEW YORK

A C.I.P. Catalogue record for this book is available from the Library of Congress.

ISBN 90-411-1870-5

Published by Kluwer Law International,
P.O. Box 85889, 2508 CN The Hague, The Netherlands.

Sold and distributed in North, Central and South America
by Kluwer Law International,
101 Philip Drive, Norwell, MA 02061, U.S.A.
kluwerlaw@wkap.com

In all other countries, sold and distributed
by Kluwer Law International, Distribution Centre,
P.O. Box 322, 3300 AH Dordrecht, The Netherlands.

Printed on acid-free paper

Printed in the Netherlands.

DEDICATION

To my daughters Marian and Marta

TABLE OF CONTENTS

INTRODUCTION

Although the chapters of this book are placed in a chronological order this aspect is not what matters most. In this sense, the order only shows the evolution (if any) of the author. In my view, what matters most is the set of common features that underlie these works. These common features, basically, are methodological and ideological. Roughly speaking, the methodology is analytical hermeneutic. I am not going to explain at length, now, what is already developed in the book. It is enough to say that I am placed not in the Galilean tradition, based on explanation, but in the Aristotelian tradition, based on understanding. At the same time, I am not within the legal positivist tradition (more specifically, within methodological legal positivism, which I take to be the "best" within the legal positivist tradition) but share a post-positivist view. The ideological stance is better seen in the chapter related to the Rule of Law. I think it shows a concern for certain conceptions of freedom and equality that are close to the first of Rawl's main works *A Theory of Justice*.

In this respect, I owe a deep intellectual debt towards A. Aarnio, A. Peczenik and N. MacCormick because they gave me the opportunity to participate in fertile criticism within a cordial and respectful atmosphere. It is clear that the intellectual debt (as any other intellectual debt) cannot be sharply drawn between those who have influenced you and those who have not. Among other reasons because you could not be conscious of the influence some authors have had in your intellectual evolution. Nevertheless, while reading what one has written it is possible to place the author in a certain tendency and, doing so, one can see who, or what tendency, have basically influenced the author. However, this should not be seen as a kind of label, that accompanies the writer for life, but as a kind of inevitable skin. On the contrary, when a researcher does not take the risk of freely searching for the "truth" he is not a researcher any more and becomes an arteriosclerotic academician. Now, I think that the reader will better understand why the term "truth" is placed in inverted commas while reading this book.

In the first chapter, **"On Legal Method"**, it is claimed that we cannot see the world as it is because we face it in a "contaminated" vein. Namely, our conceptual scheme (or a certain interpretation of it) and our biological constitution condition certain perspectives of the world and not others. When we face legal orders and legal method we are placed in a kind of second world that is not possible without the first. Nevertheless, this normative world, let us say second world, has some special features, *inter alia*, the primacy of practical reason over theoretical reason and the primacy of the internal point of view over the external point of view.

Related to these cited features there are others, like "institutional facts", "justification" and "hermeneutics", etcetera, that play an important role for understanding this special part of the reality that we can call "normative legal field". Although it is not a feature of all legal traditions we can say that "legal dogmatics" is a privileged way of knowing our normative object, that is, legal orders and legal rules. One of the problems relates to the word "know". Granted that practical reasoning has the primacy, should we say that we could reach knowledge of legal orders? If our main concern was truth and description (as it is in Physics, for example) we could claim that legal dogmatics can reach truth, granted neutral descriptions of the object.

Unfortunately or not, we are not undertaking an empiricist enterprise. In this vein, our basic epistemological task (as legal scholars) is not to describe properly the reality as it is, or to verify empirical regularities. Why not? Among other reasons because we are not mainly interested in the reality but are interested in the "relevant" reality. One could say that scientists are also interested in some "relevant" reality, granted that they do not search for reality as such but reality according to a given theory. Granted this, there is the following difference. Legal scholars do not basically depend on a theory but on "legal sources", that is, on legal formulations of certain authoritative persons, according to certain procedures, to guide relevant social behaviour holding a coercive institutional apparatus.

If this complex set of legal meanings, values, interests, political power, legitimacy, etcetera, works, legal scholars develop legal theories that try to describe, justify and improve the legal normative object. Why? Because they share, generally speaking, an internal point of view. It means, *inter alia*, that participants are not simply neutral observers of this complex legal set. All this also means that some methods are more adequate than others. What for? In this case, we are not trying to discover the truth of nature or of some aspect of nature. We are trying to live together, *inter alia*, with authoritative rules in order to better solve the problems of co-ordination (any society has) and to better reach some relevant, at least for us, purposes.

Granted this we deal with hermeneutic methods because we, as participants, try to understand this normative field and ourselves, and also because we want to "optimise" this normative field and, in doing so, to "optimise" ourselves and our purposes and expectations. This "optimisation" cannot be properly done without a "commitment" to this normative field, that is, at least with the basic values that, explicitly or implicitly, underlie it. Some values could be seen as instrumental (related to desires) and prudential (related to interests) and both could be considered as consequentialist values. Any legal order also has moral values that, at least according to our cultural world, are seen as ultimate reasons. All these values form a complex stratification that may generate conflicts either within a person or within interpersonal relations.

The above-cited task of optimisation is undertaken both by legal scholars and by judges because they, usually, share the so-called internal point of view. Nevertheless, addressees, in so far as they also share an internal point of view, collaborate in this endless optimisation task. As is clear in the text, I hope, it is not claimed that participants, all the time and in all legal items, behave as a "good man", to use O.W. Holmes's expression. In any case, this normative task cannot be undertaken on the basis of some algorithm. On the contrary, we cannot avoid "judgement" because rules (no matter how many and how perfect they are) are unable to solve in advance all legal conflicts in a justified and acceptable way. At the same time, this social effort to improve or optimise our legal orders channels through "social practices". They state in a more orderly manner the judgements of correctness that underlie certain social actions. This shows the basic and critical commitment of participants in a given practice or some important aspects.

Without this commitment social practices would decline and, probably, disappear. This is related to the cited concept of "optimisation". Granted that social practices relate to legal normative fields they are basically interpretative, that is, they try to reach the "best" interpretation according to a given legal order and this interpretation requires a justificatory reasoning. This justificatory reasoning has to deal not only with posited legal rules but also with positive and critical morality. From this stems the most important source of principles, no matter whether they have been accepted or not (by judges) according to what has been established by a given rule of recognition, because we do not have criteria of validity for legal principles or, if we had them, they could not exhaust any close "list" of principles.

The second chapter, "**Essentialism, Conventionalism and Primacy**", allows me to place myself in a post-positivist methodological point of view. I would say that my concern for a rigorous meta-language is one of the main objectives, but it is neither the only one nor the most important. In this vein, conceptual clarification is a main task of any respectable philosophical work but not the only one. Moreover, methodological issues, that are not neutral, allow me to distance myself from the view that we (as participants) can adopt a neutral-descriptive approach. In other words, that we (as participants) can be neutral observers of a given reality. At the same time, I deny that it is equally important to adopt a neutral-descriptive approach (if this was pragmatically possible), or a constructive-committed one, towards our legal orders. I claim that, legal orders being a practical task, the participant's approach (a constructive-committed one) has primacy over the external one.

We are committed participants (although not necessarily all of us, all the time and for all items of our legal orders) but we also try to describe our legal orders, not for the sake of description, but for viewing better how we are, what has been successful or not, and for solving better our social problems. When we design what we "ought to do" it is a sound attitude to realise where we are. This does not mean that I accept a kind of metaphysical materialism where we are able to "copy" the world outside through our language or certain type of language. From the rejection of this metaphysical materialistic dream one does not need to embrace cultural relativism because I do not accept that the only truth is the "internal truth" of the participants. In this respect I would say: First, in our legal fields we should change "truth" for "correctness", which is a normative concept. Second, our rationality (not in the positivistic-reductionist sense) is related, *inter alia*, to criticism, dialogue and universality. Not to algorithm.

Although I support a participant's approach it should be understood as if it were a parochial one. For example, we do not only believe that "freedom of speech" is good for us but also for any other human being. This would show a claim of universality. Otherwise, the term "better" (related to the task of participants) should not be understood in the abstract sense but as forming part of a social and critical morality of a given society, at a given time. There is, then, a dynamic interplay between our "internal truth" of participants and the search for universality.

In this chapter, therefore, I claim that the practical features of the object (legal orders) require the primacy of the internal point of view over the external one. It does not mean that the descriptive approach is of no use for participants. On the contrary, participants are especially interested in the good working of their legal orders, and description is a good tool for better fulfilling their goals and to check what has been done according to previous plans and expectations. Participants are also "realists" in this sense. However, our legal object, a legal normative field, is a dynamic object. We should firmly adapt our present "is" to the permanent modification of the reality or parts of it. Moreover, this also explains why the polemics between natural law writers and legal positivists has not been a sterile one, as some legal scholars believe.

In chapter three, "**Identification of Legal Orders**", I try to show that it is not possible (pragmatically speaking) to identify legal rules only on the basis of syntactical criteria. This legal positivistic view understands legal rules as factual entities that can be observed. In this respect, there would be two criteria of identification of legal rules, rules that state the conditions under which a legal rule (understood in the above sense) belongs to a given legal order and the rules that state that a legal rule does not any more belong to a given legal order. I claim that these syntactical criteria are necessary but not sufficient conditions for identification of the legal rules that shape a given legal order. In this vein, I do not agree with the strict separation between the act of establishing a legal normative text (pragmatic dimension), the legal normative text itself (syntactic dimension) and the legal norm (semantic dimension), the latter of which I understand as the meaning of the legal normative text.

I accept that the act of positing a legal text is not the same as the norm itself but, although there can be customary laws that do not need (for their existence) a legislative act (pragmatic dimension), some pragmatic dimension is needed for the existence of legal norms that are legally binding for given participants. The pragmatic dimension, emphasized here, is not only the legal speech-act but the whole legal enterprise. Everything is pervaded by this pragmatic dimension. Any other dimension is and should be (at least from a participant point of view, which has the primacy) subordinated. When any other dimension has the primacy (at a given time and context and for solving a concrete conflict), it is because from this pragmatic-participant's view it is so stated.

From this approach we can see that we cannot understand legal norms from a pure conceptual stance and, in consequence, it would be closer to an Expressive conception of norms that stresses the pragmatic dimension but understood in the wider sense commented on above. From this pragmatic dimension we can see the differences better between orders, assertions, questions, etcetera, and not from the semantic dimension that sees norms as purely conceptual and not as a result of the prescriptive use of a given language. In this chapter it is claimed that we do not discover the legal meanings (that are chronologically provisional) but we, as participants, assign meaning to the legal normative texts in an endless process. Hence, we are in a different position to the scientist who scrutinises a volcano. The scientist can put himself in the position of an external observer of an outer material object. We, as participants, have a different position. Our main concern is not to describe the legal normative texts (because this is a poor task) or to discover the hidden meanings of these legal texts, because our task is not a discovery task granted that there are no meanings waiting for us to be discovered.

Our main task is to assign legal meanings in the "best possible way, here and now". This means, *inter alia*, that we have an ideological background that conditions (although not determines) our constructive work. We do not assign legal meanings in the abstract but within a certain tradition, in a given social context, in a given legal order, accepting some values and not others, certain interpretations and not others, etcetera. Then, we do not discover legal meanings but we assign legal meanings. Nevertheless, we do this within limits that are direct, that is, the limits that legal orders establish which are, nevertheless, disputable. There are also indirect limits. The latter are those not incorporated (or not yet incorporated) in legal rules but that can influence not only the existence of certain kinds and levels of limits but also their interpretation.

I have said above that direct limits are disputable. This should be understood in the following sense: for participants, legal limits have to be respected because they are seen as legally binding, in other words, as "must sources" of the law. Nevertheless, one way of respecting must sources is to adapt them for better fulfilling their goals. This methodological attitude depends, *inter alia*, on a given interpretation of the doctrine of separation of powers, a methodological attitude that can be more formalistic or more finalistic. In this dynamic balance neither is eliminated but one is emphasized. This emphasis depends on direct and indirect limits. Moreover, goals (necessary elements of legal orders) are usually, although not necessarily, formulated in rather vague terms for pragmatical reasons. This does not mean that the level of vagueness is the same in all branches of legal orders.

The previous comments lead to this conclusion: the identification of legal orders calls for argumentation and justification in so far as legal norms cannot be discovered, that is, legal meanings cannot be discovered but they can be (in the best case) properly justified. Why do we want legal meanings to be justified? Because we expect "correct" decisions, although correct decisions are not necessary conclusions of given premises allowed by the legal order. In this respect, internal justification is a rationally acceptable derivation from premises to conclusion. However, this "rationally acceptable derivation" means that we have moved within the legal limits previously stated. This is an interpretative task although it can be logically reconstructed *ex post*. We are in a world of contingency and choice (within limits), not in a world of necessity.

This is why some legal scholars do not emphasize the pragmatic dimension. They prefer to place themselves in the world of abstract entities and their logical relations, that is, the world of necessity. My approach is a "contaminated" one, a "committed" one, not falsely neutral and descriptive. Consequently, we do not know (at least not always) when a legal norm belongs to a given legal order only on the basis of a legal act which has authorisation of another legal rule that belongs to a given legal order. At most, we can know which legal texts belong to a given legal order but not which legal norms belong to it because an interpretative task is required, whose result is not completely known in advance. In relation to the individualisation of legal orders, if we accept that this issue is related to the fact that different officials appeal to different coercive institutional apparatus we would be able (in the best case) to individualise different legal orders.

When I claim that we cannot identify legal orders (on the exclusive basis of a legal positivist approach) I claim that we cannot identify the legal meaning contents that make social relations obligatory, prohibited or permitted because to identify the legal meanings is, at least sometimes, a constructive task. Finally, the expression "legal systems" is only an idealisation. We cope with legal orders, that is, with incomplete aggregates of legal rules. We never complete them. We have some regulative ideas like completeness, justice, justification, etcetera but we cannot reach them completely.

In the same way as we cannot reach freedom but only (to a certain extent) some conceptions of freedom to a certain extent, we cannot reach completeness in legal orders. Perhaps, as in theories of normative ethics, we could rely on an ideal legal observer. A legal order would be a legal system when an ideal observer believes that the former is complete and perfectly coherent. Unfortunately, we have neither these ideal observers nor addressees able to survive in this world of perfection.

The fourth chapter is **"Models of the Rule of Law"**. Some legal traditions say that there is a conceptual separation between law and morals, not in the sense that law lacks morality but in the sense that we can always know which is the existing law without appealing to extra-legal considerations. As is known, communitarian and contractarian approaches are usually considered as the most influential political tendencies, at least at the present time. Generally speaking, communitarian views claim that the foundations of morality rest, exclusively, on a given community. Hence, morality is fundamentally linked to certain traditions of a given community. On the other hand, contractarian and neo-contractarian views claim, generally speaking, that there is a necessary step from a natural situation (where causal explanation is adequate) to a social situation that has to be understood and justified, not only explained. A social situation in which human beings are not only links of a natural chain but also citizens with rights and duties, with ideas of right and wrong, with legal institutions, with social and critical morality, etcetera.

A contract is required for this step but this is only a hypothesis and not an historical fact. In any case, some of the criticisms against these contractarian or neo-contractarian tendencies are objecting to their underlying assumption that individuals are rational, autonomous and isolated individuals able to determine for themselves, to a certain extent. I put the Rule of Law in this context. The Rule of Law can be seen, *inter alia*, as something particularist or something universalist. At the same time, the Rule of Law can be understood from a "thin" or from a "thick" perspective. I claim, *inter alia*, that the Rule of Law necessarily stems from a particular context, in a given society, but need not be particularistic. My claim is a normative claim, that is, the Rule of Law has a universalistic vocation if understood as a relatively "thick" model. Why cannot "thin" versions of the Rule of Law have this universalistic vocation?

This is related to a fundamental point. The Rule of Law, understood from a "thin" perspective, has only bones and no flesh. That is, to be able to create an internal point of view (a moral point of view) on the side of the addressees, the Rule of Law has to offer not only legal certainty, predictability, freedom from arbitrariness and political control of the government but also some moral values. The Rule of Law, understood from a relatively "thick" perspective, is able to introduce some basic moral requirements and, in this respect, is able to obtain not only mere obedience but also fidelity to law. Of course, obedience or fidelity to law are not necessary consequences. As I have already said, when dealing with legal normative fields we are not in the world of necessity, either logical or causal, no matter whether we can make, *ex post*, logical reconstructions or not.

In relation to these values I have commented above that the most fundamental one is the requirement that human beings be treated as ends in themselves. I take for granted that for human beings to be respected as ends in themselves (and not only as means) they should have personal autonomy to build up their lives implying ethical (not methodological) individualism because the former is not incompatible with co-operation and solidarity. Hence, the Rule of Law understood in a "thin" sense is unable to give human beings the contextual conditions for seriously furthering personal autonomy. Only the Rule of Law, understood in a relatively "thick" sense, is able to promote social conditions that allow us to say that personal autonomy is taken seriously. However, it should be emphasized that in any social construction, especially in a normative social construction, there is always (explicitly or implicitly) a conception of human beings as a kind of fundamental living basement of the whole building and of the whole human enterprise.

I would say that several concepts I use in each chapter intertwine with each other and support each other. They are recurrent and form the common background of the whole dissertation. For example, the first chapter emphasizes, *inter alia*, the primacy of practical reason, the idea of "optimisation" as a characteristic task of "committed" participants; the idea that we cannot properly undertake our legal task only on the basis of deductive reasoning because participants require "judgement". Judgement is required to fulfil properly our task as participants because we, as committed participants, are not only interested in legal interpretation but in the "best interpretation, here and now".

In the second chapter, the idea of the primacy of the internal point of view of participants is stressed, developed and compared with the external point of view. This latter view is sometimes (wrongly) understood as a neutral and scientific one. Moreover, the internal point of view is usually neglected as a "subjective" view because some people (supposedly the external observers) would have the "God's eye view", that is, the view that tells us how reality really is. There is also an interpretation of the secular polemics between natural law thinking and legal positivism and a certain view of essentialism and conventionalism. In the third chapter, the pragmatic dimension of language is emphasized, *inter alia*, related to "users" of a given language, in a given context. It is also stressed that the identification of legal meanings is a constructive task, especially in the so-called hard cases. Generally speaking, we do not "discover" legal meanings that are already there, in the legal order. The legal normative task is, at least basically, constructive and justificatory but is also related (although not exclusively) to intentional action. The idea of "neutral observation" and "pure description" (legal positivists) that would distinguish scientific scholars from subjective participants (post-positivists) is also criticised.

In the fourth chapter, there is an analysis of the two basic models of the Rule of Law and their respective features. The idea is also stressed that any legal normative construction (like the models of Rule of Law) has to begin stating (explicitly or implicitly) a certain conception of person, basically related -in this chapter- to personal autonomy.

It is also emphasized that we cannot expect "fidelity to law" only on the basis of the so-called "thin" models of the Rule of Law. This is basically because we cannot expect it only on the basis of legal procedures and legal certainty (understood in a legal positivistic sense) but also on some moral values. We, as committed participants, cannot have "fidelity" to procedures and (void) predictability alone. We are committed, *inter alia*, to certain moral values and a relatively "thick" model of the Rule of Law incorporates them.

All this means that argumentation and justification, *inter alia*, (more than demonstration and truth) are fundamental elements of our task of committed participants. As H. Putnam puts it:

> "... then we see that what we are trying to do in science is to construct a representation of the world which has the characteristics of being instrumentally efficacious, coherent, comprehensive, and functionally simple. But why? I would answer that the reason we want this sort of representation ... is that having this sort of representation system is part of our idea of human cognitive flourishing, and hence part of our idea of total human flourishing, of Eudemonia."[1]

Similar considerations apply when we, committed participants, deal with law, legal interpretation and legal science. And they would show, I expect, that a certain post-positivist perspective should be supported as an alternative to positivist ones.

[1] Putnam, Hilary. *Reason, Truth and History*, Cambridge University Press, 1991, page 134.

CHAPTER 1

ON LEGAL METHOD

1. WHAT IS METHOD?

In a wide sense, we can say that any procedure to reach a given end would be a method. But method, even in a wide sense, refers to a certain regular activity. A way of doing certain things that can be repeated by others in similar conditions. From this very wide beginning we can see that there are, at least, two important features: regularity and predictability. For some people the ideal method would give us full regularity and predictability. In this view, the importance of the person using the method would be insignificant, or non-existent, because the method would work -let us say- by itself. Otherwise, as is known, methodology would be a second order discourse related to the methods used.

The object of this brief overview is not to scrutinize the existing methods. This is a task that exceeds, by far, my goals. The aim is to show that there is a plurality of methods. We can, with no intention of comprehensiveness, distinguish among rational, axiomatic, descriptive, historical and psychological methods. First, although there are several rational methods I will only mention two; the transcendental method, used by Kant that implies an analysis of the conditions and limits of knowledge, and the intuitive method that supposes the immediate perception of the given. Second, the axiomatic method. Once certain logical rules of inference are settled we can deduce some theorems from the axioms. Nevertheless, this is only syntax. In this respect, each axiomatic system may have different empirical interpretations. Only the semantics of an axiomatized theory allow us to talk of true-false. Third, the descriptive method implies, *inter alia*, procedures of observation, classification and statistical order. Fourth, the historical method is mainly used by those who investigate the past. It implies, *inter alia*, selection, classification and interpretation of facts, testimonies, etcetera. Fifth, the psychological method, basically used by those who investigate the behaviour and development of human beings, not only by means of introspective analysis but also by means of empirical procedures.

Finally, there are two -let us say- universal reasoning models, deduction and induction. Deductive reasoning is usually called "truth-preserving" because (when it is valid) it is impossible that premises are true and the conclusion not. Differently, the inductive argument cannot give conclusive grounds for the truth of the conclusion. It gives more or less grounds. In this respect, they are gradual. They can be better or worse but the deductive reasoning is, contrarily, valid or invalid. However, some people believe that scientists, even scientists of the so-called mature sciences, are fully equipped to do their job just using deduction and induction. This is a wrong view.

As we shall see, it is supported here that both empirical or formal axiomatic methods are of little or secondary importance for legal experts in general. Contrarily, methods based on understanding are much more important for us. However, understanding is related to interpretation and application. We shall see the relationships of legal tasks to hermeneutics. This will also lead us to the problem of participants and observers. Granted that we try to understand our own legal and social relations, who is better placed for undertaking this job? It is supposed here that we understand better from within, not from an external-realistic approach. In addition, there is another basic point related to this emphasis on understanding. We are not mainly interested in describing regularities of behaviour.

We are mainly interested in a normative task. We try to justify certain behaviour. This fundamental aspect conditions the basic methods legal experts use in fulfilling their task. Nevertheless, a formal approach that, as some say, could lead us to certainty is not supported here. My main concern will be with justification not with truth. In this respect, the problem of justification is related to foundationalism, coherentism and internalism-externalism. All these matters are dealt with in the following pages. In any case, it is very difficult to give a precise report of the methods or method a person is using. What should be the reliable criteria by which we can identify the proper description of the method a person is using?

Finally, let us briefly outline how Marx, Durkheim and Weber, see the problem of method.[1] For Marx, method is basically a conception of the world, whereas for Durkheim, method is basically comprised of procedures that differentiate what sociologists do from what philosophers, historians, etcetera, do, and for Weber, method is both objectivity and moral responsibility or moral compromise. In relation to legal normative fields I would say that we have elements of all three. From Marx, because any legal order is based on a given conception of justice that justifies it. From Durkheim, because we, *inter alia*, differentiate law from other social practices on the basis of the so-called must-sources (legislation) and authoritative decisions (adjudication). From Weber, because participants share an internal point of view that is a kind of moral compromise. Nevertheless, this moral compromise does not allow arbitrariness. The internal point of view has a compromise with objectivity, which is understood as intersubjectivity.

2. ADDITIONAL REMARKS

We should neither understand ourselves as neutral observers of our own form of life, nor believe that some magical method will make irrelevant the presence of historical subjects that use it in a given context, at a certain time. We, as participants of a given legal order, try to reach the "best" possible solutions and this is related, *inter alia*, to judgement and justification.

At least from Kant, we know that some conceptual schemes are prior to our experiences. In other words, we face the world "contaminated" and, from this perspective, the Baconian methodology is an ideal that is impossible to reach because, *inter alia*, observation without hypothesis does not exist. Our conceptual scheme conditions how we see the object, in other words, our conceptual scheme and our biological constitution make it possible to see the world from a certain

[1] Fernández Buey, F. *La Ilusión del Método*, edit. Crítica, Barcelona, 1991, pages 23 and ff.

perspective, not as it really is. Furthermore, when we place ourselves in the legal normative realm we (that is, some people) can create the object within certain limits. In this respect, we can recall a well-known distinction, since the so-called external point of view (proper according to methodological positivism) and the internal point of view (proper according to hermeneutics) is the importance given, respectively, to theoretical and practical reason. While practical reason relates to action (that is, to *praxis* in the Aristotelian sense), theoretical reason relates to propositions (that is, propositions that can be true or false).

In relation to practical reason, human beings can, for example, regulate a certain behaviour in a certain way, with this regulated behaviour constituting a "marriage". In other words, the known distinction between brute facts and institutional facts. The latter would need the support of the former, since without brute facts we could not have institutional facts. For example, legislators can decide (without implying success) that private property of means of production does not exist anymore in a given society, but neither legislators nor scientists can decide that earthquakes do not exist anymore. In addition, a legislator could legislate that there is no mode of production in the society he is ruling on, although this would be useless.

However, I am not claiming that subvenient properties (brute facts) supervene supervenient properties (institutional facts) in the sense that the latter are logical or causal consequences of the former. Consequently, I would say that facts do not determine values and values cannot be exhaustively defined in terms of facts. In this respect, we should not claim that certain institutional facts are the result of certain brute facts, meaning that there is some kind of logical or causal necessity. In any case, what I reject is not that there is a link between normative and natural properties but that normative properties can be reduced to natural ones. This supposition could lead us to some kind of naturalized epistemology, which is outside of my concern.

It is also known that explanation and understanding are two basic methods to deal with different objects. Therefore Galilean tradition (within which methodological positivism can be placed) and Aristotelian tradition (within which analytic-hermeneutics can be placed) represent two different ways to cope with basic issues such as; what is law?, what is the proper concept of law?, which is the proper method used to know what law is?, etcetera. In this respect, certain legal tendencies that try to reach necessary conclusions from clear and explicit premises lead to a known illness, the so-called Cartesian anxiety.

They try to fossilize legal normative language, stressing either empirical method or formal logic, or both. The result is the absence of the subject and the presence of a pure and neutral object and method. In this paper the idea is supported, *inter alia*, that interpretation has no sense outside the historical framework where this legal language exists and outside the historical subjects that support, or not, this legal language. In addition, legal formalizations also tend to neglect the importance of time, which is fundamental in the understanding of law.

I shall support that adopting an external point of view, in relation to "our legal orders", is misleading. We cannot be external observers of our legal orders because we cannot be external observers of our form of life. I shall deal with the idea of "objectivity", which is understood (by methodological positivists) as something possible from an external point of view but not possible from a participant's view.

Nevertheless, methodological positivists claim that they are external observers only when they are working as legal scientists, but not during the rest of the day. I shall claim that this is pragmatically illogical, although not a logical inconsistency. The interpretative turn does not look for any essence but claims that we cannot avoid "seeing" from somewhere, since we have a given conceptual scheme and a given biological structure.

Bearing this in mind, it is not sound to claim "objectivity and neutrality" as if the subject could be removed from the spotlight, for a while, in order to eliminate subjectivity, that is, personal "contamination". Another related chimera is the claim that they (the true legal scientists) can describe the object as it is, because they are able to utter "detached statements".

I shall try to show that a prior presupposition of any social research is a shared set of meanings.[2] It is a necessary presupposition for a proper understanding of any social normative fact. A surreptitious move of methodological legal positivists is to "say" that they are able to utter detached statements. Nevertheless, they are really participants of the same world of meaning as the legal theorists that claim to be unable to utter detached statements. The latter legal scholars though should only be able to utter committed statements, since one thing is what people "say" they do and another thing is what people actually "do". In this respect, methodological legal positivists are not neutral describers (as they usually claim) of legal reality as it is. It can be accepted that certain legal approaches tend to emphasize "description" and others tend to emphasize "construction", especially in cases where it is not clear what the law in force, of a given legal order, "is". Nevertheless, description is always selective.

Some approaches claim that there are strict boundaries surrounding the law, as if law was a kind of fortress that could avoid the entry of contaminating elements. In this vein, when we do not find a legislative legal text able to solve a specific legal problem, we would have to look for something outside the law, that is, the field of no law. In this respect, law is (for these supposed scientific approaches) a technique for solving legal conflicts, in other words, an instrument. Since these scientific approaches have problems (for example, Exclusive legal positivism, mainly represented by Joseph Raz), certain other scientific approaches (for example, Inclusive legal positivism, mainly represented by Waluchow) try to occupy the place of the proper methodological positivism. The last step, as far as I know, is to include social morality within the realm of positive law, given the problems Exclusive legal positivism has to explain how adjudication works on the exclusive basis of posited legal rules.

I will try to show that this is not methodological positivism (if we have to separate law and morals conceptually) and, in case this move is accepted, I would claim that we cannot clearly separate social and critical morality. Hence, we cannot clearly distinguish in advance (in all cases) what the law "is" from what the law "ought to be". This is so because the initial meaning of the legislative legal texts (granted that there is agreement about it) never (from a pragmatical point of view) lasts forever. All this means that law always (from a pragmatical point of view)

---

[2] Lagerspetz, E. *The Opposite Mirrors*, Kluwer, 1995. Especially his Conclusions.

changes its meaning (not necessarily all laws at the same time though), even without the intervention of the legislator, because, *inter alia*, the constructive interpretation, in hard cases, solves the problem of adaptation of law. Adaptation of law means change of law with no legislative intervention.

This is made through acceptable legal solutions, based on legal positive materials and meta-legal materials, the latter including social and critical morality. As Inclusive legal positivism includes a standard of positive morality, this leads to two remaining problems: first, why only positive morality and not also critical morality?; and second, can we "discover" what positive morality states or which interpretation is needed? In this case, the standards to solve legal conflicts would be void and something like "obey the positive morality when there is no clear legal rule" would apply. In relation to the first problem, a usual answer could be the following: critical morality is not included because the legislator has ordered only positive morality. However, we could ask, why? In this case, the answer can rest on authority or on reasons. If we take the first option we are in the field of legal positivism, perhaps ideological legal positivism. However, I would prefer to accept the option of reasoned authority. If we accept this option though it is not clear why we should not also accept, in hard cases, critical morality.

In order to deal with these and related issues I will cope with terms such as "facts, objectivity, legal positivism, hermeneutics, method and justification".

I shall take for granted that the known distinction between brute facts and institutional facts should be included, at least in legal normative realms. We should remember here though the distinction made by Alf Ross between "creative facts and conditioning facts", that they are both within the common label of "operative facts". The former would be specifically relevant (for example, the fact of homicide or the fact of a promise) and the latter would include the possibility of modifying the application of the expected legal effect. Nevertheless, I shall start this paper based on the cited distinction between brute and institutional facts.

In this respect, A. Aarnio says, in relation to J. Searle:

> "I want to defend the idea that there is a reality that is totally independent of us ... Brute facts require the institution of language in order that we can state facts, but the brute facts exist quite independent of language ... "Social fact" refers to any fact involving collective intentionality ... A special subclass of social facts are institutional facts, facts involving human institutions ... The structure of institutional facts is the structure of hierarchies of the form "X counts as Y in context C" ... Institutional facts exist thus only within systems of constitutive rules ..."[3]

In a very brief way, I would say that the main idea I intend to show is that our object, the legal order, and our main task, to solve certain conflicts in the best possible way, call for judgement and justification. We are not in a world of truth and propositional knowledge. Neither legal experts nor citizens deal with or are interested, basically or exclusively, in empirical proofs or logical inferences. This does not mean though that we can live against logic or the empirical world. On the contrary, because we want the best we cannot dispense with logic and the laws of nature. However, they are not our main concern as in natural and formal sciences. It

---

[3] Aarnio, A. *Reason and Authority*, Dartmouth, Aldershot, 1997, pages 127 and 128.

has been repeatedly said that we ascribe reality although we do this within certain limits. Some of these are natural, some of them are logical, and some of them are evaluative. The latter dimension in particular is extremely important for the task of the legal scholar. I hope this will be clear in the following discussion.

3. ONTOLOGICAL COMMITMENTS

I am a "weak representationalist" in relation to brute facts and a "constructivist" in relation to institutional facts. However, when constructing institutional facts, which is my direct concern, we have limits. At the same time, I believe that collective entities have no existence in themselves (that is, even if they are neither physical nor mental entities they do not objectively exist in a Popperian third world) and, in this respect, they are not autonomous. Moreover, our legal normative language does not try to "reflect" the world but, mainly, to justifiably guide certain basic human relations in certain contexts. In this respect, I believe we should not strive for a physicalist language, *inter alia*, because we inevitably have to make, in fulfilling our legal tasks, judgements of relevance. Our legal orders are full of dichotomies such as legal certainty-material justice, among others. In this vein, legal theories are traditional ways to solve (or try to solve) these dichotomies. To avoid idealist tendencies we should not only rely on internal coherence but we should also have an eye on our social relations. In any case, the legislator's language alone is not enough to properly put in motion legal normativity. Jurist's language is also required.

It is usual to be upset, when dealing with ontological commitments, with the accusation of idealism, especially if one is neither idealist nor materialist, although these are not unanimous terms. I am a "weak representationalist" in relation to "brute facts". This means, *inter alia*, that the external world is as it is, independent of our constructions, because we can only have access to the external world through our constructions and sense-experiences. Hence, we do not describe the world as it really is because, *inter alia*, we creatively participate in its constitution. However, in relation to "institutional facts" I am a "constructivist". This means, *inter alia*, that although we produce our object it is within certain limits.

In this respect, I deny that our object of research is only a construction of the mind. Granted my conception of "person" (that tries to avoid an atomistic Hobbesian stance), constructions should not be seen as a kind of solipsist utterance but as a social product. In other words, that produced by individuals in a social network of meanings, values, interests, means and goals. All this provides a pragmatic point of view that should not be forgotten. We do not only try to determine what a given legal order is but, also, how to reformulate it better and how to justifiably propose "just" legal solutions to certain legal conflicts, at a certain historical point in time. In other words, we are mainly interested in contextual human action, undertaken by individuals in several social contexts. Therefore this means, *inter alia*, that collective entities do not have an autonomous existence, no matter whether they are communities, systems, etcetera.

In legal fields, the positivist tradition, represented by Scandinavian realism, has often even accused certain legal positivist approaches as idealist, on the basis of their ontological commitments to ideal entities. Kelsen is a known example of this criticism. Currently, positivists do not enjoy the best of things and they had better days in the past. They usually do not support such strong claims as the Scandinavian realists did. They even accept things like "positive morality", although not all of them. On the other hand, the philosophy of science has shown that "facts" can be complex and difficult entities to grasp and justify, since they are not simple, packaged objects that can be taken, like a stone can be, and classified in a neutral way. The confidence in Baconian methodology has disappeared and it is therefore hard to claim that we can just pick up such an object, as it really is, without any constructive human intervention.

As jurists, our position in the world is somewhat different from, let us say, doctors or astronomers. The first deal with human beings while the second do not. We are closer to the former because jurists also deal with human beings. Doctors experiment with human bodies using the mediation of instruments, medicines and theories. Legal scholars deal with certain human relations using the mediation, mainly, of a legal language, that is, a legislator's language and a jurist's language. Hence, our object can be equated with certain human relations seen from a legal normative point of view. In other words, they are authoritatively solidified in sentences through certain procedures. I know that custom does not fit in this description but I am not worried about formulating exhaustive general laws that encompass everything. Wittgenstein wrote in his Tractatus,

> "We can describe the world completely by means of fully generalised propositions, i.e. without first correlating any name with a particular object."[4]

These questions are related, *inter alia*, to the theory of language. If the meaning of a term should lead us to ask for its reference, perhaps, we would not have difficulties in relation to the word "chair" for instance, that could be considered a member of our social brute facts. Nevertheless, we have to deal with institutional facts and it can be very problematic to decide what terms such as "just", "justified", or others, refer to. In our legal context, the main use of words is not to "reflect" the world but to justifiably guide certain human actions. In this respect, not all members of the same linguistic game share the same properties. We not only have to deal with different linguistic games though, having only a family resemblance, but we also have to deal with the fact that inside a linguistic game not all its members share all the same properties. Nevertheless, we shall put aside the anxiety for the sake of generality.

Nevertheless, this should be properly understood. In legal fields, we know that criminal law requires this generality to a different extent than private law. Hence, analogical reasoning is widely accepted in private law but not in criminal law. This is due to certain goals and values that certain communities have in dealing with certain behaviour. Hence, it is not an anxiety of generality "in itself" but, let us say, instrumental generality. We value certain goals and we believe that generality or predictability are good means to reach these valuable goals. Sometimes though we

---

[4] Fogelin, R. *Wittgenstein*, second ed., Routledge, London, 1987, page 67.

believe that other goals are not so important and we accept, more easily, exceptions and analogies.

3.1 Ontology and Society

The ontology I am dealing with requires a certain kind of society with a certain level of institutionalisation. In this respect, the claim "*ubi societas ubi ius*" is not true but the contrary "*ubi ius ubi societas*" is. At the same time, a society with problems of co-ordination is also required, with certain conflicts that show the relative scarcity of certain goods, with judges, or similar arbiters, for solving these conflicts and many other matters authoritatively. All the former shows that our ontological commitments are the result of a construction, although we cannot construct from scratch. At the same time, the membrane that separates the legal field from outside is a porous one and no logical reconstruction of the legal language can avoid this inevitable and puzzling fact. It is wrong to suppose that the uncovering of the logical forms of legal language will show our object as it really is. Let us say, "its essence" or "deep structure".

This metaphysical dream is similar to the discovery of Platonic forms. Instead of ideas as objective essences, we would have logical forms. In any case, what matters for our purposes is that they would be the true ontological basis for our imperfect grammar or our imperfect legal language. They would be the infallible "foundations" of our future knowledge building. Law, from my ontological point of view, is a complex mixture of materials (such as chairs -not my chair because it is not required for the proper working of the law in force-, buildings, etcetera) and ideal entities (such as legal concepts, legal meanings, legal reasons, etcetera) that may have sense, granted certain contextual purposes, which some historical human figures may have.

All this is put in motion by persons because it has sense for them, because they are engaged in certain relations and because it fulfils, more or less, certain goals that are valuable to them. From a materialist point of view, we could say that minds or meanings would be non-existent entities because they are non-material. This is a contentious view because of, *inter alia*, the "existence" of theoretical terms. Scientists cannot dispense with quarks, black holes or magnetic fields even when they have not observed them, as a stone can be observed for example. With these examples, I am not trying to show that legal dogmatics is like physics or that we also have non-observed entities, such as legal concepts that could be compared to black holes.

I am not worried by this because it seems to me wrong to strive for a physicalist language and a physicist mentality. My concern is how we deal with some problems (legal problems) and to what extent we can deal with them successfully, although "successfully" is a historical and complex term. In order to do so we require certain means. In so far as these are required for a proper working of a given legal order, they could be understood as ontological elements. However, this is also a relative construction. We can decide, for example, that some buildings are ontological entities in so far as they are required for a legal order to work, but we exclude the dust inside the building although it is a material entity. We have to make judgements of relevance, in relation to both brute facts and institutional facts.

3.2 Physicists and Legal Scholars

We are not trying to discover how the world really is. This is a metaphysical enterprise. We are not trying to discover the constituents of the reality. If this were possible, which I doubt, it would not be our concern as legal scholars. In a similar vein as physicists, we do not deal directly with our reality but do so through a given theory. Legal scholars do not "see" the object (a given legal order) directly. They need conceptual schemes for doing so. They have "seen" the legal order from various legal schools, using different ontologies and methodologies. Even when they agree that the legislator's language is a basic ontological entity, they can see it from a different view.

Hence, we do not see law as it is but we see law from a certain theoretical perspective. In this vein we could distinguish, for example, between the "will theory of law", the "pure-norm theory of law", the "psychological theory of law", and the "behavioural theory of law".[5] These theories of law include diverse ontological commitments. For example, according to the "will theory" a positive legal rule is to be equated with an act of wishing, while according to the "Pure theory" a positive legal rule is to be equated with an ought or may meaning-content.[6]

Hence, in order to have ontological commitments we have to interpret a given reality because it is not "given". That is, a given reality (a legal one) has many features and we select those that we believe important, given certain purposes. I will not deal with the weberian problem of whether we can avoid value judgements (Werturteil) using only a reference to values (Wertbesiehung). This will be clear in the text, I hope. Anyway, the former comments force us, at this point, to consider the problem of "reality". Should we be upset if somebody tells us that we have ontological commitments with "non-real" entities? Let us take a first step. Suppose that a normative legal text (a given sentence) is a reality because, for example, we can see it or we can touch it.

Even if this is so, it is not enough when we talk of legal positive rules. Why not? Because we have to decide what is their "proper" sense? As an act of wishing or as a pure meaning-content? If we decide, as an example, that they are pure meaning-contents we would say so on the basis of a legal theory. In this case, a Pure theory of

---

[5] Harris, J.W. *Law and Legal Science*, Clarendon Press, Oxford, 1979, page 25 ff.

[6] Ibidem, page 24. On the other hand, I would say that the so-called legal science does not work apart from legal theories. If dominant legal theories are a kind of accepted lense through which legal orders are seen and understood, legal dogmatics will, usually, develop its work within this conceptual framework. Only when the legal theory in question faces a crisis (more or less in a Kuhnian sense) will some new legal alternatives be seriously undertaken. Something similar to this happened when von Kirchmann gave his well-known lecture in Berlin. He said, inter alia, that legal science was neither a science nor a reliable technique for solving social legal conflicts. This was an expression of the weaknesses of the Jurisprudence of Concepts legal theory. However, although we can distinguish between high and low legal science (or theoretical and practical) there is both a continuous interdependence between them and a nebulous frontier.

law. The former means that we cannot dispense with ontological commitments and we cannot dispense with theoretical constructions. Even when we have adopted certain ontological commitments we have not exhausted our problems. Suppose, as in my case, that participants (at large) deal with a positive legal text (understood in any of the former senses).

They have, especially if they are jurists, to justify their "proper" meaning-content. "Proper" relates to "correctness" and it relates to an internal point of view. In my ontology, there are not only legal positive rules (as basic units of the legal orders) but also a generalised dispositional attitude, an "internal point of view". This is not though a logical or causal necessity. My modest ontology does not try to reflect the basic units of the reality itself, expressing the infallible foundations of our knowledge. I do not have the anxiety of certainty and universality typical of rationalist law thinkers and logical positivists. What worries me is Ockam's warning, although it is a formal one because neither the razor nor the reality at stake can tell us when to stop. In order to do this, we require a judgement of relevance, which includes an evaluation of consequences. Hence, it is important to emphasize, once again, the requirement of decision and interpretation.

The question about the ontology of law should be translated into the following one. Which ontological perspective do you support? Logical positivism and the model of Physics have pushed some legal scholars to strive for a unique paradigm in our legal normative field. However, it is disputable that this is so. In this respect, I will quote A. Aarnio when he deals with the problem of "matrix", granted that Kuhn substituted the notion of paradigm for disciplinary matrixes. He says,

> "... matrixes typically consist of the following elements: a) symbolic generalisations, b) shared norms and values regarding the conduct of scientific inquiry, c) shared models about the subject matter, as well as d) exemplars, i.e. paradigmatic patterns of scientific problem solving."[7]

Aarnio's conclusion is that the basic matrix of legal dogmatics has remained the same because the changes have been changes inside the basic matrix. In this respect, he cites three basic changes: conceptualist jurisprudence, jurisprudence of interests and analytical legal dogmatics. The point is about the meaning of "change". In relation to interpretation inside a given legal order, it has been said that most jurists do not accept that a change in the interpretation of law, made by judges, could be equated to a modification of this legal order. Why would this be so? Because, it is said, legal certainty and separation of powers are strong commitments for most jurists. Hence, judges would not change the legal order when they authoritatively state a different meaning to some legal positive rules. Only the legislator could do it.

To claim that the changes in the basic matrix of legal dogmatics have been changes inside it, or not, poses a problem of relevance for us. We have to evaluate and decide whether some changes can be equated to a change of the basic matrix or not. Why should this be important? In my view, the stability of the basic matrix of legal dogmatics is a reason that favours the prestige of legal dogmatics. I am not saying that Aarnio does it for this reason though. We should not forget that under the

---

[7] Aarnio, A., op.cit., page 79.

influence of logical positivism the search for permanent stability (logical forms) has been a strong commitment for many jurists. It is not necessary to be a logical positivist for valuing permanence instead of contingency. Nevertheless, neither permanence nor mutability are good or bad in themselves.

3.3 Justification and Reality

In my view, what matters most is whether changes have been justified and are useful or not. Moreover, I would add that it is easier to claim the permanence of the basic matrix of legal dogmatics if we rely on the basic elements that shape it, that is, general concepts. On the contrary, it would be easier to see them as qualitative modifications of the matrix if they are understood as conceptions. In a similar vein, as happens with classical liberalism and egalitarian liberalism, they can be seen either as changes inside liberalism, or as qualitative modifications. My conclusion is that we should move away from this positivist anxiety forever. On the other hand, I believe that one of the virtues of legal dogmatics is the capacity of its members to change and adapt to a changing society in a justified and useful way. In this respect, the most permanent elements are usually formal ones, although not always. Some material contents can be deeply rooted in a given society.

Let us, at this point, go back to the problem of "reality". Granted that to deal with reality "in itself or as it is" is mistaken, I will confine myself to a given context, the legal context. This would be preferable because ontological research cannot sharply and clearly separate the worlds and entities each science has constructed for its own purposes. Our main ontological concern, then, refers to a given conceptual scheme, the legal one. Our legal conceptual scheme (or schemes) does not try to represent a given reality like the conceptual scheme of Physics. It tries to describe certain objects of legal relevance and, also, to interpret the legal reality that is not static.

This legal reality is partly given and partly decided by some human beings, following certain procedures. From the legislator's point of view, it is usually said that he must be able to choose if we are going to see him as a legislator. This is sound in relation to certain aspects of the legal order but not in relation to others. What is "given" for a legislator is, roughly speaking, the mode of production in force. This is, at present, the market. At the same time, certain strongly internalised beliefs are also the "given". A legislator cannot reject any penalty for murder, kidnapping or rape. Again though, this is not a logical or causal impossibility. Nevertheless, he must be able to choose in many other cases. This vague and changing "given", plus the so-called must-sources, is the foundation for those who share an internal point of view. However, these foundations should not be seen as a kind of unshakeable bedrock.

3.4 Crossbreed-Ontology

It is important to emphasize that our contextual ontology is not, and does not try to be, an autonomous world of ought. Our interpretations, our theories, refer to something outside them although they do not represent them in a pictorial form. Our ontology is crossbred. Using Searle's terminology we should say that we have to deal with brute facts and with institutional facts. The latter are not a logical or a causal consequence of the former. I believe that our legal ontology expresses a tension between dichotomies. For example, between brute facts and institutional facts, between legal certainty and material justice, between rights and duties, interests and moral values, between legal entities and meta-legal ones, etcetera. The different schools, such as Conceptual Jurisprudence, Jurisprudence of Interests, and others, are ways of harmonising the dichotomies that pervade the legal normative field. That is, they are ways of solving the tension between these dichotomies. Although these solutions are provisional, they are usually more provisional (in its regular recurrence) than the solutions or theories of mature sciences, understood as those that have a unique paradigm.

It should be clear that this tension cannot be exclusively solved by appealing to coherence. This is a necessary but not a sufficient condition. One legal textuality can be coherent with another but it should also fit with certain social relations, as they are understood and evaluated at present. We deal permanently with a legal is and a legal ought, with past and present. The basic units of our legal ontology are legal positive rules (understood as normative texts - in legislator's language- and as legal norms -in jurist's language), not in isolation but joined together in institutions. These rules and institutions would be nothing without certain social facts, human relations and purposes. In this respect, I disagree with the "construction" typical of Jurisprudence of Concepts where the internal combination of legal concepts would produce new implicit legal material.

The acceptance of the above cited interplay can avoid idealist ontologies, in other words, ontological commitments should not refer to transcendental entities divorced from the historical background where this ontology may have sense. It means that our legal ontological commitments should have an eye on social relationships, social interests and social values and on the sciences, in general. Nevertheless, the problem of the existence of certain entities remains in relation, not to chairs, but to legal concepts or legal norms, which are understood as the meaning result of an interpretation of a given normative text. What is the "reality" of these entities, if any?

If we deny that linguistic expressions are objective universally valid structures, we could be invited to accept that they are mental subjective contents. To avoid this solipsism we should understand legal meaning-contents as normative societal products. However, I recall that the weaknesses of the correspondence theory for reaching an acceptable solution to the word-world relation, do not justify exclusive reliance on a coherence theory, for reasons already commented on.

If we understand a legal order as a coherent field of meaning-contents, we could say that this is an idealistic approach. By this we would mean one in which the external world is a mind-dependent construction. However, one can deny this by claiming that legal orders are not only more or less coherent fields of meaning-contents but, in addition, contextual human actions and brute facts. We cannot have legal orders without brute facts, although institutional facts are not logical or causal consequences of the former. Human actions, although related to mind, are not exclusively dependent on it. In a similar vein, as we have language and parole, we have "momentary legal orders", and "non-momentary legal orders". The former are a more or less coherent set of posited legal rules stating, in a given country, what is permitted, prohibited and binding. The latter are sets of written choice-guidance devices, available to officials for settling disputes.[8]

Although I have quoted Harris, I suppose it is clear that I have a different understanding of the matter. He believes that "non-momentary legal orders" should not be confused with "legal systems", understood as the present valid law of a country. Perhaps, in this instance, we could use the metaphor that legal orders are like boats. They require people to put them in motion. The problem is, then, whether legal orders could work without participants and without the jurists' language. I believe not. Legal orders are the result of the legislators' language but, although it is a necessary step, it is not a sufficient one. Therefore, legal ontology requires two types of language. The legislator's alone cannot move the boat.

3.5 Final Remarks

In summary, brute facts, as the subvenient entities, and institutional facts, as the supervenient entities form our legal ontology. The latter are mainly of two kinds: legally authoritative (must and should sources, which depend on what concrete legal orders state) and rationally authoritative (those items able to justify or help to justify legally authoritative decisions). Only must sources are members of the legislator's language. All these ontological commitments have sense in relation to a given background. We should not understand ontological entities as having sense in themselves, or as forming part of the reality as it is. Nevertheless, we could settle, for example, the formal claim that all legal orders require must sources.

Furthermore, we should bear in mind that these ontological entities or how they are understood, are a result of the acceptance of a given legal theory. In other words, the acceptance of the scheme of general concepts is able to organise our legal experience in a certain way. Hence, our ontological conclusions are not the result of a formal logical clarification or, alternatively, a purification of our linguistic impurities. Therefore, we have not been looking for the logical forms that, supposedly, would reveal the logical structure of the legal world. This means that the rational reconstruction of the legislator's language is, basically, the result of practical reasoning and practical concepts.

Consequently, certain abstract entities that pertain to a given legal tradition will help us to organise legal experience to reach certain practical goals, although they do not exist in space-time as brute facts do. At the same time, they are not entities existing in a platonic third world because they require, *inter alia*, intentional human actions to put them in motion. In addition, the hardware of these intentional actions, human beings, cannot be exhaustively explained and understood as physical things, exclusively dependent on causal laws.

---

[8] Harris, J.W., op.cit., pages 65 and 66.

4. FACTS, POSITIVISM AND HERMENEUTICS

We should bear in mind two kinds of facts: primary facts (which are the object of the so-called mature sciences) and secondary facts (which are the object of legal dogmatics). In relation to the former, we can say that the world is as it is and does not depend on how we see it. In relation to the latter, the legal normative world does depend on how we see it, especially how certain powerful groups see it. In this respect, "objectivity" does not mean the same in natural sciences and in legal dogmatics. Although both are related to a "community test" in the latter case there can be deep modifications in the legal dogmatics' task, due to changes in political power. In natural sciences this is much more difficult. In this respect we can quote the known case of Stalin. He rejected Planck's, Bohr's and Heisenberg's work for ideological reasons with the help, *inter alia*, of Lysenko. However, this is rare.

Moreover, the results of the so-called mature sciences usually spread out all over the world irrespective of the legal borders. Differently, our legal normative fields are worlds of "intentions and good reasons", although not exclusively. In this respect, it is stated that we cannot formulate "detached statements" of our accepted legal orders, as an anthropologist can in relation to a primitive tribe. It is also claimed that there is primacy of the internal point of view over the external one. Practical reason and justification also have primacy over theoretical reason and truth. Finally, the legal epistemology supported (normative in any case) is not based on knowledge (understood as justified true belief) but on *prima facie* justifications. This means, *inter alia*, that they can be defeated by further justifications although legal certainty imposes an end. The legal justification task is closely related to a basic dichotomy in our legal orders: stability and adaptation.

For the moment we have distinguished between "brute facts", which exist independently of ourselves and of our will, and "institutional facts", that depend on our will and reason. It is known that von Wright distinguishes between changes in the world, that depend on the intention of a subject (changes that he labels as "results"), and changes in the world that do not depend on the intention of a subject (changes that he labels as "consequences"). While the former relation is interpretative the second relation is causal. Granted this, we can take a further step and distinguish between primary facts and secondary facts.

In this respect, N. MacCormick says,

> "Supposing that this woman had herself impregnated by a process of artificial insemination, does that amount to, count as, or constitute adultery? Certain "primary facts" have been proven, or assumed as if proved for the purposes of debate: do these primary facts count as an instance of the required "secondary fact" -adultery- in order to find a claim for a divorce?"[9]

We have, then, two kinds of facts: primary facts (in our example, the fact that this woman is pregnant or not) and secondary facts (in our example, the fact that this woman has committed adultery or not). It is important to emphasize that these two kinds of facts are inescapable elements in legal orders (at least in our culture). This makes a basic difference in relation to the world of "brute facts" that would be the

---

[9] MacCormick, N. *Legal Reasoning and Legal Theory*, Clarendon Law Series, Oxford, 1978, page 93.

object of mature sciences, such as physics or chemistry. In this mature scientific realm there is no "normative reality" as there is in law and legal dogmatics. In our example, the first fact (the pregnancy of this woman) can be the object of a study of a mature science. However, the "secondary fact", whether this woman has committed adultery or not, cannot be the object of physics or chemistry. This basic difference can raise some problems, since, on the one hand, it can be claimed that the world is a world of facts *tout court*, whereas, on the other hand, we can face the problem of whether this basic difference allows for a different method.

It could be said, as A. Aarnio claims, that natural sciences are no more mature than human ones, and yet they are different. However, this is a disputable matter. It can be accepted that they are different but also assemblies of witches are different from assemblies of legal scholars, and we do not believe that they are equally "mature". Nevertheless, I do not believe that there is an epistemologically sharp cut-off between science and philosophy. Hence, these differences should be seen as differences in degree, with boundary problems, because there is no distinct line between science and philosophy. Nevertheless, the unity of method is not a strong requirement in the latter while it is in the former.

In relation to the first issue, that is, whether the world is a world of facts, we could believe that the world has an objective entity, in other words, the world does not depend on how we see it. The conclusion is that the true scientific task is to describe and classify it. I shall suppose that we are not gods and we have no direct access to the world. The necessary mediated access to the world is through our biological constitution and our conceptual scheme. We cannot see outside ourselves. This is not to deny that we are perceiving the world, it is only to deny that we perceive it as it really is. In legal theory, or in legal dogmatics, "objectivity" is related to "legal community test", in a similar (but not equal) vein as happens in mature sciences.

A. Peczenik poses a profound question here when he says that the object of knowledge is whether the woman committed adultery, not whether there will be public agreement about it. Granted that we are not dealing here with knowledge (implying that if we know something then it must be true) but with legally justified beliefs, I would say that law is a social practice and it has no sense to evaluate legal behaviour from an exclusively individualistic point of view. Legal justification necessarily stems from individuals but it is a social matter regulated by socialized and authoritative rules that look for, *inter alia*, legal certainty.

It is usual though to hear some complaints in this respect. Methodological positivists usually claim the risk of subjectivity, persuasion, etcetera, if we rely on this "legal community test". What can they offer? Either themselves, as true representatives of the observers of the world as it is, or as representatives of the true method. Normally, both proposals go hand by hand. Be that as it may, I will deal only with the possibility that they have the true method for obtaining true results or, to put it in other words, that they are in the position to reach the dream Kelsen and others had, that is, to articulate a purely descriptive legal science. Hence, the claim that a given sentence corresponds to the facts, in the sense of an independent state of affairs, should be distinguished from the claim that a sentence corresponds to certain agreed truth criteria.

Recalling the above example, we have criteria of truth to know when a woman is pregnant and we have criteria of truth to know when this woman has committed adultery, according to a given legal order. The difference is that the former criteria are objective (in the sense that it is possible to test them in the most objective way our scientific community is able) and the second are, or can be, intersubjective. In the latter case, there can be an agreement of the legal community and, if this is the case, this is what "objectivity" means. That is, public agreement, in a certain place and at a certain time, by experts. This agreement is based (at least in our legal realms) on a legal tradition, on positive rules, on legal reasons and on explicit (or implicit) moral reasons. It is not an *argumentum ad populum* fallacy. In the first case, (whether the woman is pregnant) we can claim that it is true, or not, according to the facts of nature.

In this example, not only can scientists objectively test that this woman is pregnant but also people can normally "see" it after a certain time has passed. However, not all examples are equally clear and it would be a mistake to generalize from this particular one. In some legal cases, we could also use the term "truth", although it is not related to the world outside and even if it were, it could not be the last word because lawgivers do not try to describe the reality but to evaluate it and guide human conduct. For example, in order to be valid some contracts must be written in the public record. In some cases though, we can claim that it is true that a certain contract is not valid according to a certain legal order. A basic difference between this case and the case of the pregnant woman is that, in the latter case, there is an empirical verification of a biological state of affairs while in the former we are not dealing with "natural nature". Moreover, the legislator can modify the validity requirements tomorrow morning and then the "truth" of the cited contracts will also change. However, pregnant women are pregnant women, no matter how happy or unhappy the legislator is.

In the former case, we can either infer or (normally) place certain legal facts in the interpretative limits of a legal text. In this respect, I agree with MacCormick that once the ambiguity of legal rules is eliminated, through an interpretative task, all rules can be formulated as sentences having the structure "if p then q". The problem is that once this is done, it will not last forever because certain "distinguishing" can modify the older understanding of the rule. For the moment, I would say that our legal realm calls for justification and acceptability (not for truth) and this is closer to hermeneutics than to an external and causal view of the object. In the example of adultery, we are justified in claiming that the woman has committed it when we have enough evidence for this claim, evidence accessible to the legal community.

In the case of legal orders and legal theory, the predominant form of justification should be internalist, that is, it should include a deontologist aspect that is representative of the participant's point of view. To adopt an externalist stance would imply placing the emphasis on an objective perspective, in the sense that it would refer to the relationships between the world as it is and our beliefs about it. This is too strong a claim though and useless for legal normative realms because "intentionality and good reasons" play an important role in "understanding" the object. The object is a legal text, although it is not only a text. When we deal with law and legal dogmatics, we are not in a causal world that calls for explanation, but a world of institutional facts (although not exclusively) that calls for understanding and justification.

4.1 Detached and Non-Detached Statements

In this respect, Hart says,

> "Of course those who make such "detached" statements must understand the point of view of one who accepts the rule, and so their point of view might well be called "hermeneutic"."[10]

The question is whether western methodological positivists may have a "detached" stance towards their own legal orders. Judges and normal people (at large) would be participants and would have a "committed" stance towards their legal orders. In this respect, methodological positivists would always have an external perspective (first possibility) or would just have it when they work as legal scientists, and then change to an internal point of view when they are not working as legal scientists (second possibility). I shall support the idea that this is a neurotic possibility. Very few people are able to resist this split personality.

We deal with a different case when a western anthropologist, for example, "visits" a primitive tribe. In this case, it is sounder to claim an external point of view, because the anthropologist is more able to utter "detached" statements given the "distance" between conceptual schemes and social relations. Be that as it may, if, as Hart says, those who make "detached" statements must "understand" those who participate, what is the difference? The only relevant difference is that one is a participant and the other is like a participant, that is, he does not share the internal point of view of the participants, although he could be taken as one of them. If this is correct, the difference is not between an internal point of view and an external point of view. The method is always hermeneutic. One uses it and the other mentions it.

If the methodological positivist did not understand the internal point of view of the participant, he would adopt an externalist stance, ignoring "intentions" and "good reasons". In doing so he would be a bad describer because he would not be a hermeneutic describer. In addition, an internalist approach has logical and chronological priority over an externalist one. We should bear in mind though that with no participants there cannot be describers. At most, methodological positivists can be good hermeneutic describers of relevant aspects of our form of life, such as individual rights, pluralism, tolerance, certain types of adjudication, etcetera. This is a fundamental point because gaps in law and hard cases cannot be properly filled unless some basic commitments are assumed. Description can be easy in easy cases, because there is social agreement on which description and understanding are the proper ones, although legal orders also have hard cases.

For example, if there is a positive legal rule saying, "it is prohibited to smoke in aeroplanes" a description could be, "in this legal order there is a rule stating it is prohibited to smoke in aeroplanes". However, not all descriptions of the rules of a given legal order are so easy. Sometimes construction is required because there are

[10] Hart, H.L.A. *Essays in Jurisprudence and Philosophy*, Clarendon Press, Oxford, 1983, page 14.

hard cases, although neutral describers cannot construct. They have to wait and see what participants do and, then, describe the relevant aspects in the proper way. Not everything merits being described and not all descriptions have the same level of abstraction. Only once the best possible construction is proposed and accepted by the legal community will it have the sense to describe what the law is. This should not be understood though as if the "true right answer" was discovered or recognized.

This is a regulative idea that participants, at large, share as a dispositional attitude. They look for and want the "best solution", whereas methodological positivists cannot because, if they did, they would not be neutral. In other words, participants, although they are not angels and may have conflicts between them look for (and expect) the "best solution". This also shows how normative meaning is not an individual matter. The meanings of the legal positive rules, although not members of the "is world" but members of the "ought world", have sense within a social practice. This means, *inter alia*, that normative meanings should not be placed in a popperian third world because they have sense in so far as some participants share these meanings and undertake (on this basis) mutual action. I hope we can see here that there is no strict "outside point of view", except perhaps for a Martian's.

The misleading point is to believe that the neutral relationship we may have, say, with fossils is the same as the relationship with what constitutes ourselves, for example, our legal order, our cultural traditions, etcetera. This is not to claim that we cannot adopt a critical stance towards our social world. We can and, I would say, we should, although another thing is to believe that we may reach an external point of view when we are looking at ourselves. This critical stance towards ourselves, towards our most important social practices and basic institutions, cannot be properly carried out if our "true scientific task" is to describe neutrally the existent. When we are dealing with our basic institutions, we are looking at ourselves because these basic institutions and social practices constitute us as social individuals; they are part of our "skin".

I very much doubt that we can do this from a "detached" view, whether or not it is undertaken by methodological positivists. However, this is not a "privileged" view. At most what methodological positivists can try to do is to describe accurately the different meanings of certain rules and social practices, in certain contexts and times. Even supposing that this can be done properly, participants in a social practice want to know more than just see how many meanings some rules have, in a specific language game, at a certain time. That is, they play, *inter alia*, the game of "justification" and justification is related, *inter alia*, to choice and action. In due course though this will be a basic point to be developed.

Hence, far from autonomy and independence of logical structures and far from subjectivism and essentialism, what a hermeneutic stance tries to do is to "understand" a human project, situated in a given context and expressed outwardly by texts and actions. In our case, these are legal texts and normative actions. However, at this point, another difference appears. Methodological positivists radically separate the context of discovery from the context of justification. The text would be seen as autonomous and it is usual to criticise those who search the origins of the text as committing the genetic fallacy. However, we would commit the genetic fallacy when the causes of someone's belief are criticised as if they were the justification of this belief. In other words, when we try to refute a claim by rejecting the cause of a person's belief rather than his justification. In this respect, hermeneuticians would not appeal to causes when they refer to normative meanings.

4.2 Justification and Truth

This means, *inter alia*, that in order to justify a normative legal statement it is not enough to show its cause, that is, the fact that the legislator enacted it, unless we believe that this fact is a sufficient reason for action. When we believe this, it is easier to move to exclusionary reasons for action. In other words, I doubt that hermeneuticians appeal to natural causes to justify normative meanings. In this vein, we should say that to take into account the "social context" when interpreting a legal text, for example, is not only a methodological possibility but it can be a legal obligation, as in the case of the Spanish civil code, article 3.1., which states,

> "Rules will be interpreted according to the proper sense of their words, in relation to the context, historical and legislative antecedents and the social reality to which they have to be applied, bearing in mind, fundamentally, their spirit and purpose."

To avoid bare subjectivism, our legal tradition and our positive laws have settled legal procedures, legal reasoning, legal means, legal goals and several judicial instances, and among these is the obligation to justify judicial decisions. What happens is that the ideal of the Vienna Circle has developed another language game. This is centred on an ideal logical language that makes any other language game inevitably vague and neglectable. It is probable that (at least) the most radical legal theorists of both sides (methodological positivists and analytical hermeneuticians) had very little in common, thereby making fertile communication between them very difficult or impossible.

In this respect, although it is not my aim to deal here with Luhmann's work, I would say that it does not fit into my contribution, among other things, because he over-emphasizes "structure, system and procedure" and undervalues "human beings as actors of the legal system, values and material legitimation". It is not necessary to agree with the requirement of the Habermasian "emancipation" to criticise Luhmann's very conservative approach. To over-emphasize the legitimating character of procedures means, *inter alia*, to accept uncritically the present power's structure and its material contents.

Recalling the above cited problem of legal method, it is interesting to note the criticism of N. MacCormick made by C. Alchourrón and E. Bulygin.[11] They say,

> "science is interested nearly exclusively in settling the truth, while law is basically interested in solving social conflicts."

[11] Alchourrón, C. and Bulygin, E. "Los límites de la lógica y el razonamiento jurídico" (pp. 303-328). In: *Análisis Lógico y Derecho*, Centro de Estudios Constitucionales, Madrid, 1991. In this respect, it seems interesting to remind ourselves of some of Herbert Simon's words, "There is a final difficulty, first pointed out by Gödel, that rich systems of logic are never complete, there always exist true theorems that cannot be reached as outputs by applying the legal transformations to the inputs." *Reason in Human Affairs*, Blackwell, Oxford, 1983, page 7.

My point is that law is not only interested in solving social conflicts but also in doing it in the best possible way, granted that most addressees are participants. Otherwise, some empirical or deductive tasks could be done equally by neutral observers. Nevertheless, the most interesting aspects, like selecting (or constructing) the proper normative premise and selecting (or constructing) the proper interpretation of a given normative premise, are better undertaken by participants because they are mainly interested in the "optimisation" of their legal order.

They also say, in relation to MacCormick,

> "But, if -as MacCormick and many jurists seem to believe- truth would depend on what the judge decides through an authoritative act ("truth is what courts say what is truth"), then, judges would be really infallible ... Facts are what they are and not what judges say what they are."[12]

I do not know whether MacCormick believes this but, in my view, we should distinguish between formal truth and material truth. Judges (like scientists) are fallible but the highest courts are formally infallible for legal certainty reasons. In this respect, truth -in this legal formal sense- is what judges say it is. Another thing is material truth. It is possible that something has happened, materially speaking, but from the point of view of the legal order it can or cannot be legally true.

If we understand this as saying that it is not materially true then it is illogical. However, if we understand it as saying that it is not true from the point of view of this legal order then it is not illogical because legal orders (differently from Physics) rely on some basic values, such as legal certainty and others. For example, although a rape could have happened (materially speaking), it could be known through means and procedures that are radically illegal. It can happen that (formally speaking) there is no rape. Hence, if this is correct, there could be a material truth (something really happened) and a formal truth (what the legal authority states that has happened, according to the rules of a given legal order and certain "legal" facts).

It is surprising that they claim,

> " ...in this respect, the concept of truth used in law is exactly the same as that used by empirical sciences."

I think that (granted the distinction between truth in a legal formal sense and truth in a material sense, and granted -as they also say- that law is mainly interested in solving social conflicts), even when facts are what they are (that is, according to what our mature empirical sciences say), they are dependent (at least sometimes) on legal fictions and basic values. Hence, "real" facts do not always have the last word. This does not happen in empirical sciences. Therefore, it is confusing to claim that the concept of truth in law is exactly the same as it is in empirical sciences.

In other words, it is correct to claim that the truth of propositions is independent of linguistic conventions but not the sentences. In this respect, it is usually said that propositions are bearers of truth and falsity, but do sentences expressing commands express propositions? In the negative case, they would not be true/false and this would actually be the case for most legal sentences. Even if this were correct though, it would not modify the fact that a fact is what it is, but it would show that

---

[12] Alchourrón, C. and Bulygin, E. Ibidem.

the importance of material truth is rather different in empirical sciences and in the so-called legal science.

In the same vein they see judges as neutral observers that describe and put labels on the correct boxes,

> " ...we tend to believe that in many cases (not all) judges do not evaluate but limit themselves to register the evaluations of the social group they belong to."

I hope that in this paper I have already expressed my contrary view to this "neutral-observer-position" and therefore I will not repeat it again at this point. Nevertheless, we do not know what "many cases" mean and what happens with the rest. They also distinguish, as is usual, between norms and normative propositions,

> " ...a factual proposition cannot justify a prescription and normative propositions are factual, even when the facts to which they refer ... are "institutional facts"."

This seems to show that, if legal justification plays a basic role, as I believe, prescriptions and not descriptions play the fundamental role in legal orders.

This does not happen in empirical sciences since, alternatively, they claim that,

> " ...to justify it the judge has to use the norm uttered by the legislator."

In my view, this means that in order to justify we have to adopt an internal point of view. If this is the case, the "point" is not description and truth as correspondence, but prescription and justification. Of course, granted that these prescriptions and justifications are made by human beings and are directed at human beings, they have to be (to a certain extent) realistic, although not in Ross's sense. In spite of my comments, I agree with their final conclusion,

> " ...the reconstruction of the justificatory judicial reasoning can be done within the limits of deductive logic."

In my opinion, if this means that this step (from premises to conclusion) can be reconstructed as a deductive inference it is only to claim that it is possible to translate the language of judges to the language of logicians.

I am not qualified to claim whether this is so but I accept what they say. The aspect I want to stress is that, granted that this is correct, a logical reconstruction would show what judges did in the past, showing the moves from premises to conclusion in the simplest way. This is very interesting because it can show the existence of reasoning mistakes that can, perhaps, be avoided in the future. Nevertheless, in so far as legal decisions are interested in solving social conflicts in the best possible way, here and now, deductive logic is not decisive because it is an *ex post* justification and because legal reasoning is not exclusively logical reasoning. What matters most is that the judicial decision be just (the other basic value is legal certainty), according to the values of the legal order, the values of the legal institution at stake, the positive norms, the precedents, the social reality, certain justificatory reasons, etcetera.

However, they are not necessarily logical conditions. They are sources with different justificatory strengths that call for interpretation. The "users" will make new proposals to "best" adapt the legal order to new "relevant" social circumstances. This is, basically, an evaluative justificatory process. It is interesting to note such deep differences between some methodological positivists and some analytical hermeneuticians (although it can also be frustrating in so far as it shows the practical impossibility of agreement) because they show different understandings of the object and different ontological commitments. In this vein, Aarnio asks,

> "What methods does legal dogmatics have in establishing truth/falsehood?"

In his view, instead of truth we should talk of rational acceptability of interpretations.[13]

Even if we accept that truth is correspondence with reality we can say that this theory applies to statements like "there are three chairs in the room", but when we deal with an evaluative statement we have more difficulties because we may doubt which is the state of affairs to which it corresponds. It does not mean though that there is a complete separation between empirical and evaluative statements. Our evaluative statements may change on the basis of new empirical knowledge. Nevertheless, in legal normative fields jurists try to justify their statements and decisions, not to demonstrate they are true. If truth is a relation between propositions and facts we can say that jurists, mainly, deal with institutional facts not with brute facts. That is, jurists deal with facts (institutional facts) that, at least in part, depend on us. It is usually said that brute facts do not depend on us. I take for granted here that our task is basically practical not cognitive. We try to justify, not to demonstrate. We do this in certain contexts that we can, partially, change.

4.3 Legal Meaning and Common Understanding

Criticising Aarnio's and Niiniluoto's view of legal dogmatics E. Bulygin says,

> "The above claim that the problems of identification are empirical requires some clarification ... In this vein, it is important to distinguish between the discovering of an existing meaning and the adjudication (totally or partially) of a new meaning. The first activity is empirical although the meanings are non-empirical entities. The meaning of an expression is given either by the common usage of the ordinary language or the legal language, or by the intention of the author's expression."[14]

This shows, in my view, the deep difference between methodological positivists (let us say, the Carnap tendency) and Hermeneuticians (let us say, the analytical tendency). Bulygin seems to believe that although meanings are not empirical entities they can be discovered.

In this respect, it would not be surprising to claim that "some ramblers discovered a dead man on a mountain near a town". Now, suppose a newspaper says, "Some ramblers discovered a meaning, hidden in a bush". Bulygin does not claim that this is possible because meanings are not empirical things. However, in this case, can we discover God, granted that it is not an empirical thing? It seems that we can discover the common usage of a given language. For example, John discovers that Peter uses the term "justice" with the meaning "J". However, this

---

[13] Aarnio, A. *The Rational as Reasonable*, Reidel, Dordrecht, 1987, page 24.

[14] Bulygin, E. "Dogmatica Juridica y Sistematización del Derecho" (pp. 465-484). In: *Análisis Lógico y Derecho*, op. cit.

meaning can be the common usage of a given group in a given society, or the intention of Peter. For the first, we should suppose that this society is unitary, that is, all of its members use the same term with the same meaning in the same contexts, both intralinguistic and extralinguistic ones, and at the same time. For the second, the difficulty of discovering the intention of the legislator has been repeatedly commented on. The same applies to Peter.

In my view, Bulygin's basic flaw is to support the unity of method, typical of logical positivism. I believe that this tendency and hermeneutic analytic tendency have very few relevant aspects in common. He recognises this though, in an elegant way,

> "... differently from Aarnio I am sceptic about the need of a special method (hermeneutic method) to determine the meaning of legal statements."

Finally, Bulygin believes that two different legal interpretations are two different legal norms and not two interpretations of the same norm. He also says,

> "Hence, when Aarnio talks of interpretation of a norm, by "norm" it should be understood the normative formulation and not its meaning."[15]

Suppose that there is a legislative text, in a given legal order that is usually interpreted by judges as having the meaning "M". We have, then, an interpretation of this legislative text that produces a legal norm with the content "M". Suppose that, in due course, judges interpret the same legislative text as having the meaning "M-1" and not as having the meaning "M". We can say that we have interpreted the same legislative text in a different way. Another question is to claim that this new interpretation produces a new legal norm. Is this so? If the meaning of "M-1" does not contradict the meaning of "M", we would have two legal norms that are the result of the interpretation of the same legislative text. If the "M-1" meaning does contradict the "M" meaning, the usual result will be that judges will not apply the former meaning ("M") and it will then disappear. What will not disappear, until legislative decision, will be the legislative text that appears as the formal valid must-source.

"M" or "M-1" are, for the legal community at large, the proper representation of the legislative text (when they are not contradictory) in the sense that they properly represent the legislative will. The force of the Rule of Law doctrine favours this situation. Otherwise, the legislator's will model would not accept the idea that two contradictory legal norms are both existing and applied (to the same situations) at the same time, in the same legal order. Hence, a legal norm should be understood as the meaning of a legislative text, granted that this interpretative result is accepted by the legal community and not rejected (at least) by the community at large.

Let me return to hard and easy cases. I think that there is a relevant basic difference between our western societies (in spite of the differences between them) and the ancient Greeks. *Inter alia*, we have no common good or, at least, not in the same sense as ancient Greeks. This is a reason for having more hard cases than in unitary societies where there is a unifying common good. In a society with a shared

---

[15] Ibidem.

common good, the existence of hard cases would be more surprising. It would be, probably, considered as an apparent difficulty. This is not what happens in our societies. We cannot expect the "one right answer" in all cases. In this situation, "justification" of one "second best" answer is fundamental, granted that logic can solve the problem only once a choice has been justified and accepted by the legal community. Although I am not interested, at least for the moment, in the "right answer thesis" I would say that it is close to a neo-conservative stance, in so far as it expects that tradition will give us certainty.

This neo-conservative perspective is very close to a communitarian perspective because only a common good could give us, *inter alia*, stability, happiness and "one right answer". This would not be possible (pragmatically speaking) in a pluralistic society, at least with the same extension and intensity. Even democratic political regimes and dictatorial political regimes can share "one right answer". For example, they can agree on traffic regulations or certain requirements for a contract to be valid. This can be seen as "one right answer" both as a premise and as a conclusion of a premise. However, we should not confuse neo-conservative or communitarian nostalgia for old unified communities, sharing a common good, with the basic social need of a certain level of common understanding.

The problem, then, is neither common understanding nor selfish individual solutions. We should not confuse the change in the level of common understanding with the absence of it. We have to decide within a given tradition, that is, within certain interpretative limits, which level of commonality and individuality we believe is best, here and now. This is not written in the past, although the past we have (and we necessarily have some past) places us in a certain cultural tradition. From it, we have to decide what we want and what is possible for us to reach.

4.4 Epistemological Remarks

As we saw when we dealt with ontological commitments, we cannot (or better said, we should not) do this irrespective of a specific background, in our case, the legal background. In dealing with Epistemology, we could say that we are dealing with a general theory of knowledge but, in so far as we do not have knowledge, we could say that it is useless to talk of Legal Epistemology. It would be a spurious way of giving (or trying to give) prestige to legal dogmatics. This is a complex and disputable matter and therefore I will make only a few remarks here. As a first step I would agree with claims such as those of R. Chisholm when he says that epistemology is normative. It is probably so in any social field, although I am limiting myself to the legal field. Claiming that legal epistemology is normative means that we have some epistemic purposes, which are the most important for improving our belief-sets. It should be clear now (if not, I hope it will be clear later on) that this is coherent with my support of the primacy of the internal point of view over the external point of view.

"Knowledge", in the limited sense I am going to use it, is not something conceptually separated from opinion. In this respect, I would not back Plato's view (the so called "incompatibility thesis") that knowledge is infallible while opinion is not. In my view knowledge is not infallible. Moreover, my view of knowledge should be separated from causal theories of knowledge because of the causal connection claimed between knowledge and facts. Hence, knowledge should be seen as a belief (placed within a set of sufficiently coherent beliefs) on the basis of sufficient justifying evidence. This means that a judge, a legal scholar or a citizen know that a valid contract of sale exists (at a given time, in a given legal order) when there are sufficient justifying legal reasons for having this belief. This though is not exclusively an individual task.

In relation to the "existence" of the cited contract it seems clear that it is not a physical existence. However, it does not matter, since, for instance, we cannot touch "friendship" or "love" although we are in touch with them. We require them for reaching a certain psychological stability. On the basis of these concepts and certain biological and social features, we both receive and create social networks. These and other things "constitute" us, as we are, as individuals that live in a social context. That is enough for my present purposes. We can dispense with the global sceptic. We should not waste our time because we are limited, also in a chronological sense. We (participants in a form of life) should only be interested in the local sceptic. All this means that "justification" is a basic concept for us, as participants in a common enterprise, in order to improve our legal order. This means to improve ourselves and improve our social relations. Only when we believe that the social background, as a whole, does not deserve our "effort", our "internal point of view", should we strive for a global alternative. Nevertheless, this is exceptional.

Therefore, legal justification is not only related to what the legal order "is" but also to what the legal order "ought to be". This means, *inter alia*, that legal dogmatics is not, and should not be, only descriptive. It also means that the Kelsenian distinction between the "subjective sense" and "objective sense" of legal acts is mistaken. Everyone knows his example about the captain of Köpenick, in which a secret society condemns a person to death for being a traitor. Subjectively, this act was an execution but objectively it was a crime.[16] Legal dogmatics should only deal with the objective sense. The problem with this Kelsenian distinction is that we can see this difference in "routine or easy cases" but not in the so-called "hard cases", because in the latter we do not know which is the objective sense. It is a disputable matter but, nevertheless, the objective sense should be understood as an intersubjective sense, unless an essentialist view of the language is supported or we expect the objectivity of Physics.

Consequently, our Legal Epistemology should be normative and based, *inter alia*, on *prima facie* justifications. This means that they can be defeated by further justifications, either on the basis of the same legal premises (but with new justifications) or on the basis of different legal premises. This shows the fundamental dynamic aspect of the legal task. This balance between stability and adaptation should be understood as a balance between stability justifications and adaptation justifications, which is a balance that will depend, *inter alia*, on the social circumstances and goals. That is, whether they are normal or not. However, "normal circumstances" is clearly a vague expression that calls for interpretation. Recalling

---

[16] Kelsen, H. *Teoria Pura del Derecho*, Editorial Universitaria de Buenos Aires, 1976, page 38.

Bobbio's view we could say that when some social and institutional variables are given we would have a tendency towards a formalist conception of legal dogmatics. Therefore, "normal circumstances" would refer to situations where jurists appeal (mainly or exclusively) to formal sources of law when, at the same time, we are living in a relatively stable society. Although this also calls for interpretation, I will not try to define all these expressions more precisely. For our present purposes I believe this is enough.

4.5 Stability and Adaptation

Granted that (at least in our cultural realms) we cannot completely reject stability or adaptation, our Legal Epistemology would have to take account of this basic feature, that is, a permanent justificatory effort to improve our legal normative field on the basis of a balance between these two ideal types, stability and adaptation. I have already said above that the importance, for participants, is the "improvement" of our object. This means, *inter alia*, that stability-adaptation are means for reaching the best possible contextual legal solutions.

I reject, then, that our input be certain sense-stimuli and that our cognitive model should be psychology plus linguistics, in a naturalised epistemology vein. We do not try to explain our brain processes but to justify our decisions, or at least certain decisions, that are taken on the basis of certain legal norms, legal procedures and selected facts, at a given time. Perhaps, Epistemology *tout court* should have to settle the conditions under which a statement has the property of being objective knowledge. Otherwise, Legal Epistemology would refer to the conditions under which legal statements are more or less justified. The expression "legal statements" refers both to legislator's language and jurists' language. No matter whether the first is authoritative and the second not, because the latter is not a self-referring language. In so far as legal scholars share an internal point of view they try to improve the legal order. When they improve their meta-language they do this for improving the legal order and their solutions to changing circumstances. Hence, pure description (if possible) would be poor.

We, as legal scholars, are mainly interested in knowing how a subjective judgement becomes an objective one. I would say though, an intersubjective one. Nevertheless, granted that we are not in the realm of mature sciences, we may have more than one paradigm, which is different from what happens in mature sciences such as Physics. If this is correct, we could say that we have a methodological approach (with its own ontological commitments) that is interested, on the one hand, in truth and description from an external point of view and, on the other, mainly in judgements and justification from an internal point of view. That is, the so-called Analytic-Hermeneutic approach appealing to concepts as a way to categorise a certain world, the legal normative world.

Once we (basically, but not exclusively, the participants of a given legal community) have accepted these legal concepts, we have a sort of map of the field we are going to live in. From these concepts we shall draw inferences, with the most interesting ones not being logical consequences, because we have to make judgements of relevance. Even if a logical chain is valid, we have to decide where to cut the chain because not all logical inferences are necessarily relevant for us, here and now. This means that, within limits, we construct the world we are going to interact with. However, while it is wrong to claim that we can deal directly with facts (because we require a previous conceptual map) it is also wrong to believe that there is only one way from concepts to reality. In any case, the next step from concepts is judgements, because (in a Kantian vein) concepts have to be applied in judgements. In short, we cannot rely on algorithms.

We interact between concepts and reality. One of the reasons of this interaction is the dynamic feature of legal orders and interpretation-decision. Another one is that our concepts have no clear and sharp boundaries. Sometimes we try to widen or restrict these boundaries, or try to interpret old and new boundaries in a new way. This is so because we are not looking for essences (either material, so beloved by natural law thinkers, or formal, so beloved by logical positivists) because our legal concepts are neither true nor false and because our legal solutions do not last forever. It is interesting here to recall Quine's "entrenchment". Essentially, we decide in the best possible justified way which legal concepts (that is, their accepted interpretation and application, at a given time) should be more protected from change or adaptation.

Judges (in an official authoritative vein) and legal scholars (without it) support, or not, this entrenchment until a legislative decision decides otherwise. Nevertheless, I have already commented that the legislator must be able to choose between alternatives in order to be a legislator, although this capability is not unlimited. Hence, granted that legal concepts are, let us say, universal and have the property of being instantiated in many particulars, there is always room for argumentation. That is, we could argue whether some particulars should be in or out of the legal concept at stake. This is one of the reasons why justification and *prima facie* reasons, *inter alia*, play such an important role in legal argumentation. Another reason is that our legal concepts are basically normative.

The connections we make between them are not, and cannot be, just logical connections. We do not undertake this task for enjoying ourselves, looking at a geometrical world, but to help improve the working of the legal order, that is, human beings. In this case, I believe that a further step, from Hart's view, should be taken. It is not the case that officials should share an internal point of view with it being sufficient (although not desirable) that citizens be obedient donkeys. We should reject either systemic or positivist approaches that enhance officials and diminish the role of citizens. We should also reject a pyramidal view of the legal order that is close to the Kelsenian idea of "sanctions" as the essence of legal orders.

This view has been considered by some legal scholars as a proper representation of the legal order itself. Nevertheless, once pure and neutral conceptions of legal dogmatics have failed, we should accept the moral and political dimension of both the legislator's language and the jurists' language. A pyramidal map of legal orders does not reflect reality itself, but represents an authoritarian view of the object. This is not to deny what imperativists and supporters of Critical Legal Studies, among others, emphasize, that is, the institutional coercion linked to any legal order.

However, one thing is to recognise this feature and another one is to see it as the "essence" of legal orders.

This shows that our form of life makes room both for those who see legal orders as expression of domination and manipulation, and for those who, without denying it, do not see them as exclusive features. Concepts or conceptions of freedom, for example, are not seen by all as tricky devices of capitalism through the mediation of corrupt and alienated jurists. On the other hand, those who see things in the other way are not "pure" beings fighting against the devil, that is, the market. It is probable that our epistemic commitments make it very difficult to leave our conceptual scheme that has been built up through our lives. Moreover, it is not clear, at all, that universal agreement on substantive justice (on which items?) would be pragmatically possible.[17] In any case, neither is a neutral position.

5. ACTION AND SOCIAL PRACTICE

A basic presupposition is that adult agents are purposive, intentional and able to commitment. Nevertheless, we should not see them in an either-or way, that is, pure participants or pure observers. It is also stated that we cannot claim objectivity in relation to values, except in a trivial sense. That is, once we have accepted a general claim like, "it is morally wrong to steal from someone", then it is true that it is a morally wrong action that Peter steals John's book. If there were truth in relation to values we should accept the "one right answer" in the so-called hard cases, but I do not. It is assumed here that the intersubjectivity of value premises depends, fundamentally, on forms of life. We are embedded in values through social practices. At least some values are seen as objective by those who share certain social practices in a similar way as certain basic beliefs are not put in doubt.

---

[17] Unger, R.M. *Law in Modern Society*, The Free Press, New York, 1976, pages 241 and 242. "I have argued that these ideas of solidarity and equity can be seen in two different lights, which correspond respectively to the two senses of custom. On the one hand, they can be devices with which to defend the established beliefs and values of a particular community, as articulated by those who have governed it in the past or control it in the present. But in conjunction with a program of substantive justice, they may also serve as the primitive form taken by the struggle to discover a universal given order in social life". Even accepting that our best possible goal would be a program of substantive justice the problem is how we should do it and what price should we pay for it. Otherwise, what should we do with those who do not agree with it?

From a related point of view, J.A. Pérez Lledó says, "The transformer value attributed at "CLSers" to ideological criticism appears then as something extraordinarily optimistic and idealistic ... And if the Law forms a fundamental part of this constituent conscience of society, to transform the juridical conscience is also to transform the society. The academic jurist can contribute in a decisive way to this change in the juridical conscience. Of course, CLS does not claim that this is the only route for transformation of social conscience ... but CLS encourages Law professors to work in this direction ... it has to do with the idea that Unger christens as "*internal development*", the one working "*from within*", sharing what there is, strengthening the repressed possibilities that are already present." As a kind of general view, he says, "The already described CLS could be as heterogeneous and paradoxical as is wanted and still however be relatively accessible if they at least showed a certain "clarity in the contradiction". But if, as Boyle said, conciseness is not one of its virtues, clarity, I add, is neither." *El Movimiento Critical Legal Studies*, Tecnos, Madrid, 1996, page 399 and 21.

We grow as human beings "contaminated" by a complex web of social practices, although we are not determined worms but conditioned human beings. Individuals and social practices develop in communities but they should not be seen as unitary sets. On the contrary, communities have (to different degrees) a permanent tension between the private and the public spheres, between individuals and the community, between positive and critical morality. The entrenched background of individuals, social practices and the community is a form of life. It can be seen as an ideal place where communities overlap allowing individuals to feel members of wider contexts than their own strict local community. In this respect, Human Rights could be seen as a higher normative level where different normative conceptions come close to one another.

When we want to describe the outside world we do not "constitute" it, because the world is already there. What we can do is select a piece of the reality according to a given theory or methodological perspective. However, we cannot describe the reality as it is but, granted certain biological features (ours) and a certain basic conceptual scheme (ours) we take a certain theoretical perspective that allows us, or justifies us, to select a certain piece of reality and, then, to describe it from a certain point of view. Therefore, in the so-called normative sciences, human beings (or, at least, certain human beings in certain contexts) can "constitute" reality. For example, article 1.254 of the Spanish Civil Code says,

> "The contract exists since one or several persons agree to put under an obligation, in relation to another or others, to give something or to render a service."

We can see that human beings can put into "existence" certain social facts like "contracts". In this respect, we could distinguish between "sense" and "reference". Before a person under an obligation has given something or rendered a service to another, there is no present reference. However, it has "sense". We, human beings, have given sense to certain social facts. Afterwards, when this person has given something or rendered a service, there is reference and sense. We can see that this social fact (a valid legal contract) "stands by itself" because it has sense even without present reference. Nevertheless, in the end, although some fact has to happen, it will be a fact "mediated" by a given sense that has not been discovered, because there is nothing to be discovered. When we deal with these "normative facts" we therefore realise several things:

First, that there is a commitment, in other words, some people commit themselves to give something or to render a service.

Second, it is a commitment in relation to the future, or at least, a commitment in relation to certain actions that will be undertaken in the future.

Third, although there can be degrees of intentionality, "normative actions" are basically intentional. Some of them are so strongly intentional that we, for instance, do not say, "he married intentionally". We simply say "he married" because normative actions are basically intentional. Some of the less important actions convey little intentionality or can even be fulfilled mechanically. For example, to buy a newspaper is not as intentional as marrying. Nevertheless, if we are asked, we can explain, later on, that we wanted to buy a newspaper, or, even more accurately, a specific newspaper because we like it or for other reasons. We can rationalise our "mechanical" action. We can also say, "John ran over Peter but he did it without intention". In this case, John did not perform the action of knocking down Peter under a given description, a teleological description. Perhaps this can be so under a causal description but this is not usually sufficient in legal normative fields.

Fourth, what has been mentioned above entails certain presuppositions: that adult agents are purposive and intentional beings, especially when they deal with "normative actions". An "ideal" normative action not only has a social symbolic content (that does not depend -or not exclusively- on the agent) but it also has intentionality, consciousness and commitment. I would say that although "commitment" is a subjective element it also has a social dimension. Peter and Mary can marry not only because they commit themselves to marry, performing certain facts, but also because there is a community that understands this commitment and these facts in a certain way, giving them a certain social importance. Nevertheless, it is possible for a person to pretend to marry, that is, to perform the external formalities without sharing the expected internal commitments.

In other words, to fulfil all external appearances that can cheat the other persons that have a "true commitment" about this concrete normative action. If all persons (or a certain number of them) from a given community did not have this commitment, it would make no sense to undertake a pretence. All this means that agents, as participants, are the main actors of this complex web of meanings and facts, because they are logically prior and because "non-committed agents" (or some of them) try, usually, to simulate being "committed" agents.

Fifth, it is not correct to claim that there is no privileged description of actions. On the contrary, depending on the field we are talking about, we do have a certain privileged description of actions. For example, if actions are understood as bodily movements or as factual regularities, the privileged description is a causal one. On the other hand, if actions are understood as having the normative features mentioned above, the privileged description is a teleological one. If this is so, the agents are supposed to be purposive and conscious agents able to know what a commitment is, and which social symbolic content a concrete normative action has. The normative fact would be the normative action when it is seen from a third person viewpoint. Recalling Wittgenstein we could say that there are no private normative actions.

From a first person viewpoint, somebody performs some action. This action converts into a social fact when others identify it as a normative action undertaken by a participant (or a pretender). This normative action then "solidifies" into normative facts. The first person viewpoint originates a normative action in the sense that puts in motion a social web of meanings and consequences. If not, it is not socially understandable. This social web is chronologically prior to individual action, although the interplay between "participants" and this social web is a fundamental aspect that does not exist in the causal world. Human beings interact with the world outside but the "answer" is not the same. We deal with the world outside with the help of theories but we can do it consciously or not. Some of the theories are so internalised that it is difficult to be conscious of them.

Therefore, properly speaking, only the social web has "answers", because the social web is basically managed by participants and conveys a conceptual scheme. We, as individuals, interact with this, more or less entrenched, conceptual scheme.

In any case, participants should not be seen in an "either-or" way. Participants and observers should be understood as ideal types in a Weberian sense. We cannot see "pure participants" and "pure observers" in the real world. For this reason, methodological positivists are not (and cannot be) neutral observers *tout court*, and participants are not (and cannot be) types of angels, always and exclusively acting as conscious, intentional and critical beings, on the exclusive basis of moral reasons. In relation to this issue, the problem of objectivity arises. In this respect, A. Peczenik claims that either one must be value-objectivist or value-nihilist because an intermediate position is a chimera.

Value-objectivity could be understood in the sense that certain values are morally good in themselves, no matter what the subjective opinion of certain persons is. Value-nihilism could be understood in the sense that there are no values, only desires or wants. I would say that values can be understood as something different from desires. Suppose Peter desires to have a sexual relation with Mary but she refuses. If Peter (1) sees his desires as ultimate reasons, he could use sexual violence against Mary. This behaviour would be coherent with his premises. Peter (2) may refuse to use sexual violence because, having the same desire, he does not want to go to jail and he therefore makes his prudential reasons prevail. In addition, Peter (3) could refuse to use sexual violence because, having the same desire, he believes that human beings are ends in themselves and Mary ought not to be treated only as a mean.

If values are reasons for action we could understand moral values as the strongest reasons for action. However, claiming that values (or practical judgements) are objective, should mean that they are not only feelings, in a Humean vein. What are they in a positive sense? The objectivity of values (and value judgements) would imply a kind of "one right answer", either in the acceptation (or discovery) of value premises or in the application of accepted value premises. Nevertheless, a problem arises when another individual does not accept either the value-premises or the conclusion (if it is not a formal deduction). On the other hand, how can we objectively choose between two value-premises belonging to two different communities? What happens if both sides claim objectivity?

We can claim that (1), (2) and (3) are only subjective psychological states. In doing so, we are using a natural sciences view (basically, the idea that a certain effect comes necessarily from a given cause) for explaining human social relations. Although this is one possibility, there is another that contemplates human beings as capable of judgement, and not only as a link in a causal chain. If this is accepted, we can deal with the issue of value-objectivity commented on above. If values are subject dependent, they cannot be objective in a certain sense. For example, volcanoes are objective but values are not because the former are not subject dependent. Moreover, one can say that legal dogmatics or mature scientific tasks are both subject dependent because, *ipso facto*, they depend on subjects.

Nevertheless, scientific tasks and scientific theories have certain features that legal dogmatics (much more value laden) do not have. For example, the empirical approach, a much more developed logical apparatus, tests predictability, with the main goal being to explain how reality is. On the other hand, some basic features of legal dogmatics are systematization and justification, with the main goal being to justify a certain systematization of a legal order and a justification of certain normative proposals that try to "optimise" the legal order or certain aspects of it. In this respect, it should not be surprising that legal positivist tendencies (in general) claim that the proper task of legal dogmatics is only description of a legal order. I have already commented that this is an insufficient task, either as a matter of fact or as a matter of normative proposal.

Recalling the issue of "value-objectivity", we could say that there is one sense in which we can talk of the truth about values. Another sense will be commented on later. For example, if you accept that no one ought to hurt anybody, it will be true that John ought not to hurt Peter. This is a trivial truth and it is dependent on a previous acceptation of a certain value premise. Therefore, even if everyone (in a given society) would accept a value premise like the one commented on above we would still have trivial truths, although we would also have "hard cases", that is, cases where more than one answer is sound. This is very different from the other case where what John ought to do is logical inference from the value premise. Even if we believe that we can make true moral statements (in a non-trivial sense) we have to cope with the problem of time, change and adaptation.

Assuming the former is correct, (let us suppose it is) we could not make this claim ahistorically. Certain prehistoric ancestors did not have terms such as "freedom" and others. Hence, what does "objective-values" mean? I believe that this term is related to the participants' judgements, that is, they use this term (or a similar one) and justifiably believe that they are reasons for action at a given time, in a given society. This term is also related to observers, but in a different sense. They may describe that participants judge these values as "objective". The question is whether this is only a dream or not. I would say that this is not a practical question for participants because they (generally speaking) cannot avoid believing that murder, rape, fraud, etcetera, are morally bad.

When many people, in a given society, judge that certain values are ultimate reasons for action, we deal with "objective" values. In this judgement, the closer we are to the general conditions of a rational Habermasian discourse, the stronger the claim of "objectivity" can be. However, when we engage in practical judgement we already have some presuppositions. In a Kantian vein, we could say these are not only categories (like substance and causality) or forms of intuition (like space and time) but also more concrete determinations, like basic values and basic beliefs. Nevertheless, they are not "transcendental" in the proper sense, because although they are presupposed in the social experience (at least for participants) we also interact with them. Among other ways of interaction, any society interacts its values and judgements through positive and critical morality. In relation to basic beliefs we also have scientific revolutions, that can make us change some basic beliefs.

In my opinion, this is the acceptable sense of "objective", when we are dealing with values. Granted certain natural features, certain social relations and certain cultural constructions, we cannot dispense with certain "objective" values. Nevertheless, we do not only have scientific revolutions but also moral revolutions as well, although they have different features. At the same time, even within the realm of "objective values" we have "hard cases", especially when we try to apply them to specific circumstances. Finally, even if we accept the existence of "objective values", in the above commented sense, this should not be seen as a static picture. "Objective values" do not only exist for participants in a changing society at large, but they also have to deal, as I said, with critical morality. That is, they exist in a realm of tension and conflict.

Sometimes there is an internal tension and sometimes there is an external one, that is, the latter occurs when value premises or basic value functions are questioned. Recalling the use of the term "truth" within normative fields, I would agree that in the ordinary language we sometimes use the term "truth". For example, John says, "Peter is a bad person" and Mary asks, "Is it true?" In my opinion, this means that Mary asks for the commonly accepted features that make a person a "bad person", at a given time in a certain society, for an important part of its members. I think that this is dissimilar to what Physicists call "truth". If this were correct I would say that most of us (sharing the same form of life) use certain basic values as objective. Most of us use certain basic beliefs as true. No one denies that "John is riding a bicycle" but some may reject the claim that "Peter is a bad person". It would mean that some basic beliefs are more "entrenched" than some values, not only in their acceptation but also in their application to concrete cases.

This would mean that we expect (at least from a practical point of view) truth in relation to basic beliefs, that is, intersubjective agreement on certain beliefs. Moreover, we do not expect truth in relation to attitudes or in their application, except in logical inferences. We know that different persons may have different evaluations of the same beliefs. This is a feature of our democratic societies, where different political parties interpret differently what is good for society, even using the same data. Summing up: "truth" qualifies our basic beliefs, that is, we do not even say that it is true that we are sitting on a chair, when we are. We take this for granted, as a basic presupposition of the reality as it is. In a similar way, science tries to tell us how reality is, although in a more complex and precise way. On the other hand, values do not try to tell us how reality is but how we ought to behave, granted certain rules, institutions and social contexts. In this respect, I would not say that we are looking for truth (in normative fields) but rational consensus. Differently from truth, this rational consensus tries to solve, impartially, certain practical conflicts.

In case we are talking of "truth" (when dealing with values) it should be applied to certain human behaviour (understood as observable facts), not to the values themselves. In this respect, normative legal fields are more dependent on justice than on truth, because law (in this normative sense) is a practical enterprise. It means, *inter alia*, that guiding and justifying certain conducts have primacy over the discovery of how the legal reality is. One could claim that before judging a conduct as just, we must know which is (in fact) the legally expected conduct. I will not though repeat my arguments here, but merely say that "description of law as it is" is not a neutral matter and cannot, on the other hand, be equated with "description of nature as it is", although this is also selective and theory dependent.

Can participants be objective in relation to their own world and their own normative actions? This is a problem for the meaning of "objectivity". Do "contaminated" participants, on the one hand, and observers, on the other, claim the same when they talk about "objectivity"? First, let us see what importance social practices and the form of life have for human beings. Let us remember what I said above about the pretender. The basic point in relation to social practices is that they constitute a complex web of guidance, justification and support for individual normative actions. Let us take the example of a private contract. We suppose that both parties have undertaken a commitment. It is not necessary though that these commitments be of the same importance and/or intensity.

No one expects that to buy a newspaper conveys the same kind of commitment as to marry. Then, confidence in the seriousness of commitments (no matter the degree of intensity or importance) allows for a person to rely on a normative social practice and to identify other people as participants. We can be mistaken in relation to the commitment of specific participants, but not to the existence of commitment as a social practice. Of course, it is logically possible that all "participants" cheat each other all the time. When there is this commented commitment, the web of social practices is constitutive of the society and of the individual. However, this should not be understood in a strong communitarian sense, because individuals have (at least in democratic societies, to a higher extent than others), and ought to have, freedom for shaping, to a certain extent, their own lives, although this can never be so starting from scratch.

In any case, I reject both "higher and objective goods" that are superior to the individuals and also the supposed happy community of integrated communal beings. At this point, I will go back to the issue I am now dealing with. Why can a social practice serve as a guide and justification for normative actions? The answer is because social practices are not seen, at least by the participants, as a collection of causal facts but as a created and dynamic web of normative social relations that have a justificatory dimension. Once we accept that these normative social practices have a justificatory dimension, as they have for participants, we can see the necessary interplay (from a pragmatical point of view) between the present situation of a social practice and what it ought to be.

Once again though this is a matter of degree. It is not the case that participants are anxious all the time, trying to do their best to improve the social practice. However, if they do not bear in mind that a social practice is not only something to be repeated but also something to be improved, this social practice will impoverish itself and may die, that is, may lack justificatory force (not necessarily in a yes-no or true-false form). This means, *inter alia*, that any social practice ought to be adapted to new circumstances and this adaptation, undertaken by participants, should be "the best" it can be. This requirement is sound because participants, when doing this, are, at the same time, doing what is "best" for themselves. This is so because participants constitute themselves, not only by private individual actions, but also by the influence and interaction with social practices.

Now some final remarks. It is supposed here that human beings, at large, are rational agents in the sense that they are capable (not necessarily all of them, all the time, for all items) of understanding and desiring certain ends. At the same time, they are able (within biological and social limits) to undertake intentional actions that, in general, lead to the fulfilment of these ends. This intentionality should be understood in a loose sense, since, it is not necessary to have a conscious intention of all steps and a clear, precise understanding. Intentional actions are only a probable result of practical deliberation.

There should be, then, a balance of reasons and this is a contextual matter. There are no ahistorical and supra-contextual practical deliberations. In this vein, we should remind ourselves that causal explanation and intentional interpretation do not have the same *explanadum*.[18] Hence, our basic beliefs and basic values could be seen

---

[18] Ricoeur, P. *El Discurso de la Acción*, Ed. Catedra, Madrid, 1981, page 129. "Von Wright solves the paradox in the following way. In the first place, the causal explanation and the teleological explanation (besides the intentional interpretation) do not have the same *explanadum*; on the one hand, what is explained are natural events; parts of the body move; what is explained teleologically are actions already interpreted as intentional: in effect, the conclusion of practical syllogism is that an agent begins to do something that he thinks is required to reach such an end, the teleological explanation goes back from this conclusion to homogeneous premises."

From a similar point of view, "What I wish to claim is that none of the things that can count as reasons, viewed intentionally -and that is the kind we are interested in- have the right *ontological status* to be causes. And that is because they have *no objective being at all* ... Thus I conclude that reasons are not causes and that explanations in terms of an agent's reasons are not causal explanations ... So none of that controversy is germane to the point I wish to make, namely that reasons, being either propositional contents, which are intentional objects, or subjective states, or both, have *no objective or independent existence*. They exist wholly within the intentional world of the subject who thinks or feels them. Hence they cannot qualify as causes, since causes must have an independent existence as events." E. J. Bond. *Reason and Value*, Cambridge University Press, 1983, pages 22 and 23.

In relation to rational choice theory and game theory, M. Hollis says, "Admittedly, these theories are ideal-types; and we should be wary of assuming that ideal-types are as helpful in social analysis as in the natural sciences. Rational agents, abstracted from the social life and idealised, may turn out to be a source of the problem they are supposed to illuminate. But they bring a welcome clarity to a tricky subject. Ideally rational agents have three basic attributes: perfect information, fully ordered preferences and faultless computing." I suppose it is clear, that I am not dealing with this type of agent in this work. Nevertheless, M. Hollis sees one of the basic problems that does not seem to upset methodological positivists, (at least, "qua scientists"); "What could be more prudent than a system of justice and property which lets two farmers form a binding agreement and thus both get their harvests in? Yes, but the problem is not to spot the solution but to see how it could work. How can justice, as an artificial justice, bind *in foro interno?* How can prudence forge the missing link between truth, virtue and happiness?" *Trust Within Reason*, Cambridge University Press, 1998, pages 45 and 66.

In relation to action, P. Smith and O.R. Jones say, "To repeat: to explain an action we must do more than simply specify beliefs and desires that would make the action comprehensible; we must say that the agent acted *because* of those desires and beliefs ... Putting together the strands of our discussion, we can sum up things by saying that a doing is an action only if it involves something done intentionally, i.e. something done *because* of an appropriate pro-attitude and corresponding belief ... To answer Wittgenstein's question: the difference between your arm going up and you raising your arm is a matter of appropriate causation by beliefs and desires." *The Philosophy of Mind*, Cambridge University Press, 1986, pages 132 and 134.

In any case, we should distinguish between a desire that is a fact, and the propositional content of this desire, that is a normative judgement. In a practical reasoning, a fact cannot be an operative reason because the conclusion of a practical reasoning is not a fact but a decision or an intention or an action. Hence, an operative reason must be an "ought", although in the premises of a practical reasoning we also require an auxiliary reason, that is, a factual judgement. Moreover, I would say that the specific character of legal action is due to the rule constraints over beliefs and desires. Those believes and desires that are relevant for legal purposes are those stated (or allowed) by legal sources. Then, legal human action would not only have biological constraints and social constraints but also legal ones. This means, *inter alia*, that when a human being is acting, several levels, such as biological, social and legal, interact together. Not surprisingly, "legal fiction" is a useful device for ascribing and combining such different forms of reality.

It is interesting to note that "action" has been usually considered as "social action", at least in sociological realms. Colin Campbell criticises situationalist sociology because it rejects either the existence of subjective meaning or absorbs it in intersubjective or social meaning. The result would be the extinction of human action, in the weberian sense, that would be sucked or slurred in the concept of social action. Nevertheless, irrespective of whether his criticisms are correct or not, they do not seem to be especially applicable to the legal normative fields, as can be seen, I hope, in the following quotation: "As we saw above, some essentially communicative or expressive acts are indeed instances where meaning is constituted by the rules or conventions governing the context of their occurrence. As we have just seen, there is also an argument which logically connects meaningfulness and rules. However, neither of these arguments provides any basis for assuming that the majority of human actions have a social meaning, even though, of course, most human actions could indeed be adjudged to be "rule-governed". This then constitutes the final situationalist confusion over rules and social meaning, the confusion between actions which are rule-constituted and those which are merely rule-governed. It may be reasonable to contend that acts that are constituted by their rules deserve the designation of "social acts". But activities which are merely rule-governed certainly do not warrant this designation." *The Myth of Social Action*, Cambridge University Press, 1996, page 125.

Carlos S. Nino, says, "... the confusion between justificatory reasons and explicatory reasons or motives. Effectively what causes an action and serves to explain it are the desires and beliefs of the agent conceived as facts (it does not matter if they are irreducible intellects or in the final instance are reduced to neuropsychological phenomena). These facts can be presented as "reasons", but only in an explanatory sense that is equal to the valid meaning of "motives" ... What justifies the action, *from the agent's point of view*, are not the desires or beliefs conceived as facts, but its propositional content: that is to say, the *judgements* that constitute the premises of practical reasoning to which Davidson refers ... Evidently the judgements, such as those that establish that the object opposite is a diamond and it is desirable to take possession of it, cannot be *causes* of the action, since to constitute any type of entities they are not the sort that can cause phenomena that occur in time and space like the corporal phenomena that constitute the action. Those which are causes of the action of taking possession of the diamond are psychological *facts* for adhering to or adopting the judgements that the object opposite is a diamond and that it is desirable to possess it. When the agent's desires and beliefs are seen "from outside", as causes of the action, they can effectively be conceived, as Davidson emphasized elsewhere, as consistent events in adhering to certain valorative and factious judgements." *El Constructivismo Etico*, C. de E. Constitucionales, Madrid, 1989, pages 23 and 24.

Anthony Kenny says, "When an human being does X in order to do Y, the achieving of X is his reason for doing X. But when an animal does X in order to do Y, he does not do X for a reason, even though he is aiming at a goal in doing so. Why not? Because an animal, lacking language, cannot give a reason for his action. Does this mean that an agent only acts for a reason if he gives a reason? No. It is possible on a given occasion to act for a reason without giving to oneself or to others an account of the reason. But it is only beings who have the general capacity to give reasons who have the ability to act for reasons.. Humans are rational, reason-giving, animals ... Intentional action presupposes language in the same way as self-consciousness presupposes language." *The Metaphysics of Mind*, Oxford University Press, Oxford, 1992, pages 38 and 39.

In relation to method and individuals I distance myself (I don't know how far precisely) from Werner Krawietz's view, "In my conception of legal and social theory I have never fallen into the individualistic misunderstanding that society exists basically only of individuals or of groups of individuals. Against this view of moral and legal individualism, according to which all law is simply a result of the properties and decisions of individuals, that is, it results from the expressed and unified will of the assembly of such individuals or of their formations in groups, and in this way serves as a universal means for bringing about a binding order I am putting forward a version of legal thinking that is informed and shaped by history and society." *The Law in Philosophical Perspectives*, edited by Luc J. Wintgens, Kluwer, Dordrecht, 1999, page 73. Both Wintgens and Krawietz seem to agree on the following, "The relationship between the issuing of norms and rules and the compliance with rules is always the core of legal communication ... It may, therefore, be possible to say -with a degree of exaggeration- that *it is communication that communicates*- and *not* its authors, human beings, individuals, persons, subjects or even legal subjects.", page 108. I do not know how they expect "compliance" unless they see "individuals" as obedient donkeys or mechanical puppets. Either the basic unit of the Legal Communication System is a sham person or it is a structural set. I believe that

as kinds of Kantian categories, in the sense that any reasonable world should have, for us, its appearance settled by our categories. However, I do not rely on a metaphysical doctrine about time but about shared meanings, values and beliefs. In any case, interpretation is required and the method for solving our doubts comes from inside, that is, from the participants' point of view.

5.1 Community and Morality

I would like to develop, a little further, the concept of social practice. For this, I would use as a reference Dworkin's conception of it and, then, I will take a critical view. I think it is clear that my approach toward legal positivism is a critical one (understood as methodological positivism that accepts: one, what counts as a legal order in a given society is a matter of social facts, and, two, there is no necessary link between law and morals) but, although I believe Dworkin's approach goes in a better direction than methodological positivists, it has a basic aspect which I believe to be mistaken. It is known that Dworkin talks of "law as integrity" and compares it with conventionalism and pragmatism. However, it is not my interest here to scrutinise these conceptions but to scrutinise Dworkin's option from a critical stance.

This is because, although I believe that a hermeneutic stance (for the moment, let us say analytical hermeneutics) is a better viewpoint to cope with legal normativity than methodological positivism, I reject a basic point of Dworkin's approach. I agree though that legal texts, as normative facts and legal decisions, should be seen as forming part of a coherent whole, with the principles playing a fundamental role.

However, it is not my aim to deal with "principles" at length. Hence, I will only briefly refer to them. In this respect, A. Peczenik says,

---

these approaches have not convincingly eliminated "individuals" from the stage and it is hard to see how they can properly work, at least for the moment.

I am closer to J. Elster when he says, "The elementary unit of social life is individual human action. To explain institutions and social change is to demonstrate in what way they appear as the result of the action and the interaction of individuals. This view, which is usually referred to as methodological individualism, is, in my opinion, trivially true." *Tuercas y Tornillos*, Gedisa, Barcelona, 1990, page 23. Nevertheless, although much more should be said about this, I always repeat that individuals cannot start from scratch but from within the contextual circumstances in which they are living.

Werner Krawietz criticises Analytic Hermeneutics and its method of interpreting and understanding. He says, "The legal attribution and imputation of collective rights and duties has been largely missing from the point of view represented by legal dogmatics and, precisely for this reason, requires a thorough analysis from the stand point of legal theory. An information- and communication theory of law which seeks to include organized social action must, therefore, attempt to balance and compensate potential deficits of an entirely agent -and subject- based, individualistic theory of action." *The Law* ... op.cit., page 81. This is a very important matter that I will not deal with here. Nevertheless, I agree that an entirely individualistic legal theory, or legal dogmatics, is misguided. On the other hand, the emphasis on collective rights and duties seems to be more the result of a philosophical political point of view (communitarism) than a neutral methodological proposal that takes into account modern communication networks, society and history.

A classical book is, *Explicación y Comprensión*, George Henrik von Wright, Alianza Universidad, Madrid, 1979. A. Aarnio deals with collegial judicial decisions as a form of human actions, in *On Collective Actions. Some Remarks on the Theory of Legal Actions*. Ratio Iuris, Vol.11 No.1, March 1998 (1-11).

"The most characteristic feature of principles is that they collide with other principles and that such collision can be solved only by weighing. There is a direct relationship between the claim to correctness, the idea of coherence, and the theory of principles. The claim to correctness demands a consideration of all reasons possibly relevant. The consideration of all relevant reasons is at the same time a corollary of the second element of coherence, the idea of comprehensiveness, and an old postulate of hermeneutics."[19]

Bearing this in mind and also that Principles are, according to Alexy, optimisation-mandates, in the sense that they include a normative content to be optimised through weighing, I will deal with the conception of "law as integrity". It is known that Dworkin talks of "personification of the community". He says,

"We cannot explain the special responsibilities of political office, therefore, we try to build these directly from ordinary principles of private morality. We need an idea that cannot be founded there: that the community as a whole has obligations of impartiality towards its members, and that officials act as agents for the community in acquitting that responsibility."[20]

When dealing with the term "community" we could appeal to a stipulative definition but it seems better, in Wittgenstein's vein, to try to scrutinise the conditions of use for this term. In this respect, I suppose that there are many contexts in which this term is used and that these uses have no common essence but they do have a family resemblance. In this respect R.J. Fogelin says,

"In the end, I think that the notion of family resemblance has two chief virtues; (i) It helps dispel the commitment to definiteness of sense but exhibiting a set of concepts that violate this standard but are still perfectly serviceable ... (ii) Somewhat differently, recognising the existence of family resemblance classes will lead us to abandon the idea that definitions, of the standard kind, are always possible and, if we are doing this right, actually necessary for the systematic development of a subject matter."[21]

Therefore, I believe that in spite of the different uses of the cited term there is no common essence, but there are some basic meanings related to two basic moralities, private and public morality. Let us consider the first example. Suppose that a person of a given community is awarded a Nobel prize. Another member of this community could tell her: "Our community is proud of you". In this example, a member of a given community is saying that most, perhaps all, members of the community are proud, and ought to be proud, because another member has received a Nobel prize.

---

[19] Peczenik, A. and others. *On coherence Theory of Law*, Acta Societatits Juridicae Lundensis, Nr 131, Lund 1998, page 45.

[20] Dworkin, R. *Law's Empire*, Fontana Press, London 1986, page 175. Moreover, I reject Raz's view, since it is, among others, more or less communitarists. It is one thing that our abilities and capacities are linked and influenced by the society we have grown up in, or to a certain interpretation of it, because we are not clonic beings sharing a unique group. It is another thing that we are determined by these links. I think we are not, but in some societies, where individual autonomy is less respected and protected, the determination is harder and, perhaps, oppressive. I would not like to live in these societies where the state actively and directly participates in the apology of the "true" national identity and the consequent rejection of other interpretations. We, fortunately, live in plural societies. I equally believe that individual autonomy is a basic value although it has (as any view) some problems. One of them is the intent of fulfilling all personal capabilities we have in so far as the others are involved (directly or indirectly) in these personal plans. Nevertheless, I will not deal with this problem here.

[21] Fogelin, R.J. *Wittgenstein*, Routledge, op.cit, page 138.

In this case, the community is related to certain "oughts" that the members of a given community should have if they are "participants". It has sense for participants to participate in the achievement of the "best" possible results. If they cannot participate directly in these results they are, usually, proud of other participants, and they, usually, believe that they ought to be proud. Nevertheless, this does not deny the social importance of envy but it is not my concern here.

This can be understood as an analogy of the family, which is supposed to be a basic institution within the private domain, although not exclusively. For example, the parents are proud of their daughter because she won a prize. The more nationalistic the feelings of the members of a community, the more they see the community as a family. We can suppose that the community allows them to have personal identity. In this respect, there is a degree of intensity that changes according to diverse communities. Some of them are more proud than others but I suppose that even in more reasonable communities, their members are proud, at least on these occasions, although without hysterical nationalistic reactions. If I am right, this is a basic use related to private morality, although the difference between private and public morality is not a sharply defined one. Here it is only stated that there is a difference. In this respect, Hegel said that one of the main features of modernity is the separation between private and public spheres.

Therefore, one basic use of the term "community" would be related to the private sphere, as in the example cited above. Citizens have feelings towards other members of the same community that make them feel members of the same community. This is compatible with other, let us say, negative feelings. I believe that there is another basic use of the term community, and it is related to the public sphere, to the public morality. Let us consider the second example. A citizen having certain problems in relation to public hospitals or public education or personal safety in the streets, says, "The community should take these things seriously". In this case, the emphasis is put on the public sphere because it can be translated into this other sentence or another similar one: officials and/or politicians ought to behave in a more responsible way towards public health, etcetera. Or, in other words, they ought to undertake certain actions to reach certain goals or to reach them in a better way.

If I am right, the term "community" should be understood, basically, as a place where social individuals interplay, given a certain complex web of institutions, traditions and relations. This interplay is an interplay between the private and public sphere and also an interplay within each sphere. Hence, I do not believe it is correct to state that "the community as a whole has obligations of impartiality towards its members", as Dworkin says, because it does not emphasize the dynamic aspect of a living community. To see the community, as Dworkin does, as a unitary moral agent that has obligations and rights, is only a possible theoretical construction. I disagree though with his strong unitary view which forms the basis of his approach. However, I do not deny that personal identity presupposes the existence of a community.

The problem is whether the supposed rights of the community are, or not, over and above the rights of the individuals. A possible solution (which I reject) is to claim such a close interdependence and fit between individuals and community that this problem disappears. The community should be seen as something "we" (participants) have created (within limits) for a better development of ourselves, as social beings. Nevertheless, the more we respect personal autonomy the more we shall see the community, not as an end in itself but as a necessary complex web that serves (although not understood as a mere fact or tool) for our improvement, which is, otherwise, a basic and interpretative concept. In fact, political regimes may enhance the "rights of the community", "objective goods" and so forth.

If this is done, laws and legal decisions could also be understood within a coherent set of principles, although these principles would be of a different kind. Hence, in my view, the best approach does not over-emphasize either the private sphere or the public sphere. We cannot dispense with individuals or the community. On the contrary, we have to undertake a provisional and complex balance between them deciding, *inter alia,* when internal coherence is sufficient and when we have to introduce new empirical or evaluative premises. We should try to maintain a balance (always provisional) between them. If it has been said that the collision between Principles can only be solved through weighing, I would say that the tension between individuals and the community should be solved through weighing too.

This is not, and cannot be, an aprioristic task. It cannot either be a numerical task. What we can do, after weighing and interpretation, is to accept faithfully the results obtained through the best possible rational agreement. However, this can be so only for a while. In so far as the principle of *stare decisis* does not mean that certain legal decisions will last forever, although they try to give a certain amount of stability and predictability, the same happens in relation to this balance between individuals and the community. It would not only be a kind of reflective equilibrium but also an unstable one.

5.2 The Form of Life as a Background

Lately, the "background" of a community and of individuals is this relatively unstable interplay (between individual and community, private and public, stability and change) in which important parts of the private and public sphere are taken into account. This "background" is closely related to the known Wittgenstenian form of life. I understand it as an ideal place where communities overlap, allowing for individuals to feel members (at different degrees) of wider contexts than their own strict local communities. In this respect, the form of life can be narrower or wider depending basically on the intensity and exclusiveness to which a community conception is lived by its members. The more intensive and exclusive a conception, the more local coherence will be because it is difficult to maintain this intensity in huge territories and large populations.

In this case, more difficulties may arise for a wider understanding. Let us take an example. If we accept that the application of a concept (that is, a legal concept) to a particular situation cannot be decided on the exclusive basis of formal logic, we could claim that the basic way to approach it would be argumentation. The concept of argumentation, or practical argumentation, is linked, *inter alia*, to the concept of audience. In so far as some of the main features that shape human beings (both perceptual beliefs and fundamental values) are not understood in the same way, we shall have more difficulties to convince a specific audience than another with a different understanding, no matter whether both audiences are addressees of the same legal order.

As is known, L. Wittgenstein didn't elaborate on a definition of "form of life", although it is usually believed that it is an important concept. Why should it be so and why should this be relevant for jurists? The first thing to say is that the so-called first Wittgenstein is not so important for jurists, although the so-called second Wittgenstein is, at least for jurists within Analytic-Hermeneutic tendencies. To dive into the form of life concept would require us to deal, *inter alia*, with the theory of meaning but it is not my aim, here, to talk about Wittgenstein. It is enough just to say that, for my present purposes, the form of life is a kind of background over which we can develop a certain theory of meaning that moves away from a pictorial view, denying the logical independence of elementary propositions, and superseding the true-false dichotomy for another one that is contextual.

The second Wittgenstein is important for us because he emphasized the social and pragmatic understanding of language by seeing language as a social activity. This activity, although undertaken by individuals, has sense in a given community because to undertake this activity we have to obey rules and to obey rules (in our case legal rules) is a social institutional practice. To learn a language is to learn a form of life. The form of life is "the given", the justificatory bedrock of our language in the sense already explained. Although in a different sense, we should be reminded that the French jurist F. Gény talks about "the given", but in reference to basic principles of natural law. What is important is that although we are not condemned (in a similar way as worms are) to a determinate interpretation of our form of life we cannot dispense with it.

We can connect with our form of life, we can criticise it, we can even leave it but, like a skin, it will be a permanent constitutive part of ourselves. Nevertheless, I want to emphasize that these attitudes towards our form of life are only attitudes towards a certain interpretation of it, because the form of life is vague enough to allow a variety of possibilities, in a similar way as our language gives us a cluster of alternatives. Our legal language should be placed in this complex situation. Our legal language, first cousin of our ordinary language, is not for the geometrical enjoyment of the so-called legal scholars. On the contrary, legal scholars should help citizens and judges to walk through the maze of streets better, not on straight and comfortable avenues. The danger is that they can use a language as if it were on holiday.

I do not mind whether Wittgenstein understood it as I do. I want to emphasize (and this is a normative emphasis, because we are not in a field of empirical verification) that we are not slaves to our form of life. In this respect, the more open the society is, the more we shall be able to interact critically with our form of life. I should say, more accurately though, interact with a certain conception of the form of life. In a similar way, as within an open society, the interaction between social and critical morality is easier and more fruitful. This dynamic interaction is a basic feature of ours. We can facilitate it or make difficulties for it but social practices, granted that we are neither worms nor slaves, have sense derived from the interaction between stability and adaptation.

Linguistic communication can fail for several reasons. To facilitate linguistic communication we have to be able to capture not only what has been explicitly said, but also what is implicit. It is true that legal language is not exactly like ordinary language and that it has developed more precise rules and procedures for eliminating the implicit implications of linguistic communication. Hence, the dangers for a clear and precise linguistic communication are not only vagueness and ambiguity. In this respect, we can rely exclusively on general and abstract rules when dealing with legal communication, but we can lose these implicit meanings or intentions. Heisenberg showed us that the more precision we have in measuring the position of a particle, the less precision we shall have in measuring its speed and *vice versa*.

Some legal scholars should bear in mind that the high precision we may reach in legal communication is not a value in "itself" but it has to be balanced against other values, at a given time, in a certain context. I repeat though that legal language is not for the enjoyment of legal scholars. Once again, the permanent problem of law arises here, which cannot be solved by only betting for precision and predictability, on the one hand, or equity on the other. These, let us say, extremes represent basic values, legal certainty and material justice. My view is that we should strive for a justified and provisional balance between conflicting basic values. Furthermore, in so far as we do not believe in the "scientific" isolation of legal dogmatics we should bear in mind that legal linguistic games permanently intertwine with other linguistic games of the same society.

Sometimes the legislator's language authoritatively reflects this intertwinement, but sometimes not. In the latter case, it does not mean that this intertwinement has not taken place. On the contrary, legal argumentation represents a way, a justified way, where intertwinements are rationalised even when they are not officially existent. They form a legal tradition that, at least in principle, does not call for justification. What can require a justification is a concrete formulation of a legal argument within the legal tradition at a given time, although not the tradition itself. Something extremely important should happen for this to be the case. This only means that we cannot doubt everything.

Although, contrarily to Wittgenstein, we should distinguish between normative and factual statements, some of them are fundamental for any form of life. In this respect, we cannot doubt some basic perceptual beliefs and, at the same time, we cannot doubt some basic values. I will not deal, here, though with the question of the relativity of Wittgenstein's proposals. I will just say that this (relative) relativity is more important in relation to normative fields than factual ones. However, this is not an "essence" of the form of life. Different persons pertaining to different forms of life (although this is disputable because of the flexible limits) agree in relation to many factual statements and scientific theories.

In relation to the normative field, Human Rights could be a normative meta-level where different normative conceptions come close to one another. One of the main reasons is that Human Rights deal with human beings as such, not with white or black, with Europeans or Americans. In any case, the form of life is not a fixed bedrock but a changing one. When it changes we do too. When we change, the form of life, or our perception of it, also changes. Is it a vicious circle? I do not believe so. It shows a fundamental feature of our form of life and of ourselves. We have never in the past had the present possibility of an intense and extensive interaction of beings within forms of life and between different forms of life. The consequences of this new situation cannot be settled in an *a priori* way.

6. METHODOLOGY AND PRIORITIES

It is usually stated, especially from certain philosophical tendencies, that we should explain the object (no matter which it is) instead of trying to understand it. Nevertheless, it is disputable whether some legal researchers can reach neutral and objective results through the use of the so-called scientific method. In this so-called scientific task it is also required to be an observer or, better said, to adopt an observer's view. From this privileged perspective they would have to clearly separate the context of justification from the context of discovery. However, in so far as a legal scholar has to undertake a conceptual clarification of the object they would have to undertake a selection of what they consider as relevant. It seems that any legal scholar (or legal philosopher) would have to take decisions and make evaluations. In this respect, two models conflict: logical and rational reconstructions.

The former are close to the observer's point of view and explanation while the latter are closer to the internal point of view and understanding. The former are also looking for infallible methods in so far as they have not abandoned the hope for safe algorithms, while the latter believe there are no safe algorithms for solving our normative conflicts. While purposiveness and evaluation are absent in logical reconstructions they are present in rational ones. At least sometimes, to scrutinise legal rules alone is not enough to solve our normative conflicts, or some of them, properly. Intentions, interests, social expectations and values can also play an important role. Underlying any approach there is some concept -or conception- of person and rationality. It seems that the Positivistic and the Hermeneutic approaches have different views on these.

When we talk of method (let us say, what legal scholars usually do in a systematic and procedural way, when trying to solve certain legal problems, coherently and purposively) and methodology (let us say, what legal philosophers usually do when dealing with the use of methods by legal scholars or other legal philosophers) we should bear in mind, first, what we should not do. Granted that there is no God's eye view, I will just mention some of the things we should avoid, from an Analytical-Hermeneutic perspective.

We should avoid the confusion between Internal Point of View and Idealisation. This idealisation, the most terrible sin of a serious legal scholar, would be the result of confusing two separate worlds, "is and ought". Although I have talked about this point several times already in this work, I will briefly repeat my opinion. When we deal with clear cases, that is, when competent jurists agree what the legal order is (in reference to a specific legal problem) it would be easy to separate what the law "is" from what all or some would believe it "ought" to be. Nevertheless, when competent jurists deal with "hard cases" they do not know what the law "is". If they knew, it would not be a hard case. In this situation, to talk of idealisation would be misleading.

Once there has been a justified agreement among competent jurists or when a court of a certain level has decided authoritatively what the law "is", it would be easier, again, to differentiate between "is" and "ought". This shows that we cannot know (always) in advance what the law "is". One solution is to believe that the legal conclusion that either competent jurists will give or a higher court will establish, is (mysteriously) embedded in the wording of the legislator's language. This is a bad and useless idealisation.

Another misguided view, that should be avoided, would be the claim that Hermeneutic tradition makes knowledge subjective. There is no doubt that some Hermeneutic approaches can do this but we should bear in mind some caveats. In some sense, "knowledge" cannot be made "subjective" because, in this case, it is not "knowledge" anymore, granted that "knowledge", by definition, is objective. In some other sense, "knowledge" cannot avoid to be "subjective". In the latter case, this means that "knowledge" comes from subjects and, in this sense, it would be subjective. Granted that this would not be denied, we can deal with the former sense. In this sense, Hermeneuticians would make knowledge subjective while others, for instance, methodological positivists, would not. This is not acceptable.

It would imply that methodological positivists have either personal abilities, not available to hermeneuticians, or that the method of methodological positivism avoids this terrible sin. If it is the latter, we are dealing with the old and discredited view that we can have "science without subject". Hence, while hermeneuticians would be idealist, ignoring the difference between "is and ought", methodological positivists would be "realists" in the good sense, that is, they would explain (but not understand) the object, although not exclusively from a causal approach. A related accusation against hermeneuticians is their vagueness and the flexibility of the boundaries they are using. Supposedly this refers to the language they use. Nevertheless, the accusation of vagueness is vague in itself.

Methodological positivists should have a precise reference (like the famous Paris metre) to be able to compare two items with precision. If they do not have it, which precise measure do they use for referring to meanings? The most usual way is to compare deductive logic with other non truth-preserving processes. Nevertheless, the most important problem is not "precision" but "usefulness". Not "usefulness" in a vacuum but a contextual one, which is also limited, *inter alia*, by values. In this respect, we could obtain very precise results with very little benefit. On the other hand, the flexibility of the boundaries of Analytic-Hermeneutic methods is close to what Hart said, when talking of the "natural sins" of natural languages.

Another usual accusation refers to the distinction between context of justification and context of discovery. This is another metaphysical idea that could be justified when logical positivism was in fashion but it is risky to say so now because it is in crisis (at least in some spheres). At present, we have received the benefits of Philosophy of Science and, although there is no unanimous view, it should be clear that it is hard to support (with the smugness of the true describers of law as it is) a radical separation between these two contexts. The membrane that separates academic research and society, context of justification and context of discovery, is flexible and porous. I know though that this is rejected by methodological positivists who claim to know how to clearly separate is-ought, law-morals, discovery-justification, etcetera. A usual accusation is to confuse causes (context of discovery) and justificatory reasons (context of justification). However, Hermeneuticians would confuse them while methodological positivists would not, because they would use precise and neutral methods.

When we deal with a legal conceptual clarification we have to undertake a selection of the relevant facts. I will suppose, for a moment, that Hermeneuticians cannot do this in a proper way, while methodological positivists can. Even in this hypothesis, they would have to undertake a selection. In order to do this, they would have to decide what were the relevant features of the legal concept at stake, granted that they cannot search in reality without concepts. If they have to decide this (instead of deducing it) they would have to select and justify the selection. This means that everyone deals with "constructed facts", that is, we decide (in a justified way) the relevant features of the object. At the same time, we have to decide the relevant properties of the legal concept at stake and decide, at least partially, which items are "in" the concept, granted that this is not a deductive task.

Legal scholars usually agree on this complex and constructive task because they are members of the same form of life and members of the same culture or community, sharing the same legal tradition or legal order. They are "contaminated" researchers from the beginning. They do not "explain" the object as something radically different from "understanding" it. Furthermore, "explaining" does not give a better view of the object. All this means, *inter alia*, that we make a rational reconstruction of the object, not a logical reconstruction or a neutral description of it. A germ-free description of legal orders is only wishful thinking. In other words, I suppose that it will be seen, in this work, that "justification" fits better with Analytic-Hermeneutic approaches than "explanation".

6.1 Reconstruction and Purposiveness

It is easier to claim what methodology should not be rather than stating what it should be. In this respect, I will follow on with some tentative opinions but not with a precise and clear-cut model. One first step is to claim that we are not members of the natural world, in the sense that we cannot be exhaustively understood from a causal explanation. This shows, from the beginning, that I support a methodological tendency based on "understanding" more than "explanation". Related with this, I claim that we should look for the meaning and intentions of our actions more than their causes. It also means that I emphasize the view from within, among other things, because I take for granted that there is no view from "outside". That is, the members of our form of life cannot see themselves from "outside".

If this is correct, methodological positivists would be mistaken and therefore before going ahead, we have to emphasize something known, that social facts are not neutral but are value-laden. Granted this, we cannot believe what methodological positivists claim, that is, a neutral and external explanation of our legal orders. A methodological view is not only a decision about a "proper" starting point (I began talking of a "conventional starting point") but also a decision about the emphasis we put on certain items and not on others. Methodological positivists emphasize neutral description and logical reconstruction. I believe that a neutral description is a pipe dream and that rational reconstruction is more useful than logical reconstruction, although the latter should not be excluded as a kind of *ex post facto* revision of our rational reconstruction.

In other words, whether or not we have fallen into logical contradictions. Nevertheless, we should bear in mind that the discovery of a logical contradiction is not, by itself, the final judge. In this vein, Ziman says,

> "... any person who would try to refute the theory of relativity would not achieve it through, let us say, the demonstration of a logical fallacy in the original Einstein's work ... any change in the fundamental results of a so proved theory would have incalculable consequences that would go much more further than the facts for which it was conceived."[22]

The decision to adopt a certain methodological perspective is, *inter alia*, a philosophical compromise. In my view, epistemological problems cannot be reduced to logical problems. I also believe (contrary to Quine) that neither can they be reduced to psychological problems, although this is not my concern here. It means, *inter alia*, that our legal concepts are not the exclusive result of factual input but also of our human capacity, structured through legal traditions, legal theories, legal orders, needs and desires. In other words, we are not only discovering the object but also producing it. It also shows that methodological positivism over-emphasizes rules in the sense that certain rules will guide us, with certainty and necessity, from the premise to the conclusion.

We can see then how important logical reconstruction is for them. Alternatively, I believe that this smooth path of certainty is, in the best case, of secondary importance in our legal normative fields. The more or less hidden desire of methodological positivism is to eliminate human decision. All the work would be done by rules that are controlled by rules. From this stems the scorn against the Analytic-Hermeneutic method. They only accept infallible methods and the only infallible method is a logical one. Alternatively, I believe that instead of dreams of infallibility we should rely, *inter alia*, on our legal experts, who share an internal point of view. Not exclusively though, because a normative requirement is that participants should avoid, as much as possible, being obedient (or disobedient) donkeys.

We should emphasize rational reconstruction over logical reconstruction (not only because the former uses a wider view of reason) but because we should adopt the legal decision (respecting certain limits) that most favour our legal purposes. This cannot be done by a logical reconstruction alone. To know what favours our purposes most, here and now, also requires evaluations. Purposiveness is absent from logical reconstruction but not from rational reconstructions. For similar reasons, neither are we interested in causal explanation. Another important aspect of our Analytic-Hermeneutic methodology is its dynamic character, in which the audience has an important role, although it does not in logical reconstructions. Legal experts (sharing an internal point of view) can influence the audience and can be influenced by it.

---

[22] Ziman, J. *Introducción al Estudio de las Ciencias*, Ariel, Barcelona 1986, page 67.

At the same time, we are "condemned" to rebuild our rational reconstructions. On the other hand, basic features of logical reconstructions, such as necessity and certainty, would avoid the "weaknesses" of argumentative methods, which are unable to be truth-conducive like logical reconstruction. Generally speaking, methodological positivists believe that it is possible to drawn a sharp line between legal method and legal content. This would explain, *inter alia*, the overemphasis on form. They do not want the results of their research to be contingent. If this is correct, it is hard to see how they can rely on justificatory reasons, granted that they can be fallible. On the contrary, fallibility is a basic feature of our relationships with our world, and the world of Analytic-Hermeneutics too.

Why, then, should we not rely on methodological positivists? Because they are also fallible and try to understand us from a supposedly external point of view. This is not to deny the usefulness of the clarification-simplification of the logical reconstruction of an argumentative discourse. It just means that this is neither all we can do, nor the most important. One of the lessons we could learn from the appearance of Non-Euclidean geometries is that there can be alternative geometries, internally consistent but non-consistent with Euclidean geometry, which for centuries was considered as the "true one". Should we decide which is best for us by appealing to a formal method? It seems not.

6.2 Logical Deduction and Normative Expectations

Translating this to a legal normative field, I would say that the most important and complex task is to settle, in a justified way, the legal premise in a given legal problem. The rest is deduction, usually so easy that any practical jurist can do it without more ado. Do we have any logical reason for constructing, for example, ten thousand legal premises of a given legal problem? We haven't. We can answer this though within a wider concept of rationality and the answer is the "reasonableness" of the legal experts that share an internal point of view. They strive for the best possible solution, here and now. In this respect, some of the possible legal premises are not even constructed because they are not "sound", granted certain purposes and certain values. If this is correct, the concept of rationality that methodological positivists claim to use, is too narrow because it rejects (as useless or non-existent) practical reason.

Our main concern, as legal scholars, as judges, as participants, is to know the normative requirements and the normative expectations we justifiable have under a given legal order, at a certain time, in a given society. For doing this to a reasonable extent, we should know meanings, intentions, rules, beliefs, interests, etcetera. Not only this, we should also know the way in which they are joined, because this helps to shape a certain model of society. This is one of the reasons why a logical reconstruction is not sufficient for a proper understanding of our normative world. In a rational reconstruction we cannot put aside this changing set of rules, meanings, intentions, interactions, beliefs, etcetera, that is, the changing view of participants.

It should be clear, by now, that a rational reconstruction should neither be a repetition of the existent, nor a logical reconstruction. It should be a normative proposal on the basis of the existent social net but with an eye on our purposes. Rational reconstruction should be placed in between a strong utopia and a repetition of the existent. Rational reconstruction should help participants to improve their existing network of relationships. The future will tell us whether a rational reconstruction is useful (and just) for a society or not. Meanwhile, neutral observers can take external pictures. Either they would collect data or they would fail to be neutral-external observers. I do not believe they are able to do anything useful without a certain level of "understanding" of the participants' expectations.

These expectations should be understood as normative expectations and they are linked to a normative concept such as "duty". In this respect, it is hard to believe the claim that we can draw a sharp, clear line between legal and moral duty. Duties tend to create regularities of behaviour, which are the external sign of a rich and hidden variety of reasons for action. With the passage of time, the external appearance -the regularity- may remain the same, especially for an external observer, while the reasons for this social regularity change. I will not deal though with the difficult question of how to understand the "participant". Very briefly, however, I would say that participants are not individualistic atoms. They cannot do what they please. At the same time, we cannot simply talk of participants because there are different levels, depending on their degree of understanding and commitment. These features could lead us to different conceptions of "understanding". Clearly, one can choose other variables such as wealth, professional role, etcetera.

My view of participants should not be understood as if they were, all the time, "moral citizens". "Participant" is an ideal concept. There are no pure "participants" in any society. It should be clear that citizens can behave, for a certain time, "more or less" as a participant or as a prudent person. In a similar way, human beings cannot be completely placed either within the realm of positive morality or in the realm of critical morality. I would also say that although legal rules cannot be understood in isolation, while they can be within legal institutions and institutions within a legal order, I believe that neither represents the "essence" of legal orders. However, the point is to solve certain important problems (at least for us) through certain institutional procedures in the "best" possible way.

I do not deny that we live and behave in systems and that these even have systemic requirements. In this respect, fulfilling these systemic requirements would be functional for the system itself. What I reject is the idea that individuals are "pawns", "puppets" or "obedient-disobedient donkeys". However, if they are not, some margin of decision, freedom or "movement" should be accepted. In this respect, we can make sense of the expression "reasons for action" if we can understand them not as an inevitable chain of causal connections but as a chain that, having some causal connections, has certain alternatives for action. This would be possible because our world is not exclusively a world of facts ("is" world) but also a world of shared meanings ("ought" world).

Finally, legal rules do not determine the extension of a legal concept. This means, *inter alia*, that what is analogical in a concrete case, does not depend on formal logic. If this is correct, and granted that analogical reasoning is a fundamental legal method (at least in private law), we should conclude that contextual argumentation and evaluation play a more important role than formal logic. That is, rational reconstruction of the legal order, either undertaken by practical jurists or by legal scholars, is more important (at least by participants) than logical reconstruction. Methodological positivists, at large, would try to impose their method, claiming that there is one rationality, theirs.

A participant's rationality would be subjective and relative, while a methodological positivist's rationality would be objective and universal. Nevertheless, it is doubtful that, unlike Physics, we can state an objective and universal overview that condemns any participant's perspective to the lumber room. Even Carnap claimed that we should be tolerant with all rational reconstructions because they should be seen as proposals. Nevertheless, some of his heirs tend to see themselves, not as representatives of a conception of rationality but as representatives of the true concept of rationality. It is doubtful though that we should see this as an epistemic virtue. They are also heirs of the Cartesian language tradition where some features are emphasized, such as an individualist perspective and the view of the mind as a computational system that helps to understand the importance they have always given to form or syntax.

The individualist perspective can be understood in the sense that representation is individualistic. This would mean that a representation of a given individual would supervene from subvenient physical properties of this individual. On the other hand, Analytic-Hermeneutics tend to reject the physicalist view of the mind and this individualist perspective. On the contrary, they tend to emphasize the social dimension of the individual because basic aspects of our representation and understanding depend on the interaction of minds with a social and historical context. In this vein, the so-called internal point of view and intentional states of mind cannot be properly understood from an individualistic perspective only. However, I have already stated that the IPV is not an all-nothing or yes-no aspect.

This is even more so when this individualistic perspective is computational. We can see how Analytic-Hermeneutics, at large, rely on a different view of mind and language. Language is not a mirror of the mind. We have to start from a given form of life that we have not chosen, where successful communication will be possible when we understand each other, at least to a certain extent. Understanding is possible because we share, *inter alia*, (in several and conflicting degrees) not only meanings but also normative expectations, needs, desires, etcetera. In this respect, intention and purpose will play an important role. Nevertheless, while it is possible for a person to fail, repeatedly, when communicating with another person, this is not possible for the community itself or, in other words, for the bulk of the population. Of course though, I am not talking of logical possibility.

7. OBJECTIVITY, METHOD AND ORDINARY LANGUAGE

"Objectivity" is one of the central terms that differentiates Positivist approaches from Hermeneutic ones. Within the former approaches we can distinguish between tendencies based on logical syntax and others based on conceptual clarification. I believe that a fertile communication is possible between the latter and Analytic Hermeneutic approaches. Be that as it may, positivists claim that to bridge the gap between subjectivity and objectivity we should adopt the view of neutral observers and utter "detached statements". It is doubtful that legal positivist can transmute into neutral observers and, then, utter "detached statements". They also claim that participants cannot utter neutral statements and I agree with the claim that we cannot utter completely neutral statements, as everybody else. Nevertheless, we should distinguish between "committed statements" on the one hand and irrationality or arbitrariness, on the other.

Participants utter committed statements and undertake actions (at least normally) on the basis of reasons. The other participants usually understand them because they share, *inter alia*, a complex conceptual scheme. We, as legal scholars, try to articulate this conceptual scheme better, that is, more clearly and coherently. Moreover, the term "observer" is not univocal granted that it is not the same to observe the natural world as the social world. In relation to Hermeneutics we can emphasize two tendencies: Hermeneutics of Tradition and Hermeneutics of Suspicion. Both tendencies would try to show hidden aspects of a text but the latter moves from the discovery of these hidden aspects to an emancipatory interest. On the other hand, Hermeneutics of Tradition would not have a basic point from which to make a radical criticism of the present time. Nevertheless, we should not dispense with any of these because they represent -at least tendencially- the static and the dynamic aspects of social practices. Finally, a wide view of method (not for an algorithmic one) would imply an interplay between tradition and change, not understood in the abstract, but in a concrete place, time and legal order.

The term "objectivity" can be understood from an ontological point of view. In this case, basic propositions have a paramount importance. It is usually supposed (at least within positivistic and empiricist realms) that there are some basic propositions that exist independently of our awareness. Why is this possible? Because they are objective. For example, some basic propositions refer to atoms or stones, or mountains. However, can there be "uncontaminated" reports of reality that give us truth? It is usually supposed that these basic propositions are not the result of a theoretical construction. Granted this, their insistence on a physicalist language can be understood better, although this has been a platonic ideal that has never been achieved. A further step is to claim that these basic propositions give us knowledge in a strong sense, that is, they are conclusively true and, over them, we can confidently build the rest of our knowledge. Who are the Gods that will have this immediate encounter with experience *tout court*? Certainly not Hermeneuticians.

I believe that we can forget this dream and scrutinise "objectivity", not from an ontological point of view but from an epistemological point of view. In this case, we are not burdened by these protocolary statements. We have to confront the problem of method, having accepted that we do not have a privileged access to reality, not even the kind of reality cited above (e.g. atoms, stones or mountains). Granted this, we should remind ourselves of something well known, that the methodological perspective we decide to adopt will condition the priorities we shall undertake. In other words, given certain method, we shall give preference to certain objects, or relations, more than others. In this respect, it is of paramount importance to adopt a methodological positivistic method or a hermeneutic method. Methodological positivism would establish a radical separation between science and philosophy, between law and morals. For the moment though I will not deal with the hermeneutic method.

Nevertheless, it should be noted that the distance between methodological positivism and analytic hermeneutics can be strong or weak, depending on which analytical tendency we are talking about. If we understand it as logical analysis, then, the epistemological method would be based on logical syntax. Here, the difference between methodological positivism and hermeneutics would be radical. On the other hand, if we understand analytical tendency as conceptual clarification, the difference is not radical and communication between them is possible. From another point of view, language has a paramount importance, although it is not understood in the same way as the other analytical tendency is. On the contrary, some Wittgenstenian concepts, such as language game or form of life, appear to be basic. Language, in this other view, is a human activity with different language games. Hence, context, rules, purposes, etcetera, assume a fundamental importance.

From this point of view, the meaning of a sentence or the meaning of a legal text, depends on a particular context, on the different types of rules that govern this specific use of language, etcetera. In this respect, the legal order as a whole (whatever it is) is basic for the determination of the meaning of a sentence. This point relates to the importance of coherence,[23] especially if it has been accepted that

[23] It is not my aim, in this paper, to deal mainly with this important issue but Joseph Raz scrutinises some methodological questions in, *The Relevance of Coherence*, Boston University Law Review, Volume 72, Number 2, March 1992 (pages 273-321). One of his main theses is that coherence should be understood in a local sense and not in a global sense, *inter alia*, because of moral plurality. Although I agree with this point, he states some disputable claims. He says, for instance, "I will be concerned with constitutive coherence theories of law and adjudication, which claim that coherence makes legal propositions true or judicial decisions right." (p.275) ... "Coherence theory may seem plausible when attention is focused on the believer alone. But it is seen to be plainly false to our entrenched understanding of justified belief when we consider our judgement on the belief of others."

Although this seems very heretic it can be seen in a softer tone when we see that local coherence (not global coherence) can solve this problem. Coherence will fail when it is understood as global rather than local. However, the main disputable points are these: "I do not mean that the law is as it is, independently of human beings and their activities, only that what it is, is independent of my, or anyone elses, inquiry into its nature. Therefore, our preferences or value judgements are immaterial. Our account of the law should be faithful to the nature of legal phenomena". On the one hand, it is surprising to claim that cultural constructs like law can be something in themselves, independently of human values, preferences, interests, etcetera. It is hard to claim that physical things are what they are independently of our beliefs but it is even harder to claim that third world constructions have a life in themselves and are what they are.

We would simply discover what they are. Hence, moral plurality would not affect this basic point. The process would be the following: we would discover the reality (or the nature) of law and, then, (granted the existence of plural morality) we would have different evaluations. Especially from Kant onwards, it is hard to claim that we simply discover reality, even cultural reality. On the other hand, he claims, "Furthermore, epistemic coherence is relative to each person. The justification of each person's beliefs is relative to that person's totality of beliefs ... A constitutive account of law cannot enjoy the same luxury. It cannot be person-relative. What is or is not the law in the United States today is one thing, and what people believe it to be is another ... Their base must be, practically speaking, the same for all believers, so that the coherence imposed on it will yield one legal system per state, however much people may disagree about its content." (p. 284)

It is surprising that Raz criticises global coherence and also emphasises coherence in the whole legal system, independently of moral pluralism that would justify local coherence. Perhaps he believes that moral pluralism is immaterial in relation to the global coherence of the whole legal system.

truth as correspondence has no relevance in legal normative fields such as in Physics, for example. Moreover, once we stress the pragmatic perspective of language, the primacy of the participant (who uses the language, not who mentions it) over the observer is clear. One of the problems will be to scrutinise how "objectivity" can be achieved from the participant's point of view. I take for granted that "observers" cannot reach "objectivity" (in a strong and neutral sense), although I will scrutinise later on what "observer" means.

In any case, "objectivity", when talking of normative actions in legal normative fields, can be understood as properly placing actions in shared rules or in shared concepts. The criteria by which these actions are placed in these concepts and rules require an interpretative stance. It should be emphasized, once again, that it is unsound to talk of "objectivity" from outside, as if something was objective in itself, independently of us. On the contrary, something is objective within a specific conceptual scheme that includes, *inter alia*, purposes. This view of objectivity gives preference to the conceptual scheme of participants. To make this conceptual scheme more coherent and clear is a basic methodological task of the legal scholar. Moreover, his task is both descriptive and normative. We can understand the positivistic insistence on legal dogmatics as descriptive. In this case, it would incorporate the dichotomy true/false and it could be the object of logic. In this respect, many scholars support the view that there cannot be a logic of norms but there can be a logic of normative propositions.

Moreover, what is the difference between hermeneuticians and logical analysis and the tendency of conceptual clarification? They would say (that is, methodological positivists) that a "scientific task" cannot be done from an internal point of view. Hence, a basic point is to differentiate between "committed statements" and "detached statements". The gap between subjectivity and objectivity would be bridged when we, as neutral observers, utter "detached statements". I wonder how this is possible. I have observed some of these "scientific legal philosophers" many times and I have been unable to see anything special. I mean that they had similar appearance, similar habits and we, usually, understand each other, although we do not necessarily agree. Where should the difference be? Probably in the method. They have decided to use the "proper" method. Why haven't we hermeneuticians? We do not know because mental states (and Wittgenstein said so) are non-intelligible aspects of human behaviour. Furthermore, they are placed in the context of discovery.

Therefore, the move should take another direction. We do not know why but they have decided to adopt the proper method. Why is theirs the proper method? Because it leads to objective results. Why are hermeneutics not the proper method? Because they lead to subjective results. Hence, it seems that we have to scrutinise what "objective" and "subjective" mean. Nevertheless, it should be clear that these answers are given from the methodological positivist point of view. From a hermeneutic point of view this is wrong. Therefore, perhaps we do not have the same conception of "objectivity" and "subjectivity".

Consequently, even if epistemic coherence is relative to each person, it is not necessary to have this mistaken conception of person, understood as an isolated monad.

In my view, one of the basic mistakes made by the supporters of the methodological positivistic method (MPM) is that they claim what cannot be achieved, although this is not a logical impossibility. They claim that they are participants (they cannot deny it) but when they put a white coat on, their minds change. They are no longer participants, they are neutral observers of their own world. When they are tired of being neutral observers, they take off their white coats and become participants again. No one can see what happens though because this is an internal change. We can only see the results they have achieved, that is, "objective" results.

The supporters of the hermeneutician analytic method (HAM) need not suffer such deep transmutations and, at the same time, do not need to step outside their own bodies. A common basis (including supporters of MPM and HAM) is an intersubjective context. Granted this intersubjective context, meaningful actions are possible. How do we know that there are meaningful actions? Because we are members of a given community and have been constituted, as social beings, within this community. However, we have to distinguish between first level concepts, those used by the participants, and second level concepts, those mentioned by the supporters of MPM or HAM. A basic problem though is if these second level concepts are the cement of "detached statements". This could be so if these second level concepts were neutral.

First, the concepts used by participants cannot be neutral, but neither are they arbitrary. Hence, we should separate "committed statements" from "arbitrariness or irrationality". Why do the supporters of MPM very easily condemn others to be irrational, or claim that they use an irrational method? Because they have a narrow concept of rationality. They behave as the Prince with Cinderella's shoe. The Prince used the shoe Cinderella lost as a test for knowing who was the true Cinderella. The supporters of MPM use their concept of rationality to decide who is rational and who is not. Unfortunately for them the "physicalist times" are gone, especially in relation to legal normative fields. Fortunately, there are supporters of MPM, like Hart, that adopt a more open perspective and make a fertile dialogue possible between positivists and hermeneuticians.

In this respect, a fundamental point in order to identify human actions, undertaken by participants, is that normative actions are meaningful because they go together with reasons. We can understand these actions-reasons because we share a conceptual scheme and because we share a legal order. We, normally, understand these actions-reasons because we also understand their purpose. Although it is logically possible for a participant to undertake actions for nothing, the normal behaviour of participants is to undertake actions for something. In other words, they have purposes shaped by the social context, traditions, the legal order and individual personality. In summary, these normative actions can be understood by us (no matter whether we are supporters of MPM or HAM) because there are intersubjective categories, that is, because we share a common conceptual scheme related to basic features of our social life.

Consequently, "objectivity", in the strong sense, is of no use in this normative field. There are few relevant aspects of our legal orders that are independent of us. Some natural features (for example, the so-called "minimum content of natural law" by Hart) required for the permanence of legal orders, such as some form of property, sanctions, etcetera, even leave room for human choice. We partly create, although not from scratch, this normative world. We understand this normative world because we, as participants, put it in motion. We, as legal scholars, try to articulate this intersubjective conceptual scheme better, trying to make it more clear and coherent. However, legal scholars or legal philosophers should not see participants as an entomologist observes insects, because the legal philosopher is also an "insect", that is, he is also a member of what is observed.

7.1 Participants and Observers

Hence, any social scientist participates in a double dimension: as a participant and as an observer.[24] This should not be understood though as a change in what I have been saying, because it is a mistake to believe that the term "observer" is univocal. There is, on the one hand, an observer of the natural world and, on the other hand, an observer of the social-normative world. To believe that the second type of observer can be like the first type would be both an ontological and an epistemological mistake. Nevertheless, from an epistemological point of view, there are more interweavements because both methodologies, in spite of the differences, look for, *inter alia*, clearness and coherence.

Returning to the legal normative fields, I would say that the second level conceptual scheme of legal scholars is not available to the participants. From a pragmatical point of view, this is not usually dramatic, although when the distance between the legal scholar's work and citizens is very high, there can be relevant problems. It is known that the lecture given by Kirchmann in 1847 in Berlin, claiming, *inter alia*, that legal science was useless, both as a science and as a technique for solving conflicts, was due, basically, to the exaggerations of the formalistic *Begriffjurisprudenz* (conceptual legal dogmatics). These types of exaggeration have no place in mature sciences because people do not expect to understand what N. Bohr or A. Einstein said. Therefore, legal dogmatics is closer to the daily interests and values of citizens.

Even if scientific discoveries, in a strict sense, have direct influence on our lives, this is normally seen both from a causal point of view and as a beneficial result, with no necessary understanding of the procedure. We use the telephone but, in spite of its usefulness, we do not know how it works. This is rarely a problem though for most citizens. Therefore, citizens are more interested in legal normative matters because they have an influence on their lives not as an external and unintelligible knowledge but as an internal regulation of their daily life. This daily life depends, in part, on normative actions that anyone (or nearly anyone) can fulfil. At the same time, these normative actions constitute us as citizens, as members with equal rights compared to the other members of the community (at least in democratic political

[24] A classic book is, *The Idea of a Social Science and its Relation to Philosophy*, Peter Winch Routledge, London, 1988.

regimes). These and other matters shape us as human beings with autonomy and dignity. This is why they are so important for us.

It does not seem difficult to see that "observation" cannot be the same in all cases. In legal normative fields "observation" is, or is mainly, a question of grasping the "sense" of certain external regularities. There is not, then, a sharp distinction between "subjective" (the world of participants) and "objective" (the world of neutral observers). Both are members of the same intersubjective public network of meanings. We, as "committed observers", have to clarify and systematise this first level conceptual network. This entails, *inter alia*, that these committed observers have to look back to the participants' conceptual scheme and try to clarify and systematise it. In order not to be "contaminated" by the participants' point of view some legal tendencies prefer to dive into a logical analysis, as was previously mentioned.

Far from metaphysical dreams of "strong objectivity", (as something conclusively true, in a way that would be independent of us) "objectivity" should be understood in a weak sense (at least in legal normative fields), that is, as justified agreement. Even accepting a HAM, there is a danger in relying exclusively on existing language games of given communities. In this case, "legal dogmatics" would be, in the best case, a rather accurate description of these conceptual networks. This view leads to "acceptation" rather than "rational acceptability". As participants, (and legal scholars are "committed observers and participants") we are not only interested in what things are but also in what things ought to be. For this reason, we cannot rely exclusively on positive morality.

On the contrary, "committed observers" are interested also in critical morality because we want "the best" for our social practices. We need this interplay between these two levels. We are not historians trying to describe past events of dead people. "Committed observers" try to describe our social conceptual schemes and also propose the "best" it can be, here and now, because we are dealing with live categories. Therefore, second level conceptual schemes are descriptive and prescriptive, and it is a good thing to separate, as clearly as possible, what is description and what is prescription. A reductionist view would make legal dogmatics either "poor" or "useless".

Participants and observers should be understood as kinds of ideal types, in the sense that they have a methodological value for a better understanding of normative actions, understood in the first and third persons' view. They should not be understood in the sense that they perform clear-cut roles. However, legal rules have motivating force for human behaviour, but not in the sense that they have causal motivating force. Fire has a causal motivating force. For example, it forces us to take our hands away when we are too close to a fire. If our body were like iron the fire would not have the same causal motivating force as it does. On the other hand, legal rules have motivating force in a normative sense. They are, generally, seen as reasons for action, at least for participants.

In this respect, they have motivating force but in the purposive sense. In the first example we do not have the purpose of pulling our hands away, we just do it as a "natural" reaction. Contrarily, we would be surprised if a member of our community undertakes normative actions without any purpose. Everyone understands the difference between, why did you marry Peter?, and, why did you pull your hands away from this fire?

Consequently, there are, on the one hand, participants that critically reflect on legal rules and principles, because they are seen as authoritative (although not exclusionary) reasons for action. Observers would be persons and their only concern would be to observe regularities, either by understanding the internal point of view of the participants, or not. As I said, these should be seen as ideal types, although preference has to be given to the participant point of view, for the reasons already outlined.

7.2 Some Hermeneutic Tendencies

Methodological positivists believe that accepting any method other than their own, would produce "subjective" results, that is, results that are not supported by "scientific criteria". It is not clear what "objective" results could be in our legal normative fields and which sense the "unity of method" could have, granted the diversity of objects. However, either we are able to achieve objective results (in a strong sense) or not, and we have to be interpreters to undertake any task, to be strictly scientific or not. In this respect, a hermeneutic point of view would be something, let us say, "normal" when we want to understand any object. What happens, in legal normative fields, is that we have to interpret normative texts, that is, we have to deal with intentional action, based on normative rules placed in a specific and dynamic social context, which is all based on a specific conceptual scheme.

Intentional legal actions are closely related to "meaning", and this is so in a special way. When a scientist is observing a volcano that, after a long dormant period, is erupting lava, he may comment to his companion, "what does it mean to you?" If he says this, he is just asking for a causal explanation of what they are observing. In a different vein, when a legal scholar observes an (presumably) intentional action and asks a companion, "what does it mean to you?", its meaning is different. In this case, he wants to know the purpose and reason for this intentional action. However, at the same time, he wants to know what is intended to be performed. For example, does she want to perform a valid will? We also know that this specific intentional action, that has a concrete goal, can be properly understood because it is an element within a whole.

It has certain relations with other legal elements within a whole (that is, a given legal order) and this whole works and has sense within a wider whole (that is, a given society). This would show that legal orders are not autonomous and that legal discourse has no sense in itself. This is not the end of the story though, but, for our present purposes, it is sufficient. In this respect, as has already been mentioned, social practices have a paramount importance because any rational enterprise (and legal orders are very important ones) has some external and observable manifestations. A social practice is a typical example. Hence, to understand a given rational enterprise we have to understand the social practice (or social practices) that gives rise to and justifies this rational enterprise.

It does not mean though that we have to look at these social practices as something justified in themselves, because we would be condemned to accept strong relativism. In other words, only each group could understand and be understood through these social practices that would "constitute" the members of these groups and would be, by definition, justified. We cannot avoid having a form of life, that is, certain ways of understanding the world outside, the social world, ourselves and a certain economic form to produce and reproduce our existence. Nevertheless, our form of life is not univocal. This is a very important feature. I will take an example. Being a member of the Afghan society, at present dominated by Talibans, gives the members of this community a basic univocal possibility of being a person. If not, they will suffer serious or dramatic consequences.

In our form of life, we have plurivocal (although not infinite) possibilities of being a person. This has consequences for social practices because these open possibilities give the opportunity for developing diverse social practices or, at least, different interpretations of them. Some social practices, such as legal dogmatics, allow for pluralistic approaches, although there are some basic shared features. For example, legal positivists and hermeneuticians differ in important legal issues but they also agree on important questions, for example, that positive laws have to be considered as "must-sources" and not as "may-sources".

This does not mean that this agreement precludes any differences. It is not so because, following the above example, what positive laws are in some cases (that is, whether they exist from the formal validity point of view, or how they can be understood) gives room for divergence.

For example, Hermeneuticians believe, generally speaking, that parts cannot be properly understood without the whole, in this case the legal order. However, at the same time, the legal order cannot be properly understood without a certain relationship with its parts. All this depends on legal data that, in their turn, exist as legal meanings. Another difference between positivists and hermeneuticians, generally speaking, is the conceptual separation between law and morals, or between the subjective and the objective. Although positivists (at large) are usually relativists on material moral grounds, they claim to know very well what morality is, granted that they claim a sharp conceptual distinction between law and morals. However, if we cannot clearly and precisely identify morals, on the one hand, and law, on the other, it makes little sense to claim this sharp distinction.

Methodological positivists usually criticise others for not being precise enough, or for not having precise criteria to identify the object we are talking about. However, in which sense can we claim that we have objectively described a given morality of a given society, as it is? When we deal with Hermeneutics, as an alternative perspective to methodological positivism, we may ask what Hermeneutics has to offer. It does not have, neither as a matter of fact nor as a dream, an algorithm to offer. It does not even have universal rules of interpretation to be applied to any text, in any context. If objectivity, in the strong sense, has to be superseded by justified agreement, the main point will be to identify which are the criteria that make an agreement justified.

Once again, the Cartesian temptation is to suppose that there will be some "if p then q" that will work, no matter who does it, in which time, or context. Following this line of thought, a legal text would have universal meta-rules for their application. However, positive legal texts may remain in force (that is, have formal validity) while social reality changes. How can universal meta-rules work (everytime-everywhere) unless they are understood as purely formal? And if they are formal, how can they determine the result? This has been one of the main methodological positivistic lines of research that have led to a remarkable sort of "useless precision". According to Wroblewsky, there are two main ideologies of legal interpretation. One is supported by values, such as legal certainty, legal predictability and stability. The other is mainly based on the idea that legal interpretation should adapt law to changing social needs and interests.[25]

I believe that any sound ideology of legal interpretation should include both aspects because, as a matter of fact, one cannot dispense with the other. The difference should be, in my view, only a difference of emphasis. Depending on social circumstances, such as the dominating legal doctrinal tendencies and existing legal valid rules, jurists would stress legal certainty or justified adaptation. However, in any case, no legal order can survive only on the basis of legal certainty, or on the basis of justified adaptation. In a pre-industrial society, social stability could more easily cohere with legal certainty because relevant changes were slow. In post-industrial societies, legal certainty cannot be understood in the same way because accelerated change is a basic feature of these societies.

Therefore, while we cannot begin with complete doubt (according to Peirce) we cannot begin either with complete change. We always need (as a pragmatical need) some stability. With no stability we cannot give sense to the concept of change. We must know what stability is (at least as a contingent historical-societal understanding) in order to understand change. Change requires the contrast with stability. Consequently, it is a human societal feature to combine stability and change and, hence, to combine these two legal ideologies of interpretation. Now, we can introduce the idea that we need not choose between the so-called hermeneutics of tradition (basically represented by Gadamer) and the hermeneutics of suspicion (basically represented by Nieztsche or Focault).

If we choose one, we would have to abandon the other. In fact, we cannot do this in so far as they are basic societal features. These hermeneutic tendencies (cited above) emphasize, *inter alia*, the static and the dynamic aspect of any understanding of a social practice such as the legal social practice. In this vein, Nietzsche told us, *inter alia*, that language can deceive us. This would be so because language pushes us to believe in fixity that would underlie the changing world of experience. He also emphasized the hidden selfishness of the apparent disinterestedness of religious individuals. He also wanted to change or destroy Christian morality. In Habermas,

---

[25] Wroblewski, J. *Constitución y Teoría General de la Interpretación Jurídica*, Cuadernos Civitas, Madrid, 1985, pages 72 ff. Moreover, according to A. Aarnio, when we deal with "legal positivism" we should bear in mind the following: "If values are excluded from the theory, then we will have legal positivism. This holds good irrespective of whether we take positivism as a doctrine of the origins of law, as a theory of the application of law, or as a doctrine of the study of legal regulations." In: *Philosophical Perspectives in Jurisprudence*, Acta Philosophica Fennica Vol.36, 1983, "Form and Content in Law".

we can find, as in the case of Nietzsche, a certain standpoint from which it is possible to criticise and overcome the present.

In Habermas, emancipatory interests would be this basic standpoint related to communicative action, consensus and understanding. In his turn, Nieztsche had "master morality" as a basic standpoint to change or destroy the "slave morality". Habermas tried to change or overcome the social circumstances (power and domination) that obstruct new and superior forms of social life. On the other hand, it seems that Gadamer does not have, at least explicitly, this basic standpoint from which to overcome the present. He stresses the understanding of the meaning of a text, instead of the discovery of certain hidden interests, which would obstruct the achievement of the "authentic" form of life.

The radical historicity of Gadamer's hermeneutics means, basically, that the subject is "condemned" to understand the meaning of a text (although it cannot only be a text but also an event) based on his own conceptual scheme and prejudices. I believe that this should not be denied because we cannot see ourselves from outside. The problem is that our form of life has, because of its pluralistic structural basis, diverse conceptions and prejudices. In this respect, there is no one right answer that can be adopted from our historical situation. In addition, hidden aspects of the text that were unknown by the author, can be disclosed by the present interpreter. Hence, what is the main difference between Hermeneutics of Tradition and Hermeneutics of Suspicion?

They both try to show hidden aspects of the text but, in the case of Hermeneutics of Suspicion, this "disclosure" would be a sufficient reason to criticise the present. This criticism would be made from the adopted basic point of view, emancipatory interest or master morality. Gadamer does not seem to have this basic point, from which to make a radical criticism at the present time. However, in spite of the fact that our historical perspective does not determine the answer, it allows us to state that our interpretation does not start from scratch. In the case of legal interpretation this is even clearer. The smooth "fusion of horizons" between past and present is more akin to legal interpretation than the Hermeneutics of Suspicion.

A new legal interpretation tries, *inter alia*, to change and enrich the past, but we can only enrich our present if we have some past on which to stand. In cases of dramatic revolutionary changes this claim could be modified but not completely eliminated.

Finally, we could ask whether hermeneutics is a method. One possible answer is to say that it depends on the definition at stake. If definitions are not real, we could conventionally define "method" in a way that hermeneutics were in and not out. Or we could do so the other way round. I believe that hermeneutics is not a method if we understand a method as a bunch of clear and delimited rules that leads us, precisely and clearly, from premises to necessary conclusions. Existing and useful legal methods are not like this. Even more, there is room for sound disagreement, especially in the so-called hard cases. Be that as it may, I prefer to talk of hermeneutics as a metaphor. As is known, the idea of metaphor as the ability to discern likeness among unlike things is as old as Aristotle. Nevertheless, I will not only refer to the important function of metaphor for naming other ideas or to objects for producing similarities between them. In this respect, there is a fruitful discussion between M. Black and R. Boyd on metaphors in science and scientific communities but I will just focus on Kuhn's comment where he rejects the old empiricist frame and supports more open conceptions, where metaphors have a justified place,

> "Can we suppose that nature -and society- have one and only one joint of articulations to which scientific concepts, theories and metaphorical formulations should come near by successive cuts?"[26]

7.3 Hermeneutics and the Rule of Law

I would say that the "principle of inertia" (one of the important legal principles) fits in better with Hermeneutics of Tradition, not in the sense that tradition, or the past, should be seen as something sacred, but in the sense that, in the best case, we can only take a step forward. This link between legal theory and Hermeneutics of Tradition could be seen in the following sense: we can move a step forward but providing we maintain a foot in tradition. If we translate this to legal normative fields, we would say that we can move a step forward (basically in hard cases) but with a hand on must sources. When old legal normative texts remain and the change of relevant social circumstances requires new legal solutions, legal interpretation should move a step forward.

In doing so we must put material justificatory reasons beside some must sources. These material justificatory reasons and the must sources would represent, respectively, the present and the past. I recall, again, the dynamic aspect of critical morality. Nevertheless, an excessive demand for legitimacy of validity claims would make our legal orders useless. Hence, we should carefully reflect on the accusation made by Habermas (one of the representatives of Critical Hermeneutics) against Idealistic Hermeneutics. The latter would assume that self-interpretations undertaken by given participants are the final referee of any approach that tries to understand their interests, desires, etcetera. On the other hand, Critical Hermeneutics would see that there are material factors determining or conditioning (the alternative is extremely important) these self-reflections of the participants. Supposedly, Idealistic Hermeneutics would not notice them.

The above cited difference is very important because if we accept the former alternative, that is, "determination", let us say, of the legal-political superstructure by the economical structure, one cannot see how representatives of the so-called Critical or Materialistic Hermeneutics are so fortunate because they can see the truth, while the rest of the dominated human beings are only undertaking alienated social practices. On the contrary, if we accept the alternative of "conditioning", I do not see serious problems for accepting it, granted that there is some room for choice. In this respect, it is doubtful that any social researcher wants to deny that she is not conditioned by the society she is living in, even when she is behaving as a social researcher.

There is a balance between the past and present, with moments in which there is more stability and moments in which there is more change (for example, it is

[26] Fernández Buey, F., op.cit., pages 170-179.

supposed that in the Victorian era there was more stability than in the era of the levellers and diggers). This process of justified change can produce a new legal meaning, so distant from the initial meaning of the legal text, that we would have a new must source from a justificatory point of view, not from a formally valid point of view. This is not exceptional because legislators do not legislate so often and so perfectly that they can avoid changing legal meanings. These legal changes should be undertaken on the basis of the purposes of the legal text (understood from an intralinguistic and extralinguistic point of view). This can be problematic, and a legal theory (that cannot avoid moral and political considerations) should underlie the justified election of the purpose and its meaning. Obviously, there can be conflicting purposes and a justified choice would have to be undertaken.

Moreover, the legal theory that is based on these justified decisions can be disputable, either because there is another alternative legal theory or because there is another internal interpretation of the same legal theory. In any case, methodological positivists would not have a better alternative than hermeneuticians because, either logical preciseness or criticism of others' impreciseness is not enough. The "fusion of horizons" that Gadamer talks about could be reached through them (that is, past and present). This connection will allow us to see new problems, new horizons and, it is expected, new solutions. This view, and similar views, cannot satisfy methodological positivists because they see method from a narrower point of view, that is, as a delimited collection of techniques and procedures that will lead, safely and precisely, from premises to conclusion.

In this respect, we should distinguish between logical and empirical problems. In relation to the so-called legal science, the latter refer to the criteria that allow us to know when a rule is a member of a specific legal order (if this is so, interpretation plays a basic role). The former refer to the necessary consequences of the legal rules (if we accept them, the problem for participants is to delimit which necessary consequences are relevant). On the other hand, if we see method from a wide point of view, we understand it as a collection of conventions and flexible procedures that delimit the object and the legitimate problems a given group can deal with, at a given time. This delimitation cannot be geometrical because we are in the realm of practical reason where justified adaptation (the "best") to changing circumstances is fundamental.

If we adopt this wide point of view we cannot see method as a supra-personal and neutral collection of techniques and procedures that have to be "objectively" accepted, if we are going to behave as true scientists and obtain the necessary results. On the contrary, we should look at what the community of legal scholars and practical jurists do when dealing with legal conflicts, granted that they adopt an internal point of view. At least in our culture, this wide view of method implies an interplay between tradition and change. This wide view of method stresses the importance (and expertise) of the subjects who use the method, and rejects the positivist tendency of emphasising the autonomy of the method. Granted that method should not be understood as an algorithm, the more heavily we break our legal tradition the more difficult it is for us to have reliable methods (even in this weak sense of method).

This can be better seen in relation to historical revolutionary changes, such as the Revolution of 1917 in the Old Soviet Union. They can be seen as either conservative-progressive or intelligent-stupid, depending on the likes and dislikes (or values, if they are not likes or dislikes), not on verification. To change our past, showing new aspects of the text that were hidden until now, would be safer than completely breaking (if possible) our present and dominant form of life. In this respect, the problem of method and Hermeneutics transcends these concrete issues and dives into the problem of market society and the Rule of Law, on the one hand, and the rejection of market society and the Rule of Law, on the other.

In the end, the main problem is whether our present form of life justifies our efforts for improving it, or whether it is better simply to burn it, granted that any improvement is illusory. Those who believe in the calorific answer would support Hermeneutics of Suspicion and neglect any concern for the legal method. If we take the view of the Critical Legal Studies Movement, for example, we should assume that the indeterminacy of the market society makes the efforts to elaborate determinate rules useless to protect the interests of the legal actors. At the same time, legal methods, generally speaking, should be seen (from that point of view) not as descriptive of a given reality but as a political device for shaping a re-shaping of the citizens (that is, consumers) of the market society.

This would be done by favouring the -more or less hidden- interests of the market society itself. However, one thing is to see legal methods only as political devices held (or indirectly held) by those who hold the "real" power, and another is to be "method fetishist", as methodological positivists tend to be. I will not deal, here, though with the first suspicion. Let us repeat that we should not see Hermeneutics of Tradition as an option against Hermeneutics of Suspicion, providing the latter is understood in a weak sense. Or in other words, representing the dynamic side of interpretation, which is one of the main ideologies of legal interpretation. This ideology understands interpretation mainly as an adaptation to changing social needs and interests.

The other main ideology sees interpretation as a task of discovering the proper meaning of a given legal rule. If there is going to be a fertile "fusion of horizons" between past and present there must be coherence, which is understood from our contingent historicity. This coherence though is difficult or impossible in cases of dramatic economical-political change. In any case, this historicity is too vague and, for this reason, useless for legal purposes. Consequently, we have concrete legal social practices that develop in a concrete society, by a concrete legal community, on the basis of a concrete legal order. This development is a dynamic tension between tradition and adaptation. Only in a few cases, such as the French Revolution or the Soviet Revolution, does the above cited coherence fail because a radical new tradition begins, although not from scratch.

In this respect, Habermas is right when he claims that we can go beyond the framework of tradition. However, Wittgenstein and Winch are also right because we, normally, develop ourselves and our social practices within the limits of our tradition. As an analogy, we could say that scientists usually live and work within "normal science" and when they do this, they have a somewhat conservative stance because they cannot leave the limits of the paradigm in force. However, from time to time, a "revolutionary period" arrives. In this period, scientists can leave their tradition because they cannot find the correct answer in it. In any case, neither in mature sciences nor in legal fields, are we very often able to begin a new tradition, or to live a revolutionary period. On the other hand, certain traditions, like ours, (that stem, *inter alia*, from Greece and the Enlightenment) foster creativity and critical reason. I know that our culture also includes Hitler, but I am interested in the "best" not in the "worst" traditions.

These traditions (seen from their best viewpoint) allow or even encourage change, although not the radical change that destroys traditions, our best traditions, if this is possible. In a similar vein, a democratic political society allows, or even fosters, political change, but not the radical change that breaks the rules of the game itself. Only those who believe that our world does not deserve to survive any more can reject any effort to improve our world and ourselves. They would see any "fusion of horizons" as an indecorous prolongation of a lost cause.

8. SOME REMARKS ON LEGAL INTERPRETATION

Although there are several types of legal interpretation, I am talking about normative interpretation of valid legal texts or legal norms. I mean by the latter, the interpretative result of a given valid legal text, that is, a working interpretation and, hence, one accepted by the legal community on the basis of justificatory reasons. This legal norm will (probably) be the object of future interpretations when new relevant circumstances justify a new legal interpretation. This would be so unless we believe that the legislative legal text has, within it, all the future possibilities that future jurists could discover, granted the legal techniques. Legal interpretation should neither be understood as a creative task of the interpreter each time she specifies the meaning, nor as a mechanical task of the interpreter. As I claim in this work, there is a hard core of legal meaning, but it is not understood as if it was a meaning in itself but rather as a result of the rational acceptance of legal experts. The population should not reject, at least, these legal meanings because it is the citizens that usually make legal application. When this is not possible or it does not work, judges, authoritatively, apply the law.

At least in legal normative realms, the absence of algorithms implies that the stress should be put, not on neutral procedures, *tout court*, but on both legal procedures and subjects who interpret and apply them to specific cases, in certain contexts, at a certain time. Hence, we do not have "one right answer". It does not matter whether we use formal logic or normative construction. If we accept this, a certain language game appears as dominant. Instead of "one right answer" (or a necessary conclusion) we have (in some legal cases) several sound possibilities. It has some similarities with Strawson's criticism of Russell's definite descriptions, that is, the former would have attributed to statements certain properties that should only be attributed to the uses of these statements. Be that as it may, instead of "proof" and truth we have "justification". When we deal with "legal facts" we can have proof, understood in a scientific sense, although the legislator may modify the results of a scientific proof because "legal fiction" is an accepted element of legal orders. Finally, therefore, causal explanation cannot be the relevant aspect, as it is in physics. In legal normative fields, the primacy rests on teleological explanation and intentional action although not necessarily for all items, such as in objective liability.

We have to deal with choice. Nevertheless, a rational choice can be considered from different perspectives. Some theories of rational choice emphasize the idea of ideal rational agents and rationality itself as logical inference. These rational agents are usually seen as irrepressible maximizers of the expected utility. They are usually seen as atomistic Hobbesian individuals. My view of rational choice is especially related to hard cases, where competent and responsible legal experts can firmly disagree. In a similar way, a competent judge may have problems of rational choice in a hard case, that is, there may be more than one reasonable answer to a given legal problem. In this respect, rationality is not only concerned with the choice of means to given ends. Ends can be "open" requiring a rational choice of how to concrete them in concrete situations. In a similar way, although legal premises are given, legal experts have to select whose premises are adequate to a given case. A justified rational choice is required. Moreover, a rational choice in legal normative realms, should not see addressees as irrepressible utility maximizers and as atomistic Hobbesian individuals, in so far as they share an internal point of view. In addition, addressees should not be seen in an either-or way or a moral-prudent way. They are both. Consequently, the moral theory that underlies the rational agent I am dealing with cannot only be a prudent *homo economicus*.

These and other aspects shape a different understanding of human action and rationality, that is, intentional action and practical reason, with the latter considered by methodological positivists, such as Kelsen, Ross and others, as a contradictory concept. At this point, I am going to scrutinise "justification" and "practical reason" in relation to "legal method". Legal interpretation is a necessary, not a contingent, task of legal orders. If we take operative interpretation as the basis, that is, a normative interpretation of valid legal texts to reach a valid legal decision, we can see that it depends, *inter alia*, on "relevant" facts, values and interpretative decisions, settling whether there is or there is no doubt in a legal text. At the same time, as J. Wroblewski says,

> "Interpretative directives of both levels, that is, D1 and D2, are decisive factors in the justification of the interpretative decision."[27]

However, these interpretative directives are full of evaluative terms such as "sufficient reasons", "intention of the lawgiver", etcetera. In summary, evaluations play a central role in legal normative interpretation. Granted this situation, a possible option is to claim that this is a realm of irrationality and the only rational task could be to describe, *ex post*, the process of decision. However, before condemning us to bare irrationality, in relation to one of the most important social practices of our life, we should explore another possibility. This possibility is to neglect the positivist insistence on logical and empirical rationality as the only kinds of reliable rationality.

---

[27] Ibidem, page 63.

What does this mean? It means, *inter alia*, the predominance of a certain language game that is not a physicalist language game. If this is correct, causal explanation cannot be, as I have said, the relevant explanation in legal normative fields. Granted that any legal order establishes social goals to be fulfilled, since it utters legal rules that require certain citizens to undertake certain intentional behaviour, and legal rules facilitating the private goals of citizens, etcetera, we can claim that teleological explanation seems the proper and predominant one. This would be so because human action is mainly understood on the basis of purposes, purposes of the agents (legally conditioned) and purposes that solidify legal rules and institutions.

Granted this, we have to deal with "purposes", "rational and legitimate means", "rational actions", "justification of decisions", "normative theories", "rights", "duties", "justice", etcetera. In this respect, there is a normative interplay between normative theories and legal rules. This means that legal rules, at least in hard cases, are interpreted through the lenses of normative theories that justify the importance given to certain facts, in certain contexts, and the relevance of certain purposes and not others (in certain time-situations). This would be so, no matter whether we are talking about the linguistic, systemic or functional context. Once again, we have to decide whether all this is no more than an irrational enterprise, or to neglect the narrower sense of rationality typical of methodological positivism. Hence, in due course, my aim will be to scrutinise the importance of "justification" and "judgement" in legal normative fields.

Let us consider the following type of propositional knowledge: "A knows B if (1) C believes D, (2) C's belief in D is justified, (3) D is true". Most, if not all, methodological positivist approaches support the idea that to be rational we have to know and, in order to know, we must reach truth. How can we reach truth? By logical inference or by empirical statements describing facts as they are. The problem, for us, is whether we should accept that justification necessarily implies truth. On the other hand, if it is the case that truth is not a necessary element of justified beliefs, then, we may have justified beliefs without truth. "If Peter knows that Mary has a right to freedom of speech in this specific situation, then, Peter cannot be mistaken about it". We should distinguish though between the meaning of "knows" when it refers to the normative existence of a legal text, and when it refers to the application of this normative legal text to a concrete situation.

While Peter may have knowledge, in relation to the first case, Peter will not have knowledge in relation to the second, because several interpretations of the same normative legal text can be possible and sound. Granted this, we may have knowledge of the language of the legislator, in the sense of its existence at a certain time and place, but we will not have knowledge of legal norms, understood as the interpretative result of the legislator's language. Some could say that we might have knowledge of the legislator's language, understood in its literal meaning content. However, if knowledge is only empirical or logical we could not have knowledge of a legal premise, understood as its meaning content. If knowledge is understood as propositional knowledge, it seems difficult to apply it to legal normative fields. Nevertheless, a purely descriptive legal science should be able to utter true legal propositions, such as "It is true that legislator X stated that "it is prohibited to smoke in Parliament"", in a given legal order.

As I said, with the passing of time an interpretative result (that is a legal norm) can be the material object language (instead of the legislative text as a formal legal object) whose new interpretation may produce another legal norm. For example, when a legal norm (understood in the above-cited sense) has received support from the legal community and it is considered as the correct representation of a legal normative text, at a certain time, it will be taken as the material object language. In other words, it will be taken as the stable normative-meaning point from which a possible future change may take place. This means that a new legal meaning-change may arise, not from a formally valid point of view, like a must-source, but from a legal norm, that is, the result of the interpretation made of this must-source. The formally valid legal text may lose or decrease its legal material relevance while holding up its relevance as a formal must-source.

It is not clear whether methodological positivists claim that their analytic method produces fallible or infallible results. Nevertheless, the first understanding, fallibilism, is accepted by most legal theorists. The second understanding (supposedly accepted by methodological positivists) is problematic. However, methodological positivists do not claim that they, personally, cannot be mistaken. They know that they can be. What do they claim, then? In my view, that the method they use leads to "objective" results, while the method used by non-methodological positivists leads to "subjective" results. It seems that they do not defend a strong version of infallibilism. They accept that they, as individuals, can be mistaken but the method itself cannot be, when properly used.

If this is correct, the characteristic method of methodological positivists would be a logical one, because empirical methods cannot claim to be infallible, even when properly used. Nevertheless, methodological positivists seem to rely on empirical method (external point of view) and once the "objective" results have been obtained, they apply a logical method. However, logical correctness of an argument is not dependent on the truth of its premises. In this respect, to have true premises would be logically irrelevant, since the logical correctness (or incorrectness) of an argument depends on the relation between the premises and the conclusion. In this respect, a logically correct argument may have one or more false premises. Nevertheless, granted that the premises are normative it would make no sense to talk of the true/false dichotomy.

Summing up, methodological positivists would have to describe legal premises (sometimes understood as the normative texts uttered by the legislator and sometimes understood as the constructive result of these normative texts undertaken by participants) as "non-committed observers". We should distinguish though between the "external" observer who does not understand what participants are doing, and the "hermeneutic" observer who understands, and then describes, what participants are doing. Here we can remind ourselves what Einstein said,

"In so far as mathematical laws refer to reality, they are not true; and in so far as they are true, they do not refer to reality."[28]

It seems that methodological positivists have difficulties to reach infallibilism because it seems difficult to find an ordered and finite set of operations that allows us to find the solution to a problem, that is, an algorithm. However, if they do not have an algorithm, that is, an algorithm for solving practical problems, what is the superiority of their method? In summary, both (methodological positivists and hermeneuticians) can be mistaken but the probability of being mistaken would be higher in hermeneutic methods because it leads to subjective results, no matter how good legal hermeneuticians can be. Here we are facing two different approaches. It is known that one is called "internalism" and the other "externalism". The two main lines of internalist theories of justification are "foundationalism" and "coherentism". First though, let us have a look at some of the problems internalism and externalism have in relation to justification.

8.1 Internal and External Justification

Internalism and externalism are not clear-cut approaches and, in this respect, more or less radical versions can exist. The softer versions of both approaches allow for a close harmony and, perhaps, fertile communication between them. Be that as it may, internalist approaches are taken from the first-person viewpoint, in the sense that our epistemic evaluations are, in the end, grounded in what is "available" to the participants. I will use here "participant" and "observer" as the basic human reference of internalist and externalist perspectives. At first sight, it seems that there is a basic flaw in internalist approaches because its first-person approach does not fit in with social reality. Our body of knowledge *lato sensu* (whether *episteme* or *doxa*) has a fundamental communal dimension.

Granted that this is correct, it would represent a strong reason against internalism. Fortunately, internalism does not need to be understood in this way. Internalism emphasizes a first-person approach, in the sense that it emphasizes the "participant point of view", although this person is not an isolated monad. On the contrary, because the person is a participant he has a special relationship with the rest of the participants. They do not see each other as aliens but as persons sharing basic aspects of societal life. One manifestation of this is the understanding of legal normative texts. At least in principle, they understand actions performed by other participants and understand them to be intentional. This aspect of "intentionality" is related to the idea that internalism is based on a first-person approach. However, participants create a complex web of social relations that transcends it. Nevertheless, although they could be seen as a kind of Popperian third world, it does not exist in itself but has to be put in motion by human beings.

In a similar vein, we have seen how important social practices are from a participant's point of view. Hence, if internalism has to be criticised, it should be

[28] Einstein, A. "Geometry and Experience", 1923. In: *Readings in Philosophy of Science*, Feigl and Broodbeck (eds), page 189.

done from another perspective. I would say that although a strong view of internalism is untenable, a weak version is not, because it combines participants as social individuals with shared social practices. On the other hand, externalism can be seen from a strong perspective. In this vein, in so far as we do not rely on a first-person approach, we do not need to have reasons for accepting a belief. It should be sufficient that others (or some others) have these reasons. In some cases, this can be rational. For example, we are usually passengers of aeroplanes without knowing how they work, but we suppose that others (experts) know. This supposition seems to be rational.

However, not everything is like this. For example, I can use the same structure of reasoning and say that I do not understand a very important political decision of my Government, but I suppose, at the same time, that others do understand. Although having the same structure, it does not seem to be acceptable for a "committed participant". The question is not whether few or many persons behave in that way, because we are not facing, here, a descriptive sociological approach. I believe that the basic purposes of legal orders (at least those based on a Rule of Law view) require something more than participants as "obedient donkeys". It is known that Hart supposed this to be sufficient (although not desirable) for a working legal order. On the other hand, it is not a basic purpose of Physics that all citizens "self-reflectively participate" in this scientific enterprise. In this respect, it should be unsound to require all passengers of aeroplanes to know the scientific problems implied in their flight. These differences, *inter alia*, would justify a different methodological approach.

A problem, for a strong view of externalism, is that it excessively relies on "experts". These experts are different from the experts that share an internal point of view. The former would tell the rest of the people which is the "truth", because they would make a logical reconstruction of a given language. The latter would make a rational but fallible reconstruction. Another danger is that it excessively relies on "exclusionary reasons for action", in Raz's sense. These are serious dangers though, in so far as participants (understood from a soft internalist approach) almost disappear as self-critical participants. If experts know what we should do and we rely on them, because what really matters is not what is "available" to me, then, we would have to move a step closer to the concept of participants as "obedient donkeys".

On the other hand, if "exclusionary reasons for action" are so compelling, that participants have no room for reflection and rational criticism, then another step should be taken towards our ideal "obedient donkey". Although there is no logical necessity, methodological positivism is closer to this picture than hermeneutician approaches. No matter whether methodological positivists are, as individuals, "progressives" or "leftists" or "revolutionaries". As legal researchers, they are closer to this view where participants are impoverished as autonomous and rational beings. However, perhaps, their view is the true one. No matter how unpleasant this result can be. If they use a scientific method that produces "objective" results, then, although they can be mistaken (because they have abandoned infallibilism) they would probably be more right than hermeneuticians.

In this respect, we could distinguish between factual probability, on the one hand, and epistemic probability, on the other. Suppose Peter kills John. According to factual probability, there is a certain probability of Peter being arrested by the police of the town where he killed John, at least following a certain lapse of time. Although legal theorists should be interested in these matters, their main concern is not with sociology but with legal theory, that is, the normative aspect of law. Nevertheless, some realists' approaches have emphasized the probability of future events, although I will not deal here with Scandinavian Realism. In this respect, it seems that epistemic probability is closer to the cognitive interest of legal theorists. What is the main difference between factual and epistemic probability? In the latter, the degree of epistemic probability depends on me, while in the former the frequency of a given event does not depend on me.

If we bear this in mind, some could say that a justified belief should be based on factual probability, not on subjective evidence. The evidence of a given subject could be based not on the structure of the world as it is, but on wishful thinking. Then, it seems that for a belief to be justified it should be factually probable, and it is factually probable because it is based on the laws of nature. (We should remind ourselves here that a person living in Copernicus's time would be wrong, if relying on certain laws of nature). If this is correct, and if the beliefs of methodological positivists are more factually probable, because they rely on externalism, we should conclude that their beliefs are more justified. Is this correct? From a deontological point of view, justified beliefs depend on our evidence. This is closer to internalism.

At the same time, this is closer to our cultural background, because one can be blamed (at least generally speaking) for a concrete action, according to our own evidence. Although there can be exceptions, we blame a person for a wrong he has done, granted that he knows the relevant information, not when he ignores it and is not expected to know it. This is an aspect usually incorporated into legal orders, although not completely, because liability, as I said, can be subjective or objective.

This means, *inter alia*, that we expect persons to have a certain average knowledge in certain matters. We punish murderers, *inter alia*, because we suppose that everyone knows that murder is a morally bad conduct and because we suppose that everyone knows that shooting a person, for example, implies (normally) to kill, or to hurt somebody. If someone really does not know this, we do not blame him. It means that epistemic probability and epistemic justification are the proper and more important basis of our deontological beliefs. If methodological positivists want to produce justified beliefs on the basis of an externalist approach, they should accept that some persons-observers (let us call them, Opv) know better than participants (Ppv) whether the behaviour of the latter (that is, Ppv) is justified or not.

One of the main tasks of methodological positivists would be to convince lawgivers that their proposals are made on the basis of scientific methods, which differ from those of analytic hermeneuticians, who use non scientific methods and do not achieve true results. One problem is that lawgivers are participants and addressees too. Even a methodological positivist, like Hart, claimed that officials should share an internal point of view. What is the importance of scientific and neutral descriptions of what they do, if this is a possible task? They want to know what they ought to do. What is the purpose of neutral and scientific descriptions of the participant's behaviour? Post-positivists' legal approaches (in so far as they are descriptive and normative) have the purpose of being useful for the legal community because they try to give justified solutions to hard cases and, also, try to improve the systematization of the legal order.

While quantitative sociological tasks should use externalist approaches, legal theorists, when dealing with positive legal orders, should use internalist ones. Generally speaking, the epistemic duties of participants depend on the evidence that is accessible to them, after reflection. However, it should be accepted that this is not the whole story. Coexisting with the former, there is, as I said, "objective responsibility". In these cases, an externalist approach would fit because the agent's intention would not be so relevant. This would be another example of the uselessness of reductionist approaches. Hart partly supported this internalist view when he emphasized the "reflective and critical attitude" of some participants, especially officials. He also emphasized the externalist view, in so far as he saw participants as "obedient donkeys".

In my opinion, this internal point of view (here and now) would have epistemic preference and chronological priority over external observers, even accepting that they are able to understand (not only to describe) what they observe, in other words, the participants' internal point of view. This means, *inter alia*, to be able to understand it from the participants' point of view. If this is the case, it is doubtful what observers could add to the participants' view. I have recently said that reductionist approaches are useless. In this respect, we should remind ourselves that Physicalism used to be reductionist and its present heirs have a similar attitude towards other not "truly scientific" approaches.

Leaving aside this methodological tendency, let us see how "justification" applies to a hermeneutic point of view. A first basic point is that justification allows for error and error can be seen from a first-person viewpoint. In this respect, similar to the Cartesian Cogito, we could say that it would be an error (or an existential inconsistency) to claim "I do not exist". Similarly, others could not claim that John's utterance "I am in pain", is false. Therefore, a problem is whether private data can warrant knowledge. Granted the possibility of error, neither participants nor observers can claim to have knowledge about the normative social practices undertaken by participants, in a given community. Nevertheless, granted that we cannot have knowledge of these normative social practices because we can be mistaken, can we only have "subjective appraisals"?

Methodological positivists would claim that they have knowledge because they use a scientific method that truly describes the object as it is. It is hard to see how this is so. In a purely formal language, logical properties and relations are determined by syntactical features. If we accept that there is no privileged interpretation of logic symbols, and that this purely formal language considers material content as irrelevant, it is problematic to see what is the practical usefulness of this enterprise, especially when they claim to be the only rational legal theorists. On the other hand, it is doubtful that all semantic properties of natural languages can be properly represented by a logical symbolisation. If we accept that only some semantic properties are relevant, this would put doubts on the idea that we can properly represent semantics based only on form.

Related to what has been said, we face the following problem: if we reject an internalist approach, what does it mean that John has a reason for action (B), when this is said by Peter? How can John have a reason for action if he does not know it, or if he is not motivated by this reason? One answer could be the following: legal orders cannot rely on the acceptation of participants because laws are not morals, in other words, law is heteronomous. If someone has no reason for action (and does not perform the action) legal orders have legal-institutional punishment as a proper answer. In this vein, legal orders can be understood as devices for guiding behaviour and reaching certain goals, no matter whether there is internal acceptation by the participants.

Although this is a possibility, once we move away from this view of legal orders, we come closer to internalist approaches, where the understanding and acceptation of the participants is more important and, hence, gives a different view of what human persons and legal authorities are. This does not mean that, in this new perspective, all participants in all circumstances are perfectly aware and consciously accept the legal duties settled by a legal order. Once reductionist approaches are rejected, the emphasis is put on participants as rational agents, and not as obedient donkeys. It also means that "punishment" cannot be the "essential" aspect of legal orders because participants, at large, share an internal point of view and "fidelity to law" is important for most of them, although it is not exclusive.

Punishment can be seen as the "essential" aspect of legal orders, once we stress legal form, discard material content and dispense with fidelity to law, among other things. In summary, sentences about what other participants "ought to do" are not factual expectatives about future behaviour based on an external stimulus. Even accepting the importance of these external stimuli, they should not be seen as the determinant aspect. Why not? Because participants are not exclusively seen (at least from an internal point of view) as Holme's "bad man". It is known that the bad man would only be interested in making legal predictions related to his own interests. Hence, a legal order is not a guiding and justifying whole but a bunch of orders in a den of thieves.

Once again, the angelical view that all participants always behave like "good men" is not claimed here. What is claimed is that our communities need not be organised as police states, *inter alia*, because participants, at large, share basic values, rights and duties. These are seen as beneficial for their interests (individual and social) and, also, as important in themselves. That is, they have internalised reasons for action, both from a consequentialist view and from a deontological view. Nevertheless, to see addressees only from a consequentialist view or from a deontological view is mistaken. Moreover, a hypothetical external observer and a real participant can both make predictions about the future behaviour of other participants.

However, both can be mistaken (granted that methodological positivists have renounced infallibilism) although participants know each other better and, at the same time, they require these predictions to be fairly accurate, because their own individual and societal life is concerned. Last but not least, I recall here a distinction A. Aarnio establishes,

> "This means, that from the organizational point of view the judge works within the official system and the scholar examines legal norms from outside. The judge, but not the scholar, is a part of the power wielding machinery ... However, in a certain sense both the judge and the scholar have a similar internal point of view. Let us call it an epistemologically internal point of view ... The perspective of legal dogmatics is essentially different from that which is typical of social science. In the latter field it is normal to put the question "What happens?" or "What regularities can we find here?""[29]

8.2 Hermeneutic Circle and Justification

Now, it is time to focus on "justification" and its importance, both from an external point of view and from an internal point of view. What does "justification" mean from an external point of view? Why and how should a "bad man" justify what he does? In this position, "justification", from his own view, is to anticipate properly the legal answers of the legal institutions. If I only go after my own interests I will see legal institutions as a means to obtain the best possible results for me. If we suppose that the lawgiver is also a "bad man" (why should he be otherwise?) he will act in a similar way, although with one basic difference, that is, he will proclaim certain social goals. These social goals would be fostered by the lawgiver because they help him to keep his post.

Differently from these "contaminated" human beings, methodological positivists would be able to purely describe reality as it is, and their personal interests would not influence the application of their "scientific" method. In this respect, I insist that the dichotomy between legal theorists and citizens, although logically possible, is extremely difficult in practice. Hence, I cannot see the force of basing a methodology on this ethereal dichotomy. Methodological positivists cannot "decide" that they have no pre-understandings or prejudices, or that they are not influenced by them. Perhaps, to avoid them they only rely on logical reconstructions. Granted this, we again face the problem of distinguishing what we do as "legal scientists" and what we do as "citizens". Taking this distinction to the extreme we could say, "Peter works as a legal scientist for the Nazi regime during the day, but during the night he is a member of the Resistance".

I agree that not all situations are like that cited above but, in any case, what this should show is that a sharp distinction between these two realms is untenable. There are distinctions, but no sharp distinctions, between John as a citizen and John as a legal scholar, in so far as basic assumptions or values are at stake. "Justification" is a socio-historical concept that changes with time, as other concepts do, although some of them are more "entrenched" than others. For a participant, "intentional action, best interpretation, individual rights" etcetera, would be examples of "entrenched" concepts that are related to justification. Another feature of "justification" is that it is gradual. You can be more or less justified in relation to a certain case, given a certain context. This can be very disappointing for a person expecting to deal with

---

[29] Aarnio, A. *The Rational as Reasonable*, Reidel, Dordrecht, 1987, pages 9 and 10. For this and other related issues, Jerzy Wroblewski, *Sentido y Hecho en el Derecho*, Edit. Universidad del Pais Vasco; *The Judicial Application of Law*, Kluwer, 1992.

truth, because it is not gradual. In this respect, if methodological positivists are on the true path and are using the true method, analytic hermeneutics are on the wrong path and using a false method. However, which method should we use for knowing this?

It is related to the confidence in "truth conditions" that would supersede the subjective beliefs of the participants. Granted this, the "subjective" opinions of participants would be irrelevant and experts and exclusionary reasons may take a hand. Another problem for the epistemic concept of justification is that it should not be understood in one exclusive direction, from basic beliefs to non-basic beliefs, in a foundationalist way. Put in legal words, justification would not be based on only one direction, from legal normative text to an interpretative decision. This can be so in "routine cases", where the clarity of the normative text and its application to a specific case, is not put in doubt by the legal community. Moreover, when we deal with a "hard case", this foundationalist view fails and we come nearer to a coherentist view or closer to the hermeneutic circle, used in advance by Roman jurists.

In this case, we face the "hermeneutic circle" (so much rejected by methodological positivists) because it is disputable (even by legal experts) which is the proper legal premise, or the relevant facts or the proper conclusion, etcetera. Now, justification is not linear but circular, and Hermeneuticians have to support the accusation of a vicious circle, which is supposed to be sufficient for them to be expelled from the rational world. However, is legal reasoning (granted that it is circular) a proper example of the fallacy of arguing in a circle? I think that, before we have settled the proper normative premise(s) for a given legal case (that is usual in hard cases), circular argumentation is inevitable. Once the normative premise(s) is settled, the reasoning can be deductive, at least *ex post facto*. Suppose we face a hard case. The legal argumentation could be the following, granted that the steps of the reasoning process can be explicit or implicit:

1) The legislator is, *inter alia*, just; 2) A general normative premise (N) has been uttered by the legislator; and, 3) This normative premise in relation to certain facts, will lead to a just legal decision, granted a certain interpretation. In (3) we face a deductive reasoning. In this step, the reasoning is not circular. Once we have at our disposal a constructed and selected normative premise we can infer a legal conclusion. However, (3) depends on a circular reasoning because in order to construct and select the proper normative premise (N) a circular reasoning is required. We look forward and backward, from principles to specific cases and from specific cases to principles. At any given moment, we believe that a proper legal conclusion is either clearly seen or presupposed by the constructed premise. This belief is not reached in a deductive way. If this was the case though, the process would not be typical of hard cases but of routine cases.

Therefore, the normative premise is supposed to be able to produce an interpretation that implies a just decision because it is a product of (1), a just legislator cannot want unjust results. Why is this reasoning process fallacious? In the fallacy of arguing in a circle, the conclusion to be proved is presupposed by the premises used by the arguer. A typical example could be the following: if somebody wants to prove that God exists he could claim (1) that the Bible claims it and (2) that the Bible speaks the truth. These claims presuppose what has to be proved, that is, the existence of God. We can see that in a reasoning that begs the question, it fails to advance our "knowledge". However, this is not the case for legal reasoning, at least in hard cases. Participants have accepted the ideology of the "rational legislator" (that includes, *inter alia*, that he is just) and strive for a "better adaptation" of the legal order to changing circumstances.[30]

In some cases, we do not know which is the proper normative premise from which to infer a legal conclusion. We have to construct the proper normative premise and this increases our legal knowledge. I will take for granted that "legal knowledge" is not propositional knowledge. That is, it gives us a better justification for doing something we did not know before. Methodological positivists, at large, believe that normative premises cannot be rationally justified. For this reason, they have focused their interest on internal justification. It is known that this kind of justification refers to the justification of the conclusion, given certain premises. In this respect, only justice in the application of law could be rational. Ross, Hart and others are good examples of this type of approach. Also, as Kelsen said, the legal scientific task can tell us which are the meanings of a given normative text, although to choose the "correct" one is not a scientific task, it is a political one. This approach is linear, from premises to the conclusion, and rejects circles.

For example, if we want to justify (N1) and for doing this we rest on (N2) and for justifying (N2) we rest on (N1) then, we would have a vicious circle. Here, we can place the "hermeneutic circle". Nevertheless, we should bear in mind that legal normative fields are not the fields of the causal world. In the causal world (for example, in Physics), we cannot use some premises to prove the conclusion and, also, to use the conclusion to prove these premises. In legal normative fields we try to understand (not to prove) from within a given complex whole, but the understanding of this whole depends on the relationship of their parts. At the same time, these parts cannot be understood in themselves, only in relation to the whole. Even more, these systemic relations have sense in a given extra-linguistic context that is not static either.

In this respect, the ideology of the rationality of the legislator (implicit in jurists that share an internal point of view) implies, *inter alia*, the rejection of non-coherent normative texts because it is supposed that a rational legislator will not regulate the same situation in two incompatible ways. Therefore, coherentism fits with the

---

[30] The hypothesis of the legislator's rationality (supposedly embedded in the practice of jurists, at large) has been dealt with by several authors. I will just mention, L. Nowak, Z. Ziembinski, N. Bobbio, M. Van de Kerchove, J. Lenoble and F. Ost. In the Spanish language, J.C. Nino is, probably, the most relevant legal scholar who dealt with this issue. Very briefly, we should be reminded that the usual virtues of the rational legislator would be the following: immortal, omniscient, just, coherent, inclusive, precise and economic (not redundant). This assumption by jurists, at large, would facilitate a better adaptation of the legal order to the changing circumstances. Otherwise, this assumption by practical jurists has important methodological consequences. Just to mention some of the most important ones: the *reductio ad absurdum* argument, because we should not accept an absurd legal interpretation; and, the economic argument, because we should not accept a legal interpretation that makes a legal normative text redundant, that is, if it just repeats what a previous normative text had already stated. These and other methodological requirements rely on the acceptation of a rational legislator. I would say that this acceptation is linked to the Internal Point of View of participants.

process of reasoning that deals with hard cases, while foundationalism fits better with the process of reasoning that deals with routine cases. In the first case, we deal with a holist justification while in the second case we deal with a linear justification. In the first case, no vicious circle is inevitable, whereas in the second case it is of no use, because we can go directly from an already settled normative premise to an already expected legal conclusion.

At the same time, this kind of justification is gradual because coherence is also a matter of degree. In principle, the more we increase the coherence of the whole, the better the justification of our decision. A possible objection against coherence is that it does not permit us to move away from the empirical world as it is. Fortunately, legal coherence is not only a theoretical exercise but also a practical one. *Prima facie* coherent solutions are expected to be better for solving legal conflicts. A complex feed back goes from the intra-linguistic field to the extra-linguistic field and then to new legal interpretations. These *prima facie* coherent solutions should fit (more or less) in a given form of economic production, in a given political regime, in a given legal tradition, in a given complex cultural tradition, etcetera. This "more or less" means, once again, that we are in the field of practical reason not in the perfectly consistent field of geometry.

Not everything that coheres, from an intra-linguistic point of view, is finally accepted by the legal community and/or the social community. This does not imply the irrelevance of formal validity but the primacy of practice. This primacy makes it possible to supersede or modify (in some cases) these *prima facie* coherent solutions. In this respect, social experience represents an additional test for *prima facie* coherent solutions and, in this way, the objection that experience has no effect on our coherent belief system can be denied. This adaptation has two basic routes, legislative normative texts and coherent interpretative construction. We cannot dispense with either of them, at least in our legal culture, we can only stress one or another. In any case, there is a dynamic interplay between them. In a similar way as individuals and the community, on the one hand, and legal order and its application, on the other, also have a permanent dynamic interplay.

This interplay is more similar to a circle than to a linear movement. It also shows how a reductionist justification, either internalist or externalist, cannot work. In internal justification, justification is a matter that should be determined only by considerations accessible to the subject. This view is closer to the legal private relations, as understood in the XIX century or at the beginning of the XX century, that is, commutative justice as the proper justification of these private relations. On the other hand, external justification is closer to a distributive justice perspective. In this case, the main problem is not who is guilty, or who made the promise, but how to distribute the burdens derived from certain legal events, such as a car's accident or the unjustified breaking of a promise.

Both aspects are basic elements of our legal and political culture. In spite of their differences, methodological positivism with its emphasis on "neutral" description of what law is, and hermeneutics, that emphasizes normativity and construction, are basic elements of our legal culture. In this respect, legal dogmatics should avoid any reductionist view, relying exclusively either on description or on construction. Both elements are needed for a rich and useful legal dogmatics. We should, finally, be reminded that Hermeneutics primarily leads to understanding, not to sense-data. This is also directed to texts and human actions, which could explain why methodological positivists do not accept pragmatic contradiction but only a logical one. Nevertheless, if someone would tell me "I am not eating" when he is, I would believe that he had fallen into a pragmatic contradiction.

This denial is not, generally speaking, acceptable for Hermeneuticians because we (participants) have normative expectations, not exhaustively understandable only on the basis of formal logic. Finally, Hermeneuticians go beyond the textuality (in the so-called hard cases) because they are interested not only in legal certainty but also in other values, such as material justice. This is not understood as a deductive task that goes from a given legislator's language to necessary conclusions. I will just mention here though that going beyond the textuality can also be done by methodological positivists, when the legal order has no answer to a given problem. One difference, that I will not scrutinize here, is that they claim they have to go "outside" law, while Hermeneuticians would say that this is not necessary because, *inter alia*, law is not only made of black letter rules but also principles and underlying purposes, even if they have not been explicitly formulated.

The backcloth is, *inter alia*, a different conception of legal orders and a different conception of the jurists' task. Finally, the so-called Hermeneutic Circle is more than a method, it is an ontological situation. We can cope with particular problems, in certain ways, because we have an inevitable "pre-understanding" that constitutes us historically as human beings. It is certain though that this is not like a prison, because we are not determined in the same way as worms are. A. Peczenik claims that the Hermeneutic Circle occurs in legal justification.[31]

9. LOGICAL AND RATIONAL RECONSTRUCTION

The interaction we have, as participants, with our legal orders is not the same (and cannot be) as the Physicist with his object, the world outside. Instead of impersonal observation of the object we have to make, *inter alia*, evaluations. However, we do not evaluate capriciously but on the basis of legal sources, legal procedures, legal reasons, legal theories, purposes, interests, etcetera. This bundle of elements allows for a relatively controlled adaptation of the legal order to new social circumstances, granted that the legislator cannot (as a matter of fact) always be up to date. This means, *inter alia*, that there is always a gap between the legislator's language and the changing social relationships. Moreover, it is contended here that logical reconstructions based on ideal languages (following Carnap's path) are prone to be less interesting for participants than logical reconstructions based on Waisman's view of philosophy.

Nevertheless, in the latter case, it is doubtful that these approaches can be free of evaluations. If this is correct, the difference between logical and rational reconstruction is not clear. In other words, it is not clear whether there are important

[31] Peczenik, A. *The Basis of Legal Justification*, Printed in Sweden, Infotryck AB, Malmöe, 1983, pages 81 and 82.

differences between methodological positivists (Waisman's view) and Analytic Hermeneuticians. It is also contended here that rational reconstruction of our legal orders is a normative (and not only descriptive) task in so far as legal scholars, at large, share an internal point of view. That is, they not only try to tell us which solutions the legal orders has stated (if this is possible in a precise way) but also how these solutions, or some of them, ought to be. This is mainly done on the basis of evaluations. Axiological gaps and their posterior fulfilment could be one example of the so-called rational reconstructions. In any case, the descriptive and normative task of legal scholars is not, in practice, a sharp and clear-cut one.

It is recognised that one of the most relevant legal theorists of this century is H.L.A. Hart. He rejected empirical method in legal tasks and backed a hermeneutic method.

> For the understanding of this the methodology of the empirical sciences is useless; what is needed is a "hermeneutic" method which involves portraying rule-governed behaviour as it appears to its participants, who see it as conforming or failing to conform to certain shared standards. My explanation of the distinction which I have here called crucial is in terms of the idea of "acceptance" of preferred patterns of conduct as guides and standards of criticism, and so of an attitude which I call an "internal point of view."[32]

If Hart is a legal positivist and rejects empirical method, what does "external point of view" mean as a supposedly scientific approach? As I said, some suppose that certain persons (methodological positivists) are able to utter "detached" statements. If they do not make these by empirical method, what is the method? Does it mean that they have a different psychological attitude? In this case, can we scientifically test this different psychological attitude? However, if it is not a matter of psychology, what else can it be? We cannot say that they produce better results because it would be a begging question. Perhaps it is the method. But, what is the difference?

That is, what is the difference between a methodological positivist, who accepts the legal order, and a hermeneutician who also accepts the legal order? Some say that when a methodological positivist accepts a legal order he does so only as a citizen not as a scientist. He knows how to separate sharply the context of discovery and the context of justification and also the individual as a citizen and the same individual as a scientist. I have already commented on this dream. Therefore, the difference could be in logical reconstruction. Let us see.

When Hart deals with *Begriffsjurisprudenz* he states several features of this famous kind of legal dogmatics. I would like to stress two of them:

> "Excessive preoccupation with concepts considered in abstraction from the conditions under which they have to be applied in real life ... A false assimilation of the concepts and methods of legal science to mathematics; so that all reasoning is a matter of pure calculation in which the contents of the legal concepts are unfolded by logical deduction."[33]

---

[32] Hart, H.L.A. *Essays in Jurisprudence and Philosophy*, opus cited, pages 13 and 14.

[33] Ibidem, pages 265 and 266.

It seems that Hart rejects both empirical method and logical reconstruction. He also claims that American and English analytical Jurisprudence (both the first phase and the modern phase) cannot be assimilated to *Begriffsjurisprudenz*.[34] If this is correct, what is the distinctive feature of methodological positivism?

From our point of view, judgement and practical reason should be emphasized because we have no algorithm to solve our legal problems. Method is not an external collection of criteria and procedures that jurists apply in a neutral manner. The relation between the legal normative premises and the legal decision is relatively indeterminate, granted that we have no algorithm. One example of the absence of clear rules (and according to methodological positivists, this should be an example of irrationality) is the change of precedent. One thing is to accept the principle of *stare decisis* and another is to know when we have to change or maintain a precedent. There are no clear rules that determine the result. Does this mean that we are facing an irrational task? That anything goes? I believe not. We, participants, are interested in the "best" solution, here and now. Consequently, not everything goes.

Therefore, method is not related (or mainly related) to clear, precise steps that show how we move from a given premise to a necessary conclusion. The legal methods are rational devices that justify themselves because we, participants, rationally accept that they are useful enough for fulfilling some of our relevant goals. The main problem, then, is not whether we have an algorithm or whether we are able to show with geometrical precision what we have done and what we shall do in the future, on the basis of precise methodological criteria. This does not exist, except in geometrical minds that do not understand that legal method and legal dogmatics are, mainly, a practical task. If someone says, "Participants, don't be so happy because you cannot explain with precision what to do, on the basis of your legal methods"; it is irrelevant for participants. Moreover, we should realize that data (no matter whether factual or normative) underdetermine theories.

This is similar to the challenge of the deep sceptic, although in effect we can dispense with him. We require local sceptics who want to improve something, and this is another basic feature of our legal method, we expect it to help in our improvement. In this vein, what can a radical sceptic contribute? Once we abandon the useless search for certainty we can dispense with them too. We require persons that react to "injustice", the reaction being a discourse with justificatory reasons. What is the sense of taking into account the discourse of people that do not believe in "justice", in practical reason and other basic ideas, beliefs and dispositional attitudes of the participants at large? Is it rational to deny ourselves or to accept that we are irrational? We should simply reject their ontological commitments, and insist that the game be played in our field not in theirs because it is useless for our main purposes.

This means, *inter alia*, a rejection of the causal-explanation framework, which is understood as having the ontological and methodological primacy in legal fields. The hermeneutic framework, based on understanding, is a basic ontological commitment and a methodological trend that differentiates us. Our legal conceptual scheme imposes itself over physical reality because we characterise this reality, we

---

[34] Ibidem, pages 271, 272, 273, 274, 275 and 276.

do not aim at purely describing it, even if it were possible. Our interaction with the object, the legal order, is not the same as the interaction of the physicist with the world outside. Our "participant" interaction emphasizes the role of our conceptual scheme in the characterisation of the object (and even in the constitution of the object), the importance of contexts (intralinguistic and extraliguistic) and of values and goals.

The importance given to evaluations and legal meanings may help us to see the importance of the normative approach, where the participants' view, and not the impersonal observation (if possible), takes preference. Nevertheless, this dichotomy should not be understood as radical separation. We want to have success in our practical enterprises and, for this reason, we cannot dispense with the working of the world outside, according to our best mature scientific knowledge. However, we, participants, decide in a rational and purposive way what can be accepted or not, with an eye on the main goals and values of the legal order.

We have experts, we have procedures (that can be flexible or not), we have a legal tradition, we have legal positive texts and we have values and goals we believe worth pursuing, using certain justified means. Here, we have another important difference between methodological positivists and hermeneuticians. The former believe that only infallible method has cognitive importance, although they have no infallible method. Granted this, legal judgement, legal decision and material content take paramount importance. At the same time, legal hermeneuticians believe that the description of the legislator's language is one of the basic tasks of legal dogmatics, although it is not the only one. The basic reason is that participants are not only interested in reproducing what the legislator stated because they are not only interested in legal certainty and in law as a bundle of legislative texts. For reasons already given, we, as participants, are committed to improve the basic institutions that regulate and constitute us.

Participants, at large, have a commitment with "justice", which is not only understood as the proper application of given normative premises. Participants participate in the social task of legal orders not only as passive receptacles of judges' decisions but as participants who contribute to the settlement (and permanence) of the underlying basic values of the legal order. This is not a descriptive statement because in authoritarian political regimes citizens have to obey the commands of the authority without participating, as free actors, in the legal-political life. However, even in democratic political regimes, many citizens do not participate and others participate basically as voters. Nevertheless, our best legal culture does not see participants as "obedient donkeys" and does not believe that this should be so.

Hence, the participation of the participants can be seen both as a descriptive and as a normative statement. It is also a regulative ideal. Participants do their "best" because they have fidelity to law and want the legal orders to work as well as possible. If participants, in our legal orders, have sufficient reasons to share an internal point of view, they will be interested in making the "best interpretation" because this helps the good working of the legal order. The existence of participants is, also, a necessary condition for the existence of methodological positivists because without "committed" statements there cannot be "detached" statements. Nevertheless, it is not clear what is the difference between "committed statements" and "detached statements", granted that a competent legal participant and a competent legal observer (not a Martian), can utter the same statement in relation to the same legal case. If this is possible, and in fact it is, how should we explain it?

Practical jurists do this task of best adaptation to new social circumstances in a more specific way, and legal scholars do the same in a more abstract and systematic way. However, both undertake a descriptive and a normative task (although with several differences, such as the scientific attitude of legal scholars that is lacking in practical jurists, as G. von Wright says) that are mainly dependent on normative premises and on normative goals. Coherent interpretations with these basic premises and goals compete with each other to receive the acceptation of the legal community and of the social community. This competition (in hard cases) is a consequence of the open texture of legal concepts and of the acceptation of pluralism. It is doubtful, in a monolithic and authoritarian political regime, whether competing interpretations would be accepted. Who wins in this competition?

9.1 Legal Sources and Commitment

Although there is no logical necessity, a coherent interpretation that fosters the basic values (in a deontological sense) and the basic goals (in a consequentialist sense) better is a good candidate for reaching acceptation. If this is the case, a new legal interpretation will be considered, *rebus sic stantibus*, as a new legal "is". Of course, it cannot be known, precisely, in advance, whether, in a specific case, deontological or consequentialist reasons will win or whether a given priority order will be maintained. We can see how far we are from the view that gives an exclusive importance to must sources (legislator's language) as "exclusionary reasons for action". According to what has been written, exclusionary reasons for action should be seen as strong *prima facie* reasons. Their "entrenchment" will depend, in fact, not only on their formal status but also on their material status. Some reasons for action are stronger than others. However, this cannot be the case if formal validity is always emphasized as the exclusive criterion for the existence and binding of legal rules.

Hence, if this view is neglected, not all must sources of a given legal order would have the same material force, at a given time. Consequently, we can rely on those who share, like us, the basic values and goals of our legal order. We rely on, let us say, "external observers" when a problem of chemistry, for example, is at stake, because we believe that the "truth" of chemistry is independent of our values. We do not believe the same when we deal with legal orders, because we are not dealing with something external to us, that can be grasped neutrally and impersonally. We are involved in these issues that constitute us as citizens (and as human beings) with certain basic rights and duties. For these reasons, *inter alia,* those who believe in a neutral and criteriological method for solving our basic human problems are not as reliable as participants (or at least some) are.

We want to know whether our normative practices are justified, and this cannot be done through an algorithm. At the same time, our preferences change with time. Sometimes we value legal certainty more than justice of the case, but sometimes not.

In these cases, legal interpreters and legal scholars make rational reconstructions, that is, they make rational proposals to solve, in the best possible way, these meta-legal conflicts. They imply a value preference, given certain circumstances, that is not (necessarily) a necessary conclusion of the legislator's language. This is an example where we cannot always rely on exclusionary reasons for action because, even if we want to act according to the reasons of authority, we could doubt what they are. For the sake of ideological clarification, I would say that I am not thinking of the market when I talk of "competition". These rational reconstructions cannot be something independent of the concrete legal order, legal tradition and basic values that underlie the entire social practice. Hence, rational individual maximization cannot be the only justification for our rational reconstructions.

In relation to "rational reconstructions", we could say that methodological positivism can be seen as one of the heirs of logical positivism. Although we cannot claim that all methodological positivists believe the same, in relation to law and legal dogmatics, since there are some basic common features that differentiate them from the rest. In so far as they are the heirs of logical positivism (and we have seen that American and English supporters of analytical jurisprudence are not the same thing, according to Hart), they believe that the central task of philosophy is the clarification of propositions. This clarification should be a logico-linguistic analysis. Their interest is the syntax of the legal language. This seems to be coherent with one of their basic claims: law is form.

This would be, let us say, the rationalist dimension of methodological positivists. The empiricist dimension would be related to their exclusive interest for positive laws and predictions about legal human behaviour, which seems to be coherent with their view of the world as consisting of facts, *tout court*. Once we have brute facts (through observation and experiment) and true statements about them, we can begin with logical inferences. The analytical legal method (excluding American and English legal theory) could show us which elements form these facts and how they themselves combine. Nevertheless, it is very doubtful, to say the least, that law is made of facts *tout court*, in a similar sense as a mountain is made of facts.

It is very doubtful, even if they were able to show the constituent elements of these facts, whether this would be something useful for the society in which the legal order works. It is also very doubtful whether this logical reconstruction would be able to show anything new about what we should do (as participants) in relation to the legal order. In this respect, Hart took from Waisman the notion of "open texture" and showed, *inter alia*, how "vagueness" is an inevitable feature of legal languages. In this respect, legal philosophers who follow Waisman's view of philosophy, as solving the conceptual confusions of our ordinary language, are prone to be more interesting (at least for participants and for non positivist legal scholars) than those who follow Carnap's logical reconstruction based on ideal languages.

If this is correct, it is hard to see how conceptual legal clarifications, based on Waisman's line and similar concepts, can be free of values. That is, how a member of our culture, "manipulating" our ordinary language, using practical concepts, can make a logical reconstruction rather than only a rational reconstruction. If this is correct, what is the difference between these conceptual clarifications and the legal hermeneuticians's task? Is it a difference of degree? Is it, let us say, a qualitative difference? Although it is not possible to draw sharp lines between philosophical tendencies I would say that, in so far as methodological positivism is dependent on the idea that "deep analysis" (supposedly, once a neutral description of the legal reality is given) is able to reveal the deep structure of the legal language (its supposed essence), it is not a fertile approach for a participant's view.

This would be so because language is not a calculus of rules, because there are no hidden logical forms that analytic method can discover, revealing the logical structure of the world. This is only a metaphysical idea that stems from the basic-data, as supposed immediate experiences, over which logical constructions (sense-data) could be made. If we do not believe that there are some privileged human beings who, through the true method, are able to discover this deep logical structure (the essence), how do we decide to prefer one kind of legal description over another? In summary, in so far as methodological positivism adopts a more interesting and fertile approach, similar to Hart's for example, it can be doubted whether it deserves the label of legal methodological positivism.

This would be so because law is, fundamentally, a practical matter closely related to practical reason. On the other hand, legal positivist approaches (generally speaking) claim to be formal, although they have explicit or implicit purposes or evaluative justifications. For example, Kelsen and Ross, in spite of their differences, see legal science as being capable of "comprehension" of legal behaviour. That is, although it could be expected that Kelsen and Ross would defend the unity of method (following the path of the Vienna Circle) they rejected the causal-explicative method, typical of natural sciences. However, if legal science is not an empirical science (I will not deal now with the suitability of the label "science") it should be a formal science and undertake a logical reconstruction of the object.

In this respect, it should take into account the logical consequences of legal norms. Nevertheless, granted that we are finite beings and legal orders deal with finite practical purposes, a problem of relevancy is at stake. We have to decide which consequences of the legal norms are relevant. Granted that legal norms are a result of the interpretation of legal normative texts, and granted that legal norms are not necessary conclusions of legal normative texts, we have to wait until a proper legal decision is taken (by participants). Hence, we shall have to infer legal consequences and, then, we shall have to choose which are relevant for us, here and now. If this is correct, the importance of practical reason and judgement in legal science are fundamental.

In other words, the importance of a logical metalanguage for legal science is weak. One of the main reasons being that legal science is not exclusively descriptive. In this respect, Kelsen's rational reconstruction of legal language would be of more interest than Carnap's pure formal attempts. Kelsen's approach would be closer to the followers of the ordinary language than Carnap's. As I said, Ross introduced a basic term, "comprehension", that does not fit in with an empirical verificationist theory. The failures of both empirical and logical reconstructions make sounder attempts like Hart's possible. In my opinion, Hart could be an example of this "weaker" and sounder legal positivism. Elsewhere though I have claimed that Hart is not a legal positivist.[35]

9.2 Theoretical and Practical Reason

Legal positivism (generally speaking) sees law as a tool or as a technique to reach social order or social stability. Granted that we cannot "scientifically" justify that a given social order is better (normatively speaking) than another, legal positivists put the emphasis on the means and not on the ends. That is, what matters is whether a mean is effective to reach a given end, a social order. To reach a social order is, at least in principle, a way to reach survival. If the mean (that is, law) is able to reach a social order and the social order is a mean to reach survival, we should have to obey the law and exclusionary reasons for action. All this can explain how institutional coercion is so important for legal positivists. Kelsen is a clear example of this reductionist approach. At the same time, facts *tout court* and form seem to be insufficient for any interesting and useful legal science. Moreover, once we accept Searle's institutional facts, we dive into practical reason, which has been considered, by legal positivists, as a contradictory concept.

I have commented elsewhere[36] that to state what is a fact and which facts are the foundations of our knowledge, has important difficulties. Either we take them to be "perceptual states" (because they involve perceptual beliefs that can be true or false and because false perceptual beliefs may appear to us as true ones) or as "the given" (the very dubious claim that there are undefeatable and original data that experience provides for the human mind). The difficulty is even greater if we bear in mind that methodological positivists do not deal with brute facts but with institutional facts. It is not surprising that, granted the "weakness" of these types of facts, they rely more heavily on form. Hence, even if methodological positivists believe that the world is made of facts *tout court*, the problem is whether they have any object to deal with, granted that law is not made of facts *tout court*. If legal orders necessarily need institutional facts, practical reason seems to have something to say in this scrutiny, because institutional facts cannot be built and understood only on the basis of theoretical reason.

In any case, they cannot reject institutional facts if they want to deal with legal orders, although they have tried to treat them with the same method as brute facts. Granted that this has been a failure, they, as I said, have emphasized form. Form is what is not contingent, that is, they look for something necessary, the logical form. How should this be done? Although there are differences, a good model is chemistry, where a given substance is decomposed into its components. In legal fields a good example could be "justice". The statements including the term "justice" can be analysed as either having a certain logical form (which is supposed to be permanent) or as having a contingent content. The latter aspect is irrelevant because it is contingent and because it is irrational. It is not rational because we

[35] Urbina, S. *Reason, Democracy, Society*, Chapter One, Kluwer, Dordrecht, 1996.
[36] Urbina, S. *Identification of Legal Orders*, paper not yet published.

cannot verify it. In other words, they ignore evaluative implications when they deal with evaluative terms like "justice". Is this possible? Is it relevant?

Even if methodological positivists could know the "deep logical structure" of a given normative statement or collection of statements, what does this "deep structure" mean for the participants of a given legal order? Is it any guide for justified intentional actions? Is it a fertile contribution to the practical problems participants have to deal with? Is this "deep logical structure" a neutral starting point? If this was possible, why would a neutral starting point be useful for deciding, let us say, our value premises? Are we condemned to have contaminated starting points, and, in this case, how do they justify the perspective they are upholding?[37] In this respect, some methodological positivists claim that they only work within the context of justification while non-scientific legal theorists (like hermeneuticians) work within the context of discovery.

---

[37] In this respect, P.M.S. Hacker says, "Frege's concept-script -"a formula language of pure thought", as he called it- was conceived to reveal the true structure of thoughts which natural language obscures ... Russell, cleaving as he did to metaphysical atomism and to correspondence between true proposition and fact, held that "In a logically perfect language, there will be one word and no more for every simple object ... The language which is set forth in Principia Mathematica is intended to be a language of that sort. It is a language which has only a syntax and no vocabulary whatsoever." In relation to Wittgenstein, Hacker adds, "When he returned to philosophy in 1929, he realised that the independence thesis for elementary propositions could not be upheld. Incompatibility relations, hence entailments, between propositions attributing a determinate of a determinable to a given object are not reducible to the entailments of a logical sum or product of logically independent elementary propositions. Although he tried briefly to budget for this (in "Some Remarks on Logical Form" (PAS 1929)), he rapidly came to see that the collapse of the independence thesis implied the collapse of the Tractatus picture of the essence of logic and of logical relations between propositions ... Given that the metaphysical picture of the relation between a proposition and the fact that makes it true is misconceived, then to say that one understands a proposition when one knows what is the case if it is true is to say virtually nothing." In: *Wittgenstein's Place in the Twentieth-Century Analytic Philosophy*, Blackwell, Oxford, 1996, pages 20, 21, 53, 54 and 55.

In relation to philosophical task and reductive analysis, J.O. Urmson says, "Thus, the analysis, that both for the logical atomist and for the logical positivist had constituted the central activity of philosophers, was seen later, and as a result of the most patient efforts, as something impossible to obtain, except in relatively trivial cases, outside the field of mathematical logic in which Russell had obtained his successes. It was necessary to abandon the view according to which the task of philosophy is the reductive analysis of the confused declarations of our ordinary daily language to the simple atomic reports of immediate experience. It could not be this way for revealing neither the structure of the world nor the structure of our language." *El Análisis Filosófico*, Ariel, Barcelona, 1978, page 187.

From a view that claims the primacy of practical reason H. Putnam says, "The problem was that very soon it became evident -as happened to me when I started out- that Mach and his followers from the Vienna Circle had not done anything else but substitute one metaphysic for another ... To support that, I am speaking of observable entities when I state that electrons circulate in a thin metallic wire, equivalent to being a metaphysicist (if only it were a Berkeleian metaphysicist) as much as supporting that electrons themselves are indeed things. To understand the concept that positivism was in itself metaphysics -and to tell the truth not very credible metaphysics (why would we have to believe, after all, that the world is only composed of observable entities?)- has led to the utterance of a true plethora of metaphysical theories -including those of Princeton, in New Jersey- according to which, other possible worlds are as real as our own actual world ... I want to conclude maintaining precisely that the philosophy of Wittgenstein also has a moralist intention and that it explains, in a different way, the same theme: the primacy of practical reason, enunciated by the philosophy of Kant, although from a particular redimensional perspective." *El Pragmatismo*, Gedisa, Barcelona 1999, pages 66 and 67.

I would like to clarify that the above claim that we are "contaminated" beings does not mean to reject, for example, the ethical construction of an "ideal observer". It means that even this is constructed from a "contaminated" view, although not all contaminations are equal. In any case, the former view would be neutral, befitting of external observers, whereas the latter would be characteristic of committed participants, unable to utter "neutral and aseptic" statements. I take for granted that methodological positivists are, more or less grudgingly, participants and this status makes it possible to reach easy agreements about what is a "routine case", in a concrete legal order. Although not necessarily.

Nevertheless, granted that our form of life is, *inter alia*, pluralistic there are disagreements in certain cases. When competent jurists seriously disagree (at least legal scholars) we may be facing a "hard case". This is possible not only because we live in a pluralistic culture but because their object, a legal order, is a normative object (open texture problems) and because we deal with it, basically, on the basis of practical reason. These disagreements among competent experts are not acceptable in Physics (or, better said, they are not accepted to the same extent) because, *inter alia*, physicians have empirical proofs and sophisticated logical apparatus that are not comparable to those of legal scholars. The belief in the unity of method pushes methodological positivists to scrutinise law as physicists scrutinize the world outside. As we have seen, Kelsen and Ross claim this unity of method but they do not go very far with it.

The above cited disagreements do not mean that it is pointless to insist on the idea of "the best answer" to a legal interpretative matter. I have said that our form of life includes, *inter alia*, pluralism, as one of its structural features. For example, members of the Legal Studies Movement and legal theorists that support the Rule of Law (in some of its varieties) may have incommensurable (or at least with difficulties for understanding each other) evaluative judgements. Does this show that the search for "the best answer" is pointless? I do not believe so. It is only pointless for the members of the Legal Studies Movement because they believe, *inter alia*, that in our liberal legal orders, adjudication should collapse into politics. This only shows that the form of life is inseparable from pluralism and that our liberal legal orders are the most liberal (until now) in relation to any other real order.

Instead of killing competitors, or putting them in jail, liberal legal orders give them the same fundamental individual rights, while trying to protect (as any human organisation does, although not in the same manner) the basic rules of the game. It should be clear that any supposedly incommensurable evaluative judgement of legal theorists for these two legal tendencies would imply, *inter alia*, a different moral basis. That is why the constructive solution, given in hard cases, cannot be a neutral answer but rather is one rooted in the underlying basic moral concepts (or conceptions) that justify a given legal option. Nevertheless, different interpretations of different participants, although different, can be (and usually are) commensurable. Incommensurability may appear when someone does not participate in the basic values and rules of the game. My former comments should not be understood as if we were living in the sky but to emphasize that any theory (even the critical ones) has, more or less, important flaws in its application and implementation.

It is interesting to note how "Inclusive Positivism" tries to supersede some of the basic problems of "Exclusive Positivism". Although Inclusive Positivism intends to create a descriptive/explanatory legal theory, justice and injustice play an important role that would be ignored by Exclusive Positivism. In this respect, W.J. Waluchow says,

> "We will merely assume that people do appeal to standards like the principles of equality, liberty, fairness, and justice in assessing social institutions and their products; that these activities are not totally nonsensical as some radical moral nihilists might argue, but are open to at least some degree of rational argument and assessment; and that it is these kinds of standards that we have in mind when we ask about the possible role of political morality in determining the existence and content of valid laws."[38]

The underlining for emphasis is mine.

I doubt that this approach can be called a legal positivist one but, in any case, the problem of identification of the legal order by way of exclusive legal sources is not solved because, *inter alia*, the kind of political morality Waluchow is talking about is only "positive morality". The main reason being that we cannot clearly separate and distinguish between positive and critical morality. On the other hand, detecting what constitutes positive morality is not, for instance, like detecting walnut trees, but it is an interpretative matter with borderline problems. At the same time, different competing interpretations may claim to be the "proper" interpretation of a certain item for a given positive morality.

Finally, although legal orders have settled moral tests for the validity and content of laws, they are either "empty tests" (in which case they are not a guide for solving conflicts, and do not give exclusionary reasons for action) or they rest both on positive and critical morality, with the inherent problems cited above. An empty test could be something like Ulpiano's "*suum cuique tribuere*" and similar formulations. Hence, the idea that moral reasons are relevant, but only to the extent that the legal order recognises them as such, is a misleading idea. It is similar to a father recommending to his son to "be good" with no further explanations. In this respect, it is interesting to note different meanings of "describe" as R. Guastini puts it.[39]

I believe that legal dogmatics (at least a legal science made by participants) describes the interpretation of a legal text, once its formal validity has been recognised, although this latter point may lead to interpretative problems. Although there is no logical necessity, this kind of legal dogmatics also makes deontic statements and, hence, does not only state that a given legal text can be understood in the sense of one, two or three. Therefore, a rational reconstruction of the legal order has a normative dimension in so far as legal scholars also share an internal point of view. They do not only try to detect the imperfections of the legal order (even if we suppose this is exclusively a descriptive task) but also try to solve them in the best possible way, granted certain legal rules and principles, certain legal means and certain legal goals, at any given time.

---

[38] Waluchow, W.J. *Inclusive Legal Positivism*, Clarendon Press Oxford, 1994, pages 2-3, note 3.

[39] Guastini, R. *Dalle Fonti alle Norme*, Giapichelli editore, 1990, pages 56 and ff.

10. MAKING SENSE OF LEGAL ORDERS

When scrutinizing legal orders, legal scholars have to deal, *inter alia*, with legal rules and human actions. When they do this they have to take causes into account. One problem is to know which type of causes and which of them would have primacy. In this respect, human actions are scrutinised here in relation to individualism and holism. It is contended here that an individual approach will not be enough because individual actions, although arising as individual action performed by concrete individuals, may be converted into social actions. That is, there would be room for a distinction between individual and social actions. Nevertheless, individualism and holism should not be understood as two sharp and separate worlds. On the contrary, they intertwine. Moreover, there have been, and still are, refusers of practical reason, normally on the basis that it is a contradictory concept.

In this respect, a venerable tradition claims that reason only refers to knowledge but reason, in its practical dimension, refers to will. It is contended here that practical reason is required for making sense of legal orders, no matter whether we are not able to reach the "one right answer" that is not, moreover, necessary for an acceptable legal justification. In any case, we have the "last legal answer" for legal certainty reasons, although this should not be equated to arbitrariness. Judges, at large, internalise the requirement of justification of legal decisions that is usually a legal positive requirement. In addition, the so-called hard cases (where legal experts can disagree with the proper legal decision) represent a minority of cases. This is so, *inter alia*, because participants of a given legal order have been socialized in a certain culture, language, values, basic beliefs, etcetera.

If strong disagreements among legal experts would represent, for example, ninety per cent of legal conflicts we should deal with the problem of the soundness and reliability of our legal standards. But this is not the case. One can see the importance of practical reason in the light, *inter alia*, of the permanent task of adaptation of the legal order to changing circumstances. This permanent task cannot be done, *inter alia*, without values and evaluations in changing contexts. Be that as it may, we cannot avoid (from a pragmatical point of view) a complex intertwinement between theoretical and practical reason. In summary, we are not dealing with knowledge in the realm of practical reason but with justification and the latter is related to rational acceptability, not to truth as correspondence.

To deal with legal method, with legal dogmatics, we have to deal, *inter alia*, with human beings, human actions, a variety of other things and legal orders. As is already known, there are a variety of definitions of legal orders. I will suppose, here, that legal orders are historical sets of statutes, principles, policies and precedents that ought to be used to justify legal decisions and for guiding and justifying an important part of a citizen's behaviour. Nevertheless, legal scholars deal directly with language and we also have to make sense of this bundle of elements. Suppose I want to make sense of an ant's nest. I begin by saying that the intention of the slave-ants is to break the chains that link them to their ant-owners. They have decided to fight for their freedom and dignity and convert everyone into ant-ant beings. It is rather probable that neither methodological positivists nor analytical hermeneuticians would accept this picture because it would be considered a nonsense. However, is it a nonsense if applied to human beings?

I do not mean, necessarily, the specific case of slaves and their owners but the case of human beings deciding what to do (in given socio-historical circumstances) and why. I refer to human beings as able to combine their individual actions with social actions because some kind of consciousness is at stake, etcetera. Is this a nonsense? In case it is not, we should accept that by trying to make sense of a "why" question, we have to look for some causes. The problem is what kind of causes. Is it enough to explain (or perhaps to understand, which we shall scrutinise later) the legal behaviour of our citizens to appeal to psychological causes? Is it enough to appeal to social causes?

It is known that, in the legal positivist tradition, there have been attempts to explain legal behaviour from an empiricist account, but it seems that their acceptance has not been, until now, relevant enough. I will suppose that we cannot dispense with the laws of nature when we deal with legal behaviour. To take an easy example, legislators do not order citizens to fly because it is physically impossible. This would be an absurd order from a physical and from a pragmatical point of view, although not from a logical point of view. Hence, the laws of nature impose certain restrictions on legislators. For our present purposes it is enough to remember, as is known, that empirical necessity is not the same as logical necessity.

Therefore, the laws of nature represent a necessary condition for the explanation (or understanding) of legal behaviour, but they are not sufficient. This means that a realist account, claiming that the action undertaken by Peter, in given circumstances, is explained by social and economic factors, is also not sufficient. Although there are different lines of research (as happens with any important doctrine) in this realist view, what matters here is that the last word depends on a causal explanation. Hence, it does not matter whether these approaches give room, or not, to rational reconstruction because they all give the last word to causal explanation. I will suppose that interpretative understanding, given certain laws of nature, gives us a better account of legal behaviour. I assume that the laws of nature face different possible interpretations, although I am not trying to support a specific one, only to claim that this is a necessary condition.

Over a particular interpretation of what human nature is we can construct (or not) practical reason, intentional action, etcetera. For example, on the basis of B.F. Skinner's approach these items would not be acceptable because conditioning processes of human conduct is his main concern. We would have a different conceptual scheme if we accepted, for example, the J.P. Sartre approach, because a basic assumption is that human beings are condemned to be free. It is not clear which conception of human beings methodological positivists have (or whether they believe this is important, granted that they are dealing with the true scientific method, which is neutral and impersonal). It is assumed, here, that human beings are purposive and social individuals, able to have, *inter alia*, moral and prudential reasons and hence able to be guided by both, although they can be a source of conflict. This means, *inter alia*, that fidelity to law and obedience to law go together.

Once we are placed in the line of interpretative understanding (as opposed to causal explanation) we have to stress the difference between what an agent means by an action he is performing, and what the action actually means. This dichotomy confronts the problem of individualism and holism. However, I am not trying to be eclectic in the vain intent to avoid intellectual difficulties. I believe that intentional human action is a necessary condition for the existence, and the understanding, of the meaning of these actions, although it is not a sufficient condition. This means that an individualistic account will not suffice because individual actions, although arising as individual actions performed by individual human beings, may be converted into social actions.

When Peter smokes a cigarette as he is walking in the park, he is performing an individual action, but when he participates in a political meeting with one thousand other people, he is performing a social action. This social action needs individual actions as a necessary but not as a sufficient condition. Or, in other words, these individual actions are not of the same kind as Peter's smoking in the park. We can explain Peter's "smoking" by talking of Peter's activity but we cannot explain the "meeting" by only speaking of Peter's activity, or any other individual activity as if they only had sense in an isolated way. We have to take into account other participants and we have to do this in a certain way, that is, under a certain description. Namely, they should be, to a certain extent, conscious of what they are doing.

If all of them ignored what a political meeting is (and didn't realise it during the act), a political meeting would not have taken place. However, the most important point in relation to individualism and holism is that they are intertwined. In other words, there is a feedback. The attitudes of the individuals and of the group influence each other. Hence, individualism and holism are not accounts that we simply put close to one another without any influence. On the contrary, they are like the two faces of the same coin. Institutional facts have no sense in themselves (in so far as I do not believe in the Popperian third world as having existence in itself) but they need individuals to give them sense and put them into action. In their turn, individuals have no sense in themselves (as isolated monads) once we deal with legal orders.

We should distinguish clearly between the idea that individuals "have no sense in themselves" and the idea that the individuals "are not important in themselves". Individuals (at least in our cultural context and in my approach) are important in themselves, in the sense that they should not only be means but ends as well. This implies, *inter alia*, the rejection of certain utilitarian approaches (or certain interpretations) that make basic individual rights depend on collective welfare or similar considerations. Nevertheless, individuals have no sense in themselves because they cannot be properly understood without a certain historical web of social relations and conceptual schemes.

This complex web gives sense to the idea that, although individuals are ends in themselves, they cannot be properly understood in isolation. As a social web it allows for common understandings (and also misunderstandings and divergence) because they are put in motion by fallible participants and because this complex web is not (and cannot be) mechanically understood. Among other things because of the existence of "implicatures", in Grice's sense. This means, *inter alia*, that participants share certain basic features that make it possible to talk of social action, common understanding, understanding of disagreements, etcetera. This also means that participants are the main actors of legal behaviour. They put the legal order in motion, by understanding a given language and acting in certain ways, given certain circumstances. Some of them are legal scholars and, while working as legal scholars, mention the legal language that is used by the participants, although this is done from an internal point of view. It is not, at least as a whole, a neutral metalanguage.

Legal scholars use this legal language for most of their lives (because they are also participants) but try, when working as legal scholars, to reach a higher degree of objectivity than participants. However, there is no sharp division between participants and legal scholars, in so far as basic values are at stake. I have just now been talking of a feedback between the individual and the whole, in this case the legal order. This means that a legal participant does not enter into the legal game with his own subjective meaning. On the contrary, he enters into the game while he is able to understand, at least, some basic intersubjective meanings. The interplay means that participants (although they know, at least, some basic intersubjective meanings) are neither passive containers of such meanings nor obedient donkeys.

On the contrary, they try to elaborate new meanings or new understandings, because of the need of adaptation to social dynamics. This is especially undertaken by participants-jurists. They do not simply accept the existent intersubjective meaning at a given time, in a given legal branch, etcetera. While accepting the legislative texts (formal must sources) they sometimes give new adaptive interpretations to them. It should be said, in this vein, that some rules and practices are more entrenched than others. Nevertheless, this depends on socio-historical circumstances, although some features are common. For example, it is difficult to find a culture where torturing children is a morally or a legally good thing. It does not matter whether we could consider certain behaviour as torture and another culture not, because the point is whether both reject "torture".

Hence, the important thing, for present purposes, is that they reject torturing children. If there are some basic common features in human species, they would constitute the "bedrock", or at least a kind of very basic form of life, that would make sense of the idea of Human Rights. If we (as human beings) had nothing basic in common, this idea would have little sense for anyone. However, we are not dealing here with this issue but with legal orders. Although legal orders are rooted in some form of life their manifestations are not one-sided. One can ask whether the existence of an authoritarian regime, for example in my country, and the posterior existence of a democratic political regime, are both expressions of the same form of life or not.

If they are, the form of life is just a basic "bedrock" allowing a huge variety of possibilities. I think that we should use one concept and one conception for the form of life in any society. The concept of form of life would be this very basic bedrock that no specific historical development has violated. If this is the case, I would say that only survival of the group (not necessarily of all of its members though) and certain formal basic concepts such as "justice", "love", "interest", "friendship", "envy", and some basic others, would shape this form of life concept.

10.1 Justification and Legal Dogmatics

One could take J. Finnis's basic idea in a different sense than he does. We could take his objective goods (life, knowledge, play, aesthetic experience, friendship or sociability, practical reasonableness and religion) as constituting (with the addition of self-interest and equality, granted that freedom is implied in practical reasonableness) our western form of life. Nevertheless, this basic form of life materialises in different form of life conceptions, according to the combination of these elements and/or the emphasis put on some of them at the expense of others. These contingent combinations can produce different social practices that can be felt (for a time) as something that we "cannot" change, in so far as it is internalized by a community or the majority of its members.

For example, it is hard to believe that we can, now, decide to dispense with private contracts. We suppose, generally speaking, that contracts are part of our form of life. These combinations (although they are usually felt as non-contingent) are conceptions of the same concept of a given form of life. Probably, self-interest plus certain economical and technological features make it difficult to imagine ourselves without the legal possibility of private contracts. Nevertheless, if certain revolutionary Marxists imposed their doctrine on our societies, the status of private contracts would be different to what it is now, or perhaps it would disappear altogether.

In a similar way, if strong communitarists took the political power of our societies, the implementation of our form of life would take a different shape. But, how long can we pull the rope for? This is a metaphysical problem that cannot be answered in a precise way. A first step in knowing how to make sense of legal orders is to deal with theoretical or practical reason. My view is that we cannot dispense with either, although practical reason has the primacy. In this respect, when it is considered sufficiently important, a legal fiction supersedes reality. At the same time, not everything that is possible from a theoretical point of view is sound from a practical point of view.

In any case, legal orders are not scientific enterprises but pragmatical enterprises where intentional actions, human interests and basic values, *inter alia*, play a fundamental role. In this respect, it is interesting to see how it has been claimed that "practical reason account's epistemic claims are indefensible". The idea is that an assertion, such as "The statute in question means x", has two requirements: a requirement of evidence (the grounds must be evidence of the appropriate sort) and requirement of warrant (the grounds must be sufficient to warrant the assertions).

S. Walt claims[40] that, although there can be evidence (for example, text, legislative history, legislative purpose and intention, the evolution of the statute and current values), the accounts do not satisfy the requirement of warrant. As a result, he arrives at a desperate conclusion,

> "So two interpreters using the same body of evidence can reach opposite interpretations of the same statute, whatever those interpretations may be."

[40] Walt, S. "Practical Reason and the Ontology of Statutes". In: *Law and Philosophy*, Vol. 15, No. 3, 1996, pp. 227-255.

As a first point, we should emphasize what critics (better said, refusers) of practical reason claim for the "one right answer". The main difference between them and Dworkin would be that the latter believes this is possible (at least in principle) and the former do not. I agree with the former that we are not able to reach the "one right answer" (whether it is possible or not to reach it "in principle") but I disagree with them because I claim that this is not necessary for legal justification.

In my view, the refusal of practical reason is absurd because we need it for making sense of legal orders. One could say that this or another "need" is absurd. For example, we could need to believe in unicorns for making sense of certain legal orders but it would not justify them. My answer is that we do not, in fact, need unicorns. Nevertheless, to deal both with these views and also with a sceptic's views can be of some interest. Therefore, we are facing, *inter alia*, two different views of legal justification. These views (like having two different conceptions of law) would condition what is sufficient evidence. At the same time, from one view, the possibility of different legal decisions from the same legal grounds would be sufficient for denying putting the label of "rational" on practical reason. Therefore, we have to deal with evidence and justification (and the steps from grounds to decision). However, we are not interested in knowledge (understood as justified true belief) but in justification.[41]

Nevertheless, justification is not based on truth, *inter alia*, because justification can fail while knowledge cannot. If we know something it must be certain. The alternative to practical reason could be to accept logical justification as the unique answer. I will take for granted that empirical knowledge can fail and that there is no logic of norms (based on the authority of G. von Wright, in spite of this being a disputable matter). One could say that, although there is no logic of norms there can be a logic of normative propositions. This could be so according to a certain view of legal dogmatics, that is, the view that legal dogmatics neutrally and exclusively describes the language of the legislator. I believe this is wrong though.

In my view, legal dogmatics is both descriptive and normative and, in this case, similar difficulties arise for normative propositions because they are not exclusively an informative language. In which sense is legal dogmatics normative? Not in the sense that it authoritatively states the law in force, as legislators or judges can do. We should remind ourselves that the model of legislator's rationality is an assumption made by jurists sharing an internal point of view. One of their functions is to make a "better" adaptation of law to changes in society. In this vein, through certain legal methods, legal scholars try to make the legal order "better". At the same time, jurists are able to "see" the legal order through the lenses of legal concepts and legal theories that have been constructed by legal scholars.

These concepts and theories, if successful, become for jurists like a part of the legal order. In these cases, it becomes "natural" to see them (or some of them) as the "true" understanding of the legal order as it is, and not just as an addition of legal

---

[41] In relation to justification one can see, among other works, *Legal Reasoning and Legal Theory*, N. MacCormick, Clarendon Law Series, Oxford, 1978; *The Rational as Reasonable*, A. Aarnio, Reidel, Dordrecht, 1987; *On Law and Reason*, A. Peczenik, Kluwer, 1989; A. Peczenik, *The Basis of Legal Justification*, op. cit.

scholars. In so far as "evidence" is concerned, let us accept that jurists of a given community can know the legal grounds (that give the evidence) for reaching legal decisions. Granted this, although a competent jurist would take certain evidence (as a necessary step), it would not be sufficient because there can be disagreements in this step. In other words, it can be disputable whether some legal items entail the proper grounds or not. Once this problem has been solved and agreement has been reached about the proper evidence, there can be difficulties in relation to the steps from the accepted normative meaning to the so-called proper conclusion. This can be a problem granted that these steps are not (or not exclusively) logically deductive ones.

The step from legal grounds (as the evidence) to a proper legal conclusion is not (at least usually) a logical step. Hence, disagreement is possible and so hard cases result. We have to appeal to justification but there can be two different justifications of two different meanings, or two different legal decisions stemming from the same legal meaning. We can though take justification from a deontological point of view, as I take it, and claim that we have some duties in the task of justification. Granted that we are not looking for truth but for correctness, we have the epistemic duty of correctness. Of course, methodological positivists can claim either that this is not true or it is true but trivial. For the first, it is hard to believe that we are submerged in the task of truth while the basic units of our enterprise, legal norms, are not made of informative language.

For the second, it should not bother us because the presupposition of correctness is something that participants take for granted. If participants felt and behaved as thieves in a den, a claim of correctness would be trivial. This is not the case. On the other hand, precise statements can be useless because legal orders cannot equate to chemistry. In legal orders, the problem of relevance is fundamental but this implies the presence of decisions and evaluations that cannot reach the level of preciseness that chemistry statements or logical statements can reach. Nevertheless, two competent jurists accepting this epistemic duty of correctness can reach different legal decisions, on the basis of different justifications.

This is possible not only in the so-called "hard-cases" but also in the "routine cases". However, if this does not normally happen in these latter cases it is not because the words or sentences have, in themselves, a clear and univocal meaning but because the legal community has justifiably accepted that this is a correct meaning and a correct decision, at a given time. Not the true one though. In "hard-cases", this possible legal agreement has to be on the basis of sound proposals that try to give the "best interpretation". This can be seen as an illogical claim or expectation once we require a "proof" or something similar. Once an observer cannot grasp that a legal proposal of a legal expert (in a hard case) is sound, there is no proof or demonstration to be given to him, like in chemistry. A legal expert (with the epistemic virtues[42] of those who share an internal point of view) can grasp

---

[42] In this vein, George Henrik von Wrights says, "Finally, Aristotle's list of intellectual virtues mentions practical wisdom (phronesis) and the related "minor intellectual virtues" of deliberation, understanding, and judgement. Practical wisdom is knowledge of how to secure the ends of human life, or "a reasoned and true state of capacity to act with regard to human goods". It is not, however,

whether a proposal for a hard case is sound or not, precisely because he is an expert able to judge.

In summary, participants (let us say, hermeneutic-analytics) and observers (let us say, methodological positivists) have different ontological commitments and they would determine, like the conceptions of law, what is evidence, what is a sufficient proof, etcetera. Hence, my aim is to clarify my own ideas (with our language game) and participate with other legal participants (including "soft" methodological positivists, although there are no precise rules for their identification) in the task of making sense of legal orders. Granted this, we should say that there are neither necessary nor sufficient conditions for epistemic justification that have received unanimous acceptation. Hence, the connection between evidence and epistemic justification is controversial. In this respect, the only point that can be clearly maintained is the claim that there can be two competent jurists using the same body of evidence who reach different interpretations of the same statute. Nevertheless, this is neither usual nor necessary.

10.2 Disagreement and Practical Reason

The main problem is whether the difficulties outlined are sufficient, or not, to reject practical reason from legal reasoning. First, these important disagreements only happen in hard cases that represent, from a quantitative view, a minority of cases. Second, the claim "whatever those interpretations may be" is illogical. S. Walt claims that:

> "As far as practical reason accounts go, the interpretations are on a par."

However, no sound citizen would dare to say this. I will make an example. At the beginning of one of his books, A. Aarnio[43] talks about a hard-case where six interpretations of a given fact are legally possible, although none of them have anything to do with a seventh, which I am inventing now: "These persons were spies from Andromeda's galaxy." Why not? Because, generally speaking, both judges and citizens share, *inter alia*, basic beliefs and values.

This means, *inter alia*, that they are socialised in a certain language, certain traditions, in certain social relations, in basic values, etcetera. It is not a question of "whatever" interpretation goes, because accepted interpretations are related to accepted ideological options. Not everything is accepted and much less so in legal realms, where there are other additional restraints.[44] Disagreement is possible (and sometimes enriching) but participants (generally speaking) want to survive in the best possible way. Illogical decisions (although possible) are rejected by participants because they support the legal order and want to make sense of it. When there is a

---

knowledge of how to secure ends in general. Rather it is capacity to act with regard to that which is, in our terminology, beneficial or harmful, i.e. good or bad for us. This establishes a link between practical wisdom and the moral virtues." *The Varieties of Goodness*, Routledge, New York, 1964, page 144.

[43] Aarnio, A. *Lo Racional como Razonable*, Centro de Estudios Constitucionales, Madrid, 1991, page 24.

[44] In relation to the "one right answer thesis" see, A. Peczenik, *On Law and Reason*, Kluwer, Dordrecht, 1989, p. 302 ff.

disagreement, loyal and competent jurists (especially legal scholars) try to do their best in an objective sense.

A "trivial" answer could be that the jurist only tries to protect the private interest of his client. As we know though, legal adjudication is not an individual enterprise. Different interests can be defended and justified with the basic aim of "making justice". This does not mean though that we are living in a society without conflicting interests. It only means that the idea that judges are politicians defending the particular interests of the most powerful is only another idea, and a requirement for evidence and warrant should also be needed for a proper justification. However, other persons with different ontological commitments and values allow their supporters to see a different reality than others. A disagreement in attitude can even exist when reaching agreement on beliefs. Which ontology and values should we use to solve the problem and, hence, to prefer certain methods and proofs as opposed to others, etcetera?

The final stab to practical reason would come through the insufficiency of standards to state what is sufficient evidence. Without this standard there would be no point to distinguish between good and bad judgement. S. Walt seems to believe that "evidence" is a bundle of elements including texts, legislative intention, current values, etcetera. Although it is a problem to state what evidence is, basically speaking, the difficulty is whether evidence should be understood either as internal states or as objects and events. It seems though that Walt adopts both views. If this is correct, we should understand the evidence not only as events (a robbery took place), as objects (a text) and as internal states (the beliefs certain persons have in relation to certain objects and events).

If we accept that the evidence includes internal states (let us say, beliefs), objects and events, we could say that standards for the evidence of a robbery would be at least: a certain institutional fact like a robbery, the legal text(s) related to robbery, the accepted interpretations of them, the precedents related to robbery, legal theories about robbery and justificatory reasons about interpretations on robbery, etcetera. These cannot give an algorithm though that leads us to the "one right answer" (in a different sense to Dworkin's approach) but they can give us some standards to discriminate between proper and improper exercises of judgement. It also means that a proper exercise of judgement can lead us to several sound solutions, that in the minority of cases we usually call hard cases.

This is not the same as claiming that there is no difference between proper and improper exercises of judgement. We have chosen proper exercises of judgement and this is different from claiming that there is no standard at all. The disappointment comes because a sharp line was expected dividing false solutions from true ones and the old Cartesian dream. However, this is a misunderstanding of what judgement is and shows how much of a slave one can be to the metaphysical dream of "truth and certainty". On the one hand, "evidence" should not be understood as a one to one piece of reality. Facts and evidence have sense within the realm of theories, and "pieces of reality" can be as evident as the theory on which they rest.

Even in mature sciences, accreditation of evidence is also a social process. It is true that in mature sciences disagreements are less important than in law (basically, *inter alia*, because there is a unique paradigm and because they use a developed logical apparatus) but if we believe that evidence and judgement are exclusively dependent on cognitive criteria we are mistaken. Evidence and judgement are dependent, primarily, on pragmatical criteria. It is, usually, of pragmatical interest that some criteria be cognitive, although this is a pragmatic decision. Hence, what matters most is not whether legal standards reach sufficiency, according to empirical or logical criteria, but whether they satisfy, sufficiently, certain social and personal ends within certain procedures.

As I said, if strong disagreements among competent jurists would represent, for example, ninety per cent of the legal conflicts, we should have to face the problem of the utility of our legal standards, but this is not the case. It would be, then, mistaken to claim that there is no justification for favouring one statutory interpretation over another. If this were so, it could happen that (without changing legal texts) the legal winners in January were the legal losers in February. This is not the case, and it is only a logical possibility. Otherwise, if there were clear standards determining precisely when specific assertions were justified, law would have serious problems of adaptation. This clearness and preciseness is acceptable in limited branches of law, such as criminal law, because we especially value individual freedom, equality before the law and predictability, *inter alia*.

To demand such preciseness and predictability in private law would imply, *inter alia*, the elimination of analogical reasoning which is a basic method for adapting law to new social circumstances. Instead of "*Fiat justitia pereat mundus*", methodological positivists would say "*Fiat logical preciseness pereat mundus*". To forget this social, economical and ideological character of legal orders makes it possible to misunderstand these imprecisenesses. They would be completely unacceptable if our goal was, for example, to send an aircraft to Mars. In legal fields, we cannot have a clear and precise standard saying when a decision has to be modified. We may support the principle of *stare decisis*, for example, but we do not know in advance how long a decision will remain under it, or will change on the basis of sufficiently relevant considerations.

Nevertheless, the principle (no matter how vague it is) is an important principle for the proper working of our legal orders, and no sound jurist claims that it should be eliminated because it is not precise enough. If social reality could be seen as a static picture, it could be sound to demand clear, precise and predictable standards that allow us to go from evidence to conclusion, through clear, necessary and precise steps. Imagine that we could predict everything and that all lawyers agreed on everything, and so did judges on the basis of logical, necessary conclusions. In this scenario, nothing would have sense, in so far as we know legal orders and adjudication. Consequently, this nightmare should be eliminated from our minds.

We know that we need some stability and predictability and we also know that we need change, but we cannot have algorithms for these pragmatical temporal needs. We ignore not only how much change or stability we want (or is good for us, at a given time) but we also ignore when this change has to be undertaken, in the clear and precise sense demanded by positivists. This obsession is also present when S. Walt says that no logical account of the sequence of steps from evidence (premises) to a preferred interpretation (conclusion) is supplied. In this magical world of preciseness we would have a precise sequence of steps from premises to conclusion. No doubts, no disagreements, no judgements, just certainty. One of the problems with this reductionist-nightmare is that legal orders work with a continuous and complex feed-back, from legal texts to legal norms, from legal norms to legal decisions, from legal decisions to social impact, from social impact to possible new legal texts. This is a basic, vague, interpretative and continuous process.

On the other hand, it may happen that expected goals, according to a legislative text, can be barely fulfilled, at any given time. It may also happen that judges could undertake new interpretations of this text if they expect them to foster these expected goals. This has sense for a judge who adopts (as usual) an internal point of view. In this vein, new exceptions could arise in the form of "distinguishing" or other techniques. A perfect and algorithmic world would have more difficulties to cope with exceptions and to fulfil them with this pragmatical feedback. We expect a revision of legal decisions if the consequences attached to these decisions do not properly fulfil certain relevant social interests, needs or values, at a given time. And this calls for judgement.

We have to be flexible enough to adapt law to changing relevant circumstances, uttering proper justificatory reasons. No doubt there is a danger in the "power of judges" but, in my view, there is always danger. No matter whether we rely on more formal (England) or more substantial (United States) adjudicatory process, as R. Summers and Atiyah have shown us in *Form and Substance in Anglo-American Law*. I will not deal here with this problem but I would say that a debate should be undertaken for deciding which items and branches of law should be more based on form and which on substance. Even within one branch there can be parts where form should have more emphasis or *vice versa*. This is not only a legal methodological issue but also an ethical and political one.

As I have been saying, formal logic has little importance in legal normative fields, basically because relevant legal contradictions are those that jurists and citizens (not specialists in formal logic) can see and value as sufficiently relevant. At the same time, implicit-relevant legal norms are important in so far as they are "seen" by jurists (not by specialists in formal logic) as sufficiently relevant, whether they are logical implications or sound practical inferences. This is so because the addressees of the legal orders are not specialists in formal logic. Citizens want and have the right to understand, as much as possible, the meaning of this directive language and their relevant implications. However, I am not saying that formal logic has nothing to do in legal orders. I am just saying that it has little importance for legal reasoning if we look at judges and legal scholars.

As I said, the contradictions and implications that have interest in legal fields are the relevant ones, and this relevancy is decided by participants-jurists with an eye on the society where the legal norm applies, that is, a given context and a given time. They are not mainly upset for logical perfection. A logical implication can be trivial, or not, for legal purposes. In these cases, legal purposes will decide, because there can be a huge number of possible logical implications that may have no pragmatic relevance. This calls, again, for a judgement.[45]

10.3 Cognitive and Normative Dimensions

Hence, formal logical requirements would be necessary, but not sufficient, conditions for legal reasoning. The "last" word rests on a legal normative field where values, rights and duties, social consequences and social goals, at a given time, play the most important role. These considerations would not be surprising for anyone who rejects one of the legacies of logical positivism, the unity of method. Granted that we have intentions and purposes and granted that they are published and delimited in certain legal forms, we want to know, from time to time, whether we are going in the right direction. Although we sometimes change our intentions and purposes (but this is rare in relation to basic ones, whatever they are), we more usually change our interpretation of them.

This permanent task of adapting the legal order calls for practical reason, which is a process that starts from normative premises (basically including intentions and purposes), cognitive premises (including beliefs) and legal facts. If we want the success (always relative) of the legal order, we shall combine certain intentions and purposes with certain beliefs, not with others. However, intentions, purposes and beliefs may change and so can our interpretations of them. This is not a deterministic or logical process, although it could be reconstructed *ex post*. It is basically an evaluative process in a double sense: participants want the legal order to work as best as possible (what has sense in certain historical circumstances) and in the combination of intentions-purposes with beliefs, with the last word on the normative premises, but keeping an eye on the former proviso.

Let us have a simple example. We want people to have freedom of action, at least in democratic societies. Hence, people can take their car and travel from one place to another. At the same time, we believe that, on a narrow road, to allow people to drive at 150 km per hour will put the lives of people in great danger, and we value survival. This belief and this value may be the proper justification of a modification of a normative premise. If we do so, it is not because the cognitive element is more important than the normative one. The main point is that we value human life, not that we know that some people may die on narrow roads. Otherwise, the value of survival may collide with other values, such as human freedom.

In modifying the legal normative premise, on the basis of a belief, we enhance a basic value, in this case human life, on the basis of evaluations that include deontological and consequential elements. I am not denying though that some politicians may have other considerations in mind. For example, the cost of accidents. Nevertheless, to see the importance of both aspects let us again use the example of TV. Imagine a politician of a democratic country saying, "I do not mind whether you kill yourself while driving, I am upset by the costs of accidents". These

---

[45] To see the limits of practical rationality in legal reasoning, N. MacCormick and O. Weiberger, *An Institutional Theory of Law*, chapter nine, Reidel, Dordrecht, 1986.

witty comments can be made by some legal philosophers (in so far as they have no normative power) but they cannot be uttered either by politicians or by judges. It does not mean that the cost of accidents is not important, it means that we value human life more (at least for now), and not only for utilitarian reasons.

Hence, practical reason makes evaluations about costs and benefits. It would be easier to make this balance between clearly commensurable things but in legal orders we often have to take into account money and values, material things and human beings, not in abstract but in concrete changing contexts. Once the evaluation is made, computers and other useful devices should be used because practical reason wants pragmatical success. At least in our culture, there is a normative requirement of universalization, but this formal requirement can only be properly fulfilled in specific contexts (with justified exceptions, that also call for new universalizations) and for a certain time (not known in advance). Once we have beliefs (in the cognitive dimension) we have to decide what to do with them.

There is no *a priori* answer, there is no algorithm, but there is practical reason intertwined with theoretical reason. It does not matter how difficult it can be though. We cannot avoid it. In a similar vein, some political philosophers, like Nozick, have denied that we can mix freedom and equality. However, a basic problem is what "mix" means.

My answer here is the same. In spite of the theoretical and practical difficulties that can exist, we cannot avoid the complex intertwinement of normative and cognitive dimension. One option is to strive for the best possible solutions, here and now, taking a hermeneutic stance. Another option is to reject practical reason because "true rationality" is something else and we want to be "rational" and to act "rationally" (understood in another sense).

Moreover, I think that (at least in legal fields) we cannot avoid the mixture of "having good reasons for acting" and "an agent thinking that he has a good reason for acting". This means the existence of an intertwinement between internal reasons for action and external reasons for action. In legal fields, both have (not as a matter of logical necessity) intentions, purposes and beliefs (not necessarily occurrent but, at least, dispositional). In legal fields, to have a good reason for action (independently of the agent's opinion) is related not only to beliefs, legal norms and justificatory reasons but also to authoritative reasons.

The step from these reasons to exclusionary reasons is a degree-step. It would have little sense to deny that authority reasons have any special weight in legal orders, at least for participants. The problem rests with the emphasis put on officials and political power, on the one hand, and citizens, on the other. In the legal positivistic tradition, emphasis has been put more on officials than on citizens. This is not of logical necessity, it is a political option, although it is usually presented as an aseptic methodological approach. This has consequences for the importance given to authority reasons, legal certainty, predictability, etcetera. In relation to options I again emphasize the idea that practical reason is not useless even lacking clear and precise standards from which to infer univocal conclusions.

W.H. Newton-Smith says, in relation to Popper, Lakatos and Laudan:

> "In their writings they don't make any reference to the role played by judgement. No doubt they believe that the inclusion of this aspect would introduce, in a rejectable sense, a subjective element. Nevertheless, as we have seen in chapter 9, scientific method cannot be exhaustively specified in a system of articulated rules because there are cases in which the rules conflict with each other. Hence, the scientist has to exercise judgement, that is, the relative weight he has to give to the conflicting rules."[46]

This can also be applied (I would say *a fortiori*) to legal normative fields. This means that to require more specification of the criteria of evidence (with the aim of "eliminating" the person who decides, because we already have an algorithm) is to forget that, in any case, the reference to individual cases will remain relatively underdetermined.

In a similar vein to scientists from mature sciences who do not reproduce reality but "construct a map" of the reality, jurists impose certain features on reality and settle general standards. These general standards will create, in their turn, interpretative problems when applied to specific circumstances. Similarly, to discard practical reason for its inability to give "acceptable" criteria and standards for interpretation is not only vague (and here is the revenge of always demanding more preciseness) but, more importantly, it is a misunderstanding of what legal interpretation and legal adjudication is, at least in our cultural world.

As J. Ziman says,

> "Even the most elaborated economic models have failed to solve the problems of inflation, unemployment, exchange rates, etc. Even when the mathematical calculus is detailed, even when, supposedly, many factors are taken into account, this kind of analysis depends on the suppositions made when it is settled. These suppositions, like the limit conditions and the constituent equations, are submitted to all doubts and uncertainties above discussed."[47]

He basically refers to the absence of a taxonomic conceptual scheme for human behaviour with clear, distinct and significant categories, on the one hand, and the complexity and unpredictability of human behaviour that only allows for tendencies, on the other. Hence, in legal practical reason we are not dealing with knowledge but with justification, and legal justification does not deal with truth but with rational acceptability, and rational acceptability deals with judgement and with fallible and committed human beings, not with algorithms and certainty. In this respect, it is interesting to note how J. Elster sees rational action:

> "Rational action implies, then, three optimization operations: to find the best action for given beliefs and desires; to form the best founded belief for a given proof; and accumulate a judicious amount of proofs for given desires and former beliefs."[48]

We should bear in mind that from an internal point of view we also undertake optimisation operations. In these operations we also look for the "best" solution, here and now.

In relation to rational acceptability and justification, A Aarnio wrote,

---

[46] Newton-Smith, W.H. *La Racionalidad de la Ciencia*, edit. Paidos, Barcelona, 1987, page 291.

[47] Ziman, J. *La Credibilidad de la Ciencia*, Alianza Editorial, Madrid, 1981, page 253.

[48] Elster, J. *Juicios Salomónicos*, Gedisa, Barcelona, 1995, page 13.

> "The analyses I have carried out above have an interesting consequence significant for the methodology of legal research ... a prediction states something about how an authority will act, whereas legal dogmatics try to find out how the authorities should (ought) to act ... According to Albert it is characteristic of such pseudo-predictions that they are hidden valuations ..."[49]

11. INSTRUMENTS, PERSONS AND REASONS FOR ACTION

There are legal traditions that claim legal orders are mere instruments. On the one hand, J. Bentham believed that we can only justify laws by reference to utility reasons; on the other hand, A. Vyshinsky claimed that law was an instrument for the Soviet government. We can accept that law is an instrument for social change, for example, at least if we see law from the point of view of those who authoritatively make it. Even if we accept it we need not accept that this is correct in relation to all parts of legal orders or to all elements. In this respect, it is hard to state (at least for myself) that individual basic rights are mere instruments. Granted the former comments we can understand the importance of guiding reasons and participants in the working of legal orders. Participants' view and guiding reasons, *inter alia*, help us to know when some behaviour is right or not. In the so-called routine cases it would be sufficient to know the law in force.

For example, when a certain speed on the road is legally right or not. However, legal conflicts are not always so easy. In addition, the view of legal orders as instruments fit with the idea of the primacy of exclusionary reasons for action and the pyramidal view of legal orders. Moreover, when it is considered that the proper object of legal orders is the regulation of coercion there is a tendency either to emphasize norms directed to officials or to claim that they are the only real legal norms. Be that as it may, a conception of person and society underlies all legal approaches. In relation to exclusionary reasons for action we should distinguish between strongly and weakly accepted ideas. Only the first ones should be the object of exclusionary reasons for action in so far as the latter reasons exclude other reasons as valid reasons for doing something different as it is stated. In democratic and pluralistic societies exclusionary reasons for action should limit themselves to those values, beliefs and behaviours strongly accepted by all or by the majority. That is, previously accepted or soundly expecting that they will be so. This problem leads, *inter alia*, to a provisional and complex balance between legal certainty and material justice.

Once we accept this ontological commitment, that is, once we accept that we are facing an existing normative object, we can take a step forward. It is not necessary to claim that normative objects only exist in a Popperian third world. They do not. They only exist in so far as human beings create them (although not from scratch) and put them in motion. What seems, to me, rejectable of this Popperian construction, is the emphasis he puts on epistemology without subject. Apart from the non-temporality of truth, he emphasizes the independent and objective existence of structures, completely rejecting the subjective dimension as something irrelevant.

---

[49] Aarnio, A. *On Legal Reasoning*, Turku, 1977, pages 262 and 263.

In this respect, methodological positivists would go together with Popper, at least, in so far as he supports the unity of method, which is the deductive-hypothetic one.

Nevertheless, lets go back to the normative dimension, by saying that when we want to put a car in motion we put gasoline in the tank and switch on the starter-motor, then we put it into first gear and so on. It is probable that, in order to understand this, we have to appeal to explanatory reasons. These will explain how, given certain circumstances, certain things should be done in order to put the car in motion. A more usual example is the umbrella illustration. It is raining (certain circumstances exist), I want to go home but not get wet (the goal) and, therefore finally, I open my umbrella (because something should be done in order to reach the goal). It is interesting to note that this behaviour is not a necessary one. I could take a taxi instead, for example.

These diverse possibilities of action make human behaviour very complex and very difficult, if not impossible, for predicting anything with preciseness. In any case, I have a reason for opening my umbrella in this specific context, all things considered. But it can change. For example, if a man or a woman nearby loses heart, I will not open my umbrella for myself because my main concern would be to help this person, not to avoid the rain. However, now I am in the realm of justificatory reasons. Explanatory reasons do not have justificatory force. For example, Peter can explain to us that he knocked John down because the latter did not want to go to the cinema with him. This is an explanatory reason but not a justificatory reason because Peter cannot use it for justifying his behaviour.

On the other hand, the above example would show that my "opening the umbrella" was a *prima facie* reason, in the sense that it can be defeated by other considerations. This is a dispositional feature of human actions. In principle, our actions are supported (be it consciously or not) by reasons able to explain why, given certain circumstances, we did what we did. However, it is possible that some other circumstances, physical or not, make us undertake another action that we believe is "better". "Better" can be understood, at least, in two senses. Recalling the former example where it was raining, it could happen that my umbrella was very small and I could not properly fulfil my goal of not getting wet. Suppose a friend passes by with two umbrellas and both are better than mine. She says, "take one, it is better than yours".

In this case, I would have undertaken another action because I thought that the second action (to accept the umbrella of my friend) was a better one. I would say that the first sense of "better" refers to efficacy. The second action was better than the first because it fulfilled, with more efficiency (other things being equal), the goal of not getting wet. Nevertheless, some circumstances may appear that push me to balance the efficiency of my own goal with the "rightness" of my behaviour. If a person near me loses heart I can do several things. One is to stress my goal and my efficient mean. Another is to consider my reasons for doing what I am doing (to cover myself with the umbrella) as *prima facie* reasons that, in this case, are defeated by other guiding reasons, to help this person. In case I change my course of action, I take other guiding reasons as more important, because I believe that it is "better" to help this person in this context.

This second sense of "better" is not dependent, as the first one, on efficiency but on "rightness". This does not mean though that it should not take care of efficiency, it means that it is not the decisive element. The first explanatory reasons (and the first sense of "better") have been defeated (in this specific case) by guiding reasons (and by the second sense of "better"). If I accept the primacy of these guiding reasons I accept that my specific goal and my efficient means to reach it, are defeated (ought to be) by these new types of justificatory reasons. However, this does not have any kind of logical necessity. There are, probably, certain basic biological human features, that make extremely good persons and extremely bad persons rare. There are also certain socio-economic circumstances and a certain positive morality within which human behaviour takes place. In this complex context we can say that it is more or less probable[50] that a person, in these situations, will behave in one or another sense.

However, what matters, for our present purposes, is that legal orders are basically dependent on both explanatory reasons and guiding reasons. We have, either from an individual or a collective point of view, certain goals. For example, it is a usual goal (at least in big towns) to move from one place to another using, let us say, a car. It is a normal individual goal not to have an accident while driving the car, and it is also a collective goal. Individuals prefer to live and legal-political institutions prefer (that is, those who manage them) not to lose too much money as a result of accidents and, probably, not to see how their fellow citizens (and perhaps themselves) die while driving. We also want efficient means to reach these goals.

Although I believe that there are no sharp separations between explanatory and guiding reasons (because to avoid accidents may have something to do with "rightness", for example), since the former reasons would put the emphasis on efficiency, not on rightness.

Nevertheless, a previous step could have been taken that also had moral tones. For example, we should decide whether to invest more money on safety, because we believe that this will produce a decrease in the number of accidents, or to invest more money in certain social help to certain groups or minorities that need more social assistance. This is a matter of moral evaluation. It is also a matter of political evaluation because the politicians may balance (perhaps in private) what is better for themselves or their political parties.

It could also be a matter of efficiency, if there was a previous political agreement saying, for example, that in the next ten years the decrease of accidents would be a

[50] Granted that we are not dealing with deductive reasoning, this is "more or less" what we can expect from inductive reasoning. As A. Morton says, "I notice that many of these things are not black. Moreover, all the things which are not black are ravens. I check to make sure of this, and yes, every single non-black thing is a non-raven. This makes me remember that every thing I have seen in my life that was not black was not a raven. So, reasoning by simple induction, I conclude that all, absolutely all, things that are not black are not ravens. Then I remember some logic: "Everything that is not B is not R" is equivalent to "Everything that is R is B". So if I am concluding that everything that is not black is not a raven, I should also conclude that everything that is a raven is black. But this is an outrageous conclusion ... The relation between the ravens paradox and Goodman's problem is this: In both cases we have a possible pattern "All As are Bs" and a body of data which fits with it, since it consists of As that are Bs, but which does not give us reason to believe that the pattern holds for all cases." *A guide through the theory of knowledge*, Blackwell, Oxford, 1997, page 74.

preference of the government. Once again, this goal can be defeated by other considerations. For example, if the social situation of certain groups has severely deteriorated. At the same time, legal certainty or predictability is also a value, and the Government would not like to be considered as a kind of weathercock. There is a continuous intertwinement of diverse considerations that simultaneously push for change and for the maintenance of the situation. Here the principle of *stare decisis* applies. When should judges or courts prefer a different interpretation?

We have legal orders, we use them and we (most of us) rely on them (although critically), because they fulfil certain basic goals for individuals and for society. Intentionality, purpose, morality and self-interest are basic and intertwining elements of these complex orders. However, they are not only a more or less useful instrument. It is usual in legal positivist tradition, and in methodological positivists, to claim that legal orders are instruments. They usually scorn what they call metaphysical attitudes, that give the legal orders (or some of them) certain value "in themselves". What is the danger of giving legal orders an exclusive value as instruments? If they are only instruments, one can modify them at one's pleasure. If legal orders (for example democratic legal orders) are only instruments, we could consider individual rights as instruments.

However, we should bear in mind some caveats. First, I am talking of democratic legal orders, not of any kind of legal order, because only in legal orders where human rights are respected (to a certain extent) can we reasonably consider them as not only being instruments. Second, it is possible to claim that I have committed the fallacy of division because I would say that what is true of the whole (legal orders) should be true of all of their parts (individual legal rights, for example).

11.1 Law as an Instrument

As a hypothesis, let us accept that legal orders are instruments. It is not necessary to claim that this qualification is also true for all of their parts, it is sufficient to ask methodological positivists whether they believe that individual basic rights are instruments or not. If they say that they are instruments, we would have a basic different ontological commitment, at least in relation to democratic legal orders. If they say that individual basic rights are not merely instruments, but that they also have value in themselves, their claim that legal orders are instruments would have little importance, if any. In other words, we can accept that legal orders are instruments if it is accepted that not all parts are instruments. That is, we should not accept that individual basic rights are only instruments.[51]

---

[51] In relation to Instrumentalism as a philosophical school, P.S. Atiyah and R.S. Summers, *Form and Substance in Anglo-American law*, Clarendon Press, Oxford, 1987. In relation to the Interest School, R. Von Jhering, *El Espíritu del Derecho Romano*, Madrid, 1947; Ph. Heck, *El Problema de la Creación de Derecho*, Barcelona, 1961. Aleksander Somek says, "While constructivists held that elusive means-end relationships are only of marginal significance to the construction of the conceptual structure, scholars such as Philipp Heck and Heinrich Stoll adopt the idea (already expreseed in Jhering's later work) that means-end relationships provide the rational basis of legal institutions ...". *A Companion of Philosophy of Law and Legal Theory*, D. Patterson (ed.), Blackwell, 1996, page 348.

My view is that a normative order stating, for example, that women have no right (like Afghans) to be judges, doctors, teachers, etcetera, does not merit being called a "legal order". This is like the "extreme injustice" perspective. Some views, such as mine, see democratic legal orders as something more than instruments because they are necessary elements (although not sufficient ones) for shaping human beings as moral and autonomous agents. If one sees democratic legal orders as decoys for the concealment of the true malevolent goals of imperialism, it is sound to consider them as mere instruments for the benefit of the dominant class. Moreover, one can say that legal orders are techniques of social control, no matter what values they support or which ones lie underneath them.

The neutrality of an instrument, no matter for which purpose we use it, can be easily seen in relation to certain objects. For example, a knife can serve for cutting bread or for killing a person. The knife is neutral. However, to apply this example to legal orders is wrong because a knife cannot be compared to a legal order. I can easily identify a knife (it is an example of a basic perception) and no sensible person doubts that there is a knife on the table, if this is the case. If someone doubts whether there is a knife on the table or not, we believe he is joking. This is not the same thing as when we try to identify a legal order though. In other words, knives are not as important as basic individual rights. Moreover, their method of identification is different.

To see human beings as holders of basic individual rights is closely related to concepts such as dignity and autonomy. In this respect it is difficult to see some legal orders only as instruments, like a knife. At the same time, the goals and means of democratic legal orders are based, *inter alia*, on a certain conception of a person. Without doubt, there is a distance from theory to practice, not only in relation to democratic legal orders and their specific working, but also in relation to egalitarian-no-class societies and their specific working. Granted this general and common feature, I want to emphasize that legal actions cannot be properly understood by causal explanations.

Let us at this point take Moore's known open-question argument. If a scientist says that only yellow things produce vibrations of the type "V" then, he can infer that "yellow" means "producing vibrations V". This would be a wrong reasoning for legal normative fields. We can move from this example to legal actions and say that the description of causal explanations does not make us understand certain actions. Let us go back to the example of the person who loses heart near us. We can give causal explanations that will make us understand what "loses heart" means, but it is not sufficient for claiming whether the person who helped the other person was behaving "rightly" or not. However, I am not claiming that "rightly" is not analysable as, for example, yellow could be. I am just saying that theoretical reason, although necessary, is not sufficient to understand the "rightness" of our actions. Nevertheless, one could neglect this concept as a reminiscence of the religious or magical old times.

If this is the case, it should be explained how clever, cultivated and competent persons believe in "right" and "wrong". In any case, legal orders do not make sense without, *inter alia*, the concepts of "right" and "wrong", not only in the sense that doing the contrary of what is legally due will probably produce bad consequences for the wrongdoer. This is only one perspective of the problem, seen from the "prudent man" conception. However, many persons see and accept justificatory reasons for action in legal orders, and not only more or less reliable information for their predictions. Once we adopt the internal point of view, or the view of the "moral man" (in the sense I have already explained) we have to accept certain concepts as fundamental.

Among these concepts are judgement, justification and practical reason. This means, *inter alia*, that guiding reasons have a basic role in legal orders because these reasons are, usually, seen as having more weight than explanatory reasons, if there is a conflict between them. This does not mean though that guiding reasons are univocal. They are not. There are diverse guiding reasons that can be interpreted in different ways (not unlimited) and with the permanent possibility of conflict. Guiding reasons are so important because they justify (or try to justify) the goals of our normative premises. In this respect, guiding reasons say when a goal is right or, at least, when a goal is not wrong, in the moral sense of the term.

However, the justification of our actions is a main feature of practical reason, given certain normative premises and facts, and the justification of their revision, when due. Granted that practical inference does not lead necessarily from premises to a univocal conclusion, it is possible to accept the rightness of the goal (explicit or implicit in the premise of the reasoning process) and reject the concrete action that seems to be a proper conclusion stemming from this goal. This was already seen by Aristotle and by Francisco Suárez. General rules cannot be right in all cases though. When this happens, equity is needed in order to restore justice.

An important difference between practical reasoning and legal practical reasoning is based on the authoritatively stated limits for the possibility of defeating the actions or omissions, justified by the normative premise. In this respect, legal reasons are reasons specially protected from defeating facts or reasons. In normative moral grounds (or, at least, in those with Kantian influence), where the autonomy of the agent is emphasized, the agent's reasons are specially protected reasons because (normatively speaking) the agent himself, and no one else, can morally defeat his reasons for action. In normative legal grounds, legal texts (and their interpretation) convey specially protected reasons.

In this respect, if citizens have to be respected as ends in themselves, specially protected legal reasons have to be specially justified. Legal authority (in so far as it is based on democratic power) has legitimacy of origin but a legitimacy of exercise is also required. A basic difference (but not the only one) is the periodicity of justification. This is especially important because we are not dealing with commands (that imply a personal relation that finishes with the fulfilment of the command) but with rules that are impersonal and do not exhaust themselves with their fulfilment. If a legal reason is an exclusionary reason for action, it means that citizens are not allowed to think by themselves and evaluate either the general rule or its specific application.

In more liberal circumstances (Benthamite circumstances) you could be allowed to think what you like quite freely, although you would be necessarily obliged to obey. Doing this, you emphasize legal authority and legal certainty, at least in a legal positivist sense. You also show distrust in citizens and a static view of society.

Nevertheless, our societies change rapidly. This view says, no matter how illogical and unjust the legal solution can be, it is the legal solution. "*Dura lex, sed lex*". Consequently, practical reasoning would be an exclusive task of legislators. Also judges, in so far as they only apply them. I believe that practical reasoning should also be the concern of citizens. I do not doubt that obeying a democratic legal order (generally speaking) has beneficial consequences for citizens at large.

Predictability, stability and co-ordination are relative but important requirements for a society that can be more easily fostered if citizens obey the law. Hence, the point is not whether the citizens should discuss every law in every application. The point is not properly understood if one remains exclusively within the limited scope of legal thinking. Supporting, or not, exclusionary reasons means to support a certain kind of conception of a person and of political power and society. To emphasize exclusionary reasons means to support a kind of paternalism towards citizens. The political power says, we know better than you do what is better for you, even if you disagree. This is a new kind of enlightened despotism. We should also foster freedom, reflective criticism and responsibility, not mere obedience. In this respect a previous assumption is needed, that citizens are rational agents who have, at least in principle, valuable purposes.

We can do this on the basis of a certain conception of a person, of a legal order and of political power. If operative reasons state valid legal goals, they cannot be stated apart from the view of citizens. Granted the very rapid changes of our societies, the act of voting -from time to time- is not sufficient to take citizens seriously. As a result, even just laws can be unjustly applied, although it can be said that we have legal procedures for solving these problems. I agree, but it is a danger (granted a certain view of citizens as free and autonomous beings) to try to renew legal-political legitimation only through legal procedures. If content is every time less important, we would be closer to the Kelsenian view that law is form (or Luhmann's view of legitimation as procedure).

I am not going to discuss though whether we are, in fact, moving towards this situation. What I say is that a conception of a person as an obedient donkey is a dangerous move that diminishes, more and more, the legitimation of the legal and political system. Moreover, although it is not my concern here to deal with political philosophy, I would like to stress that Communitarian tendencies (at large) are prone to underestimate individual rights, granted the supremacy given to the community good. No matter, here, the soundness of certain criticisms towards certain formalistic-idealistic versions of Kantian tradition. At the same time, some of these versions have ignored the importance and chronological priority of certain conceptions of the good. I have criticised, elsewhere, these views when dealing with the Rule of Law.

In any case, the dominance of the positive morality over the critical one, the dominance of the majority over the minorities, the dominance of tribal attitudes, etcetera, are usual manifestations of these doctrinal tendencies. Although these doctrines are not responsible for them, I very much doubt that doctrinal tendencies based on the primacy of individual rights are favouring such worrying manifestations for peaceful human coexistence and pluralism. There is just one addition though. One thing is to impute these consequences to Communitarian doctrines, which is absurd from a logical point of view, and another thing is to show (if I am right) the intellectual origin of these undesirable manifestations, which is not absurd from a practical point of view.

11.2 Conception of Person and Exclusionary Reasons

Certain liberal dreams, where individuals are completely free to state operative reasons, are also unacceptable. If there is going to be a balance between individual and society, neither exclusionary reasons nor individual moral or interest reasons can be accepted as undefeatable reasons. It is a dangerous dream to organize legal and political institutions as if human beings were completely free and autonomous. On the other hand, the nostalgia for the lost unified community (in a communitarian sense) cannot be reached by imposing exclusionary reasons for action on citizens.

In this respect, we should bear in mind the distinction between primary reasons (the agent's desires, interests and needs) and secondary reasons (those reasons an agent may adopt because other citizens have certain primary reasons). In this vein, I would say the following: democratic legal orders may rely on exclusionary reasons for action in so far as positive legal rules (understood not only as legal texts but as legal norms, that is, interpreted legal texts) are officially justified by the similar reasons the citizens (at large) had for holding their primary and secondary reasons. It means that when the legal authority states such strong reasons they should not be reasons against the basic citizen's views.

Moreover, these reasons and the legal rules that are justified on the basis of these reasons, should be limited by the democratic majority principle, where majority ruling cannot be exercised if it implies violation of the basic human rights of the minorities. This is related to the distinction, drawn by Raz, between the normativity of the law (the moral content of legal standards) and the authority of the law (its moral force). If it is understood that law, because of its authority, has moral force we have to accept a kind of ideological positivism, that is, the view that we ought to obey the law in force because, for this reason, it offers certain levels of social peace, co-ordination and stability.

Hence, the law may be morally authoritative for those who adopt this point of view, no matter the content of the law. On the other hand, other people can reject ideological positivism and claim that the authority of law is a necessary condition for obeying it, although not a sufficient one, at least in all cases. For example, a reflective and critical participant may have a different attitude in relation to traffic-laws and euthanasia-laws, considering that one is justified but not the other. In this respect, traffic-laws do not need to be the object of moral scrutiny. We usually rely on experts and obey traffic-laws. Why? Because driving cars and bikes do not directly affect our basic values and because we accept that there must be some co-ordination. On the other hand, when laws directly affect basic values (such as euthanasia, the death penalty and others) we cannot blindly rely on authority of law, unless we accept ideological positivism.

Furthermore, unless we want pyramidal democratic regimes full of donkey-citizens, we should criticise ideological positivism and foster critical and responsible attitudes, befitting of ideal participants. By the latter I mean, not people like Hercules' judge, but the best participants (reflective and critical) of a given community. Therefore, it seems generally accepted, by myself as well, that legal orders state authoritative rules to guide and co-ordinate certain relevant aspects of human life. In addition, it is also generally accepted, and by me too, that these legal rules claim to have "primacy" over the practical reasoning of participants. That is, they are not just another element to take into account. However, if participants are going to undertake practical reasoning (as something more than a witty entertainment) legal rules should not be, *tout court*, exclusionary reasons for action.

At the same time, these cannot simply be additional reasons but privileged reasons. In other words, the balance of reasons cannot be the same as when other reasons distinct to the legal ones are shuffled in. In this respect we should differentiate between strongly accepted ideas and weakly accepted ideas. We do not need to make a special effort to accept some kind of punishment for murders, or that we have to pay a price for the table we have just bought. In this respect, legal exclusionary reasons can be understood as strongly accepted ideas. Granted that this is the interpretation, these exclusionary reasons are our own reasons, not only the authority of law's reasons. Metaphorically speaking we could say that, while obeying the law we would be obeying ourselves. In relation to this field of strongly accepted ideas, legal orders would add co-ordination, predictability, and institutional support, not the basic content.

Nevertheless, legal orders are not only repetitions of what we already believe. To clarify, elaborate and systematize our intuitive basic ideas is an important aspect of philosophy, in general, and legal philosophy, in particular. Even if it were the case that legal orders were repetitions of our basic ideas, they would have the above commented functions and the coherent concretion of these ideas. In addition, legal orders also state weakly accepted ideas (from the point of view of the society as a whole) because we live in pluralistic societies. In these cases, legal reasons cannot be exclusionary reasons for all citizens in the same sense. Citizens can accept a compromise for the good working of the society as a whole but cannot necessarily accept, as something of their own, all legal rules with the same degree of acceptability.

If this is correct, to claim that legal rules are exclusionary reasons is a rather strong fiction. I believe that this approach could be stated as a normative one (not as an empirical description of reality) but in this case the normative approach would seem to me rejectable, for the reasons already given. This view would show a nostalgia for strongly unified communities, in a communitarian vein or for authority with divine foundations. I believe that to see legal rules as exclusionary reasons for action is correct in relation to strongly accepted ideas, not for legal rules as such though, because no legal authority (especially democratic ones) can reasonably expect to receive such complete blind obedience, by all members, for all legal rules at any time and circumstance.

If legal rules, as exclusionary reasons for action, were the correct representation of our legal practices, we would not need the value of "justice of the case". It would be enough to use the value of "legal certainty". Moreover, it is hard to see how courts can undertake a "distinguishing" if legal rules are exclusionary reasons for action. The solution could be to claim that the rule at stake now means something different, and this new meaning calls, in its turn, for new exclusionary reasons. This approach would mean that the *ratio decidendi* of precedents could not be changed because it should be understood as conveying concrete exclusionary reasons for action. In this respect, Raz claims that courts must not alter the basic rationale of the *ratio decidendi.*[52]

Nevertheless, although it is disputable whether courts must or must not do this, Raz's distinction, in any case, between the "tame view" and "strong view" of distinguishing seems rather fictional. I believe that courts can do this when judges have enough justification, and this seems a better solution to me, at least from a participant's point of view. In a wider sense, all our reasons are guiding reasons, since we do not expect that our reasons "misguide" us. Hence, even theoretical reasons are used for our practical purposes. We take them because we believe that they are able to push us in the proper direction. If we rely on our scientists, as we usually do, and we decide that a certain vaccine is good enough on the basis, *inter alia*, of theoretical reasons, we inject it into individuals because we have a practical goal. This practical goal can be to improve the health of the citizenship and we believe that the vaccine will produce the expected result.

This is, then, a mixture of theoretical reasons and practical reasons. This practical goal "guides" us to undertake certain actions that are considered as the best we can reach, here and now. For example, we believe that to rely on our scientists is the best way to reach our practical purposes. In this wide sense, theoretical reasons also guide us to reach our practical purposes. However, guiding reasons can also be practical. When we talk of guiding reasons as practical, we move from a wide sense of "guiding" to a narrower sense. In this respect, when a person gives primacy to his desires and interests he is guided by his prudential reasons. When a person gives primacy to "rightness" (instead of his own desires and interests) he is guided by moral reasons. However, "practical guiding reasons" are not isolated items in our life. On the contrary, we have to reach conclusions on the basis of a balance of the relevant contextual considerations that include, among other things, competing reasons. Not only competing reason within our own scheme of stratified preferences but between our own scheme and other ones, at a certain time and context.

12. SOME FINAL REMARKS

First,

the epistemological task of legal scholars is not to verify certain types of regularities (already selected by non empirical means) but to justify the validity of certain regularities of behaviour (or exceptions) that are relevant for us, given certain human purposes and values. This means, *inter alia*, that a basic point of this task is not Cartesian certainty but justification.

Second,

---

[52] Simmonds, N.E. *The Decline of Juridical Reason*, Manchester University Press, 1984, pages 112 ff.

if logical analysis is a deductive process and it means the reduction of a certain level of knowledge to another level of knowledge, it also means, *inter alia*, that it is accepted that empirical reality (some knowledge) is isomorphic to a logical or mathematical structure (other knowledge). Granted this, we should thank logicians that show us how legal reality really is, either starting from observational statements or starting from theoretical statements. In any case, it seems that they need to rely on privileged items, either their appearances (that cannot be wrong but they are private) or protocolary statements (that can be wrong and, in this case, have a similar status as participant's statements, because they also rest on fallible beliefs).

Third,

a hermeneutic analysis is a rational process, not a logical process. It starts (within the dynamics of history) with normative statements and transforms these statements into other normative statements. This is not a pure normative transformation, because legal normativity is made of legislation, adjudication and (partly) legal dogmatics (with no legal-political authority) that are "contaminated" by the outer world. Supposing that this process was a definition, we would say that the *definiendum* and the *definiens* cannot be equal. This is so because the internal point of view of participants includes an optimisation view (the best here and now). Nevertheless, transformation is not a blind transformation but one justified on the basis of practical and theoretical reason, with the former having the primacy.

Algorithms should be superseded by a changing and justified process, undertaken by legal experts sharing an internal point of view, trying to optimise the basic purposes and values of the legal order, under legal and meta-legal constraints. This means, *inter alia*, that justified transformations move from a certain normative and factual situation to another normative and factual situation. The new normative situation can be a new legal text or a new interpretation of the same legal text. The new factual situation is supposed to be closer to what we, as participants of a given legal order, justifiably expect or want. It does not mean that participants form a unified group. On the contrary, our societies are plural societies that tend to make a balance of several considerations practically demanding. If our societies were unified societies, we would also require a balance of several considerations but I hope that it is clear that the balance should be different. Nevertheless, a certain level of common background is required for a society to work.

Fourth,

there is a problem in relation to the positivist methodological task. What do methodological positivists observe and describe? Supposing that they observe and describe bodily movements, how do they translate this into a neutral and scientific discourse? If they observe and describe these facts and also make legal utterances, what does it mean that isolated legal sentences have observable consequences that can be verified? On the other hand, if legal sentences should be understood as forming part of a legal order, we should also understand the relation they have with the other parts of the whole (the legal order). How can they do this without some theory about meaning, legal norms, legal orders or legal interpretation? And if this is correct, what does "neutrality" mean for them, what does "non-committed-observers" mean for them?

Fifth,

the optimisation process of adjudication (which is a necessary feature of our legal orders, granted the insufficiency of legislative power and plain meaning to fulfil this necessary process) cannot be undertaken in an individualistic-atomistic way. In this respect, methodological individualism should not be understood as if only individuals were real. The fundamental aspect should be that the basic starting point (although not exclusive) is the individuals who associate with each other, in different ways, creating relationships that transcend the individual, who does not exist as an isolated monad. Some of these relationships help to shape and constitute the individuals, allowing for a better understanding of their individuality and sociality.

The problem then is not a sharp line between, let us say, methodological individualism and holism but a problem of emphasis that leads to the eternal problem of vagueness.[53] Hence, the emphasis we put on methodological individualism or holism, for example, could show an underlying emphasis on basic individual rights or a communitarian point of view. In its turn, this also shows an underlying concept of person. This fundamental conception of person, which is in the basement of the whole building, is not a description but a normative approach, with an eye on empirical realities and knowledge.

Sixth,

granted that strict methodological individualism and holism are untenable, practical reason should be a process necessarily undertaken by individuals, but it is not understandable if we believe that isolated individuals are the only starting point and the only end, for the reasons already given. One of the important consequences of this point is the necessity of social practices, both as a result of individuals' tasks and also as a shaping and constituting element of individuals themselves. There is a continuous dynamic relation between the individual point of view and the social practice point of view. However, if there were an isomorphic relation we would have a different social world. There is not. On the contrary, there is an intertwinement between stability (legal text, legal certainty, *prima facie* exclusionary reasons, social morality, principle of inertia, permanence of certain social circumstances, etcetera) and change (legal norm, justice of the case, distinguishing, change of certain social circumstances, critical morality, etcetera).

Seventh,

reasoning (either deductive or inductive) is a formal structure that links certain premises to certain conclusions. Nevertheless, in the domain of practical reason what is more important is the so-called epistemic logic, that is, the process of formation of concepts (and their laws, if we can grasp them) that will be used in our judgements. For example, the concept "justice" cannot be discovered by experience

---

[53] K. Fine says, "If higher-order vagueness terminates at some stage ^{a} then vagueness can, in a sense, be eliminated. For each sentence A can be replaced by a perfectly precise sentence $D^{a}A$ that entails it. However, this method is unsatisfactory in several ways. First, one may not be able to specify the ^{a}. Second, even if one can, one may not be able to make much sense of D^{a}. Our intuitions seem to run out after the second or third orders of vagueness. Perhaps this is because our understanding of vague language is, to a large extent, confused. One sees blurred boundaries, not clear boundaries to boundaries. Finally, the method is too uniform to be discriminate. Penumbral connections may be lost." "Vagueness, Truth and Logic", *Synthese*, 30, 1975, pp. 265-300.

but it is important because it is used in some of our important judgements. What matters, *inter alia*, is how we can move from a subjective (understood as arbitrary) judgement to an objective one and what it means. At this point, an ontological option is required. We make sense of legal orders and practical reason, *inter alia*, because most participants have certain dispositional attitudes such as impartiality and disinterestedness that solidify in stable institutions, whose day to day working is undertaken by participants who share meanings, values, interests, etcetera.

Hence, judges and competent jurists develop not only legal skills but also legal virtues that make possible a certain level of social confidence on adjudication and its impartiality. Legal competence and legal virtues are linked to the concept of objectivity, although not in the positivist sense. Legal objectivity is closely related to the best outcomes of our best jurists, who share an internal point of view. Finally, it is wrong to suppose that only an external observer could soundly criticise these legal practices. On the contrary, participants, at large, are interested in sound criticism because this is an important way to bring forward safely one of their regulative ideals, the optimisation of the legal order.

Eighth,

in so far as methodological positivists look for "necessity", they emphasize legal form and reject legal content, because legal content is "contingent". However, it is useless to try to understand legal orders on the basis of logical necessity. As anyone knows, there are legal decisions that can be taken without moral argumentation. This is a trivial truth. What matters is that we do not need to claim all legal justifications are moral justifications. It is enough to claim that we cannot dispense with moral justification in any legal order. This would show the conceptual connection between legal orders and some type of morality. In a similar vein as Kelsen supported the view that legal orders are coercive, without requiring that all legal rules be coercive, we can say that legal orders are, also, moral orders (not all their rules though) because they have an ultimate moral justification and are based on some conception of justice. Hence, legal orders are not only a technique for social control.

In other words, it is wrong to suppose that moral justification is important only at the level of the ultimate justification of legal orders. If it is true that legal orders have conceptual connections with some kind of morality (according to some positivists this would be, even, trivially true) it would mean that some morality "pervades" the whole legal order and the whole process of justification. Nevertheless, it would be a fallacy of division to suppose that what is true for the whole, must also be true for each of its parts. Legal orders have a two-faced dimension: a prudential one and a moral one. If we want to understand one part, dispensing with the other, we would have a misguided view of the whole. What has been said refers to positive morality, that is, legal orders are conceptually linked to some positive morality. Irrespective of the existence of critical morality next to various positive moralities, there is a privileged critical morality. Nowadays, Human Rights are usually understood as a kind of meta-critical morality in relation to any other kind of morality, be it positive or critical.

Finally, what is left for methodological positivism, the best representation of legal positivism? It seems that it is the unique basic claim that we need not appeal to moral considerations to identify a given legal order or the rules of a given legal order. If this is true, this famous approach has a remarkable austerity. It is in line with legal positivist tradition. We should remember though that Hart exposed his "minimal content of natural law" in order to criticize natural law doctrines for being excessive, and he limited his approach to "survival". I have tried to show, elsewhere, that this is a misguided option. What matters, here, is that this unique claim of methodological positivism seems wrong to me. If it is true (even trivially true) that any legal order has conceptual connections with some kind of morality, how can it be claimed that in order to identify any legal order (and solve hard cases) we can dispense with the morality that underlies it?

Some can believe that morality is like a flower in a pot (something that can be nice to see but with no practical relevance for legal purposes). However, if one sees morality as something important for participants, morality "pervades" the working of legal orders and the working of participants, although with some legal constraints and human limitations. In this respect, one of the elements that shapes the ideology of the "legislator's rationality" is that he is just, according to the underlying morality, which sometimes intertwines with internal critical morality and sometimes with the meta-critical morality *par excellence*, that is, Human Rights. Also in this vein, judges create, sometimes, "axiological gaps" because of, *inter alia*, moral considerations. In other words, although the legal order has an answer to a given legal conflict, the judge may believe that a given solution is not just. Granted that the legislator would have rejected this unjust solution, the judge creates a gap and fills it with another legal material that leads to a just solution. Some jurists claim that in "routine cases" there is no need to appeal to moral considerations because legal justification is enough.

This can be so, *inter alia*, for two reasons: one, because it is a case with no moral relevance, according to legal and meta-legal considerations; two, because moral considerations have already been incorporated and accepted in the justification of the legal decision. For example, cases with moral relevance such as cases of euthanasia, abortion, or other similar issues. Nevertheless, if a "distinguishing" is undertaken, new moral considerations (or a new interpretation of the same moral consideration) will be emphasized as one of the relevant elements of the new legal justification. In summary, when participant-competent jurists do not know what the law is (in a given case) they would have to participate in a complex legal construction, on the basis of what the law ought to be. And what the law ought to be is the best it can be, here and now. This construction will have moral or political (or both) tones, not only legal ones.

Ninth,

if what differentiates law and morals is that the former is based on a given source (usually legislative) and on a legislator's will, and morals are not, we are led, again, into the typical austerity of methodological positivism. Granted this, any content can be admitted. But admitted by whom? Is it important? It is important because, unless we dispense with the opinion of the addressees, it is important to know whether they accept both the privileged source and the legislator's will. Why should addressees give a blank cheque to the holders of political power? Is it not a scientific legal answer? I believe it is an important question (also for legal philosophers) unless one accepts some of the typical sharp distinctions such as: context of discovery and context of justification, or legal fields, as something conceptually separated from morals or politics, and so on.

The question is what kind of legal justification can be developed on the basis of a privileged normative source and the legislator's will? Why should addressees accept the products of the legislator's will as exclusionary reasons, without knowing the legal content? On the other hand, if addressees accept exclusionary reasons once the legal content is known, why is obedience to this content so important that it eliminates the possibility of defeasibility, in relation to exclusionary reasons? The concept of practical reason, in this work, is based on the Kantian approach of practical reason. It is not a strictly procedural one, although (following R. Alexy) it requires an argumentative procedure that is based on argumentation and not on the individual maximization of benefit. It is not only procedural because a democratic legal order (even with its limitations) should not be confused with the "logic" of the market. I have commented elsewhere on some of these important differences.[54]

It is not supposed, here, that the legal order is a "tool" in the hands of the dominant class, or the dominant group(s) of the dominant class. The supporters of this claim should have to show, *inter alia*, what "tool" means and how the so-called legal-political super-structure has no certain autonomy and, in the affirmative case, what "certain" means. Moreover, a democratic legal order cannot have a rational foundation only based on procedures, because it rests on a concrete conception of a human being that excludes an exclusively procedural foundation. My view is that any legal order has an ultimate justification (a given morality) that pervades the whole legal order and the adjudication process, although this pervasiveness is not the same in all branches of the legal order and in all legal conflicts. This more or less explicit moral code, that underlies any legal order, has (in a more or less explicit way) a certain conception of a human being and of a society, among other things. I cannot see how a strictly procedural conception of practical reason can do justice to any sound conception of human beings and their acting.

The legal order cannot go against (as a pragmatical requirement) this concrete conception of a human being that is on the basis of our legal orders. On the contrary, the legitimation of this order is based, *inter alia*, on the steps (legal, political, economical, etcetera) taken towards the fulfilment of these conceptions. That is why legal practical reason cannot be exclusively procedural. Legal procedures convey a certain content and this content cannot go against the basic tenets of these basic conceptions. How can this work though? First, on the basis of evaluative rationality. We, human beings, settle certain goals that deserve fulfilment. It is logically possible to settle goals and believe that they do not merit our efforts, although this is pragmatically irrelevant. However, we cannot put in motion evaluative rationality without a certain world conception.

Second, on the basis of practical rationality, that is, taking certain measures to reach the settled goals. However, not any mean is acceptable. A balance of reasons is required to decide when the economy of means should overcome the legitimacy of the means (or the reverse), granted the above underlying moral code. The decision is

---

[54] Urbina, S. "The latest Buchanan: Efficiency and Ethics", *Ratio Iuris*, December 1993, Volume 6, Number 3, pp. 339-349.

authoritative and it is a privileged reason for action, for the usual reasons: legal certainty and social co-ordination. Third, on the basis of methodological rationality because we, as rational human beings, "need" a justification. The justification can be logical, although this is not the most important one in legal normative fields.

Epistemic justification has the primacy in these fields. This means that we are interested in knowing what are the grounds, an addressee of the legal order has, for holding a legally relevant belief. What are the grounds? They differ according to different legal orders but legal orders have some authoritative sources. These are the basic grounds. If we look at the problem from a methodological positivistic view, we should stress must-sources and exclusionary reasons for action. From an Hermeneutic Analytic view, the importance of must sources and exclusionary reasons for action, understood as privileged sources and reasons, is not denied. Nevertheless, these reasons should be seen as defeasible.

The alternative is not between defeasible and non-defeasible reasons but between different levels of defeasibility or, in other words, different levels of entrenchment. Especially in our dynamic societies we, sometimes, cannot wait until the legislator's will gives us new exclusionary reasons for action, because some older ones are, now, obsolete. Competence with different reasons and with different types of balance between reasons can better help a sound adaptive change towards a new understanding of exclusionary reasons. This means that when the highest courts have reached a new interpretation of certain legal conflicts, this interpretation represents a set of exclusionary reasons that have a privileged status, although they are defeasible reasons. How long these exclusionary reasons will last, depends on many factors whose specific incidence and importance cannot be completely stated in advance. Nevertheless, legal certainty is not defended any better by claiming that these above commented reasons are absolutely entrenched reasons. This is useless and is not functional for our societal changing interests and our structural pluralism.

Tenth,

according to methodological legal positivism its most fundamental thesis (or one of its most fundamental theses) is that law is form, not content. However, if people of a given society believe (generally speaking) that law requires not only certain procedures but also certain material values or principles (let us say, equality before the law, with no discrimination for race, sex, etcetera), why is the reason for supporting that law only form? Do they mean that law is form in itself and, for this reason, it does not matter what people believe? It could though be something similar to the following: the earth is not flat even if some people believe so. Nevertheless, to apply this argument to law is not correct because law is not a physical object. Hence, why do they pay so little attention to what people believe? One advantage of the methodological positivist proposal would be the following: granted that any person (or nearly any person) has his own and different idea of what is morally good, law as form would have the advantage of giving legal certainty because form is perennial. Is it?

However, law is not like this misleading picture. We are not isolated monads but social individuals. We are socialized in certain language, values, traditions, etcetera. That is, there are social practices that create a kind of "ideological paste" that unifies (to a certain extent) different ideas and beliefs. It makes possible the existence of a positive and critical morality. Moreover, law is something that is expected to work. For doing so it needs to solve, in the best possible way, certain social conflicts. How can it be done by a legal form that dispenses with the morality of a given society? This would show several things: that law as form cannot solve the practical problems we have, and that law and legal dogmatics have to deal with values, not only describing them but making normative proposals and including values in legal argumentation.

This would show, once more, the distance between legal positivism and legal hermeneutics. One answer could be: law as form refers to the permanent features of legal orders. We, qua scientists, do not take any particular position because we are neutral. We do not deny the importance of morals, etcetera, but we just want to describe how a given legal order is. If this is the answer, I believe it would show a deep difference from a Hermeneutic-Analytic approach.

At least some Natural Law thinkers believe that the essence of law can be found in some concrete basic or natural values, while methodological positivists would believe that the essence of law is form. If they are interested in the working of legal orders how can they dispense with content? They seem to be neutral scientists who deal with necessity. But, which necessity? If it cannot be an empirical necessity, as seems to be the case, methodological positivists would be limited to logical necessity. Moreover, logical necessity would exclude rational justification that is linked to the possibility of choice from among several possibilities. At the same time, it means that truth as correspondence cannot be the concern of legal dogmatics.

Legal scholars systematize and describe the legal order but they do this task for normative reasons. Their aim is mainly practical and, like judges, they both share a participant's view. They want to know what is "correct", according to the main elements of the legal order that include, *inter alia*, deontological and consequentialist values. We then face a different view of human beings when adopting a positivistic methodological approach or when we adopt a Hermeneutic-Analytic approach. This implies an ontological option. In other words, they believe (in a Humean vein) that reason is able to describe facts or state the proper means to given ends. However, human reason has no motivating force. Therefore, what we ought to do depends on feelings or will. That is why the legislator's will has such an important role in positivistic approaches. Granted that human reason is unable to state what is "correct" (we cannot derive ought from is, and to derive ought from ought would be a *petitio principii*), we should rely on a sufficiently powerful will. Once we have this foundation, we are able to reach the only possible justice that can be reached, justice in the application of the law.

Eleventh,

we can make a list of the most important legal arguments, at least in the western world, such as the following: *a contrario*, *a simili*, *a fortiori* (including *a minori ad maius* and *a maiore ad minus*), *a completudine*, *a coherentia*, psychological, historical, *reductio ad absurdum*, teleological, economical, *ab exemplo*, systematic and naturalistic.[55] These are, probably, the most important legal arguments used by jurists in our legal context. What matters, here, is that lawyers and legal scholars do not use either empirical generalizations or mathematical method as main tools for fulfilling their task. The reason is that the aim of legal dogmatics is not to reach truth, if understood in a naturalistic or logical sense. The meaning of terms and sentences changes, as does also the social reality to which these interpretations and conclusions have to be applied. This is the realm of justification and judgement.

With the change of meanings there can be a change of evaluations and *vice versa*. Legal dogmatics have to mend, in a coherent and justificatory way, these sometimes incoherent legal pieces that shape a legal order. For example, badly articulated laws, because of the compromise of political parties, have to be the object of rational reconstruction, with one eye on values and the other on consequences. Legal dogmatics should try to give a systematic picture (not a cloning picture) of this complex and dynamic human enterprise that we call legal order. However, coherence alone is not enough. In this respect, if the legislator does not give new proper foundations (new must sources) to the existing legal order, in due course, judges and legal scholars would take the responsibility of "adapting" the legal order to new sufficiently justified social expectations.

Hence, if coherence goes "against" social life expectations it can collapse into internal perfection, unless it includes critical morality and social expectations. There is, then, an intertwinement between descriptive and normative tasks[56] in a similar

---

[55] The list of legal scholars dealing with this issue is too long. I will only refer to some prominent jurists such as: Ch. Perelman, G. Tarello and J. Wroblewski, along with many others.

[56] In relation to legal method and descriptive methodology, Mario Jori says, "Non mi pare fruttuoso, e probabilmente neppure possibile, tentare una metodologia esclusivamente descrittiva delle scienze sociali empiriche ... Per quanto riguarda la sienza giuridica avverto quindi che l'analisi che segue si svolgerá prevalentemente in base a considerazioni di carattere normativo ... gli argomenti di metodologia descrittiva, basatti sulla considerazione che i giuristi "effetivamente" parlano e operano in un certo modo, verrano sempre considerati come approsimativi, condizionati e problematici sul piano fattuale, e comunque sempre come argomenti non conclusivi." *Il Metodo Giuridico tra Scienza e Politica*, Giuffre, Milano 1976, page 45. Very briefly I want to stress that M. Jori has also said (with Anna Pintore), in 1988, "Per l'intanto è bebe osservare che quasi tutti questi problemi che abbiamo chiamato metodologici presuppongono la soluzione degli altri più fondamentali problemi metafisici de epistemologici ... Molto spesso infatti non é facile determinare la natura prescrittiva o descrittiva di un discorso sulla giurisprudenza." *Manuale di Teoria Generale del Diritto*, Giapichelli, Torino, pages 92 and 108.

In relation to method and ideology, Alvin W. Gouldner says, "Opposite the old traditionalism and the rising bourgeoisie, the new positivist sociology at first filled a liberating and rational function. It put in doubt the autocomprehension of all the elites, while it could not give them an "empirical" foundation ... The unavoidable paradox of the new social science was this: the sociology was constituted for the study of society and the profound power and influence of the objects that it studied stood out -the society, the groups, the social structures-, in order to later claim that their own investigations were free of prejudices derived from these same powerful influences." *La Dialéctica de la Ideología y la Tecnología*, Alianza Editorial, Madrid, 1978, pages 40 and 41.

In "On Method and Methodology", Z. Bankowski, N. MacCormick, R. Summers and J. Wroblewski state that, "Rational reconstruction aims at a descriptive account of normative material ... But the aim to produce a purely descriptive account can never be perfectly achieved. In terms of commitment, therefore, one has a necessary commitment to certain scholarly values and to a certain theoretical framework, as well as to a conception of the possibility of practical rationality in the implementation of norms and values. These commitments are essential to the work. But beyond that, a certain

way as it has been said that there is a link between formal logic and legal argumentation, as in the T. Viehweg approach or the Ch. Perelman rhetoric. In any case, a central problem of legal method is the rational control of legal decisions.

---

detachment is also essential." *Interpreting Statutes*, edited by N. MacCormick and R. Summers, Dartmouth, Aldershot, 1991, pages 21, 22 and 23. In my view, these comments show a mistaken view of legal dogmatics. Although claiming that it undertakes a descriptive task they also claim that there are evaluative commitments. In my opinion, this should be accepted as part of the task of legal dogmatics, not as a shameful defect.

In relation to his methodological conception, O. Weinberger says, "The thesis which I have here put forward leads to pluralism in scientific methodology -that is, the thesis that the means suitable for describing brute facts are as a matter of principle insufficient for the characterization of humanly conditioned facts ... Humanly conditioned facts cannot be adequately described without the use of practical concepts." N. MacCormick and O. Weiberger, *An Institutional Theory of Law*, Reidel, Dordrecht, 1986, pages 90 and 91. Nevertheless, I think N. MacCormick is clearer than O. Weinberger in this respect, when he claims, "I am not here denying the duality of "ought" and "is", *sollen* and *sein*, *devoir etre* and *etre*. But I am asserting the primacy of "ought", "*sollen*", "*devoir etre*"." page 103.

In relation to Hermeneutics and Methodology it is worth reading, *inter alia*, J. Habermas, *La Lógica de las Ciencias Sociales*, 1988, Tecnos, Madrid, especially chapter two; and T. MacCarthy, *La Teoria Critica de Jürgen Habermas*, Tecnos, Madrid, 1987, especially chapter three.

In relation to method and philosophy, R.J. Bernstein says, "What I find more objectionable in analytical philosophy is not precisely what analytical philosophers do -I have already stressed their importance- but the *ideology* that has surrounded this movement. In the early days of reductionist and conceptual analyses, an absolute conviction existed that for the "first time" the philosophers had found the correct method and approach to solve or dissolve all the philosophical problems. Both positions maintained the promise that in no time the work of philosophy would have finished and that this would have been due to its way of philosophising. We have already seen how empty these "promises" were. Although it would be difficult to find many of these "enthusiasts" around us, the ideology persists, and there are still active analytical philosophers that are convinced that their fundamental task consists of clarifying the confusions and tangles of others." *Praxis y Acción*, Alianza Universidad, Madrid, 1979, pages 319 and 320.

In relation to method and pluralism, Ernan McMullin says, "Our investigation has proceeded on two different levels. First, we have dealt with the different factors implied in the theoretical evaluation in Science: logical, historical-practical-metaphysical, conventional. Singling one of them out could give a "pure" position that tried to reduce the methodology only to that factor. In the second place, would be the different types of justification appropriate for the support of the methodological statements ... The "pure" positions, on both levels are rarely defensible; they exist mainly for dialectical and pedagogical uses. The really plausible views are the "mixed" or pluralistic ones, in which several types of factors or of justification appear and the problem that is created, then, is one more complex: to know how they should be harmonized." G. Radnitzky and others, *Progreso y Racionalidad en la Ciencia*, Alianza Universidad, Madrid, 1982, page 224. In a similar sense, M. Bunge, says, "Not many philosophers are responsible for the circulated fable, according to which the scientists use two well defined and standardized methods by means of which they can approach any problem of knowledge." *Intuición y Razón*, Tecnos, Madrid, 1986, page 92.

In relation to formalism and rational reconstruction, F. Fernández Buey says, "It does not deal with -Sacristín argued in 1968- ignoring or denying the positive efficacy of the formal methods in the analysis of society; this attitude has always been merely reactive and sterile. What it does deal with is to secure the motive for limitation of the formalisms for understanding the social phenomena. The lack of concretion for the concepts of mathematical nature is converted with great ease into ideologies designed to conceal, under the mere analogy, or at most, under the isomorphism of formal structural elements, the concrete diversity of historical-social contents. Formalism is a traditional sleight of hand route for social contents ... The rational reconstruction of scientific theories and the approximation to science methods are tasks that cannot do without the semantic, historical and sociological focus of behaviour, of language and of the values shared by real entities, visible and invisible colleges that perform the science." *La Ilusión del Método*, Edit. Crítica, Barcelona, 1991, pages 235 and 244.

Some jurists claim that if we cannot rest on deductive logic we are thrown into arbitrariness. We arrive at the old problem that pushes us to a tragic dilemma, either certainty or irrationality.

Nevertheless, we should put aside the imperialistic claims made in the name of the true method because, as Kuhn says,

> "There is no neutral algorithm for theory-choice, no systematic decision procedure which, properly applied, must lead each individual in the group to the same decision."[57]

I think we should remind ourselves that methodological positivists, at large, when referring to the problem of method are thinking of knowledge, while Hermeneuticians are thinking of what a rational agent can do in the best possible way, here and now. Nevertheless, I do not believe they reach knowledge in a non-trivial sense, if we define it (that is, propositional knowledge) as justified true belief.

As is known, Hermeneutic theories use the method of the hermeneutic circle. In this vein, we would reach understanding of a text, in our case a legal text, through a relationship between the whole and its parts. I think that this "whole" can be understood as a kind of ideal world, as a kind of horizon to be reached. If my interpretation is correct, George von Wright describes it much better:

> "Generally speaking: it can be said that a legal order and, similarly, any coherent code or normative system has the aim of what I propose to call an *ideal* state of affairs."

And he adds,

> "Granted that (nearly all) norms are norms of action, it seems reasonable to require that the ideal world a normative order aims at should be feasible, not only logically but also humanly."[58]

Although I expect it is clear, I would like to confirm my distance from communitarian views, although I know the differences between, let us say, Sandel, MacIntyre, Taylor, Walzer and the latest Rawls should be clarified. In any case, the complexity of the matter would require another work. I will just say, here, that the rejection of the God's eye view does not mean the acceptation of bare irrationality or the acceptance of our community decision as the last word. Neither communitarian nor individual fetish can properly deal with the complexities of our actions and interactions. If it were possible, it would be unjust because we are neither isolated monads nor clonic members of a flock. We are living in an unstable equilibrium, in many senses. In this context, I only have to mention four dichotomies, self-interest

---

[57] Bernstein, R.J. *Beyond Objectivism and Relativism: Science, Hermeneutics and Praxis*, University of Pennsylvania Press, Philadelphia, 1983, page 53.

In this vein, Luc J. Wintgens says " ... it could be said that in this sense method is an "institution of calculus" which guarantees the result when the appropriate facts are fed into the system. The method of legal science is not and cannot be such ... is not a mechanical process that follows from unambiguous rules. Literally, it is a matter of weighing and balancing." *The Law in Philosophical Perspectives*, op. cit., page 1. I expect that my view of legal method will not be understood as an institution of calculus, because I have, here, understood legal method as pertaining to Aristotelian tradition.

[58] von Wright, G. "Ser y Deber Ser". In: *La Normatividad del Derecho*, Gedisa, Barcelona, 1997, pages 98 and 99.

and moral values, individual-community, social-critical morality and brute-institutional facts.

We are not beings that only pertain to one of the sides of the dichotomies but to both. For example, we should be realists in relation to brute facts (although the objects, or the world, make sense within a given theory) but we should not be realists in relation to institutional facts, because we constitute them. In any case, we cannot avoid being members of both. This is one of the reasons why we have conflicts as a constituent element of our lives. Of course, not all conflicts have the same value for us. Some are destructive but others help us to strive for the best possible solution, here and now. This is the committed view of participants.

CHAPTER 2

ESSENTIALISM, CONVENTIONALISM AND PRIMACY

1. SHORT INTRODUCTION

I was lucky enough to meet Carlos Santiago Nino in Edinburgh, August 1989, at the World Congress of Legal and Social Philosophy. Unfortunately, I could only talk with him during the Congress but, as many others, I followed his work with much interest and intellectual respect. This chapter tries to show that the rejection of Essentialism does not necessarily lead to the admission of evaluative equality of all concepts and the admission of Conceptual Conventionalism, so understood. That could be so if concepts could just be evaluated "from inside" and had no sense of any external criticism. I will try to show that although there are no true concepts against false ones (at least in certain realms) there are concepts more relevant than others what would justify the acceptance of the concept of "Primacy" and the justification of the claim that there are "better" concepts of law than others, given the kind of reality of the law itself, that is, a reality predominantly normative and intentional, coercive and moral. I am not trying to expose Nino's thoughts because it would require much more than this chapter but I need to make a brief introduction of his opinion (given in 1985) about normative concepts of law in one of his most representative books (La validez del Derecho, Edit. Astrea, Buenos Aires, pages 187 to 195), given the importance that conceptual issues have in this work.

Nino says that in a justificatory context we need a concept that alludes to the existence of certain reasons and not to a mere supposition of other people that there are those reasons ... Finnis gives arguments in favour of a partially normative definition of "Law", like the one he upholds ... One argument (A) is that the internal point of view of the "reasonable" man constitutes the most relevant point of view faced with law "because only in that point of view is of utmost importance that law, differently from other forms of social control, materializes and so converts itself into an object of theoretical description." Another argument (B) is that the theoretician who studies the behaviour of some people cannot ignore the concepts that these people, when they are reasonable, have chosen to describe to themselves what is worth doing.

Another argument (C) of Finnis is that the theoretician, in the election of certain objects of research and in the identification of certain data, is oriented by evaluations and requirements of practical reasonableness. Nino adds the following comments. In relation to argument (A), that if the interest in materializing a phenomenon that can be the object of theoretical attention was relevant for the election of the point of view from which the concept has to be defined, for example, the notion of crime should be defined from the point of view of the criminals. In relation to argument (B), that is not convincing either, because although the social theoretician who studies certain behaviour cannot ignore the conceptualizations of the agents themselves, this does not mean that he has to adopt these concepts in the formulation of his statements ... in spite of the reasonableness or moral sensitivity of the individuals whose conduct is investigated, they can use inappropriate concepts for theoretical goals, especially when they use them with no theoretical intention, only a practical one, as happens with the use of a normative concept of law to justify actions.

In relation to argument (C), the current answer is that those evaluations need not be reflected in the characterization of theoretical concepts, for example, the fact that earthquakes are investigated for their disruptive effects on human life does not imply that "earthquake" has to be defined as a harmful phenomenon for persons ... the major obstacle to the thesis I try to defend in this essay is its completely obvious nature. Legal philosophers who have got rid of essentialist biases assume without hesitation a similar approach when dealing with the analysis of terms like "obligation", "right", etcetera ... yet it does not happen when dealing with the term "law" ... it is as if a last objection existed to abandon an absolutist approach in relation to the basic notion of the conceptual scheme that has to be reconstructed, a scheme whose singularity would give unity to the whole system of concepts.

Since this has only been a brief display of Nino's opinion about legal conceptual issues in the book cited, I will just add a few words on to the criticisms Nino made of Finnis. In relation to argument (C), I do not share Nino's view, because although it is not necessary from a logical point of view that evaluations be reflected in theoretical work it is normal that this happens from a practical point of view, at least in the normative realm; this problem will be dealt with in the following paragraphs. In relation to argument (B), if "to adopt" means to accept the internal point of view, the answer is negative. Probably this means that, without ignoring those concepts, the theoretician has no obligation to use them because they can be inappropriate or insufficient. But, even if this was the correct interpretation, if the participants use normative concepts and the theoretician only uses descriptive concepts, it is doubtful he can properly understand what the participants do and why. Nevertheless, this problem will be considered widely in the next paragraphs.

Finally, in relation to argument (A), Nino's criticism implies the denial of the relevant character (or primacy) of a normative concept of law and to defend the theoretical equality of the different conceptual schemes. This will be criticized in the following paragraphs. However, the example of the delinquent seems unfortunate. The delinquent is not the only one affected by the crime. Why should we not take into account the opinion of the victim and of the others affected? What sense would a "scientific" notion of crime have that would not care about either the beliefs or the interests of those affected by the crime? Moreover, the non-delinquents (at least generally) want to materialize either the absence of crimes or the punishment of them. On the other hand, the notion of "earthquake" is different. Here, the possible fury and suffering that those affected can feel is not part of the scientific notion of earthquake. The earthquake is not "responsible", it is the cause of the possible suffering. Methods in natural sciences and normative "sciences" are not interchangeable.

2. TRUE AND FALSE CONCEPTS

There is no problem to admit that,

> "Definition is now considered a linguistic operation through which: a) a new term is formally introduced in some system of signs, and, b) the meaning of the introduced term is specified, to some extent. The expression to be defined is called definiendum and the one that explains its meaning, definiens. As purposes or ends of definition the following five could be indicated: to increase the vocabulary, to eliminate ambiguity, to reduce vagueness, to explain theoretically or scientifically a concept and to influence attitudes."[1]

Nino seems ready to accept that some basic concepts of our conceptual scheme might not properly fit with a conventionalist attitude although he believes that this is not applicable to the concept of law. Therefore, this would be applicable to other concepts. Nino says:

> "Law's concept seems to be an emergent one between more basic others which can directly allude to properties made up of empirical laws: those of social practice, institution, coercion, prescription, obligation, legitimacy, justification, etc."[2]

But, how can it be maintained that the concept of legitimacy or justification or institution directly allude to properties made up of empirical laws? I think that something more should be said for the justification of that claim. Contrarily to the concepts mentioned by Nino I think that concepts like "toughness", for example, seem to allude directly to properties made up of empirical laws. Consequently, if the concept of "legitimacy" may directly allude to properties made up of empirical laws so can the concept of "Law".

However, to say that the concept of law is an emergent concept of more basic others, as already mentioned, is like supposing that "Faculty of Law", "Faculty of Biology", "Library", etcetera, would be basic concepts of a less basic and emergent concept that would be "University". Hence, it is not the case that "Law" is a less basic and emergent concept than the other ones mentioned by Nino since those concepts shape law's concept. If we join together all these concepts we are shaping the concept of "Law", in the same way as "Faculties", "Libraries", "Professors", "students", etcetera, shape the concept of "University". If this is correct it means that if those concepts are sufficiently basic then so is the concept of law because they interweave mutually. Hence, it would not be correct to claim, as Nino does, when referring to the concept of law:

> " ... neither seems to be a sufficiently basic concept as to be used in the conventional construction of many other concepts."[3]

My provisional claim is that the concept of law is a basic concept and, therefore, it would be, at least doubtful, to roughly apply a strict conventionalist conception. Hence, what I am saying is that we can deny "essentialism" and do not necessarily have to accept "conventionalism". This is for two reasons. One of which is not

---

[1] Iturralde Sesma, Victoria. *Lenguaje legal y sistema jurídico*, ed. Tecnos, Madrid, 1989, pag. 38.

[2] Nino, Carlos Santiago. *Derecho Moral y Politica*, Ariel Derecho, Barcelona, 1994, pag. 32.

[3] Nino, C., op. cit., pags. 31 and 32.

applicable, at least directly, to law, whereas the other is applicable. Nino formulates the first one when he says:

> " ... in natural sciences the sequence of theories about the structure of certain type of phenomena or natural objects cannot be explained on the basis of classificatory and conceptual conventionalism, because it would imply a mere change of meaning of a certain word -water, for example- and not a true scientific advance."[4]

Therefore, "Law" does not seem to be an appropriate object of natural sciences, since some of its relevant constituents are neither "water" or anything similar, what leads us to the second reason. Nino says:

> "We should be open to the possibility that the conventionalist explanation does not apply satisfactorily to, at least, some concepts. That is so in relationship to concepts that denote natural classes or that they are so basic in our conceptual scheme that seem to be unavoidable in the development of the internal point of view of conventions about other concepts. But this caution does not seem to be applicable to our handling of the concept of Law. This concept does not represent a natural class -whose properties are made up of natural laws- neither seems to be a concept sufficiently basic as to be used in the conventional construction of many other concepts."[5]

The underlining is mine.

The second reason is that, as I hope to show, the concept of law is a basic concept, one of the most basic concepts of our culture, of our form of life. Now, this does not mean that, like in natural sciences, the changes in the meaning of certain terms supposes the search for the "true" meaning. Hence, concepts are conventional creations (not arbitrary ones), at least within the realm of the so-called normative sciences and, concretely, in the so-called science of law, although the consequences I derive are not the same as Nino's.

From the adoption of a conventionalist view about the concept of law Nino outlines the following principles:

> "Firstly, the already mentioned of admitting a plurality, theoretically indefinite, of concepts or definitions of Law and related notions. Secondly, that of evaluating those concepts according to the purposes and necessities of the context of a given discourse. In third place, that of liberating legal philosophy from the heavy load of spurious controversies and paying attention to substantive issues ...".[6]

3. CONVENTIONALISM AND PRIMACY

Nino's first conclusion seems to me the less conflicting so that I will refer to the other three. In relation to the second conclusion, we should have to evaluate the concepts of law at issue according to the purposes and necessities of the context of the discourse. If this only means that there are not any true concepts as opposed to false ones, it is not a conflicting conclusion. But if it claims, as it seems, that all concepts are at the same evaluative level, taken for granted that they only have to be

---

[4] Nino, C., op. cit., pag. 31.

[5] Nino, C., op. cit., pags. 31 and 32.

[6] Nino, C., op. cit., pag. 34.

evaluated from their own purpose and necessity within a given context, then some problems may appear.

According to this plan, one concept of law is as "good" as any other. Hart's concept of law would be as good as Dworkin's, as Stucka's, as John Austin's. Moreover, we could just criticize them from the "inside". An external criticism would not be correct. We should say that Hart's concept of law, for example, is not "better" than Austin's because from the purposes and necessities of its context the internal coherence is as good in one case as in the other. Or that Carl Schmitt's concept is as "good" as Dworkin's. Taken for granted that it has no sense to claim that the concept of law (A) is "better" than the concept of law (B) we should limit ourselves to analysing the possible internal incoherence of each discourse. Internal coherence is, no doubt, a very important issue, especially in those discourses where truth as correspondence does not apply. But the question is whether this is all we can do and whether the rest would be metaphysics or spurious controversy.

I go next to Nino's third conclusion. This conclusion is a consequence of the former one. If each concept of law is an exclusive function of the purposes and necessities of their own discourse it has no sense to continue with spurious controversies that try to do something more than analyse the internal incoherence, daring to suppose something like commensurability of theories and trying to justify that one is "better" than another, that, however, is usually done by most, if not all, legal theorists.

The above leads us to the concept of "Primacy". This concept means that although there is not any true concept of law as opposed to other false ones, there are concepts that are more relevant than others, here and now, not only due to the context's own purposes but also to the characteristics of its own object. It does not seem correct to claim, as Nino does, that all concepts of law are evaluatively equal because, here and now, some things, but not others, are expected from law, and some of them have more intensity than others. If a concept of law faces, for example, solutions for conflicts that worry the citizenship, the justification of decisions of legal authorities, legitimacy of power, etcetera, it is, here and now, "better" than a concept of law that eludes those basic questions that worry the citizenship and that characterize, to a great extent, what is understood, here and now, by law (at least in certain cultures).

This links, in turn, with other presuppositions. To accept that it is important for a "good" concept of law to incorporate a normative reflection about the central worries of citizens (that they suppose that law can solve) or that it has sense to talk of "better and worse" solutions of conflicts. All this means that there is not any true concept of law compared to other false ones but that some concepts are more relevant than others given the type of complex reality law is and they are not exclusive from the internal purposes and necessities of the concept. A concept, such as the concept of law, has no previous external world to correspond to (as is supposed to happen with natural scientific theories), but an object built and rebuilt by individuals based on changing interests, needs and values. That is, the concept of law should be considered as a basic concept, *inter alia*, because it encompasses (although in different material and procedural ways) the protection and/or regulation of basic concepts like 'life', 'freedom', 'property', etcetera.

Nino's fourth conclusion refers to the work of conceptual elucidation, with the task to discuss substantive issues, adding that:

> " ... not only because of the possibility that there is not a radical difference between both enterprises under a Quinean view -but also because it is obvious that relevant conceptual distinctions come determined by certain hypothesis, principles or theories of substantive character."[7]

I would like to consider two aspects. The first one refers to the mention of Quine, and the second one to the substantive determinacy of conceptual distinctions. Firstly, as Nino himself suggests, we could take seriously Quine's thesis that the distinction between analytic and synthetic is a graded distinction, a relative difference. There would not be, then, a radical difference between analytic and synthetic and, furthermore, that distinction could only be formulated within the limits of a concrete system. The difficulties of neatly separating analytic and synthetic would justify a doubt about a tradition that goes back to Leibniz, Hume and logical positivism. Quine's thesis could lead us to admit that if "everyone" in a given society or cultural context accepts that law, in order to deserve that label, ought to be just, then that would be enough for the analyticity of "law and just". Of course, that analyticity should not be understood as something permanent unless "just" is understood only in a formal sense.

The former is connected with the second aspect. Can we establish a clear difference between conceptual and substantive issues, the latter being determinative of the former? In other words, if the formulated concepts are determined by certain hypotheses, principles or substantive theories, we should have to apply, again, a conventionalist view and say that those hypotheses, principles or theories could only be evaluated in the light of their own purposes and necessities. That is, no theory is better than another, no principle is better than another because only from "the inside" can a sensible reflection be carried out, although we would have serious difficulties in establishing clear boundaries between conceptual distinctions and the substantive theories that determine them. We would live in isolation, in a world of incommensurabilities.

According to Carnap, nothing bad can follow from the puzzling philosophical problems derived from asking external, instead of internal, questions to a given linguistic or conceptual frame. So much for the absurd and millennial controversy, according to Nino, among a large part of the best minds of western culture. But although they were misled in the vain search for the true concept, the controversy was spurious unless only debates within a given frame have sense. Effectively, although you can dig your garden in the vain search for a non-existent treasure, you, nevertheless, could have improved your garden.

In relation to ontological relativities and boundaries, Quine says:

> "Physical objects are conceptually imported ... as convenient intermediaries ... comparable epistemologically to the gods of Homer. For my part, I do ... believe in physical objects and the gods differ only in degree and not in kind ... The myth of physical objects is epistemologically superior to most in that it has proved more

---

[7] Nino, C., op. cit., pags. 34 and 35.

> efficacious than other myths as a device for working a manageable structure into the flux of experience."[8]

Then, would we say that law, understood as a physical object, is more efficient as an instrument for working out an operative structure in the flow of experience? We could ask, for example, whether the normative dimension of the planet Mars is more important than its scientific dimension. An answer could be the following: it depends. For a poet the evaluative-normative dimension would be more important and the scientific dimension would be more important for a scientist. This is the type of proposal that does not allow an external criticism. Something is good or bad in the light of exclusively internal purposes and necessities, either poetic or scientific. However, I believe that this is not correct. We can regret or not but the scientific discourse, at least in relation to physical objects, is a dominant one in our culture. It does not only dominate in this realm but it spreads out trying to invade all realms.

Probably, it has to do, *inter alia*, with the extension and influence of instrumental reason. Now, our object, "Law" is not a physical object but neither is it only a physical object or basically a physical object. Its relevance is placed on its normative and intentional dimension. The matter at issue is, does it affect the relevance of different perspectives that try to understand what law is and what it is for?

4. LAW AND MORALS, A USELESS DEBATE?

Nino faces the problem of the relationship between "Law and Morals" by saying:

> "But now, what matters is that there is not a true concept of Law against other false ones. Hence, the question whether there exists or not a conceptual relationship between Law and Morals, that has obsessed positivists and natural law thinkers, has no answer. There are concepts of Law that necessarily refer to extra-legal standards, which under certain conditions can be considered as morals. Moreover, there are other concepts which only designate factual properties and that do not refer to moral principles that constitute evaluative properties of the phenomenon identified as Law."[9]

The former leads to a central issue which has no answer and that, surprisingly, has worried the best thinkers for centuries. Nino's strategy seems to be that of claiming that there are concepts of law related to Morals and others that are not. From this the conclusion can follow that there is no conceptual relationship between "Law and Morals". When the problem is proposed like this, there is no doubt that Nino is right. Nevertheless, the possibility of the existence of different concepts of law is not discussed. For example, it is not under discussion that there can be paper and metal forks. There can be. The problem is whether some concepts are "better" than others. For example, if a cutting metal fork has "Primacy" (at least in our cultural world) over a "nice" or "very well designed" paper one.

If we just see the problem "from inside" none is better than the other and it could even be absurd to discuss it. If we see the problem "from outside", that is, the objective function of cutting meat, bread, etcetera, then the metal cutting fork is

---

[8] Quine, W. *From a logical point of view*, Cambridge, Mass, Harvard University Press, 1953, pag. 44.

[9] Nino, C., op. cit., pag. 44.

"better" than the paper one. I do not believe that it is necessary here to deal with the issues posed by Fuller as to whether or not the paper fork would be a fork or not. It is enough, now, to raise the issue of "Primacy" that tries to deny the evaluative equality of all concepts of law, once the denial of Essentialism is accepted.

Hence, it is clear that a non-normative concept of law can be formulated. The question is, then, whether all concepts are equally "good", taken for granted that they can be evaluated just from their own purposes and necessities or whether the characteristics of the object, law in this case, justify the relevance of certain concepts if law has to be properly understood. To pass from the claim that a plurality of concepts of law is equally justified to the claim that some of them are more relevant than others if law has to be properly understood I will use the approximative strategy to refer, firstly, to legal dogmatics and then to law.

Nino says:

> "I have tried to show in other works that this claim of legal dogmatics is a myth and does not correspond with what in reality is done. The methodological tools through which legal dogmatics tries to make the miracle to reformulate the legal system without introducing new rules in it, are spurious; they conceal the recourse to evaluative assumptions. The concealment, obviously not generally conscious, from the part of jurists it is done due to a typical duplicity of all tools used in descriptive terms or of conceptual analysis but really used normatively."[10]

In relation to legal dogmatics or legal science, either descriptive concepts or no descriptive concepts have been offered. So, we can accept that there is not a true concept of legal dogmatics or legal science and other false ones. We can accept that, taking Conventionalism for granted, we accept a plurality of concepts. But we again pose the same questions; Are concepts of legal dogmatics equally "good"? Does it depend exclusively on the purposes and needs of their own concept? Does external criticism have any sense?

5. IDENTIFICATION OF LAW; DESCRIPTION AND EVALUATION

Let us face a perplexity. Firstly, it happens that hundreds of distinguished thinkers become absorbed, through the centuries, in a spurious, absurd debate; secondly, hundreds of eminent thinkers deceive themselves for centuries, most of them unconsciously, because they believe they are using descriptive tools but, in reality, they assume a normative dimension. I think that this supports the thesis of the primacy of a normative concept of law. Instead of supposing a collective stupidity of our best thinkers or their naïve unconsciousness for centuries, we could suppose that the weight, the strength that the normative dimension has when we are dealing with a specific object, is law. This normative dimension revives itself "puzzlingly" even when the approach to the object is supposedly neutral, scientific and descriptive. We could ask ourselves why the concealment Nino talks about is "obviously not generally conscious"? Why the best thinkers of the Western World, for centuries, have not been conscious of that mixture or duplicity? Why doesn't the same problem apply to Physics or Chemistry? Is it due to the personal capacities of the

---

[10] Nino, C., op. cit., pag. 102.

physicists or chemists? Probably not. The characteristics of the object and its purposes are the main aspect, although they are neither taken "naturally" from the world or are arbitrarily imposed by individuals. In the case of law, the characteristics and purposes relate to an object placed in the world but whose causal connections are less important than its senses and purposes. Tides and volcanos present us with a "neutral world"; law does not. It is, then, wishful thinking to believe in a complete and neat separation between descriptive and evaluative language. The historical influence and pressure of the successful methods of science in legal dogmatics meant that legal scholars appeared to behave like "true scientists". However, the object and their characteristics have their own requirements, which are fulfilled openly or surreptitiously. Among these requirements we can identify the following: to decide cases with justice, which supposes a normative concept of law in which normative concepts such as "justice", "fairness", "justified decision", "rational acceptability", "underpinning reasons", *inter alia*, have primacy.

Before showing Nino's view about some of the most influential concepts of legal science and his critical opinion, let us have a closer look at descriptive concepts of law. Nino says:

> "By the way, the use of these latter concepts of Law, purely descriptive, does not imply that Law cannot be morally evaluated or that in the creation or application of Law moral evaluations are absent. It only supposes that when we identify a normative system as Law we are not necessarily evaluating it in moral terms."[11]

I believe that this is a central issue. I also believe that we can answer from Nino's own assumptions although in a different and more correct way as Nino does. I mean that it is not correct to claim that we can identify law from, as Nino says, purely descriptive concepts. Simply, with only purely descriptive concepts we cannot do that or we cannot do "well". If it is true that we cannot, what relevance might a purely descriptive concept of law have?

The answer can be found in Nino himself. To "identify" what law is we have to overcome the substantial indeterminacies of the language of law. That is, to discover the sense of the relevant materials, to surmount the semantic, syntactic and pragmatic indeterminacies, to infer logical consequences from the interpreted materials, to surmount logical indeterminacies and, finally, to subsume the concrete case under the rule. Nino says:

> "In synthesis, we have seen that in several moments of the transformation process from legal material to propositions, which underlies the causal process that links some legal materials to others, it is unavoidable to resort to extra-legal considerations, that is, principles that have the characteristics of what we call "morals"."[12]

Does this mean, perhaps, that one thing is what law "is" and the interpretation-application of law is another? But, how could we know what law is without interpreting it? Law is not an object whose function is to be contemplated like a Modigliani painting. Law is a complex object whose function, or at least one of its basic functions, is to resolve conflicts and solve problems of co-ordination with,

---

[11] Nino, C., op. cit., pag. 41.
[12] Nino, C., op. cit., pag. 99.

partially, positive and negative institutional sanctions. If this is so, interpretation-application tasks are necessary, not contingent, and they are inescapably evaluative. Hohwever, if they are inescapable, they form part of a concept of law in which this evaluative dimension has "Primacy", an evaluative dimension that Nino has shown in the process of overcoming the inevitable legal indeterminacies.

I take up again the reference to legal science. When Nino refers to the attempts to formulate a "scientific" legal science, he criticizes Kelsen and Ross with some final words for Alchourrón and Bulygin:

> "But these additions, although important, do not overcome the extreme modesty of an activity that works according to even this enriched model: because to replace a group of rules with some principles, that are more economical but strictly equivalent, is not always necessary and seldom possible. In relation to the inference of logical consequences of the rules of the system, as we saw, a "scientific" expertise is seldom required; in most cases it is so easy an operation that we actually do it unconsciously."[13]

I think we could extrapolate these opinions of Nino on legal science to the concept of law. A concept of law exclusively descriptive is an extremely modest concept. From here stems the "mystery" of many thinkers who, influenced historically by a determined concept of science and ideal of neutrality, elaborated concepts supposedly descriptive of law. However, they did not handle just descriptions, which is why the bitter debate has continued throughout the centuries, although this debate has not necessarily been false, spurious or absurd. The mistake was, probably, not being able to clarify sufficiently, at least in certain cases, the evaluative dimension of their conceptual apparatus, which was apparently just descriptive. The intellectual prestige that a supposedly pure descriptive work has provided, that is "authentic" scientific work, has facilitated the mistake.

6. INTERNAL POINT OF VIEW AND EXTERNAL POINT OF VIEW

Nino claims the logical primacy of the internal point of view (IPV) over the external point of view (EPV), which does not seem to fit with his defence of conceptual Conventionalism, where all concepts are equally good, because since they are just linguistic conventions they should only be valued from their own purposes and necessities. Now, we could say that claiming the logical primacy is something neutral. It seems true, simply, that if there are no persons supporting an IPV there cannot be persons developing an EPV.

Nevertheless, any IPV implies a moral conception and a moral justificatory apparatus. Does it mean that the logical and chronological primacy of the IPV has nothing to do with the primacy of the values of the IPV? Is it true that Nino carries on defending the evaluative equality of all concepts?

Let us see what he says:

> "A descriptive view of the discoursive practice in the modernity, coupled with the positive morality of several societies of the West, allows for an external perspective that can explain this practice as a causal product of certain historical developments (religious wars, for example) and, perhaps, as a functional mechanism to the needs of evolutive

[13] Nino, C., op. cit., pag. 109.

> adaptation. But, again, that cannot be done if the rules, procedures and values that constitute this practice and that constitute its internal aspect are not taken into account."[14]

Nino's claim is that the descriptive view "needs" to "take into account" rules, procedures and values that shape the IPV. But, what does it mean "to take into account"? Observing and describing? Let us briefly remember what a strong defender and co-creator of realism or authentic positivism claimed:

> "We could choose, perhaps, to look at the problem from the behaviorist point of view, limiting ourselves to what can be settled by external observation of actions and discovering, in so doing, certain regularities. But, in that way we would never know the rules of the game."[15]

Hence, to properly understand law, we cannot give "primacy" to the observation of rules, procedures and values, we have to give "primacy" to understanding them. This proper understanding of the IPV allows an understanding of the revitalizing mechanisms of the object, in this case a law. From an exclusively descriptive concept we obtain, at most, a still photo that does not take into account the time factor. But this object, law, makes no sense if we see it as something fixed. But this is the most purely descriptive concept we can aim for: either formalism if the account is to remain across time (as Ulpiano's maxims or Kelsenian analysis) or accurate (although never exhaustive) reproduction of something that will certainly be something different tomorrow, at least from a pragmatic point of view.

Hence, when Nino says that the descriptive view has to "take into account" this internal point of view he is using euphemism. It is not enough to take it into account, as the Ross quotation tries to show. We have to accept the primacy of the internal point of view or to accept the modesty of the intent, not necessarily of the author.[16]

In another central point, Nino does not seem to capture what I think are the correct conclusions. Once again he seems to be conditioned by the assumption of conceptual Conventionalism as a substitute for Essentialism. Nino says:

> "The thesis I am going to defend in the rest of the chapter is that this internal perspective is indissolubly linked to the internal perspective of morality and, especially, to the internal perspective of the discoursive practice that modernity has coupled with positive morality. If that is so, the external perspective of Law as a social practice becomes distorted if it is not explanatorily related this social practice with the social practice of moral discourse."[17]

If the internal perspective is unavoidably related to the internal perspective of morals, and if moral reasons are final reasons, how is it that the IPV only has logical

---

[14] Nino, C., op. cit., pag. 49.

[15] Alf Ross. *Sobre el Derecho y la Justicia*, ed. Universitaria de Buenos Aires, 1963, pag. 15.

[16] Something similar to the following: "Thus, the momentary legal system described in an essay of legal science consists of all the rule-ideas which (predictably) will influence the verbal behaviour of the officials of the community whose law is described (Theorem G). What is affirmed when a rule is said to be part of the law is that it is likely that a rule-idea with this content will spring up in the mind of some official (s) and he (they) will justify some decision (s) by a citation of the legislative material which caused the rule-idea." Harris, J.W. *Law and Legal Science*, Clarendon Press, Oxford, 1979, pag. 49.

[17] Nino, C., op. cit., pag. 50.

primacy over the EPV? But not only that. It is not only that the EPV is distorted if not related explanatorily with the IPV, it is that such a relationship is insufficient. This explanatory relationship is only able to show factual regularities and this is insufficient to develop a proper concept of law. At least, if "proper" or "correct" are meaningful. Hence, it is not only that in order not to distort a descriptive concept of law we have to describe the IPV, it is that this is insufficient, and for that matter "worse", in order to know what law is and how it functions.

Once more it seems that Nino does not extract those consequences from his own claims:

> " ... the capacity of law as a collective practice to produce efficient results in the furtherance of co-operation through other collective practices requires that law rests on moral convictions that constitute part of the positive morality of a society."[18]

In the same way as an object "that does not rest on moral convictions", such as the objects of Physics, has characteristically required the development of descriptive concepts, such as the "best ones", in the legal realm the object requires to rest, *inter alia*, on "moral convictions". Hence, it demands the primacy of normative concepts. It also means that not all concepts are equally valuable, but some are more valuable than others. That is not solely due to characteristics of particular linguistic conventions, but to the characteristics of the object. Once more we have to say that from the denial of Essentialism it is not necessary to pass to Conventionalism in which all concepts are equally valuable.

Nino's conclusion does not fit well with other parts of his own discourse, because it is a positivistic conclusion within which it would make no sense to talk of what is "better" in relation to evaluative issues, that would not be rational. What is "true" or, failing that, what is "better" in a supposedly neutral sense would move to the descriptive concept, which is the one with justified claims of authentic rationality. Nino tries to dissolve the debate by saying that both sides are wrong because they are searching for what does not exist, the true concept.

Nino also claims that the "descriptive-normative" concepts go beyond the distinction IPV and EPV. That is, the concepts of the first type would be primary because the distinction between IPV and EPV would be drawn from a descriptive or normative perspective.[19]

Now, what is problematic is another claim related to the earlier claim that we can only distinguish between IPV and EPV from a descriptive perspective. This would not be possible from a normative perspective. Nino says:

> "If we adopt, on the contrary, a normative concept of Law -denoting the group of standards that should be recognized- the external point of view facing to Law would appear not as the perspective of an observer, which is irrelevant from the point of view of the participants, but as the situation of those who act -falling into our conclusions about which standards ought to be recognized and applied- without themselves bearing in mind reasons for or against the recognition of those standards."[20]

---

[18] Nino, C., op. cit., pag. 157.
[19] Nino, C., op. cit., pag. 43.
[20] Nino, C., op. cit., pag. 44.

To properly understand, Nino seems to think that there are two types of agents, those who act sharing the basic justificatory criteria and those who act without sharing them. These types would be grasped by the IPV, but a third type would exist, the observer. This observer does not act because if he does he would be inserted into one of the two categories. It is a strange situation that would only be detectable from a descriptive perspective. I think that this approach from Nino would be applicable to an anthropologist who would visit a primitive tribe. This supposes that there is a minority in that tribe that does not share the basic justificatory criteria and we would therefore have the three types.

Now, the anthropologist (observer) would be able to distinguish between the IPV (those who share the basic justificatory criteria) and EPV (those who don't) through his descriptive activity. Nevertheless, the members of the tribe who share the basic justificatory criteria would only be able to distinguish between themselves and those who act without sharing the basic justificatory criteria (who represent the EPV). Namely, in the EPV they would not include the observer (the anthropologist) because he would be irrelevant from the participant's perspective.

For a normative concept of law the agents that matter are those who act according to a given law (whether they share the basic justificatory criteria or not). But it does seem to be a logical impossibility for a participant sharing the cited criteria to define the EPV as; (1) those who act according to a given law but do not share the basic justificatory criteria, and, as (2) those visitors who limit themselves to observing from the fringes or making brief incursions just to observe. The problem is not that they have some logical impediment, but that they are irrelevant for the understanding of the working of a given law because they do not participate. Why should they be interested in them?

Now, it is possible that a member of the tribe is a passionate follower of the descriptivist thesis, and decides to elaborate a descriptive concept of law. What changes will happen? He will describe (because it is not logically impossible) some members as sharing the basic justificatory criteria and others as not sharing them and will say that, from time to time, some strange observers, without any participation, limit themselves to observing the two types already mentioned. What does the descriptive inclusion of those non participating observers add for the understanding of a given law? Why should we rely on their description, given that the object is not merely physical but basically normative and intentional? In what sense would the description of a non participating observer be important for the understanding of a given law by the participants?

How important is it that, from a normative concept of law, the external observation of law, that is, that of the non-participating observer, is not equally perceived? I think that it is not very important. That is why, once more, I uphold the primacy of normative concepts of law in the sense that they are "better" to understand and justify its meaning, its working and ends. Conceptual clarification is a central task of philosophical reflection but it is not the only one. That is why the concern for the linguistic frame, as if it made sense in itself as an autonomous world, has always generated philosophical dissatisfaction. Furthermore, conceptual clarification has fuzzy boundaries with conceptual revision. Both may imply, and often do, a conceptual criticism, which has developed more flexible or rigid attitudes in relation to the problem of limits. In this respect, I do not believe in the existence of convincing algorithms except for those that are convinced in advance.

If that is correct, Nino's criticism of a supposedly scientific neutrality of legal dogmatics would be correct, but not his belief in the spurious and useless character of an ancient debate. The debate between positivism and natural law doctrines or positivism and non-positivism has developed a clarification, revision and criticism of basic concepts. In this long history, the fact that some -or many- were searching for the true concept has a relative importance. Now, once conceptual fundamentalism is abandoned, nothing prevents conceptual collaboration, because "primacy" does not entail a complete conditioning of the other concepts.

7. A NEW INTERPRETATION

Nino's conception can be interpreted in a different way than it has been interpreted so far. If we bear in mind not only the book considered so far, Derecho, Moral y Politica, but also, La validez del Derecho and Fundamentos de Derecho Constitucional, we could reach the conclusion that Nino did not think that "conventionalism" meant that any concept is as good as any other, but that there are two basic types of discourse that should be considered, descriptive discourse (that of the observer) and normative discourse (that of the participant). "Conventionalism" would mean that there is not a unique concept of valid law independently of the context mentioned earlier and that those concepts are equally good if they correctly capture the type of discourse they try to show. Finally, the discourse of the participant would have a logical priority over the discourse of the observer.

Supposing that this is the most correct, or simply the correct, interpretation of Nino's thoughts, I believe that we can equally reach the same conclusion, namely, the "Primacy" (and not mere logical priority) of the concept of law of the participant over the observer's point of view.

Let us repeat some distinctions. In the first place, it seems convenient to distinguish between the point of view of the "participant" and the point of view of the "theoretician". There are two basic types of participant, the "normative participant" and the "consequentialist participant". The first type makes, predominantly although not exclusively a claim of correctness in relation to a given legal system. His behaviour, in relation to that system, is conditioned predominantly for this claim of correctness. He is especially sensitive to arguments that refer to what is "just" or "correct" or "bad" or "incorrect", although he does not reject reflection about the consequences. Only a fanatical deontological attitude would reject a consideration of the consequences but these consequences are not determinant if they collide with what is just, at least in principle.

A different case is that of the "consequentialist participant". His attitude is predominantly conditioned by the consequences that can be derived from his interaction with the legal system. The claim of correctness is secondary, in the sense that an external attitude follower of that claim of correctness would be derived from a favourable calculus of consequences, whether they are immediate or not. This is independent from the fact that his calculations are correct. Although there are many ways of knowing the others, one is -falsely- a participant as they all are, the important question is that he is hiding his true feelings because he supposes that while living among normative participants it will be better for him to make others believe that he is not a consequentialist participant, and he therefore acts accordingly.

In the second place, it would be convenient to distinguish between two basic types of "theoretician". On the one hand, the theoretician who tries to describe regularities of behaviour, the regularities of behaviour of the participants, or tries to describe the psychological motivations of the participants which supposedly provoke (interacting with other variables) certain regularities of conduct.

On the other hand, the theoretician who tries to understand and justify certain normative practices of the normative participants and of the consequentialist participants able to deceive the theoretician, in so far as his external attitude does not really correspond with his internal attitude although it is wrongly perceived by others. So then, it seems to me that the most interesting conceptual apparatuses are those elaborated by these two types of theoreticians already mentioned, independently of the possibility that the participants could elaborate conceptual apparatuses because they, at least normally, would "use" but not "mention" the legal language.

The consequentialist participant would "use" it, in so far as the other participants would believe that he is really using it and acting accordingly, recognizing him as another normative participant. This is so because the behaviour of the normative participant, his claim of correctness and related concepts, has primacy. I will not deal here with the question of the relations between the consequentialist participant and other consequentialists. In any case, it is not that the theoretician has some special and privileged view when compared with the middle man but he is usually more able to clarify relations or certain relations, certain concepts used by the participants, etcetera.

If it is accepted that the conceptual apparatus of the "descriptive theoretician" and the "justificatory theoretician" are the most interesting ones for our ends, we should identify their main characteristics and whether they allow us to conclude that, given the special object, law, one of these conceptual apparatuses has "Primacy" and not merely logical priority. We have already said that it is not the case that there is one true conceptual apparatus.

One of the founders of legal positivism, Jeremy Bentham, accepted that the simple exposition of law is not sufficient and that it must be accompanied by reasons that would give law a certain degree of coherence which, in turn, would foster the reasonable expectations of addressees. Another point, although of less interest here, is that he believed that justificatory reasons of law were not law. What is important now is that, from the first, it is difficult to establish a clear and sharp distinction between the descriptive (expository) realm and the normative realm. At the same time, this positivist attitude is indebted to the separation between two different worlds, the world of will (or the products of will) and the cognitive world. The first refers to the normative aspect and the second refers to the descriptive aspect.

Nevertheless, the claim of a conceptual descriptive apparatus, *tout court*, contrasted with a conceptual normative apparatus, is wrong. If positivist approaches, in general, and Kelsen's in particular (although he modified some of his views) have tried to supersede a legal reflection based, *inter alia*, on justice (volitive aspect), for a legal reflection based on truth and coherence (cognitive aspect), will it not affect the supposedly descriptive neutrality? Will it not shape the object? Is it the case that the legal positivist reflection just describes the object in a neutral and aseptic way? Does it not select? Does it describe "all"? Is there any impartial observer?

The claim that there is a correspondence between a statement and a fact, and that the statement is true when it corresponds with that fact, is far from clear. First, to claim that a certain statement is true (in that sense) means or usually means that it has fulfilled the truth conditions "we" have settled. However, can we claim that there is an equivalence between them? Are the true statements and the fact to which they relate really the same? And, if it is not the case that they are equivalent, how great and how important is the difference or differences between them? Furthermore, should we state, in a P.F. Strawson vein, that one thing is a "fact" (which would be the pseudo-material correlation of a statement) and another a "thing" (which would be the material correlation), rejecting the identification between a fact and a true statement? Also, which theory of truth (or criteria) should we decide is applicable to what we are talking about?

I am not trying to expound any of the existing theories of truth but to show some problems of the supposedly neutral description of facts. Nevertheless, I believe that as well as "truth-false", we should use other concepts such as "rational acceptability", "justified decision" and others, taking into consideration the characteristics of the object (law) and the goals it tries to fulfil and the problems it tries to solve.

A neutral and aseptic description of unconnected "facts" seems to have little sense (at least when the object is the law) and for that reason facts are arranged in "practices". But, how can facts be properly arranged around a practice if the basic rationality of this practice, (its "point" or "rationale") is not properly understood? The facts related to law cannot be arranged according to their weight or length, so that we need to come up with evaluations and purposes. All this implies justificatory reasons in answer to questions such as the following: Why? With what justification? For which purpose?, etcetera. A descriptive conceptual apparatus always arrives late because before it is possible that the normative participant has to build "the facts" that allow for an observation (which would justify the logical priority).

However, furthermore, when it does arrive to address the "built facts" they may have changed again. This is so because a fundamental element of the interaction between normative participants and the legal system is a continuous effort to reach "the best interpretation", which is linked to a claim of correctness. This is not reached, at least practically, just by describing "what exists" (if that even makes sense from an exclusively descriptive point of view) but through a reflective and critical process of adaptation of the law, which is an endless process. For doing that we need, *inter alia*, besides a legal system and committed participants, a background of shared ideas that are not necessarily peaceable, such as freedom, equality, dignity, autonomy, certain forms of concern for others, certain forms of distribution of wealth and resources, etcetera.

The descriptive conceptual apparatus neither elaborates nor re-elaborates. It does not make an effort of adaptation to reach the "best interpretation", here and now. Nevertheless, this is indispensable for the proper working of a legal system. A descriptive conceptual apparatus does not face the problems that most matter to the participants of the legal system. That is why the conceptual apparatus of the normative participants (within which we may include the theoreticians) has "Primacy", although it is not the true one. It has Primacy because it is indispensable to understand a given law properly (as a normative-intentional construction that regulates the most -or some- important aspects of societal life) and because it is indispensable for a proper working of the legal system, which implies a reflective and critical effort of adaptation. This cannot be done by a descriptive approach that is, then, neither sufficient nor determinant, taking for granted that the legal realm does not face only empirical facts but institutional facts and regulative principles as well. The latter are those which better allow the continuous effort of adaptation and achievement of the "best solution" to be understood and justified, here and now.

The concept of rationality linked to both the Cartesian tradition and also Leibniz, among others, believes it is able to obtain "certainty" by searching, for example, for solid foundations from which it can be deduced, without error, an indeterminate number of inferences. In fact, certain positivists and natural law thinkers follow this approach. Another concept of rationality, linked to Montaigne, Erasmus of Rotterdam and others, does not believe that we will be able to reach "certainty" although this would not signify that we renounce rationality. The position of some authors that believed they were able to achieve "certainty" was called, ironically, the God's eye view. In relation to this, there is a conception of the language derived from Plato, called essentialism, which believes the significance of words is determined by reality. Therefore, a unique and true significance would exist for the language expression. J.L. Borges says ironically:

> "Yes the name is the reflection of the thing, as the Greek says in the Cratilo, in the letters of "rose" is the rose, and all the Nile in the word "Nile".

Nino says that there is not one God's eye view but there are two and that one view is as good as the other if they do their job well. I think that once we reject the absolutist views and accept a kind of knowledge that, at least in part, depends on the context (in this case the legal one) then one of the perspectives has Primacy. In a similar way as the prescriptive aspect of moral sentences has primacy over the descriptive aspects, if we want to understand them properly.

CHAPTER 3

IDENTIFICATION OF LEGAL ORDERS

In this chapter I try to show several problems that a legal positivist method has when dealing with the identification of legal orders. I take for granted that there are both different views within the legal positivist trend and also some underlying basic features. I will begin dealing with J.W. Harris's work, Law and Legal Science: An inquiry into the concepts of Legal Rule and Legal System. I do so because this is a worthwhile contribution having, among other virtues, a depth and clearness that are lacking in some other works. Nevertheless, Harris's work is an excuse, although a good excuse, for dealing with this and other related problems.

1. A FIRST OBJECTION TO THE IDENTIFICATION OF LEGAL ORDERS

1.1 Sentence Tokens and Sentence Types

In relation to the identification issue, Harris says,

> "Two kinds of objection have been raised to the view that legal systems may be identified by reference to a source-listing rule. The first argues that such a view makes it impossible to identify as separate systems those systems which have emerged, without breach in constitutional continuity, from other systems."[1]

The core of this objection is that the identification must be based on "officials" recognition, not on a list of sources. Harris recognizes the importance of this recognition, although it could be a mistaken view because it ignores the basic value of constitutionality. What does this value mean? He says,

> "The value of constitutionality directs them to apply rules originating in the right sources (that is, rules subsumable under particular constitutional source-rules)."[2]

First of all, it can be convenient to settle a difference between a "legal order" and a "legal system". I would say that the first concept refers to the language of the legislator and the second concept refers to a metalanguage, usually used by legal scholars. This second step is not a contingent one because the legal order is not a consistent field of meaning. At least from a pragmatical point of view we can claim that this is never so, although it is logically possible. Thus, a second step is required. This step transforms the existing legal order into a "better" legal order if the elimination of gaps, antinomies, *inter alia*, can be considered as an improvement of the one given by the legislator.[3] For the moment though it is enough to say that the

---

[1] Harris, J.W. "Law and Legal Science". *An Inquiry into the Concepts Legal Rule and Legal System*, Clarendon Press, Oxford, 1979, page 73.

[2] Ibidem, page 74.

[3] Aarnio, A. *The Rational as Reasonable*, Reidel Publishing Company, Dordrecht, 1987, pages 147-149. He says, "The pre-theoretical view (PT) and the systematization theory (ST) are two different ways of systematizing the legal order. When we add to this the interaction between the systematization theory

reformulation of the legal order, as given by the legislator, is a necessary task (to be undertaken by legal scholars or not), at least from a pragmatical point of view.

Harris's answer is based on the distinction between "choose" and "to be bound". He claims officials do not choose to do what has been said about the value of constitutionality but that they are bound to do so. Harris accepts (or so it seems) that officials usually accept the right sources and apply the right rules, fulfilling (in so doing) the value of constitutionality because they are bound to recognize these sources and rules. The key concept is "to be bound". However, what does it mean? I believe that we can understand it, basically, in three dimensions. First, officials are bound to certain sources and rules because they like them. Second, officials are bound to certain sources and rules because they believe it is convenient for them. Third, officials are bound to certain sources and rules because they believe this is right, in a moral sense. In fact, we can paraphrase these sentences into the following: First, I do it because I like it. Second, I do it because it is convenient. Third, I do it because it is morally right.

If we apply Moore's open question to the above sentences, by taking "good" in its ethical sense, we could ask: First, you do it because you like it but is it good? Second, you do it because it is convenient for you but is it good? We need not apply the same question to the third because moral reasons are ultimate reasons, which is different from what happens with instrumental and prudential reasons, at least in our cultural contexts. What consequences could the recognition of moral reasons have as ultimate reasons?

Harris's tendency (as legal positivists in general) has been to keep morals apart because, in the tradition of Bentham and others, positivists defend a conceptual separation between law and morals. In a similar vein, Kelsenian tradition believes that legal science must only neutrally describe the legal system as it is, not as it ought to be. In this respect let us see how Harris understands the issue of "wrong sources". When referring to officials and the value of constitutionality he says,

> "It requires them to exclude rules originating in the wrong sources."[4]

However, here "wrong" is not a moral wrong. Nevertheless, would there be any difference if we took "wrong" in a moral sense instead of a technical or a prudential sense?

I believe that the answer to this question should be related to the so-called internal point of view. Very briefly, Harris criticizes Hart's view of this concept because it would be situated midway between a rule-situation (a social situation in which a certain pattern of behaviour is regarded as a standard) and a rule-idea (the psychological occurrence represented by an internalized normative assertion about behaviour, coupled with a positive or negative imperative stimulus). However, I do not intend to deal here with any Hart-Harris discussion. I will suppose though that

---

and interpretation, the replacing system (Sj) of necessity receives a different content than does the basic system (Sb) ... This activity is "creative" in a more profound sense than Alchourrón and Bulygin allow ... If one restricts the meaning content of the term "systematization" to the "logical" reformulation only, one also cuts off the possibility to analyse the very complex procedure of system formulation."

[4] Harris, J.W. *Law and Legal Science* ... op. cit, page 74.

the internal point of view is the view of the participant, not the observer. I also suppose that participants behave in certain ways because of certain reasons and interests and that this behaviour is, in principle, distinguishable from the observer's point of view. I accept that an observer could behave as a participant for several reasons and not be "seen" by the other members of the community as an observer. Although this is an interesting question, I am again not going to deal with it here.

What I want to emphasize is that certain behaviour (the participant's) normally supposes a reflective and critical attitude. On the contrary to Ross, I do not believe that this can happen in revolutionary situations or in ordinary life. I think that the emotive dimension and the propaganda effects are over-emphasized in revolutionary situations and it is very difficult to have a reflective and critical attitude, especially in these contexts. This does not mean than in ordinary life it is an easy task but, especially in peaceful and democratic contexts, it is easier. Going back to the concept of "to be bound", what I claim is that either from a sociological point of view or from a normative point of view, moral reasons are ultimate reasons. If this is correct, the right approach to the identification of legal systems cannot set aside moral reasons, *inter alia*, because justification of decisions is a basic value, which is even usually included as a generic constitutional duty, as in article 120 of the Spanish Constitution ("Legal decisions will always be grounded ...").

The next step is to scrutinize whether the identification of legal systems needs argumentation and justification. If what should be identified are normative texts, what can be identified are certain syntactic features of certain sentences established by certain authorities, through certain procedures. Nevertheless, if what should be identified are meaning contents, because meaning contents can direct human behaviour, then, what is needed is to scrutinize the accepted meaning of a certain normative text, at a certain time, by a given community.[5] Nevertheless, we should also bear in mind the difference between a legal order before interpretation and the "same" legal order after its interpretation. In this respect we can say that what is more important is to identify (in a given legal order) not only sentence types but sentence tokens, although the legal interpreters need a certain support (sentence types) for justifying a certain sentence token.

In other words, any meaning content must be a meaning of "something" that originally stems (and it is, supposedly, an instance of) from an authoritative source. That is, there is an intertwinement between sentence types (as an abstract meaning for a class of cases) and sentence tokens as the dynamic element that formulates, here and now, an instance of a given sentence type. This instance can become a sentence type, if a certain speech act is put into a text, for example, and it is subsequently accepted by the legal community. However, the acceptation cannot be understood as a factual acceptation but as a rational and justified one, granted that the members (or the majority) of the community share an internal point of view. This would also show that there is no private language because, in this case, we would not know whether there was any correction or not. In any case, some sentence

[5] In this respect, Aleksander Peczenik distinguishes between *prima facie* Law and all things considered Law. *Law and Reason*, Kluwer Academic Publishers, Dordrecht, 1989, especially chapter V.

token will be accepted as the correct one, granted that legal certainty is an important value for the legal community.

Nevertheless, this "something" is not necessarily the normative text posited by the legislator. Suppose a given interpretation of a certain normative text has been accepted as the proper one by the legal community at a given time. When this is the case the new possible modifications of its meaning content are modifications of this meaning content, not of the normative text. Hence, the static element is the normative text and the dynamic elements are the different meaning contents that a given normative text may have, as a result of different interpretations. These last sentence tokens are constituents of the jurist's language and of the legal order in force, provided they are accepted by the legal community. However, I will not deal now with the question of momentary and non-momentary legal systems.

In the identification of legal orders we have to distinguish between *ex ante* identification and *ex post* identification. We can identify a given legal order *ex ante* if we try to show which normative texts belong to this legal order. Nevertheless, this is insufficient because we deal with working and dynamic legal orders and it means, *inter alia*, that we have to identify not only the valid normative texts (validity in a formal sense) but also the accepted meaning contents. The latter can be done *ex post*, once there have been legal interpretations and once there has been an acceptation of them by the legal community. Then, these new interpretations will work (*ceteris paribus*) as if they were the plain meaning of the authoritative legal normative texts. This means that a descriptive approach can tell us *ex ante* which are the sentence types that form a legal order, although it cannot do so for the sentence tokens as well. For this, we have to wait until interpretation is undertaken.

One could say that jurists, in general, and judges, in particular, ought to apply the letter of the law but even if we accept it there are difficulties, although there are strong justificatory reasons for applying what democratic legislatures have stated. The main problem, not the only one, is that a literal interpretation of the law could lead us to absurdity or injustice, according a certain interpretation of the values of the legal order at stake. In this respect, *reductio ad absurdum* is usually understood in the following sense: the judge (supposedly sharing an internal point of view) supposes that the legislator is a reasonable person and would not accept an interpretation leading to absurdity (logical or not) or injustice.

Again, the identification of a legal order needs argumentation and justification. Why? Because, at least in our cultural context, the main justification of the existence of legal orders is to guide basic aspects of our behaviour and reach certain levels of order and justice. Therefore, argumentation and justification are needed because, *inter alia*, we do not always know precisely what the legal authority expects the citizens ought to do when issuing certain normative texts. The legal community proposes new legal meaning contents through argumentation and justification. Some of these legal proposals will succeed, whereas others will not. Although the meaning content is an accepted interpretation of normative texts (with the preciseness already commented on), in some cases what jurists do is something different, although in a wider sense they are also doing the same: trying to optimise, in a justified manner, the legal order.

I refer to those cases that are usually called axiological gaps, where the ideology of jurists, or internal points of view to my mind, pushes them to empty a certain meaning content of a normative text because of axiological reasons. The empty space is then filled by another meaning content that is different from the original one for that normative text, according to the supposed purpose(s) of the legislator or the *ratio legis* (the supposedly objective sense of the law). At this point another interesting question arises; is there a proper meaning content for a given normative text or not? If we accept that meaning contents are not simply discovered, then, we have to choose them (although not at random), even if we are bound to the value of constitutionality. That is to say, as participants, we have to argue and justify within the realm of a given legal order and a given legal tradition.

If this were correct, the situation would be the following: we do not discover but we assign meaning contents, although there are limits, unless we accept complete arbitrariness. These limits are basically of two kinds: direct limits and indirect limits. The former are those settled by the legal authorities or those accepted by the legal community. For this reason, in a particular legal community, certain meaning contents will not be accepted. The community in general though accepts the ideology of submission to the legislative language and understands that certain meaning contents are acceptable and others are not. There is not necessarily any unanimity, especially because there is no unique paradigm in legal realms and because of the open texture of legal language. The indirect limits are those rooted in ourselves, as members of a given culture, a given historical context or a given legal tradition. The result is that, although we choose the meaning content, we assign it to normative texts in a reflective, not fanciful, way.

If this is correct, we need argumentation and justification as necessary conditions (although not sufficient ones) for identifying a legal order. The next step is to recall that in this reasoning process, moral reasons are ultimate reasons. Again, can we set aside moral reasons when trying to identify a legal order? When Harris said that officials do not simply choose to use certain sources and rules as participants but they had justification for them, because they were bound to the value of constitutionality, he is setting aside moral reasons, probably because he accepts the conceptual separation between law and morals. Consequently, the question is whether we can know what a given legal order is without this ultimate justification. If we cannot, it means that legal reasons need the support of moral reasons and the latter are not necessarily meaning contents of the legislator's will that convey certain moral contents, although legal speech acts in a wider sense. In some cases, as with certain moral values positively incorporated into the Constitution of the United States, we can see it more explicitly. Of course, it is possible that the legislator's will imposes a certain moral content, so I need to mention here that, according to a known legal positivist like Hart, one of the differences between law and morals is that the latter cannot be changed at will.

When I claim that we cannot know the content of a legal order if we set aside, *inter alia*, moral reasons, I am claiming that a descriptive approach (typically a legal positivistic one) is a necessary, but insufficient, condition to know its content. Why? For the moment I would just say that, even sophisticated legal positivistic approaches like Hart's accept judges' discretion. Although this can be interpreted in different ways I claim that we cannot know in advance the legal content of these legal problems submitted to judges' discretion and, hence, we cannot describe the new settled legal "is". We can describe it once it has been stated though. However, in order to do so a previous constructive task is needed, at least if the judges are to behave as participants. Then, the identification of a given legal order is a partial identification.

Only a super-human jurist could describe, within a given time, the whole legal meaning content in force. The description is not even complete in natural sciences. However, in legal realms there is a permanent interaction between the subject (legislators, judges, lawyers and citizens), the legal object (a field of meaning) and the global society where both interplay. None of these three elements though are static. The subjects have changing and conflicting preferences, in order to resume a variety of possibilities in one word. In addition, the field of meaning is not a static object to be repeated only because it would be useless, at least for practical purposes, and the global society (especially our post-industrial one) is not an example of permanence but is where individual and group conflicting interests and ideologies interplay.

Nevertheless, another move could be taken. Following a Kelsenian trend we could claim that law is form and form is permanence, whereas content is contingency. If we want a scientific approach and a scientific identification for legal orders we have to look at form, because form remains and content changes. A non-contingent object would give us the possibility of a scientific approach. This option has certain similarities with Kirchmann's view, although he supported an empirical approach, which is not the case with many legal positivists, except, perhaps, for Scandinavian realism. If this was the option though, some comments could be made. In this vein Harris says,

> "The internal structural elements of each positive legal rule, it will be argued, are three in number; the act-situation which is the subject of the duty or exception from duty, an ought or may deontic operator, and the specification of the conditions under which the duty or exception from duty exists. A fourth structural element of a statement describing a positive legal rule is the specification of its source."[6]

Even accepting that these formal features are intrinsic features of legal systems, they are not enough to identify the normative field of meaning for a given legal system. As legal scholars, for example, we should say what is the content of this normative field of meaning and on reaching this answer we have, *inter alia*, to interpret the build "units" (i.e. the legal rules), using Harris's terminology. Nevertheless, this is not just a descriptive task. Harris himself says,

> "The description of the legal duties which exist at the time of writing is the primary, but not the only (and often not the most interesting), function of legal science. It is, however, crucial for an understanding of the intellectual processes of legal science that the descriptive function should be differentiated as clearly as possible from these various critical functions."[7]

---

[6] Harris, J.W. *Law and Legal Science*, op. cit., pages 20-21.

[7] Ibidem, page 21.

Contrary to Harris, I will suppose that legal dogmatics is both descriptive and normative. This idea of the scientific neutrality of legal dogmatics is a dream that probably stems from Bacon methodology and it follows on through logical positivism with the idea, *inter alia*, that only sentences that can be verified would have sense. It does not matter whether Carnap later proposed a weaker criterion because of Popper's criticisms, *inter alia*. One of the basic ideas that influence some legal scholars, even today, is that there are firm foundations. While empiricism believes that science rests on experience, which is understood as sense data, the given, etcetera, thus allowing for a firm foundation on which to build our knowledge, in legal realms we have a firm foundation (i.e. form), which supports the structural features that will show the "essence" of a given reality. It is not by chance that logical positivism emphasized the syntactic dimension of language related to the idea that philosophy is logical analysis.

Since it is taken for granted here that legal dogmatics is not only a descriptive task and that description is never complete, I will deal with a related question, namely, the tendency of legal positivist trends to sharply separate conceptual and empirical issues or to sharply separate normative and sociological issues. Personally, I think that both views are wrong. In this respect, some legal philosophers have tried to distance themselves from what is supposed to be Scilla and Caribdis. On the one hand, there is normativism, whereas on the other hand, there is realism or sociologism. Nevertheless, even if we accept that proper positivist legal dogmatics is placed in a middle ground between these two theoretical flaws, two questions remain: First, what does a middle ground between normativism and realism mean? In as far as these views are related to the analytic-synthetic distinction, there is no middle ground between them, according to the empiricists themselves; Second, could this be a question of method instead of middle ground position? I also suppose that, in legal realms, the normative point of view has precedence over the descriptive point of view.[8] Although physicalism seems officially out of date, its shadow is still cast over many fields trying to equalize any object under the same method and the same language.

1.2 Subsumable Legal Rules: Logical and Implicit Consequences

When dealing with the problem of structure Harris defines the Basic Legal Science Fiat as follows,

> "Legal duties exist only if imposed (and not excepted) by rules originating in the following sources: ... or by rules subsumable under such rules."[9]

This is not his complete definition but, for the moment, I am only interested in this particular part because he talks of "subsumable rules". I will assume that subsumable rules can be placed under two labels. On the one hand, logically derived rules and, on the other hand, implicitly derived rules. These are both derived because

[8] In this respect, see my paper "Essentialism, Conventionalism and Primacy", *Ratio Iuris*, 10, volume 4, 1997.

[9] Harris, J.W., op. cit., page 70.

they are consequences of explicit rules proclaimed by the legal authorities in force. The authority of Kelsen can lead us, at least to a certain extent, to highlight the problem briefly.

On the one hand, we have static systems with the behaviour they cover being due to their content. The foundation of validity is a rule whose content is accepted as immediately evident (which is absurd according to Kelsen, because it implies the existence of practical reason). On the other hand, we have dynamic systems. Here, the foundation of validity says nothing about content, since it just tells us how legal rules can be produced validly. These hypothetical rules will be members of this system if they have been produced according to the procedures stipulated indirectly by the basic norm. Kelsen also tells us that both principles, the static and the dynamic ones, can be unified in the same normative system when both operations take place. In other words, there is a delegation of power to produce norms and there is a formulation of rules ordering the addressees of certain behaviour. He also claims that, from these latter rules, new rules can be deduced by logical operations.

Firstly, we can see whether new rules can be deduced from certain other rules, with the latter being explicitly posited. Although I will not follow Kelsen I need to take his example. He says that from the norm of Christ to "love others", a huge amount of concrete moral norms can be deduced. This seems to be true. For instance, it can be deduced that I ought to love Peter or Mary if I have accepted that I ought to love others. However, even if "others" refers to the addressees of a specific legal order, does it mean that I ought to love equally all "others"? Granted that to know whether I love another person I have to do something (or perhaps to forbear doing something), does it mean that I ought to love all others doing exactly the same things? Is it expected of me to love equally my son and his murderer? It seems that neither the dynamic principle nor the static principle can tell the addressees what they ought to do, unless they are treated as clonic beings. Moreover, logical relations seem to belong to the interpreted norms, not to normative texts. If this is correct, before logical inferences could be made, we would need interpretation, with all its "problems", such as argumentation, justification, morals, that is, practical reason as ultimate reasons, etcetera.

Let us see, first, how an argument can fail. One of the ways in which an argument can fail is when one of its premises, at least, is false. Here is an example. P1: All legal philosophers are positivists; P2: Each positivist is a truth-teller; C: All legal philosophers are truth-tellers. Nevertheless, we can say that at least one of the premises is false. Let us say that it is "all legal philosophers are positivists". Here the reasoning is deductively valid because the logical inference is correct. Let us now outline a usual legal reasoning. P1: All persons with characteristic (ch) ought to pay (p) to (h). P2: Each person who is a legal philosopher has characteristic (ch). C: All legal philosophers ought to pay (p) to (h).

Now, in which sense can we claim that one or both premises are false? Can we decide it logically? It seems not. Furthermore, which is the object of logical reasoning, the sentence or the thought of it? Granted that the same thought or proposition can be formulated in different sentences it seems that what matters most is the thought itself. However, how can we reach it? By means of interpretation. In our case, by means of legal interpretation. Is legal interpretation a logical reasoning?

It is not, although when we have a given decision we can reconstruct, logically, the pathway already taken. Moreover, the thought that represents a given sentence or a given normative text is not "the thought" but a justified thought, and it is a justified thought, *inter alia*, because a specific legal community has supported it by more or less complex reasons.

I know that positivist tradition, in general, prefers to move from one piece of language to another and arrive at true or false conclusions, without human contamination. This view has usually, among other sources, rested on the idea that there are firm foundations, even if we take Minimal Foundationalism as the most defensible of the varieties of Foundationalism. Very briefly, Minimal Foundationalism says that whether a belief is in the foundation or not, depends not on its content, but on how it receives its justification. If it is justified by perceptual experience it is a basic belief. At the same time, it is denied that non-doxastic beliefs (that do not receive justification from other beliefs) have a privileged epistemic status. They claim that they receive their justification only through experience, since they are non-doxastically justified. The other beliefs would be doxastically justified because they receive their justification from other beliefs, which is different from the former.

Nevertheless, to step away from basic beliefs with a privileged epistemic status and the acceptation of Minimal Foundationalism also has its problems. This is because it is usually accepted that a basic belief does not receive justification from other beliefs but it is justified by perception, reason, introspection or memory. This means that we may have many basic beliefs. From very selective, privileged and firm beliefs we have passed to a crowded field of basic beliefs. Even more, it is now accepted that some basic beliefs are justified by introspection or reason. Does it mean that there are more dangers for sharp distinctions between conceptual and empirical realms? I believe so, but now I want to emphasize that, contrarily to positivist tradition, I suppose here that social practices and concrete audiences are constitutive elements (not external) of the game of justification, more specifically of the game of legal justification.

This alternative view does not draw strict lines of division between philosophy and science because, *inter alia*, neither beliefs have firm foundations nor are they timeless and uncontaminated but they are dependent (although not mechanically determined) on historical context. Although some of these views have a Quinean stance I do not agree with Quine on the idea that the aim of justification is scientific explanation. However, I do agree with him on the idea that justification cannot be the old crusade for certainty anymore and that the gap between sensory experiences and our beliefs about the outer world cannot be fulfilled by a kind of new physicalist language, that only picks up sensory experiences (which have to be based on previous theories) and nothing more. This means, again, the rejection of the sharp distinction between conceptual and empirical issues.

One way to deal with implicit legal rules is to deny them. Implicit legal rules do not exist because they are not norms, which are understood as the meaning content someone gives to a normative text. Without a given normative text produced by an authoritative speech act there cannot be legal norms. The problem, therefore, seems to be whether there can be norms, in the already mentioned sense, without a corresponding legal normative text. Here there seems to be, at least, two problems. On the one hand, there would be a certain ideology that not only understands norms exist without corresponding normative texts, but also believes that a legal order is not a finished product from the legislators. On the other hand, the ideology exists that a legal order is a finished product of the legislators, because even accepting their logical consequences as legal products means that they are a necessary consequence.

In relation to the first ideology, it is possible to accept the second part, that legal orders are not finished products of the legislators, but not to accept the first part, that there are norms without a corresponding normative text. Suppose there is a certain normative text (NT) in time one, and suppose that a given interpretation (i) has been accepted by the legal community as the interpretation that expresses (NT) in time one. Now suppose that, in time two, the accepted interpretation of the same (NT) is (ii). We can say, therefore, what happens is that (NT) can be interpreted in several alternative ways in different times.

However, what does this mean? First, a given (NT) has different alternative meanings inside it and it is, let us say, expected that jurists discover these alternative meanings according to different interpretations. Second, a given (NT) does not have different alternative meanings inside it but the indeterminacy of natural languages makes it possible to interpret them in different ways that are limited, *inter alia*, by the legal traditions and basic values of the legal order. There are more possibilities but I am limiting myself to these two because I think they are the most important, at least from a pragmatical point of view. If we reject the first possibility because it supposes a kind of magic bottomless well, that favours the value of legal certainty, at least understood in a formalistic manner, we can accept the second (although not necessarily). If we accept the second alternative we can have different meaning contents through time, supposedly taken from the same (NT).

The enormous richness of a certain short (NT), that is, short in length, can be suspicious. To avoid this suspicion we could accept that these different meaning contents of the same (NT) are not extracted from a given sentence type, our (NT). However, sometimes certain jurists, when they believe that the accepted legal meaning content does not satisfy legal-social expectations anymore, propose a new meaning content. They do so with one eye on the (NT) and the other on the legal-social expectations, values and reasons. The first eye looks at legal certainty (in the sense already commented on), whereas the other eye looks at the justice of the case. Can we always claim, sensibly, that all meaning contents are expressions of the same (NT)? If they were not, are they foreign elements of the legal order? To which extent are different meaning contents norms of the same (NT)? Are they so because it is a kind of stipulative definition that all accepted interpretations of normative texts for a given legal order are norms of this order?

If legal classifications are neither true nor false but more or less helpful, I think a narrower view of the problem, that allows for explicit and implicit norms, is more useful in the following sense. A norm is explicit when competent jurists of a given legal community have no doubts about what is the meaning content of a given (NT) from a given legal order; a norm is implicit when this is not the case. Consequently, competent jurists would have to look for justifications of different interpretations, bearing in mind, basically, the values of that legal order and the accepted consequences, either by the legal order or by the addressees, or both. They will have to look for coherence too, that is, to see whether this specific interpretation corresponds to the cited values and/or consequences. If this new interpretation (Ni) is accepted by the legal community, a possible future implicit norm will be based, *inter alia*, on this (Ni) norm.

Nevertheless, the practical jurist will cite the (NT) because it gives a greater sensation of legal certainty and because of the acceptation of the principle of separation of powers. The legal positivist ideology tends to deny the existence of implicit norms because they give, in practice, a power to jurists (or certain jurists) to produce norms. The legal post-positivist ideology tends to accept implicit norms because it sees legal orders as unfinished constructing enterprises, where not only legislators but also citizens, (especially the legal community) participate. There are though, certainly, more differences.

1.3 Acceptable and Non Acceptable Contradictions

In the previous note we saw the first part of the Basic Legal Science Fiat and we shall now deal with the second part. Harris says,

> "Provided that any contradiction between rules originating in different sources shall be resolved according to the following ranking amongst sources: ... and provided that no other contradiction shall be admitted to exist."[10]

We shall see, first, whether any ranking of sources is able to solve any contradiction. Second, we shall see whether all contradictions can be solved by means of logic and, if the answer is negative, how practical reasoning and metalegal standards can be avoided.

It is of interest to see what M. Jori-Pintore says when referring to the chronological, hierarchical and speciality criteria,

> "Those criteria do not always solve the problems because there are contradictions to whom no criteria can be applied (for example, a contradiction between two norms of the same time, both general and of the same level) or more criteria can be applied because those criteria conflict among themselves (for example, a contradiction between a special norm of lower level and a general norm or higher level; in this case hierarchical and speciality criteria conflict with each other)."[11]

It seems that there are contradictions, and the metanorms established to solve these contradictions are not able to do so, at least completely. The remaining problem is that, at least from a pragmatical point of view, these problems have to be solved. However, they are not completely solved by the authoritative settled criteria. Can they be solved by logical means? In this respect R. Guastini says,

> "Logic -it is usually said- is not applicable to norms (sentences that are neither true nor false) but only to propositions (sentences true or false) ... It has no sense to apply the notion of contradiction to those sentences that truthfulness and falseness are not applicable. It follows that two antinomic norms -for example: "You can smoke" and

---

[10] Ibidem, page 70.

[11] Jori-Pintore, M. *Manuale di teoria general del diritto*, Giapichelli editore, Torino, 1988, page 195.

> "You cannot smoke"- conflict with each other but, properly speaking, they do not "contradict" each other because being norms it has no sense to claim that one is "true" and the other "false"'".[12]

It can be accepted that the antinomic problems between norms cannot be solved by logical means. Likewise, we have already seen that the metalegal criteria are also unable to solve all these problems. Therefore, how can we identify the norms of a given legal order? We could state a validity judgement and say, for example, that a given norm such as "You can smoke" is valid and the norm "You cannot smoke" is also valid. Validity judgements would not be logical judgements and, hence, a given legal order could consider "You can smoke" and "You cannot smoke" both valid norms. Nevertheless, from a pragmatical point of view it is not very important whether a given legal order can consider "You can smoke" and "You cannot smoke" as both valid norms, because citizens cannot really both smoke and not smoke at the same time.

What matters here, is to know how we can identify a given legal order. Granted that in real legal orders there are contradictions (at least from a pragmatical point of view) and granted that we cannot know, *ex ante*, the precise content of a legal order (at least completely), we have to appeal to interpretation. After the interpretation and once a given interpretation has been accepted by a legal community as the correct one, we can know the content of normative texts, whether they have contradictory meaning contents or not. In easy cases we can see it immediately. Nevertheless, our legal tradition does not seem to accept two norms, such as "you can smoke" and "you cannot smoke", because of their pragmatical contradiction. In any case, if interpretation is not a contingent task of legal orders, can we always avoid metalegal standards?

Let us briefly see whether interpretation can avoid metalegal standards. If it cannot be avoided and interpretation is needed, to know the meaning contents of the normative texts, means that to identify the legal system, interpretation and metalegal standards are needed. I will not deal at length with interpretation because it is not the object of this chapter. I will just try to show that we cannot avoid metalegal interferences. As C.S. Nino says,

> "The task of assigning meaning to linguistic acts, texts and practices is an evaluative step, a very complex and controversial one".

In addition, when referring to the task of assigning preference to certain legal materials that are expressions of the legislator's intention, he says,

> "The option to give preference to some legal materials over others is based on evaluative considerations ...".

Finally he says,

> "... without appealing to evaluative principles we cannot choose between two or more contradictory norms, fill a gap, select the sense of a expression or of an ambiguous

---

[12] Guastini-Comanducci, *Analisi e Diritto*. "Richerche di Giurisprudenza Analitica", Giapichelli editore, Torino, 1991, page 187, note 20.

syntactic connection or fix the limit of applicability of an expression, really or potentially vague."[13]

It seems that, according to some legal philosophers, we cannot use logical means to deal with deontic sentences because they do not have true-false values. Furthermore, if it is true that legal science has both descriptive and normative tasks (and we cannot clearly and sharply separate them) it will also be the case that we cannot rely on logical means, at least as the unique or privileged rationality, to deal with legal dogmatics. Are we, then, in the realm of will, arbitrariness and feelings?

1.4 Norms and the So-Called Legal Science

It can be accepted, following R. Guastini,[14] that legal dogmatics, as one possibility, describe norms and thereby assign them validity. However, this would be wrong, he says, because two norms can be both valid or invalid and, as a result, the validity judgements can be both true or false. To avoid this possibility of two contradictory sentences being both true or false, we have to put aside the idea that validity judgements are deontic sentences that repeat the syntax of the norms. According to Guastini, there are some other possibilities for legal science: it describes norms in the sense of normative texts, while at the same time interpreting them; it describes the framework of the possible interpretations; it describes the different interpretations already made; it describes the only true meaning.

In my view, the most important thing, here, are the consequences he assumes. As a result, so called legal science is referred to as a normative science because norms can only be described through deontic sentences. I also believe that legal science is a normative science but I do not see why it too cannot be described. The idea seems to be that indicative sentences are able to describe facts but are unable to describe norms. Therefore, we need to look at what a description is and what a fact is.

Let us take, as a first step, the view that proposals such as Searle's or Austin's, etcetera, unduly try to widen the entities of the world with no need. For this reason, Guastini[15] uses Occam's razor against the idea of "brute facts" plus "institutional facts", because the world is made of "*tout court*" facts. Some believe, unduly and magically, that words can modify the ontic status of the world. Now, we have to see whether someone knows in advance what the ontic status of the world is or, whether we first need "words" (i.e. theories) in order to know what it is. If this is the case, and we cannot know the ontic status of the world *ex ante*, that is, if we cannot know the world without previous "words", the claim that Occam's razor is needed could be reopened. We have to see, also, whether there is a privileged object that can be properly described or not. The first step would be to see whether there is such an object, or whether we can know "facts" (*tout court*), as the only inhabitants of the

---

[13] Nino, Carlos. *Derecho, Moral y Politica*, Ariel Derecho, Barcelona, 1994, pages 88, 90 and 95.

[14] Guastini, Riccardo. *Dalle Fonti a le Norme*, Giapichelli editore, Torino, 1990, pages 55 and ff. Another view of legal dogmatics, among a wide literature, can be seen in, A. Aarnio, *The Rational as Reasonable*, op. cit., especially pages 17 and ff.; C. Alchourrón and E. Bulygin, *Introducción a la Metodologia de las Ciencias Juridicas y Sociales*, de. Astrea, B. Aires, 1974.

[15] Guastini, Riccardo. *Lezioni sul linguaggio giuridico*, Giapichelli editore, Torino, 1985, pages 25 and ff.

world, granted that we (human beings) are not facts (or at least not in the same sense) because, if so, how could we know them?

Empiricists' trends, in general, have searched for a rational justification of the possibility of knowledge and for certainty. Generally speaking, they believe that through the senses we can know the truth of reality, that is, how things are. George Moore (the supporter of the common sense view) tried to show reality itself by holding up his hand and saying something like "I am certain of its existence." Consequently, we may have problems with the list of things that are supposedly certain, although, in case we agree, is this a proper method to define certainty? If we adopt perception, as the privileged method of empiricism, it is said that we can know the facts of the so-called external world. Nevertheless, we know these supposed "*tout court*" facts indirectly because they affect our sensory organs and they may lead to us having an experience. If this is so, we have no direct perception. Should we say then that we see certain effects of certain sensory organs? In the affirmative case we would see certain effects, although we would not see the fact itself.

At this stage, we could ask whether we see facts as physical objects and whether we are able to describe them, let us say, from outside. A different view is that these physical objects are not seen or scrutinized in an isolated or detached way, but in a contextual one (no matter how difficult it can be to settle its limits) and that we do not perceive "*tout court*" facts independently of ourselves. In addition, "ourselves" is not a container of separate atoms in their respective cocoons. At least the claim that there is something previous to any understanding, to any public cultural scheme, could be doubted, as is usual in empiricist and legal positivist fields. Although someone calls it "fact" and someone calls it "the given", what is common is the idea that there are sensory experiences in themselves. It is usually supposed, at least in these fields, that descriptive statements describing "the given" are true or false depending on whether they describe the world as it is or not.

These sharp lines between "the given" and its description (that can be true or false), on the one hand, and what we state about "created facts", on the other, (neither true nor false and not apt for a proper description), sometimes conceal a search for a safe starting point. Namely, "the given", etcetera. This search for a safe starting point is a search for firm foundations on which we can build our building of certainties, differently from other pseudo-buildings which would be full of will, feelings, etcetera, not of the proper reason. In these pseudo-buildings there are objects that are not made of the same material of which the world is made. Here, these objects cannot be said to be true or false, they cannot be properly described, because we can only describe what can be true or false. For example, "you can smoke" and "you cannot smoke" (at the same time) are not contradictory because those sentences are neither true nor false. However, a completely different example is given by, "it is raining" and (at the same time) "it is not raining". Nevertheless, even if we accept these examples, is it all so clear cut?

In this respect N. Rescher says,

> "Innovation of the side of data can generate new theories, and new theories can transform the very meaning of the old data. This dialectical process of successive

feedback has no inherent limits, and suffices of itself to underwrite a prospect of ongoing innovation in the study of nature."[16]

Here we have a question that I will deal with, which is, namely, the intertwining of facts and concepts. In the style of Carnap it can be said that there is no sense to pose "external questions" because it only makes sense to pose "internal questions". In other words, once we have decided (not necessarily arbitrarily) to accept a certain framework (an ontological framework) we can ask sensible questions within it. What has been said has connections with some legal positivists' trends.[17] Consequently, once we accept (not necessarily arbitrarily) a specific ontological framework, a given legal system, we can sensibly pose questions within it.

For example, we can frame a sensible question such as, "Is it fair according to a given legal order to torture Jews or Palestinians?" The sensible answer would begin, "According to this legal order ...". Nevertheless, there are persons with no scientific attitude (according to some legal positivistic minds) who dare to ask questions such as, "Is it just to torture a person whether they be Jew, Palestinian or not?" In any case, does it mean that we are just dealing (in the mentioned cases) with a semantic dimension? Does it mean that we do not have any ontological commitment? If we observe the reality (although a "grubby reality" in a methodological sense) on which these semantic conventionalities are based, we have to scrutinize whether they are well founded or not. At least some legal positivists' trends believe that to talk of "well founded" only has sense in relation to ontic facts, the given, etcetera.

Unfortunately, the linguistic framework of the legal realm is founded on "institutional facts" and these are considered to be pseudo-facts, *inter alia*, because we cannot claim them to be true or false. We shall see whether "well founded" pushes some legal positivist minds towards foundationalism or, better still, some kind of foundationalism. However, firstly, let us explore the intertwining between facts and concepts, and secondly, the related question of description. Thirdly, the issue of foundationalism will be addressed.

1.5 Facts and Concepts

In relation to the issue of facts and concepts N. Rescher says,

> "One of the most basic lessons of modern epistemology is that the available observational data underdetermine theories ... . Accordingly, theories transcend data and reach beyond them, so that there is always an evidential gap between the claims of a theory and the particular facts that afforded its supporting data ... . The experiential realities determine and canalize the work of theorizing reason but they cannot impose altogether unique resolutions upon it."[18]

---

[16] Rescher, Nicholas. *Satisfying reason*, Kluwer, Dordrecht, 1995, page 49.

[17] For the versions of legal positivism you can see, among other works, Guastini, Riccardo, *Dalle Fonti alle Norme*, op. cit, page 278 ff.

[18] Rescher, N., op. cit., pages 32 and 33. In relation to the problems of facts the following can be seen among an extensive literature; J. Wroblewski, *The Judicial Application of Law*, Kluwer, 1992; A. Aarnio, "On the Interpretation of Facts", *Communication and Cognition*, Vol. 28, Nr 1 (1995), pages 77-86.

It seems, then, that not only Dworkin was wrong by expecting the unique right answer in normative fields. Some believe that he was wrong because in the field of practical reason there is no reason at all, only will, and, therefore, there is no cognitive field and no right answer. Although they were not upset because there was another field, the field of facts, the given, "*tout court*" facts, etcetera, that could give us truth, if properly described. In other words, the one right answer.

Nevertheless, this is not a safe hope. This mode of thinking lies in the Great Division between truth, that we know by experience, and truth we can know by reflection. In this respect, we should bear in mind two considerations. First, the above distinction is not a distinction between necessity and contingency, since it is not the case that what we know by experience is necessary and what we know by reflection is contingent. Although, briefly, we should bear in mind two different kinds of necessity, logical and physical. The latter tells us what is possible physically speaking, while the former tells us that, if something is not contradictory, it is possible. To order a limited period of one second for presenting a remedy to the Court of Appeal is not illogical. From the point of view of logic there is no problem, from the point of view of practical reason it is absurd. However, according to some legal positivists, practical reason is no reason at all.

Nevertheless, are those items that can be described as true or false, only contradictory? If the legislator orders, "drive to the right" and (at the same time) "drive to the left", should we say that it is as contradictory as ordering, "drive on the right on Monday, Tuesday, Wednesday and drive on the left on Thursday, Friday, Saturday and Sunday?" The concept of contradiction, particularly when it is used in normative fields, has to be taken from common usage. This does not mean, however, that concepts should repeat what common usage says but that any withdrawal from this common usage should be properly justified. This would be so because concepts (especially in normative legal fields) have some specific purposes, *inter alia*, to co-ordinate social action, to solve certain conflicts and to punish certain behaviours. Second, we cannot claim that a given belief is true by a direct confrontation with reality, "the given", etcetera. Some may have, here, the metaphysical dream of supposing that we can observe "from outside" and, in that way, be able to make neutral and complete descriptions of the true inhabitants of the world, that is, "*tout court*" facts.

As N. Rescher puts it,

> "And we can never have unalloyed confidence in the definitiveness of our data base or in the adequacy of our theoretical exploitation of it; there is clearly good reason why no finite body of observations -however large- can ever settle decisively just what the laws of nature are. In consequence, our best wrought scientific theories are transitory."[19]

Therefore, it is not only that "the given" or true facts cannot be neutrally and completely described from outside, it is also that concepts are not built as has been seen usually from empiricist (or at least some) trends. In other words, it is not the case that we make many particular observations and then reach a concept, because the identification of something particular (a particular cat, for example) is, at the

[19] Rescher, N., op. cit., page 57.

same time, an acceptation of certain generalizations. Why? Because we always start from a given culture, we never start from scratch. Consequently, it is not the case that we start, as firm foundations, from a neutral description of "the given" and afterwards are able to build a solid building of truths.

In the same way, while sentence tokens are particulars, concepts are sentence types, that is, they are abstract objects that have instances. In this sense, concepts try to clarify what people have in common or what is the common usage. It is not a psychological inquiry. Nevertheless, even after philosophical scrutiny, many usual concepts (and many legal concepts are practically everyday concepts) have a certain vagueness, although this is not inconvenient enough for them to work properly. Even if we accept that concepts have related generalizations of the form "All A's are B" (normally having qualifications of the type "provided that X is present"), it is not the case that we can put all these generalizations in clearly differentiated pigeonholes. In a Quinean vein, we can tell that these generalizations should be considered as part of a continuum. If this is correct we cannot claim that we have a clear-cut map of the world. On the one hand, there is truth-description-contradiction, etcetera, whereas on the other hand, will, feelings, emotions and the rest.

The old search for the essence, or indubitable truth, is an incorrect extrapolation of mathematical knowledge. When I talk of "essence" I am referring either to the "material essence" of Natural Law thinking or to the "formal essence" of Legal Positivistic thinking. Nevertheless, nowadays essentialist approaches have been watered down. When searching for a definition of the concept of law, Jori-Pintore agrees that we cannot dispense with philosophical elections,

> "First step consists in the selection and the use of a common sense concept of Law, to individualize the legal field, at least in a rough way; this first step is, as it is usually said, "meta-legal or meta-positive". The second step consists in the acceptation of the criteria of self-limitation and self-definition of the posited Law that can be found in different societies, according to common sense criteria."[20]

Some legal positivist tendencies try to place themselves rather in a middle ground between, let us say, pure prescriptive and pure sociological grounds. It seems that this imprecise middle ground has certain analogies with M. Weber's methodology. He draws a sharp distinction between matters of fact and matters of value, between description and prescription. Although he rightly saw that empirical science cannot properly grasp all dimensions of society. We needed, he said, an "understanding explanation". It seems clear that in the definition of the concept of law, commented on above, there are "spurious" ideological aspects. Does this mean therefore that, once this "mixed" step has been undertaken, legal dogmatics will be able to undertake a neutral and descriptive task? If that was the case I would agree with C.S. Nino in the poorness (at least for practical purposes) of those models of legal dogmatics (sometimes called legal science) undertaken by very important legal philosophers of at least some legal positivist tendencies.

[20] Jori-Pintore, M. *Manuale di teoria general del diritto*, op. cit., page 35.

1.6 Description and Truth

The view of description I will criticize is based on the Great Divide, as has already been commented on. To start with, let us water down the claim that descriptive statements are true statements, the only ones able to be called true or false. As Toulmin-Baier says,

> "... there is no end to the number of things we might put into a description of anything. So we ordinarily contrast a complete description with an uncompleted, unfinished one. Sometimes, it is true, we may be asked, "Have you completed your description?" or "Is this a complete description?" meaning not "Have you finished saying what you intend to say?" but "Have you included all the relevant information you know?" or "Have you mentioned everything required by the authorities?" But it always makes sense to talk of adding to a description, making it fuller than it is: the ideal of a complete description as one which enumerates *all* the qualities of the thing described is accordingly an illusion."[21]

While Dworkin has the illusion that there is always a unique right answer in normative fields, supporters of the Great Divide have the illusion that there is a complete description of the external world as it is. If they have lost this illusion then they should accept that descriptive sentences no longer have their privileged epistemic status, because they are fallible, incomplete and contingent. How can a serious Foundationalist view be defended on these grounds? What matters most of the above quotation is the idea that "relevant" information is needed. It has no sense to talk of information because it is, in principle, endless. We need selected information, relevant information. In order to do this, we have to know for what purpose or purposes it is required. Then, description is neither complete nor neutral. On the contrary, it is incomplete, purposive and selective.

According to Toulmin-Baier, the most extreme supporters of the Great Divide classify sentences into two groups,

> "On the one hand, there are those sentences, to be dignified with the title of "statements", which express propositions ... having to do with facts and the stating of facts; which express beliefs ... ; which are properly couched in the indicative mood ... can be spoken of as true or false .... On the other hand, there are those sentences, to which it is advisable to deny the title of statements ... which are only misleadingly couched in the indicative mood; and whose meaning consists in the affective or persuasive effect ...".[22]

It is not only description (basically understood in Toulmin-Baier vein as consisting of one or more sentences) that is incomplete, purposive and selective. It is affected by context because it would be surprising to believe that our historical conceptual scheme, *inter alia*, does not affect description; likewise, descriptive predicates can acquire, through time, emotive tones. The phrase "old man, black, divorced, etcetera," may change from a descriptive to an emotive force or from an emotive force to a descriptive one.

Can we separate the issue of descriptive statements from the problem of truth? If descriptive statements can be true or false it is supposed that there must be a basis of

---

[21] Toulmin-Baier, "On Describing", *Mind 61*, 1952, pages 13-37.
[22] Ibidem, page 31.

truth supporting the claim that there are certain true statements. Hence, let us see which basis of truth is behind the Great Divide. Some of the basic problems a correspondence theory of truth relates to are facts. However, what are facts? We have already commented on some of the problems connected with those facts understood as "the given", but another problem is related to the correspondence between a fact and a belief about this fact. What does it mean that a belief corresponds with a fact? I will not deal with this here though, since I will suppose that our knowledge of the world is imperfect. This implies that truth cannot be considered as a kind of God's eye view, and this has characterized some of the approaches of the correspondence theory.

Nevertheless, human agents increasingly try to substitute this absolute stance. For example, when Locke claims that there was no similitude between the physical object and secondary qualities such as colours. A God's eye view was maintained only for primary qualities. One important question is the following: granted that our knowledge of the world is imperfect and granted that we are not able to reach definitive truths, should we be committed to the idea that there is a truth in natural sciences? In any case, observational statements (protocol statements in Carnap terms) are neither the starting points for science, because some theory precedes them, nor are they an infallible ground for the solid building foundationalists dreamed of.

2. SECOND OBJECTION TO THE IDENTIFICATION OF LEGAL ORDERS

As J.W. Harris puts it,

> "The second argument against the view that legal systems may be identified by reference to sources runs as follows. There is often uncertainty, or controversy, about the sources of a legal system or their relative ranking. Accordingly, no line can be drawn, in terms of "pedigree", between legal and non-legal standards. Consequently, the present law of any jurisdiction cannot be identified by reference to sources."[23]

He does not agree with that argument because legal positivists in general believe, or have a tendency to believe, that law is form and that one thing is law whereas another is morals. His comment is the following,

> "Now it is true that, where there is a genuine disagreement amongst officials and other legal scientists about the existence or ranking of particular constitutional source-rules, the dispute can only be settled by reference to political considerations. But such disagreements are shaped precisely by attempts to apply the principles of exclusion and derogation."[24]

Although it is not explained what "genuine disagreement" is, I will suppose that it happens when competent jurists, after argumentation, do not reach an agreement. Harris's opinion seems to suppose that there is, on the one hand, a clear cut legal argument and, on the other hand, political considerations. This tendency to draw clear lines of separation is also a positivist tendency. Nevertheless, legal language is,

---

[23] Harris, J.W. *Law and Legal Science*, op. cit., page 75.
[24] Ibidem, page 75.

basically, ordinary language. It can be said that, in general, legislators want the citizens to understand what they enact. However, as is known, this language is more indeterminate than formal languages. A basic indeterminacy of concepts in general and of legal concepts in particular is the following: these concepts have no conditions of application, not only for all logical possibilities but, more importantly, for all practical possibilities.

In other words, we cannot solve all problems just by invoking a given concept, because it would be at worst, void, and at best, not illuminating enough. Consequently, it is wrong to suppose that a legal order is complete because it has a network of sources and rules and that semantic indeterminacy would not affect its completeness. This kind of completeness could be called "empty completeness". Harris does not support this extreme formal view but believes that when a legal argument does not settle the legal question we leave legal realm and go into political considerations.

I think that this is inadequate. Legal orders, in general, and legal concepts, in particular, have a core of meaning. This is, more or less, implied in Harris's comment,

> "But such uncertainties could not apply to all areas without making the practice of legal science pointless."[25]

Granted that there is a core of meaning that gives sense to the whole enterprise and justifies that not everything is uncertainty, the idea is that this core of meaning suffers almost continuous changes because legal concepts have no sharp boundaries and because they are incomplete, in the sense that they can never solve all problems forever. Changes of society and time dimension demand adaptations, not in the sense that we should appeal to political considerations but in the sense that a given legal concept is not perfect. Jurists, fundamentally, carry on the endless process of completing legal concepts, that is, adapting and sometimes changing them.

One of the problems is that, in this process, we do not have, at our disposal, bricks with labels such as "legal" or "meta-legal". Jurists introduce arguments within the field of a given concept when there are, for example, disagreements. However, this normative field has no sharp and timeless boundaries. In my view, these features help to explain that when the jurists introduce arguments within the field of a given legal concept we cannot say that this is, simply, a political consideration because usually a meta-legal argumentation enters hand-in-hand with other legal arguments. This new "mixture", when accepted by the legal community, (because it has overcome certain standards of legal rationality and certain value requirements) lays a new coherent brick on the legal system that helps to build a new layer that will make the legal system grow, in order to solve new problems or to solve old ones "better".

This brick would be considered as something extraneous when the legal community does not accept it, because of the reasons already given. Consequently, something is a "political consideration", in the sense of something external to a given legal order, when the legal community, in general, with its internalized

---

[25] Ibidem, page 77.

conceptual legal scheme and its internalized scheme of values and legal reasoning, decide that a given item is something external to a given legal order. If not, there must be a God's eye view that makes this decision, instead of the legal community. Another possibility is just to rely on political authority, obeying exclusionary reasons and exclusionary values.

Harris says,

> "But such disagreements are shaped precisely by attempts to apply the principles of exclusion and derogation."[26]

I cannot see why disagreements cannot also affect principles of subsumption and non-contradiction. Nevertheless, let us see what these principles are.

> "By "exclusion" is meant as that principle in accordance with which legal science presupposes a determinate number of independent legislative sources for any legal system, and thereby identifies the system ... .By "derogation" is meant as that principle in accordance with which legal science rejects a rule, or part of a rule, because of its conflict with another rule originating in a superior source."[27]

I agree that, providing legal scholars adopt, in general, an internal point of view (roughly speaking, accepting the basic values of the legal order), they should try to apply those principles and the others already mentioned. Nevertheless, this does not change what I have been saying. There is no contradiction between my comments and the attempts of legal scholars to apply these principles. What happens is that, in these attempts, they are trying to reach the "best result", bearing in mind the basic values of the legal order, their basic purposes and the concrete interests, values and purposes of the legal problem in hand. This would not be so (practically, not logically speaking) if they were not participants, that is, if they did not accept an internal point of view in relation to a given legal order.

I do not believe that this is a black and white question, not only because not all officials accept this internal point of view all the time, but because even if it was so (which is very doubtful) there would be differences in understanding, intensity and localization. In other words, once it is accepted as an internal point of view it does not mean that all the officials support the totality of the legal order, all the time, with the same understanding. Granted that critical-reflective attitudes are assumed to occur in participants (at least as a usual way to deal with non-routine situations), one cannot expect only mere obedience but also reflective loyalty. Of course, this is a normative comment. I believe that a legal order can survive with the mere obedience of the population (obedient donkeys) and participating officials, but the working of the legal system is not the same. Rome once "discovered" that slaves were not profitable enough and "preferred" free human beings, although this, of course, is not the whole story.

In relation to the principle of derogation, it has been already been mentioned that there are problems of hierarchy within a legal order, so I will not therefore repeat them here. In relation to the principle of exclusion, I do not doubt that legal scholars presuppose a limited number of independent sources. What is wrong, in my view, is

---

[26] Ibidem, page 75.

[27] Ibidem, pages 10 and 11.

to suppose that this is sufficient to identify a legal order for the problems of indeterminacy already commented on. Although it is not my concern here to talk about legal interpretation, a brief comment should be made. Granted that to know what the law is we need legal interpretation, in the sense that this is not a contingent task, we necessarily need meta-legal considerations to overcome the structural indeterminacies of the legal materials.[28]

Harris also says,

> "If a rule originating in the debatable source stipulates duty X relating to topic Y, the legal scientist who is asked for information about the law on topic Y can do one of three things. First, he may include in his description the existence of legal duty X; in that case, he has included the source within the first blank of the *fiat*. Second, he may exclude legal duty X, having presupposed the exclusion of the source. Third, he may announce that no description of the topic can, as things are, be offered with any certainty, but that one or other of two descriptions would be correct depending on how the uncertainty as to the source is resolved; he may then go on to advance arguments in favour of prescribing one resolution. In so far as he offers a description, tentatively or with confidence, he presupposes listed and ranked sources. The law he describes, the "legal system" in the sense of "present law", is identified by reference to such sources."[29]

Harris seems, here, to suppose that "present law" is identified through formal features. However, this is not so unless we have a magic view of these formal features that, through a conjuring trick, converts them into concrete substantive features. Another interpretation would see duty X with a material content (based on interpretation), and the problem would then be to decide whether material content X is a duty or not, in a given legal order. For example, what happens when two competent jurists discuss which could be the proper meaning? Here we have already settled on a meaning and we doubt whether this meaning is or is not a duty in a given legal order. I think that this could be seen as a "problem of relevancy", according to N. MacCormick.

In other words, we may have a problem of what the normative text says, while we do not doubt its existence. In my view this cannot be decided, in all cases, only from the black letter rules (wording) enacted by the legislator. Of course, there is not only a problem of semantic indeterminacy, which is called the gap of recognition. Using Alchourrón and Bulygin's terminology, we can add: absence of solution (normative gap), incompatible solutions (inconsistency) and lack of factual information (gap of knowledge).

When two competent jurists are advancing arguments to decide whether duty X exists or not, they are not doing so just by looking at the formal legal sources or presupposing them. They construct legal arguments and develop legal reasoning that tries to justify one or other decision. These arguments are not "in" the presupposed listed and ranked sources unless these are seen as a kind of magic bottomless well where we can find anything. They build arguments and, in so doing, they participate in the process of constructing the legal order. Nevertheless, they do not participate as isolated individuals but as members of a legal community and as members of a

---

[28] Nino, C. *Derecho, Moral y Politica*, op. cit., pages 87 and ff.

[29] Harris, J.W. *Law and Legal Science*, op. cit., page 76.

given society. This means, *inter alia*, that this endless process is a collective task, although for obvious reasons it must be done by individuals.

What has been said has a direct relationship to Harris's next claim,

> "No resolution of the uncertainty could be achieved by describing and applying the present law. But it would be possible to prescribe or predict a resolution. Such prescription or prediction would involve the following mixture of legal and political elements ... .He would point to paper rules and principles (Theorem (j)) to be found in legal texts, such as judicial dicta about parliamentary supremacy, or, to counter these, provisions of the Treaty of Rome. So far as such paper guides were felt to give his argument insufficient weight, he would appeal to political considerations."[30]

Harris refers to his "doctrine model of rationality" and we shall now see what this doctrine means. Later though I will try to show that his division between the momentary and non-momentary legal system is an artificial division because it expects to draw clear lines between what is law and what are legal reasoning and morals. When referring to the doctrine model of rationality he says,

> "The doctrine model alone is applied whenever, in a doubtful case, a principle, policy, maxim, concept, classification, or definition, is treated as a sufficient justification for a legal decision."[31]

Harris states that, in practice, officials use both kinds of reasons, those referring to the doctrine model and those referring to a utility model, that is, to legal consequences. In this respect, we can say that even in a doubtful case a legal decision cannot be based only on "guiding reasons". If we differentiate, as Aarnio and Peczenik do, between must sources, should sources and may sources, we can claim that a justified legal decision needs a "must source", although it usually has something more. In other words, a "guiding reason" (a may source), as a member of the doctrine model, can be an element of a justified legal decision accompanying a "must source", but it does not stand alone, differently from a "must source".

Harris believes that we can distinguish sharply between momentary and non-momentary legal systems. This distinction is required because he also claims a sharp distinction between the descriptive task of legal science and other different tasks. In this respect he says,

> "If legal science is merely describing the present law on a topic, its information can be supplied exclusively in terms of rules ..."[32].

I have already commented that legal dogmatics only describing the rules of a given legal system is poor legal dogmatics, at least for practical purposes. Moreover, in order to describe something we first have to identify the object of description.

Supposing we know the complete rules that belong to a given legal order (that requires a constructive task), what we want to know is which duties, and in which circumstances, ought to be fulfilled, by whom. Nevertheless, we need some further presumptions. We should suppose that legal duties and their circumstances are settled, once and for all, until new legislative formulation or derogation exists. We

---

[30] Ibidem, page 77.

[31] Ibidem, page 143.

[32] Ibidem, page 67.

should also suppose that the meaning contents of the rules have no problems of interpretation or that these problems can be solved through rules themselves, because it was stated that the description of legal science is exclusively in terms of legal rules, as established by the legislator. We should assume that legal rules form a consistent field of meaning.

Nevertheless, all these suppositions are incorrect. Perhaps the basic mistake of this scenario is the static character of the legal system. In order to give a breath of life to his static system, a non-momentary system is left close to it. He says,

> "The legal scientist may wish to do more than describe the valid law as at the time of writing."[33]

Why should a legal scientist wish to do something more than describing? This is not a fancy wish. On the contrary, it is a constitutive aspect of the legal dogmatics' task. Under the influence of the Great Divide and logical positivism, *inter alia*, it has been possible to develop a metaphysical dream of neutral description once the spurious and contaminated will of any legislator has been translated into rules. Fortunately, legal scholars have tried to be both systematic and useful for society too.

Once we accept that a legal order is not a consistent field of meaning, we are led to a task of construction. If this is correct, the legal order cannot be identified only from a descriptive point of view. We cannot only do this because the "proper legal building" is not yet completely built. It never is. We never complete our task because there is no fixed point that can be reached. We could say that the final point would be a complete and perfect legal system, although this is a geometrical dream that we will never reach. This static perfection would be something like death, whereas legal order is something alive and imperfect. We have different interests and goals, openly stated, that conflict with each other in different contexts. The best we can do is not to blindly repeat but creatively adapt what has not been uttered forever.

Of course, there are differences in different branches of the law and the procedural warrants are not always the same. Otherwise, we could accept an inconsistent field of meaning as a proper identification of a legal order, but this would be dangerous for legal scholars. In any case, this legal construction is not geometrical but purposive and this purposiveness is related to an internal point of view. Furthermore, the meaning contents of the different rules are closer to the "core" or the "periphery" of the system and this is not a perennial feature but a changing one. This is another problem for a descriptive approach that fits static objects better. Hence, a metalanguage rebuilds the language of the legislator. This metalanguage is made of "must sources", "should sources" and "may sources". This metalanguage not only tries to explain, but also to optimise, what the legal order is and which legal duties it includes, thereby trying to justify them.

Again, the meaning content of the legal system is a result of a process of interaction between the language of the legislator and the metalanguages of the jurists. Going back to the beginning of the second objection, we could say that it is

---

[33] Ibidem, page 67.

not true that no line can be drawn between legal and meta-legal standards. It is not true that present law is unable to be identified through sources. A line is drawn, but it is not the line that legal positivists have in mind. This line is fluid and purposive, is made by the members of the legal community and it is a changing one. It is not a line in itself, because there is no God's eye view.

I am not going to deal with J. Raz's approach to the problem of identity, only to quote his view of the problem, which suggests that there can be serious problems of communication between different legal approaches in relation to certain legal problems. He says,

> "The criterion of identity of momentary systems can be formulated as follows: A set of normative statements is a complete description of a momentary legal system if, and only if, (1) every one of the statements in it describes (part of) the same momentary system as all the others, and (2) every normative statement which describes (part of) the same momentary system is entailed by that set."[34]

On the one hand, a "complete description" seems to me to be a nonsense for the reasons already mentioned. There is never a complete description of a legal order. The term "complete" is a metaphysical one, since it does not occur in reality, only in the minds of certain human beings. Likewise, "exactly seven meters" is also a metaphysical expression. During Roman times, the Industrial Revolution and at present, the expression "exactly seven meters" is not the same, as far as length is considered, because of the existence of different tools of measurement. On the other hand, the requirement of "entailment" is too strong in legal realms. If we accept that the normative statements Raz is talking about can be equated to propositions, we would have the following: "A proposition (one) entails a proposition (two) if, and only if, it is impossible that (one) is true and (two) is false". This language game seems to me to be unsound and useless for legal normative realms.

Moreover, why do the legal positivists, generally speaking, have a scornful attitude towards practical reason, fluid lines, etcetera? Among other reasons, because they share the Great Divide and they place themselves on the "good side", the descriptive, neutral and scientific one, and because they believe in a firm bedrock that will allow us to reach certainty. In summary, they need foundations. Let us, then, explore which foundations they need and whether this is, or not, another metaphysical dream.

2.1 Foundations, Certainty and Metaphysical Dreams

Among the supporters of the Great Divide, some believe that human beings have "private" experiences in their minds. For example, some human beings would have certain tactile or visual experiences with a corresponding real object, at least in the case of genuine perceptions. Some human beings would have conscious states, that is, they would have certain experiences of the real world. According to this "deep" foundationalism we can perceive reality itself because we derive our beliefs directly

---

[34] Raz, Joseph. *The Concept of a Legal System*, Clarendon Press, second edition, Oxford, 1983, page 189.

from it, not from other beliefs. However, some very brief objections to this view could be the following:

First, my sensory impressions are part of my body that is, in its turn, part of the external world. Therefore, our sensory impressions do not see neutrally and externally; Second, if my sensory impressions are just mine I am committed to a private language and, in this respect, I could not have a criterion of correctness. Otherwise, in a genuine language it should be possible to distinguish between correct and incorrect; Third, my sensory impressions do not justify by themselves the external world because they cannot be understood in isolation. In this regard, we can reach certain sensory impressions because we are members of a form of life; Fourth, if sensory impressions are taken as psychological occurrences they cannot justify truth or falseness because they are facts.

Although there are several types of foundationalism, I will only deal with "minimal", as an example of the foundationalist softening of its requirements. This move to a softer version may mean the following: Foundationalists of the empiricist tradition do not support anymore the idea of beliefs with a privileged epistemic status, which are usually perceptual experiences. Hence, they do not support the classical foundationalist view of a pyramid. The bedrock would be formed by privileged epistemic beliefs that support the pyramid and form the infallible basement. It is now accepted that these beliefs are not different from the beliefs situated in the superstructure because of their content but because of the form of their justification. The former beliefs would receive their justification from experience (non-doxastic beliefs), whereas the latter would receive their justification from other beliefs (doxastic beliefs). In classical foundationalism, basic beliefs were based on perception, but "minimal" foundationalism accepts that basic beliefs can also be based on reason, memory or introspection. Therefore, how should the Great Divide be understood? Even better, should the Great Divide be maintained?

To sum up, some theories of justification defend the view that, although some beliefs are justified, it is not because of their relationships to other beliefs. As is known, these theories are called "foundational". As I said before, the image of a pyramid is appropriate. At its base, there are intrinsically justified beliefs, which are usually understood by using phrases such as "self-evident" or other similar expressions. The pyramid is perfectly built when there are logical relationships between the so-called infrastructural beliefs and superstructural beliefs. Although an act of faith is needed to claim that foundational beliefs are logically implied by my evidence. If we do not want to make this magic move, we can accept that we reach "fallible" basic beliefs, instead of infallible ones. Nevertheless, can we build a solid pyramid with a foundation of "fallible" basic beliefs? I will not deal with scepticism here but it is a possible way out for supporters of foundationalism and certainty; another is to make magic claims.

Furthermore, even if these magic intrinsically justified beliefs existed, they could be defeated by using some part of our global knowledge. If this were correct, it would not be true that a straight line, from basic to non-basic beliefs, properly represented justification. As the reader can realise, the introduction of the term "global" refers to another theory of justification, called "coherentism". Of course, it is possible to claim that these magic intrinsically justified beliefs cannot be defeated.

However, this would be an annoying position and an even stronger claim than those made by Natural Law thinkers.

Finally, let us say something about the regress argument and foundationalism. For foundationalists, in general, the two evils of scepticism and circularity should be avoided. The former does not refer to values but to experience. One problem is whether reality itself can be justified. If you say no, you are led to scepticism, fallible ground, lack of certainty, etcetera. On the other hand, circularity means, essentially, that you must go back until you find a firm bedrock, that is, basic infallible beliefs. If not, you must go down an endless pathway without distinguishing between circularity and vicious circularity.[35] For foundationalists, the "hermeneutic circle" for example, produces uncontrollable reactions of disdain, which means you cannot make a "feed-back" move. They believe that justification is always linear.

You have to walk until you find basic infallible beliefs. However, what happens if you do not find them? Where we have no knowledge, more and more walking is needed. Now, suppose we find these beliefs, how can we detect them? How many are needed for a firm bedrock? Do we decide it or do we just infer it? Does reality say it and we just pick it up? Which reality? The long lasting obsession for a firm bedrock is closely linked to another obsession, "certainty".

In this regard, foundationalists usually believe that among the pitfalls that must be eliminated there is a dangerous one, "doubt". If doubt enters into the building of true knowledge, it can get broken. If the world is made of brute facts and we can describe them accurately and neutrally, this description would give us the first firm step. We can then build, *inter alia*, "institutional facts" over it, that would not be facts of the world. Nevertheless, it is said, that logical relationships of contradiction can only exist between descriptions of true world facts. Where does this claim lead though?

The conclusion of this claim could be the following: if there is no contradiction between, let us say, "you can smoke" and (at the same time) "you cannot smoke", we would be situated in a language in which to give reasons has no sense. This seemingly absurd conclusion fits, nevertheless, with some supporters of the Great Divide and some supporters of some legal positivist approaches. This would be so because, in so far as theoretical reasons cannot be given and practical reasons do not exist as "true" reasons, what is left for languages such as that of legal dogmatics? It seems that it is exclusively for describing the language of the legislator. In spite of this, some legal scholars claim that if this language uses "validity" as "bindingness", their validity claims are, at the same time, normative claims.

---

[35] Rescher, N. *Satisfying reason*, op. cit. "What is at issue here is not circularity but simply good sense. Admittedly, the explanation at issue has an *appearance* of vitiating circularity because the force of the validating argument will rest on an appeal to rationality: "If you are going to be rational in your beliefs, then you must also act rationally, because it is rational to believe that rational action is optimal at the point of goal attainment". However, this sort of question is simply unavoidable in the circumstances. It is exactly what we want and need. Where else should we look for a *rational* validation of rationality but to reason itself? The overall justification of rationality *must* be reflective and self-referential." Page 24.

Hence, they cannot be placed in a descriptive language and they cannot be true or false. This sound conclusion can only be worthless for those who believe that either we have firm bedrocks and certainty, etcetera, or we are in the realm of will, feelings and other non-rational elements. This language of legal dogmatics (uttered from an internal point of view and, then, marked by the original sin) is condemned to the field of bare irrationality. Only logical formal relations and authentic descriptive statements of "*tout court*" world facts would be rational. Although the strength of this last claim is based, *inter alia*, on the correspondence theory of truth. Unfortunately, the correspondence theory does not easily apply itself to non-empirical statements, as seems to be the case with a good part of the statements of legal dogmatics.

A correspondence theory has to explain, *inter alia*, what is a fact and what it means when a given belief corresponds to a given fact. I will not deal here with these difficult issues though, since neither has been clearly explained. The traditional atomistic view of traditional epistemology does not need to be converted into a kind of non-rigorous collective chat. Rather it may mean that we should forget the obsessive search for certainty and basic infallible beliefs, etcetera, and the sharp distinctions, so beloved by legal positivists in general. For example, such as those between law and moral, theoretical reason and practical reason, science and philosophy, etcetera. The idea of a "continuum" is not precise enough for legal positivists. In this regard, even Quine's Naturalized epistemology has many difficulties in justifying its central claim that the different epistemic status of beliefs must be based on a non-normative difference that will explain the former ones.

Although this trend believes that epistemic justification supervenes (very briefly, properties such as justification and other similar ones, are supposed to be tied closely to natural properties, although not reduced to them) on the above mentioned non-normative properties, it is a poor and non-illuminating explanation. It is probably as poor and non-illuminating as a pure descriptive legal dogmatics. All this leads us to the issue of justification. If justification is needed, can a purely descriptive task justify? In so far as the task of judges and legal scholars is "productive" and not exclusively "reproductive", can we expel this task from the field of rationality or appeal to practical reason, the preferred object of disdain for legal positivist scientists? Some legal philosophers, such as R. Guastini, have rightly seen that reductionist views of norms are mistaken and, in his analysis of two sentences, he singles out seven types of juristic sentences.[36] This intertwinement among these different types facilitates the "reproductive" task commented on above.

Let us return to facts again. In this regard, Hamlyn says,

> "To say that a statement corresponds to the facts is to say that the statement conforms to whatever standard of objective truth is applicable. What that standard is in any given case depends on what are the agreed truth conditions of that statement."[37]

---

[36] Guastini, Riccardo. "A tentative analysis of two juristic sentences", *Proceedings of the Conference on Legal Theory and Philosophy of Science*, Lund, Sweden, December 11-14, 1983, Reidel, pages 571-581.

[37] Hamlyn, D.W. *The Theory of Knowledge*, MacMillan, London, 1993, page 140.

It is worth noting that the "agreed truth conditions" have sense in a concrete and common cultural framework. Therefore, this framework is a precondition for agreed truth conditions that give sense to the claim that a given statement corresponds to a given fact. If we move from the problem of "correspondence" to the problem of facts we face another precondition,

> "If there are no brute facts -and the present discussion also indicates that there are none- what is to count as a fact depends on how we have come to see the world and upon the conceptual structure that is presupposed in our seeing it in this way. Because it in turn rests on our form of life, we cannot get completely behind this conceptual ordering; but we can in principle question its applicability at any given point. That is why there can be no brute facts. What we can state about the world depends on this agreed, intersubjective system of concepts."[38]

The above quotations show, *inter alia*, two things. First, We have no direct access to reality because truth conditions and conceptual schemes are preconditions of this possibility. Second, the atomistic view is unsound; we can "see" the reality in a certain way, in so far as we are members of a specific common cultural framework. This would be a necessary rather than a sufficient condition. Moreover, it should be emphasized that to talk of truth conditions, in relation to certain sentences, is a nonsense. For example, "you ought to be just". If this sentence is neither true nor false, what is the sense to talk of truth conditions?

I think it is time to put in doubt the superiority of the "good side" of the Great Divide. People on the "good side" describe, neutrally and accurately, the supposed brute facts of the world, whereas people on the "bad side" use will, not reason, to express feelings, values, etcetera. With all due respect I will reiterate at this point a scientific observation of Kepler, made through a Galilean telescope,

> "Mars is square and with intense colour."[39]

3. WHAT DOES IDENTIFICATION MEAN?

When dealing with the problem of identification of legal orders it is a good step to differentiate between rules as an ought or may meaning content, and rules as social situations.[40] Another way to say something similar is to distinguish between rules as

---

[38] Ibidem, pages 140 and 141. I am aware that a deeper scrutiny of the problem of Foundationalism should analyse different types of Foundationalism, although this is not my aim here. For example, E. Sosa says we have to keep in mind that, in order to understand Foundationalism properly we have to distinguish between formal and substantial Foundationalism. The former says that a belief is justified by virtue of certain non-epistemic properties. If we talk of normative fields we should say that evaluative properties supervene on non-evaluative properties. The latter (substantive foundationalism) has two varieties, epistemic and non-epistemic Foundationalism. The epistemic Foundationalism concerns the justification of beliefs about the non-epistemic; the meta-epistemic Foundationalism concerns the justification of beliefs about the epistemic. Only this last meta-epistemic Foundationalism supports the view that there must be foundational epistemic beliefs. "The Foundations of Foundationalism", *Nous 14*, 1980, pages 547-564.

[39] Feyerabend, P.K. *Against method: outline of an anarchistic theory of knowledge*, New Left Books, London, 1975, page 126.

[40] Harris, J.W., op. cit., page 24.

meanings, and rules as having empirical existence.[41] The former, in both cases, refers to an ideal existence, the latter to an empirical existence. Therefore, there are two ways, at least, of talking about law or legal systems. It seems that the former criterion may serve to identify law or rules, but we cannot use the latter empirical criterion to identify law or rules as meaning contents.

A related question is the difference between non-momentary legal systems and momentary legal systems. According to some legal positivists we should differentiate between them. It is supposed there is a legal system that maintains its "identity" through the changes that occur in a subjoint of the former system. It appears to be something similar to a magic personal identity that remains the same (the essence?) irrespective of the changes that occur in a given body as a "momentaneous being". He (as a momentaneous being) changes, but he (as a non-momentaneous being) does not change, although the former "he" is included in the latter "he". I cannot see why only some Natural Law thinkers have been accused of supporting magic dreams. Let us take some examples to see whether they fit in with our ordinary language. Suppose a person tells you, "that is my non-momentary friend Peter". Or "this is my momentary home", "this is my momentary and non-momentary wife", and so on.

In relation to the issue of identification of legal systems, two aspects have usually been emphasized, the criterion of deductiveness and the criterion of legality. For the former criterion some jurists or philosophers (*inter alia*, Kelsen or von Wright) have denied or put in doubt the possibility of logical relationships between legal rules.[42] Therefore, let us briefly explore this criterion of deductiveness, related to "dependent rules", that belongs to a legal order, since other rules already belong to it, that is, rules logically inferred from either independent or other dependent rules. According to an example, sometimes used by legal scholars, a person enters onto a station platform hand in hand with an ape; there is a sign saying, "no dogs are admitted here". The railway police send them away. The problem is whether we should apply "*a contrario*" or "*a simile*" analogical arguments.

As is known, a "relevant" similarity would solve the problem. According to Giovanni Tarello the predisposition of the audience to accept one or another kind of relevancy would push (or at least influence) the official to decide one way or another. Is that legal decision a logical consequence of the previous rule? I believe it is not. One thing is the possibility to reconstruct *ex post* this decisional process and another to know *ex ante* the logical consequence that will necessarily follow.

In relation to the second criterion, legality, legal rules belong to a legal order in so far as they have been authorized by other rules (independent or dependent) that also belong to this order. In this regard, it is not surprising that Kelsen and Hart (two giants of legal philosophy) claim, explicitly or not, for a "mixed system". Namely, in Kelsen, the "ought or may meaning content" (when referred to the legal system not to a concrete legal rule) cannot dispense with "efficacy", although he argued for

---

[41] Caracciolo, Ricardo. "Sistema juridico". In: *El Derecho y la Justicia*, Editorial Trotta, Consejo Superior de Investigaciones Cientificas, Boletín Oficial del Estado, Madrid, 1996, pages 161-174.

[42] Kelsen, Hans. *General Theory of Norms*. M. Harney (translator), Clarendon, Oxford, 1991; von Wright G.H. "Is there a logic of norms?", *Ratio Iuris*, Volume 4, Number 3, December 1991.

a pure theory and rejected the dualism of the G. Jellinek theory, who was one of his teachers. If a legal system has no efficacy, it is unsound to talk of validity of a certain meaning content. On the other hand, although Hart started (differently from Kelsen) from a rather sociological legal approach, he indicated the acceptance by officials of certain criteria of identification of rules that ought to belong to the system (if fulfilling these criteria) and cannot dispense with meaning content as something that has ideal or abstract existence, as opposed to an empirical one.

In other words, the acceptance of the officials is based on certain meaning contents that can be inferred from accepted legal criteria or, at least, that do not contradict them. However, this task calls for interpretation, and the officials will use (or may use) criteria and meta-criteria, rules, principles and definitions. Otherwise, when a social practice is identified and accepted, a process of interpretation is required, because this kind of acceptation demands something more than "mechanical work" or "reproductive work". Officials and legal scholars undertake both a "reproductive" and a "productive" task because they share an internal point of view, although this is not a logical necessity but a pragmatical one.

Identification of a legal order cannot be properly undertaken by "detached observers" because, unlike physics, it is not expected that jurists describe an unchanging object (one of the dreams transformed into non-momentary legal systems) neutrally and accurately but a dynamic object that guides, at least partially, our behaviour. Our behaviour changes, the legal order changes, and so does interpretation. We cannot fix (or better, perhaps we could but it would be useless) an unchanging object with geometrical perfection as a kind of "*sub especie aeternitatis*" object. Is it correct to claim that while Natural Law thinking tried to make some content eternal, Legal Positivism tried to make some form eternal?

The whole project of a God's eye view is misguided and, in spite of some illuminating anti reductive stances (some of which are underlined), there is a geometrical tendency towards truth and certainty that, *inter alia*, have expelled values and evaluations from the kingdom of rationality. We have been thrown out of the paradise of true rationality. However, generally speaking, they act contrarily to what they claim because they, more or less, want (as the others do) to be useful to society. It is doubtful one can fulfil this legal task by claiming, at the same time, that logic is the only rationality and/or by trying to impose correspondence theory on legal fields.

Sometimes, a question such as the following is offered: How is it possible to fulfil an interpretative task if we have not previously identified what has to be interpreted? It is supposed that this question is formulated by a supporter of legal science undertaking a pure descriptive task. This type of question is surprising, in so far as some legal positivist approaches claim to have a complete description of a given legal order once they have identified the normative texts edicted by the legislator. A related intent, that tries to show constructive identification of law is impossible, is due to A. Marmor. On the contrary to these impossible projects, he explains to us who has the legal authority-capacity and what is the legitimate result of this authority-capacity. He says,

> "Raz identifies two such features: First, a directive can be authoritatively binding only if it is, or is at least presented as, someone's view of how its subjects ought to behave. Second, it must be possible to identify the directive as being issued by the alleged authority without relying on reasons or considerations on which the directive purports to adjudicate."[43]

These two features would undermine, according to Marmor, the possibility of a constructive identification of law, which is related to Dworkin's theory of law. Although I am not trying to support Dworkin's view, let us explore some features of Raz's approach. What matters is the view of a powerful person who will tell others what they ought to do. By the way, let us say that this neglects the rights of the citizens. This is confirmed by another quotation,

> "Thus, Raz's main insight is that "the only proper way to acknowledge the arbitrator's authority is to take it to be a reason for action which replaces the reasons on the basis of which he was meant to decide" ... If the authority's directives are meant to replace some of the reasons on the basis on which he was meant to decide, it must be possible for the disputants to *identify* his directive *independently* of those reasons."[44]

Although the replacement of "some" of the reasons is left imprecise (a usual protest of legal positivists against other "weaker" legal philosophers), I will focus on the problem of identification. In both the so-called normative sciences (with its special "reality") and in the so-called mature sciences, reality "itself" is not identified independently of the conceptual scheme the scientist has accepted as the proper one. Similarly, there is no directive "itself", unless Marmor refers only to the syntactic dimension or the literal meaning of a given normative text, at a given time. Nevertheless, even supposing that the plain meaning can be identified with the directive itself, it is also pragmatically true that plain meaning cannot solve, forever, the legal conflicts a legal system is expected to solve.

Reasons alone cannot justify a meaning or other content (within certain limits that are neither numerical nor aprioristic) but, however, they can affect the legal force. As A. Hernández Gil says,

> "Nevertheless, there are cases in which the determination of the sense of the rules can affect its legal force and, in consequence, in their identification. This phenomenon is usual when legislative reforms have taken place, originating problems of derogation and temporary law."[45]

Fortunately for Raz's identification thesis, these exclusionary reasons are not an essential element. As Marmor says,

> "It is quite sufficient to admit (as Dworkin seems to in this passage) that they create distinct reason that *can* override other prudential or moral reasons for action. In any case, the alleged subjects would have to be able to identify the authoritative directive independently of, and, distinct from, other reasons."[46]

---

[43] Marmor, Andrei. *Interpretation and Legal Theory*, Clarendon Press, Oxford, 1992, page 114.

[44] Ibidem, page 115.

[45] Hernández Gil, Antonio. *La ciencia juridica tradicional y su transformación*, Cuadernos Civitas, Madrid, 1981, page 53.

[46] Marmor, Andrei. *Interpretation and Legal Theory*, op. cit., page 118.

This is, no doubt, a good step unless it is believed that this possibility "can" allow, in all cases, for an identification of the legal order or the directives. Not even if the legislator would settle, in general terms, when his reasons can override other reasons. In my view, the basic reason why these kinds of identification are destined to failure is that the whole project is wrong.

The object, a legal order, is not the kind of object that can be delimited and identified in a geometrical way. This is why legal positivist trends believe that any constructive identification of law fails. They expect what neither can reach in legal normative fields, that is a useful and out of context rationality. It is probable that, at least for the moment, there is no proper understanding and fertile academic communication between these two basic tendencies, positivist and post-positivist.

Be this so or not, I will now deal with another criticism of Raz's approach. In my view, Raz is not paying enough attention to the practice of adjudication. Marmor accepts that conceptual analysis should not ignore ordinary language but this is, sometimes, misleading and judges and lawyers should not be presumed to be exempt from such confusions. In this regard, Marmor says,

> "It is presumably clear to anyone familiar with the politics of law, that at least judges sometimes have very good reason to claim that they are following the law when they are in fact inventing it. This kind of pretence is far from seeming nonsensical or mysterious. In other words, the question now facing us is not whether the pretence story makes any sense at all. It is, rather, a question of quantity: what level of pretence (and confusion) can be allowed when the result is an absurd picture of adjudication?"[47]

The opinion that judges are rascals is not a new one but it seems to me that it shows a mistaken view of what adjudication is. The main question, as I see it, is the following: when judges follow the law, adjudication is in order, when they do not follow the law they are inventing it, and pretence and confusion arise. This view supposes that it is known (perhaps by those placed on the "good side") what is necessary to follow a rule, concretely speaking. Nevertheless, when it does not happen, we can see the judges rascally simulating that they are following the law. Citizens do not know this and they ingenuously believe that everything is in order.

Two aspects should be emphasized here: on the one hand, the internal point of view of judges, in general, and, on the other hand, the concept of following a rule. For the latter, P. Winch says,

> "It suggests that one has to take account not only of the actions of the person whose behaviour is in question as a candidate for the category of rule following, but also the *reactions of other people* to what he does."[48]

What does this mean? In my view, it has no sense to claim that there is confusion and pretence in adjudication when judges, in general, do not believe so. In other words, following a rule is a social practice although only individuals can follow a rule. More indirectly, people in general form part of the "reactions of other people" that Winch is talking about.

[47] Ibidem, page 119.

[48] Winch, Peter. *The idea of a social science and its relationship to philosophy*, Routledge, London, 1988, page 30.

Winch adds,

> "... the notion of following a rule is logically inseparable from the notion of *making a mistake*. If it is possible to say of someone that he is following a rule that means that one can ask whether he is doing what he does correctly or not. Otherwise, there is no foothold in his behaviour in which the notion of a rule can take a grip ... .What Wittgenstein insists on, however, is, first, that it must be in principle possible for other people to grasp that rule and judge when it is being correctly followed; second, that it makes no sense to suppose anyone capable of establishing a purely personal standard of behaviour if he had never had any experience of human society with its socially established rules."[49]

Several aspects should be emphasized here: legal dogmatics is a matter for experts, and its task is not an individual thing, although only individuals can carry out the work. In addition, the concept of correctness is basic because the other members of the group (the legal community or society in general) must be able to know whether this concrete following of a rule is correct or not; and, finally, related to this last element, there is the concept of mistake. In other words, we make mistakes when following a rule but we know, nevertheless, to give sense to the concept of following a rule.

The other aspect is the "internal point of view". In certain historical events this kind of pretence Marmor talks about can be detected. It is said that, after the Soviet revolution of 1917, Lenin had to make use of the judges of the old regime, even though these judges, in general, did not accept the new situation and they did not share a common point of view. In these cases, it seems sound to talk of pretence. However, the judges Marmor is talking about are not these. In our societies the judges, in general, share the basic values of the Rule of Law, both in the material and in the formal sense. If we accept this point it is hard to claim that they contribute with pretence and confusion to the task, *inter alia*, of guiding and co-ordinating behaviour.

Why talk of confusion and pretence? In my view, underlying these comments is the expectation of a clear identification of the legal order or identification of its components. Two of Marmor's claims will be commented on: <u>first</u>, the problem of understanding language, and <u>second</u>, the unavoidable openness of "some" directives enacted by the legal authority.

He says,

> "As far as this view depends on the assumption that all understanding of language and communication involves interpretation, it involves a fallacy ... But law, like any other form of communication, can simply be understood, and then applied. Interpretation is the exceptional, not the standard mode of understanding language."[50]

It is acceptable that we share not only a language but also certain meanings. We are socialized in a certain culture and, generally speaking, it gives us a basic understanding. Nevertheless, while loose share understanding can be enough in certain realms it can be insufficient in others. This is because more precision is

---

[49] Ibidem, pages 32 and 33.

[50] Marmor, Andrei. *Interpretation and Legal Theory*, op. cit., page 122.

needed and some other specific rules can complicate the understanding of a given item that is not usually problematic in every day life.

However, this relative agreement co-exists with relative disagreement because specifications of agreements (and this requirement changes from one language game to another) are contextual, and contexts do not last for ever. Even if they last for a long time they can be interpreted differently. This is not a logical necessity but a practical one. This happens also when we have authoritative rules as guide lines. If the reader has followed me until now, he can see my preference for the expression "legal order" and not "legal system". I prefer the former because it gives us an idea of openness and incompleteness that "legal system" seems to avoid. We never systematise a legal order in the sense that "everything is consistent". We, as participants, try to improve the legal order but we never reach perfection. Sometimes we believe that we have done good work but, perhaps, this "good work" will not work tomorrow.

In this regard, Winch says,

> "But sometimes even if O knows with certainty the rule which N is following, he cannot predict with any certainty what N will do: where, namely, the question arises of *what is involved* in following that rule, e.g. in circumstances markedly different from any in which it has previously been applied. The rule here does not specify any determinate outcome to the situation, though it does limit the range of possible alternatives."[51]

The situation Marmor thinks about is more similar to what Ferdinand Tönnies called Gemeinschaft, where, *inter alia*, there were close personal relationships. Although Tönnies' conceptual scheme is not an isolated one, because it has similarities with E. Durkheim and Ch. Cooley, among others. What matters here, is that stability does not characterize our societies, but change, and changing contexts, have a basic importance for understanding and interpretation.

As T. Burge says,

> "There is what one might call the *context of interpretation*, the environment that one investigates in order to determine the grammar and lexical meaning of the expressions of a language. No expressions have meaning apart from a context in which they are related to various entities that they represent, to action, and to various other expressions. By varying the context of interpretation one may, trivially, vary the meaning of expressions ... . Even after a context of interpretation is fixed, thereby fixing the lexical interpretations of linguistic expressions, one has not yet fixed what one might call the *context of application*. Such contexts are approximately local and short-lived circumstances in which an expression is actually uttered or otherwise used ... . The notions of context of interpretation and context of application must each be distinguished from the notion of a *context of evaluation*. These are possible counterfactual circumstances (or circumstance-descriptions) by which necessity or validity may be evaluated."[52]

A second question, commented on by Marmor, relates to the openness of "some" directives;

---

[51] Winch, Peter. *The idea of a social science and its relationship to philosophy*, op. cit., page 92.

[52] Burge, Tyler. On Davidson's "saying that". In: *Truth and Interpretation*, edited by Ernest Lapore, Blackwell, Oxford, 1986, pages 190-208.

> "Thus, when their directives are open to different interpretations, a judge has no particular reason, that is, a reason based on the authoritative nature of law *ipso facto*, to decide the case according to the legislator's intentions (even if the legislator had such an intention and it is discernible)."[53]

We can see here that the ideal of deductiveness fails because it is admitted that "some" directives are open to different interpretations. In these cases, judges would either frankly admit that they are inventing law or they would pretend that they are following law. It seems that when different interpretations are at hand it is not rascal behaviour to invent law. Granted that some level of construction in adjudication is needed, two issues are of interest: first, how do we know that a directive is open to different interpretations and second, whether the judge is also inventing law when there are different interpretations at hand.

First, it seems that Marmor believes that directives are open, or not, to different interpretations according to features of the directive itself and that these cases are exceptional because he believes that interpretation is an exceptional mode of understanding language. This seems a sound interpretation because Marmor can justify the rascal attitude of judges granted that someone clearly knows what to follow the law means. But who is "someone"? If judges are rascals -being the experts- who are the serious and responsible persons? I think that the basic mistake here is to neglect the paramount importance, especially in normative realms, of the pragmatic dimension and the participant's view. Moravcsik says,

> "to explain to a potential agent an activity he will participate in, often requires only necessary not sufficient conditions. This applies also to scientific research. Explanatory concepts we use while research is in progress often yield only necessary conditions. These guide us in our work ... our being necessarily agents influences the structure and content of the general scheme within which we explain what something is."[54]

The second question is closely related to the former because when we understand adjudication from "somewhere", the participant's point of view and the pragmatic dimension, it has little sense to talk of "inventing", etcetera. In this other context, we can understand the inevitable constructive task in legal fields better, because the purposiveness of the pragmatic dimension and the strive for the "best" is accepted as the usual behaviour of participants (not observers or obedient donkeys).

The problem of "rule following" and "community practices" is an important issue that has also been considered, among others, by Frederick Schauer,

> "Thus, the question whether a sign reading "No dogs allowed" excludes seeing eye dogs is not a question whose answer requires direct reference, even according to Kripke and Wright, to community practices. Instead, the rule builds on and refers the rule-follower to the phrase "No dogs allowed", a phrase whose meaning exists apart from the question whether the community believes that seeing eye dogs should be allowed in restaurants."[55]

---

[53] Marmor, Andrei. *Interpretation and Legal Theory*, op. cit., page 123.

[54] Moravcsik, J.M. *Thought and Language*, Routledge, London, 1990, page 227.

[55] Schauer, Frederick. "Rules and Rule-following argument". In: *Law and Language*, edited by Frederick Schauer, Dartmouth, Aldershot, 1993, pages 313-318.

However, the "existence" of a meaning, apart from what the community in question believes, is a rather idealistic view. This is a similar stance to the Popperian third world, where ideas can exist by themselves, for example, in books. I think this is a mistaken view though. Meanings exist in so far as they are related to individuals, who share a certain language, accept a certain meaning and, related to both, support certain social practices. Hence, meanings do not exist like trees. We can come close to a tree and say, "Peter was wrong, this is not an apple tree, it is a peach tree". In case Peter does not agree, we can consult a valuable encyclopaedia of trees or ask a specialist of the flora of the region.

Unfortunately, we cannot do this with meanings. We can decide that certain officials have the last word under certain circumstances, because legal certainty requires us to stop sometime. We know that their decisions do not settle the "true meaning" but, at most, a correct meaning. Moreover, we do not expect that this correct meaning remains for ever. People, generally, accept that legal meanings can change even when the legal statute has not changed, because it is expected that legal meanings serve for correct or just legal decisions. In this regard, E. Levy and others, have shown the different stages through which a given legal concept can change. We can hardly understand a judge that says, "I will not change this meaning because this is the existing meaning". On the contrary, we can imagine an annoyed farmer accompanying his daughter to school because the teacher told her that an apple tree was a peach tree or *vice versa*. Moreover, it shows, again, how difficult the application of the correspondence theory can be to legal normative realms.

Taking into account the above comments the next view by Schauer seems surprising. He says,

> "By recognizing that rules do not determine their own application we are, thus led not to reject the possibility of rule-based constraint, and not to reject the importance of rule-formulations in supplying the meaning that is at the heart of ruleness, but to acknowledge that the tools of language as embodied in a rule-formulation are necessary but not sufficient conditions for treating a rule as a reason for action. When we look for the other conditions that contribute to the existence of a regulative rule, we see both the importance and the incompleteness of focusing on the formulation of that rule."[56]

If Schauer recognizes the importance but the incompleteness of focusing on the formulation of the rule, that knowing the meaning will, in its turn, determine the application, why talk about the "existence" of meanings apart from what the community believes? One answer is that a given meaning exists but it happens that communities, according to different kinds of conditions of internalizations of legal rules, produce distortions that are, sometimes, accepted by the officials. This would show how and why we do not know, in advance, the proper application of legal rules. The consequence is that legal rules are not necessary and sufficient reasons for action. However, this is surprising if we go into the legal positivist tradition, but not if we remain outside it.

If we recall Hobbes, Bentham and Austin, they support (with some differences) an imperative law approach. Laws were commands and the subjects obeyed or ought to obey. Even Hart said that (although not desirable) it is enough, for a legal system

[56] Ibidem, page 318.

to work, for the citizens to behave like donkeys. Remaining outside this tradition one can see, unsurprisingly, that authority reasons are not always necessary and sufficient conditions for the application of legal rules. Furthermore, outside (although not completely, because positivist and post-positivist have intertwinements) this tradition, both "context-dependence" and "meta-legal reasons" play an important role in law, because they influence the meaning of legal rules and their relative weight, through time.

Aleksander Peczenik has commented, (among other comments which I strongly agree with), that my "rule following approach" seems to be based on a consensus theory while, from an epistemological point of view, only three approaches can be accepted: foundationalism, coherentism and scepticism. I agree with this deep comment, but I have some considerations to add. I believe that legal meanings and "rule following" are dependent on social practices, undertaken by socialized individuals. This view tries to distance itself from any essentialist or intemporal approach that sees meanings, for example, as something to be discovered or something that has sense in itself. I also agree that a consensus theory is closer to legitimacy problems than to epistemological problems, although my approach is not only based on rational consensus. In legal normative realms, this rational consensus is linked to foundationalism and coherentism.

In which sense? Foundationalism applies because legal rational consensus must be based on "must sources", which are foundations for any legal rational consensus. This means, *inter alia*, that not any foundations will work (at least from a pragmatical point of view) because foundations must cohere to a certain extent with the form of life where the legal order tries to work. Therefore, legislation is not simply the realm of will and adjudication, but also the realm of reason. It is more complex and not so sharply defined. Especially in our culture, the democratic legislator cannot say, "this is the law because it is my will". The process of making laws goes hand-in-hand with reasons, not only during the process of making laws but also when the law is finally formulated. Reports of Parliamentary sessions and Travaux préparatoires allow us to see how laws cannot dispense with reasons.

On the other hand, how does coherentism apply? Because, once this has been accepted (that is, the legal foundations), the inevitable constructive legal task has to be coherent. I have already said that legal dogmatics cannot accept an inconsistent field of meaning as the result of its work. Nevertheless, this is an endless process and there is no point where the task is already finished because we never reach a complete coherent whole.

Peczenik says that I follow a consensus theory but this is, perhaps, a theory of legitimacy or a theory of communication which, in itself, must be put under the umbrella of coherentism or foundationalism, or both. It is true that my approach is based on a consensus of the legal community but, at the same time, consensus is based on the following aspects: First, law in force, which is the foundationalist umbrella (Must sources). Second, Precedents and Travaux Préparatoires (Should sources). Third, Legal dogmatics, legal and moral reasoning (May sources). The second and third aspects form the coherentist umbrella, in the sense that they try to complete, coherently, the law in force. I believe that these aspects cannot be sharply separated, because the law in force can be also a matter of interpretation, that is, a matter of the language of jurists, not only the language of the legislator.

Otherwise, even the coherentist sources may add new legal layers to the legal order that may be converted, if justifiably accepted by the legal community, into Must sources. This would be so because, once accepted certain justificatory reasons as the "best" justification of certain legal normative texts, they tend to be accepted as part of the legal order itself. This would show, once again, the "optimising" task of those who share an internal point of view.

3.1 The Legal Cartesian Anxiety

For the task of a legal scholar, or a legal philosopher, it seems that the first step is to accept the object of research, although the term "accept" can be understood in several ways. First, the posited legal rules of a given legal order can be accepted as the legal premises for their task. This first sense of "accept" can be equated to the so-called ideological positivism, that is, it is accepted because it is in force and this would warrant peace and order. Second, the posited legal rules of a given legal system can be accepted from a moral point of view, that is, they are not accepted because of prudential reasons. This second view supposes a moral compromise between these legal premises, although not necessarily for all the laws and for all time, because this is a critical acceptance. Third, the posited legal rules of a given legal order can be accepted in the sense of an "object of description". Here, it is understood that the researcher adopts a detached view towards the object to avoid, *inter alia*, the idola that leads us to error, according to Bacon.

I would claim that the first option is rejectable because, at least in our culture, moral, not prudential reasons, are the ultimate reasons. There is an extensive literature that talks about the insufficiency of proposals like Gauthier's[57] and therefore I will not dwell on this important subject. The third option is the option that has been directly or indirectly commented on in the preceding pages. Deduction alone is not sufficient to show the unity of the legal order and to identify it. Legality as authorisation (dynamic dimension) would complete the explanation with no need for a moral conception that underlies, justifies and gives unity (not in a logical sense) to a given legal order. I have tried to show that this is a metaphysical dream. We cannot leave our bodies to look at ourselves from outside. We are always committed and we are never detached, although this is different from claiming that "anything goes".

This cited trend and its conviction that we can sharply and clearly separate language and metalanguage is shown in J.L. Mackie's words,

> "These are first order moral views, positive or negative: the person who adopts either of them is taking a certain practical, normative, stand. By contrast, what I am discussing is a second order view, a view about the status of moral values and the nature of moral valuing, about where and how they fit into the world. These first and second order

[57] Doxa, Cuadernos de Filosofia del Derecho, n° 6, 1989.

views are not merely distinct but completely independent: one could be a second moral sceptic without being a first order one, or again the other way round."[58]

The solution for a true scientific legal researcher can be found here. His first step is to decide whether he will have strong moral views or whether he will reject all established morality. Once this is done, the second step would be either to believe (in the first case) that his strong moral views are simply attitudes or (in the second case) to believe that the existence of evil is an objective truth. I do not doubt that this is a logical possibility but I believe that this is pragmatically not important. As Mackie says,

"A man could hold strong moral views, and indeed ones whose content was thoroughly conventional, while believing that there were simply attitudes and policies with regard to conduct that he and other people held. Conversely, a man could reject all established morality while believing it to be an objective truth that it was evil or corrupt."[59]

I think that it is more important to explore whether we can place ourselves in the second order moral view, completely decontaminated by the first order moral view. This seems to me to be another magic dream. As is known, the logical form is a basic concept in Wittgenstein's Tractatus, and the relationship between language and the world is solved through this fundamental aspect, if any proposition has to be properly described. Namely, it must have the same logical form as reality. Thanks to this isomorphic dimension it would be possible for language to describe facts properly. However, and here is the point, a given proposition cannot say anything about either its logical form (because if it is extracted from the proposition that is going to be analysed, the proposition itself would loose its sense) or a metalanguage, because to say something it should have the same logical form as the cited proposition has, but in this case it would be self-referential.

In this regard, Baker and Hacker say, referring to Carnap:

"He followed Tarski and Hilbert in distinguishing sharply between speaking in a language and speaking about a language. He characterized a semantic system as a set of rules formulated in a metalanguage which lay down a truth-condition for every sentence in the object-language, i.e. a necessary and sufficient condition for its truth. Consequently he held that logical truth would be exhibited as a semantic concept only if it could be defined in a metalanguage for a given object-language. The straight-forward procedure would be to define a logical truth as any sentence of the object-language such that the statement that it is true can be derived solely from the semantic rules for the object language.

This formulation, in virtue of mentioning derivations from semantic rules, must belong to the meta-metalanguage, not to the metalanguage itself. Hence, strictly speaking, it fails to define logical truth as a semantic property! The very same distinction between language and metalanguage which underpins Tarski's definition of truth seems to forestall employing his idea to give a precise semantic definition of logical truth and logical validity. Carnap addressed this crisis as Russell had tackled the parallel

---

[58] Mackie, J.L. *Ethics. Inventing right and wrong*, Penguin Books, London, 1977, page 16.

[59] Ibidem, page 16.

difficulties generated by the theory of types. He adopted the tactics of judiciously relaxing the full rigors of semantic ascent from language to metalanguage."[60]

This long quotation shows that if we relax the rigor of the ascent between language and metalanguage we may have some difficulties because, how are we sure that we have avoided spurious contamination from the normative language? It is not clear that we can construct a metalanguage without any kind of contamination. In this regard, it is not surprising that those fond of clear and sharp distinctions support the idea of "context-independent sentences" or "context-independent reasons". As Baker and Hacker say,

> "Indeed, it is doubtful whether there is any such thing as a type-sentence which invariably makes the same statement whatever the circumstances of its utterance, and it is equally doubtful whether there are any features of the world or its history which may not be relevant to specifying what is said by the utterance of some type-sentence. If truth-conditional semantics is confined to "context independent sentences" thus construed, it seems to be a theory of meaning for the void."[61]

Therefore, I would say that, in legal normative realms, there is neither a common logical form between descriptive propositions and reality, nor a clear and sharp distinction (at least in some cases) between language and metalanguage. Hence, the idea of a pure metalanguage that neutrally describes the language of the legislator should be criticised. This fallacy of the neutrality should be criticised because it conceals that either this metalanguage is a complete repetition of the object language (and is poor and useless) or it is not. In the former case, what we can know for certain is whether the metalanguage has repeated the same sentences as the legislator did, although it is problematic whether the same propositions (in case it is sound to do so) have been repeated. In the latter case there is, at least, the presupposition that law is a legal order and the normal fact that legal scholars are not observers but participants of the form of life in which this law works.

If this is correct, I cannot see how a third basic element, concerned with the purposes that give sense to a given law, can be avoided, at least pragmatically speaking. Namely, if legal scholars modify the law and not only repeat what is already said, it is expected that they are improving the law, not impoverishing it. Then, neither deductiveness nor legal authorization can solve all problems of identification, because reflection of law not only has a descriptive dimension but it also has a normative one, because of the reasons already mentioned. Furthermore, what is going to be identified is not out there, waiting for our identification.

That is why a descriptive approach is not sufficient for proper identification of the legal order, pragmatically speaking. This is not even true, in all cases, for the so-called mature sciences. Furthermore, it is doubtful that the so-called "descriptive monism" (that different persons develop the same cognitive processes in relation to given objects) is sound. Fortunately, we are not clonic beings and I think that the so-called "descriptive pluralism" is more acceptable, although there is no sharp line between them. If this is correct, the classical legal descriptive approach would have

---

[60] Baker G.P. and Hacker P.M.S. *Language, Sense and Nonsense*, Basil Blackwell, Oxford, 1986, page 148.

[61] Ibidem, pages 204-205.

difficulties in convincing us that it has described the reality as it is. Particularly, when the reality at stake is not made of facts in a physicalist sense.

3.2 Identification and Premises

Another reason why identification of law is, *inter alia*, a constructive task is related to the problem of legal premises. It is rational to accept a certain premise, or a given cluster of premises, if we have accepted them through a rational process that demands, again and *inter alia*, other premises. If this is correct though, we are led down an endless return pathway. How can we stop it? In the case of law, legal scholars and legal researchers, in general, have the problem nearly solved because they already have premises. It is usually supposed that legal researchers "qua" legal researchers ought to accept the legal premises settled by the legislator. However, what does "ought" mean here? Does it mean that they have a moral ought, that is, a kind of ideological positivism? We could say that in a similar vein, as we have to obey the posited law because it is in force, we have to use the premises settled by the legislator. Nevertheless, what is more usual is the following: if you want to fulfil properly the task of describing the law in force, you have to use the settled legal premises. There are though, at least, two kinds of problems.

First, ideological problems. These have usually been rejected by legal positivist trends because it has been supposed that one thing is the scientific task of describing the legal order in force and, another thing is to adopt an ideological stance towards this legal order. The first is the attitude of the legal scholar "qua" legal scholar and the second is the attitude of the legal scholar as a citizen. We again though have the sharp distinctions so much beloved by legal positivist trends. We can cast doubt on the fact that the task of legal scholars is to "neutrally and scientifically" describe the legal order in force, or that they carry out, in practice, this "neutral and scientific" task.

I think it is rather clear that the history of legal science shows legal scholars have not carried out this "neutral and scientific" task, at least exclusively. If this were correct, supporters of the "neutral and scientific" task would have to demand it as an "ought", because the history of legal science shows the contrary. Then, the claim would be something similar to this: although legal scholars do not carry out this task of describing the legal order in force "neutrally and scientifically", we believe that they ought to do so. Is this a technical "ought"? I do not think so. If you say that to stop the car you have to press the brake pedal, you have claimed a technical ought, but is this one like the above mentioned case?

If one believes this is analytical, or it is the proper scientific method to describe the legal order in force "neutrally and scientifically", then, the "ought" would be a technical ought, granted that one wants to behave scientifically. However, this is not the case, because I would say that there is a normative claim from the beginning. In summary, they prescribe that legal scholars ought to describe. We have already seen the problems description has, if it is understood as an isomorphic statement that reflects reality itself. The second aspect refers to the opinions of the legal scholar as a citizen. It can only be claimed from the viewpoint that sees method as something that works by itself (as in the case of deductive inferences, carried out by competent logicians, using the same type of logic) and that the human subject does not influence the "neutral and scientific road from premises to the conclusion", that one can radically separate the legal scholar from the citizen. If the legal scholar is seen as a human being with no values, no feelings, no passion, etcetera, there is no doubt that we can separate both aspects clearly and sharply.

Second, technical problems. These problems arise, partly, from what has been already said and because of another problem already commented on. Should we understand premises as syntactical or semantical elements, that is, as non-interpreted or interpreted signs? If we take non-interpreted signs as the proper legal premises, legal scholars cannot "refute" these premises as far as they work "qua" legal scholars. However, this would lead to a static and useless dimension for legal dogmatics or any similar reflection about law. If this view is accepted, there will be a "neutral and scientific" road, walked by "neutral and scientific" researchers, that has little or no similarity with what law is like. Nevertheless, there will be another road, walked by those who try to solve legal conflicts and justify their decisions.

I think that legal researchers have to work on this real-societal road and not on the "neutral and scientific" one. This supposes that it focuses on the task of legal researchers as a task of both describing and constructing. This binomial and dynamic task tries to "improve" the object. However, this is done, *inter alia*, under two conflicting principles; on the one hand, the principle of inertia (that calls for the static dimension); on the other hand, the principle of justice for the case (that calls for the dynamic dimension, that is, adaptation to some changing aspects of the social life.)

It can be claimed that "neutral and scientific" description is the proper task of legal researchers, if it is believed that authority reasons are exclusionary reasons, and that purely describing these authority reasons would be better for the community. The problem is that if we do not believe that authority reasons are always exclusionary reasons, why should we rely on a "pure" description? It can be claimed that in order to behave in a clever way, we first have to know how "things are". Nevertheless, this is, again, a mistaken extrapolation from the field of physics or similar mature sciences that have, in their turn, many problems if they are claiming that they know how "things are". It is more usually accepted that even mature sciences build "maps" to represent (not to reproduce) reality.

In any case, what does it mean to claim, in legal fields, that someone has told us "how things are"? At least, we have to distinguish between the so-called routine cases and the hard cases. In the former, the members of the community, in general, would agree as to how "things are", that is, which legal interpretation has been accepted by the legal community, at a given time, because it is evaluated as the correct one. In the latter, the members of the legal community can reasonably disagree. In this case, there is no concept of "how things are" and perhaps some legal positivists would agree with this. They can say, there is no law because we cannot describe "how things are", although this is just a pretentious view. Why do they have the truth about "how things are"? What they can do is, like any other legal scholar, to try to convince the members (or part) of the legal community or the community at large, or both. Any grimace of superiority because of the mention or the supposed use of the "true method", is useless and ridiculous.

The point is, then, whether a "neutral and scientific" description of the non-interpreted signs is "better" or not for the community. If we believe that the above cited legal signs cannot foresee all conflicts, the legal community will have to complete this insufficiency. If we believe that the proper meaning (supposedly plain meaning) cannot fulfil the legal expectations forever, why should we support an exclusively "pure" descriptive task? As far as scientists (of mature sciences) can change premises, *inter alia*, if they believe there are good reasons for doing so, why should legal scholars not interpret, in a new coherent and "better" way, some legal premises? Basic values of a given law in force (at least in our family laws) should be understood as a kind of ideal state of affairs that has to be interpreted, step by step, bearing in mind the change of circumstances and consequences. Of course, one can claim that "better" (having evaluative overtones) is a nonsense. If this is the case, I believe we should admit that the doctrinal legal community has at least two separate and incompatible strands.

In any case, why is there this constructive task? Because it is not understood, or not only understood, as a "neutral and scientific" description of certain posited premises. It is as a mixed task that not only describes but also tries to foster, coherently, the basic values and other authoritative legal premises. Sometimes, legal scholars will justifiably believe that they cannot adapt a legal premise any more, within the scope of a given interpretation, and will change the interpretation of the premise. It is disputable when a given interpretation is an adaptation or a change. Granted that there is no "essential point" the answer has to be related to the accepted legal justifications by the legal community. What else? They will do so because they try to help the community to cope with new legal conflicts better, when the plain meaning (or any other) of the posited premises cannot fulfil the social expectations and the legal text has not been derogated.

I am not talking of criminal law because, at least in our cultural context, the principle of legality is rather stronger. Why should the fixity of some criticable legal premises be more important than the basic (and open) values of the community and the proper solution of their legal conflicts? I think the answer relies, basically, on the legal positivist tradition, which has a strong emphasis on legal authority. Nevertheless, it is clear, likewise, that legal authority is also political authority. Although here lies another dream, when, for example, in the extreme, a very neutral and scientific legal scholar that works "qua" legal scholar under the legal premises of an authoritarian regime, but during the night behaves "qua" leftist revolutionary. This dichotomy is, practically speaking, very rare.

I think it should be accepted that the relation between legal premises and legal conclusion is, at least in part, not univocal. Furthermore, as Wittgenstein said, following-rules and making mistakes go hand-in-hand. At this point a formalistic-geometrical mind would probably claim that there is nothing to reflect here, because we have to come across with practical reason, that is, nothing scientifically respectful. Hence, we have no deductively valid inferences and we cannot rely on inductive reasoning. In summary, there are no algorithms and we cannot achieve certainty. In spite of this failure, millions of citizens relate to each other using legal language and thousands of jurists do the same, although in a more complex way.

If we take premises as non-interpreted signs, legal scholars cannot "refute" or "deny" these premises, as long as they work "qua" legal scholars. Nevertheless, this would lead to an absurd and static dimension for legal dogmatics or for any other legal reflection. Likewise, if we take interpreted signs as premises, we accept, at least implicitly, that there is no kind of intemporal premise with a fixed meaning that exists in itself, apart from the opinion of the legal community and apart from the consequences produced by the application of this normative meaning.

Moreover, to accept non-interpreted signs as the proper legal premises rejects the possibility of any criticism of legal scholars, except for the discovery of internal inconsistencies. In this useless perspective of the legal scholars' task, they would be seen as neutral describers of the possible meanings of the posited normative texts. They go outside themselves (if our natural language is like our skin) and are able to see the object as ideal observers, from outside. Why should we believe both, that they only neutrally describe, and that to only neutrally describe (if possible) would be better than describing and constructing, bearing in mind the purposes of the law in question, purposes that need interpretation and adaptation?

It is easier to support the view of legal scholars as neutral and scientific describers, if we believe that authority reasons are exclusionary reasons. If not, why should we always rely on the neutral description of the posited will of the legislator? I believe that a central point is the following: do we believe that a neutral description (if possible) of the posited, non-interpreted signs, is better for the community in general? If we believe that the above cited legal signs cannot foresee and solve all (or a good part of) legal conflicts, the community will have to cope with them in the future. In addition, if we believe that the proper (plain) meaning cannot fulfil all social expectations, why should we support an exclusively neutral-descriptive task?

To describe meanings purely is a very difficult task (if it is possible at all from a pragmatical point of view) because of the several overlapping meanings of different terms that have sense, not in isolation, but because of certain relations with other terms. Moreover, we do not deal (at least usually) with proper names but with class names. Hence, we have the problem of membership. To decide on a membership problem "here" (in a certain sense) may have some repercussions "there" (which we do not know, completely, in advance). This would be so because the understanding of a given item (be it sentence type or sentence token), or the existence of an item, in a part of the system may have influence in the understanding of another item(s) of another part of the system. On the other hand, something can be acceptable today but not necessarily tomorrow.

As far as scientists (of mature sciences) can change (and do change) some premises if they believe there are good reasons for doing so, why should legal scholars not interpret some legal premises in a better way? One answer could be that there is certain political ideology in our society and that the Rule of Law requires division of powers. However, does it mean that this is an absolute value? Those who believe in authority reasons as (always) exclusionary reasons, should be close to that view, although this is an ideological option. Another answer could be that officials have no legitimate power to legislate (an argument already used by Bentham) although, again, these political constructions supposedly serve for a "better" autonomy, freedom, happiness, etcetera. Moreover, officials (in so far as they share an internal point of view, as they normally do) do not apply their personal opinions. On the contrary, they have to justify their decisions, and they have institutional and social values as basic points of reference and justification.

In other words, there is an ideal state of affairs that things should conform to and officials should do this task, sometimes with more flexibility and sometimes with less flexibility. In some cases, certain accepted values normatively impose a strict respect for the principle of legality, as in criminal law. It is worth noting that von Wright also talks about "ideals",

> "But even if the "classical" system does not adequately represent existing normative structures, it may have another sensible function with regard to them. Namely, as an *ideal pattern* to which a contradiction-free and gapless normative structure has to conform."[62]

Why should the fixity of some criticable normative texts (that ought to be used as premises) be more important than the interests of citizens or the values of the community? Why should a skilful and justified criticism of the law remain within the exclusive sphere of the legal scholar as opposed to a private citizen? A rejection of these points fits better with a legal positivist tradition that has previously gone, hand-in-hand, with an emphasis on legal authority and authority reasons as exclusionary reasons.

In addition, granted that legal scholars do not have at hand a formal algorithm, they have to deal with the problem of underdetermination, namely, that the relation between legal premises and conclusion is not, at least usually, univocal. If we claim, in a Wittgenstenian vein, that following rules implies making mistakes, it is probable that a geometrically minded legal scholar would claim that there is nothing to talk about here, because we are facing practical reason. The field of will, not of reason. Therefore, if we have no algorithms we do not have certainty, and if we have no certainty, anything is possible. In spite of this desperate situation, millions of citizens and thousands of jurists relate to each other using, *inter alia*, the language of law and the language of jurists. Are we going to help them or to claim that if no certainty is achieved, we are moving within the realm of irrationality? I believe that the first option justifies the existence of legal scholars, but the second does not. Instead of "*fiat iustitia pereat mundus*" the new version is "*fiat veritas pereat mundus*". However, what is "*veritas*"? Only deductive valid inferences? According to which logic?

3.3 Identification and Rational Justification

I will take for granted that an empirical approach in legal normative fields is not appropriate and I will not repeat the critical literature against Scandinavian Realism,

---

[62] von Wright, George H. "Is there a logic of norms?", *Ratio Iuris*, volume 4, number 3, December 1991, page 282.

in spite of its importance and of its positive aspects.[63] Now, let us have a look at the great importance that certain legal approaches have given to formal logic, as the kind of tool that goes hand-in-hand with a supposed true and authentic rationality. According to von Wright, logical theories have to cope with several problematic issues. First,

> "Norms *as prescriptions* of human conduct, however, may be pronounced (un)reasonable, (un)just, (in)valid when judged by some standards which are themselves normative -but not true or false ... . The representation of the conceptual structure of norms in a formalized language is controversial and difficult ... . Another unsettled difficulty in this region is how formal language can correctly represent conditional norms, i.e., norms which prescribe what ought to, may or must not be done given that certain conditions are satisfied ... . A third controversy over deontic logic concerns its applicability and usefulness as an instrument for clarifying and describing the structure of actual normative systems such as, for example, a legal order."[64]

According to von Wright it seems that deontic logic serves as a tool for avoiding contradictions and gaps. Nevertheless, it is problematic to see how gaps can be avoided, granted the type of determination of the different state of affairs,

> "I shall say that a state is *deontically determined* if, and only if, it is either forbidden or permitted. In a normative code which adopts the principle that everything which is not prohibited is *ipso facto* permitted, every state of affairs is deontically determined or has a "deontic value". In such a code there are no "gaps in the law"".[65]

One thing is that a state of affairs is determined generically and another refers to particular applicability. For example, a given precedent can settle that a certain state of affairs is not prohibited but later a new exception can be inserted into this state of affairs. When will an exception modify a previous state of affairs? We do not know. I think that we should talk of "empty completeness" because we know, for example, that "all A will behave as B in circumstances C". However, we do not know (now) who will fill A (and whether this concrete instance will be problematic), which concrete conduct will fill B, and which concrete circumstances will fill C. This is so because there are, inevitably, borderline cases and because it can be problematic to determine whether something (a norm, a situation, an object) belongs to a particular class.

Consequently, we cannot say that if something is not prohibited, it is, *ipso facto*, permitted except in a formal sense. Another example is the following: suppose that there is a rule saying "pet animals are not prohibited in this park". Generically speaking, it is clear that if it is not prohibited, then it is permitted. Nevertheless, we do not know, in advance, whether the authorities will accept or not a tame bear as a member of the class of permitted pet animals. Here, the application of arguments *a simile*, or *a contrario*, is not the result of deontic logic. In summary, we know that if

---

[63] Among a wide literature: Hierro, Liborio, *El realismo juridico escandinavo*, F. Torres, editor, Valencia, 1981; Aarnio, Aulis and Peczenik, Aleksander, "Beyond the reality. A criticism of Alf Ross". In: *Meaning, Interpretation and the Law*, edited by A. Peczenik, Kustanja A-Tieto Oy, Tampere, 1986; Aarnio, Aulis, *Acta Philosophica Fennica*, Vol. 36, 1983.

[64] von Wright, G. H. "Is there a logic of norms?", op. cit., page 266.

[65] Ibidem, page 280.

it is not prohibited to allow pet animals in the park, then it is permitted, but this does not solve all problems that citizens expect to come across.

At least in some cases, a judgement of relevance will be needed in order to achieve determination. We could talk, in relation to the above example, of "void certainty". Hence, judges are as important as legislators in order to know what the law is, concretely speaking. One could say that in order to know what the legal order is, it is enough to describe what the legislator has authoritatively said and what the judges have decided to do about the obscurities of the legislator's discourse, by virtue of their power of making choices. In this case, we would have two books to describe, the legislator's and the judges'. However, what does it mean to describe the sentences uttered by legislators and judges? If it is not enough to describe black letter rules, what else is needed?

It has been said that all logical consequences of the primitive statements or axioms, would form part of a given legal order. However, this is dubious. As G. Harman says,

> "The mind is finite. One does not want to clutter it with trivialities. It would be irrational to fill one's memory with as many as possible of the logical consequences of one's beliefs."[66]

Here it seems that, again, a judgement of relevance is needed. It has no sense, from a pragmatical point of view, to fill our time with trivialities, although it does not seem absurd from a logical point of view. As far as a judgement of relevance is a proper task for practical reason it has primacy over logical rationality, in the sense commented on above. In this respect, it is interesting to recall what G. Harman has said about the role of logic in reasoning,

> "Reasoning is not argument or proof. It is procedure for revising one's beliefs, for changing one's views ... . The question then, is whether logic has a special role to play in this procedure of belief revision."[67]

Harman believes that logic has an especially relevant role in implication and inconsistency, but implication has to be distinguished from inference, which has a basic role for changing or revising our plans and intentions, as something different to the change of our beliefs. Moreover, Harman believes that we cannot settle clearly the boundaries of logic, in so far as logical constants are expressed in natural language,

---

[66] Harman, Gilbert. "Logic and Reasoning", *Synthese 60*, 1984, page 108.

[67] Ibidem, page 107. These and other ideas have been developed by G. Harman in his book, *Change in View*, A Bradford Book, Cambridge, Massachusetts, London, 1989, pages 5, 10 and 19. He says, "Mary believes that if she looks in the cupboard, she will see a box of Cheerios. She comes to believe that she is looking in the cupboard and that she does not see a box of Cheerios. At this point, Mary's belief are jointly inconsistent and therefore *imply* any proposition whatsoever. This does not authorise Mary to *infer* any proposition whatsoever ... Furthermore, even before Mary fails to find any Cheerios in the cupboard, it would be silly for her to clutter her mind with vast numbers of useless logical implications of her beliefs, such as *either she will have Cheerios for breakfast or the moon is made of green cheese* ... Reasoning in the sense of reasoned change in view should never be identified with proof or argument; inference is not implication. Logic is the theory of implication, not directly the theory of reasoning ... I began by suggesting logic might be especially relevant to reasoning in two ways, via implication and inconsistency."

> "Whether we should count "today is Friday, so tomorrow is Saturday" as a logical implication depends on whether or not "today, tomorrow", "Friday", "Saturday" are logical constants (in a kind of tense logic). What determines the logical constants? ... It seemed to me the identification of the logical constants should reflect something about our practices, about what our reasoning is or at least should be."[68]

Hence, he believes that what makes the implication a logical implication is that it appears by virtue of logical form, in other words, by virtue of the grammatical form. He finishes by claiming that, it is not clear whether the grammatical criterion will single out a unique logic in English.

A point of Harman's approach that should be emphasized is that reasoning is a procedure for revising one's plans and intentions. If this is correct, logic arrives "late", in the sense that its basic usefulness is *ex post,* once interpretation has been fulfilled. Namely, once we have decided through practical reasoning that a given legal conflict does not have enough similarities (or relevant similarities) with a former model for solving a certain type of legal conflicts, we have to state which are the factual relevant differences and whether they fit adequately in the former normative model. We can re-elaborate it, create a new one, or elaborate a principle within which the new conflict can adequately fit. Once these problems have been decided, logic (that is, the type of logic we have chosen) can come to our help in order to avoid inconsistencies, granted that there is no unique way to formalise legal rules. Moreover, we should remember that normative contradictions are dependent on the same factual circumstances and this is (or can be) an interpretative problem.

Some of the former problems may lead us to look for meta-rules to decide between different logics. However, how can we decide which is the "right" one? It seems that there is none.[69] It seems that either we toss up a coin (bare decision) or we fall into an infinite regression. Once we abandon the requirement of applying algorithms everywhere we can cope with the problem of choice, that is, choice made by skilful people (in this case, competent jurists). Of course, there can be reasoned disagreement. Nevertheless, if this approach is not accepted, when dealing with external justification, we are led to bare irrationality. However, in this case, we can

---

68 Harman, G. "Logic and Reasoning", op. cit., page 120. Moreover, some have claimed that there cannot be a logic of norms (deontic statements expressing norms, not describing norms) because these "genuine" norms have no true-false values: Bayón, J.C., *La Normatividad del Derecho*, Centro de Estudios Constitucionales, Madrid 1991, pages 251 and ff. In *Normas Juridicas y Análisis Lógico*, Hans Kelsen-Ulrich Klug, Centro de Estudios Constitucionales, Madrid 1988, page 26, Bulygin says (in the prologue), "von Wright who supported for a long time the idea that there are logical relations between norms, is now defending the opposite view. The difficulties the hiletic conception has to overcome are very important (partly stated by Kelsen) and it is not clearly glimpsed how they can be surmounted. I believe that there is not a decisive test to prefer one to another." In addition, Alchourrón, C. and Bulygin, E., *Análisis Lógico y Derecho*, Centro de Estudios Constitucionales, Madrid 1991, page 126, say "For the expressive conception there cannot be a logic of norms because there are not logical relations between them. Deontic logic can only take the form of a logic of normative propositions. On the other hand, for the hiletic conception there are two logics: a logic of norms and a logic of normative propositions."

69 Soeteman, Arendt. *Logic in Law*, Kluwer, Dordrecht, 1989, page 21, "In other words, there is a plurality of possible logical systems based upon a multitude of different axioms and different meanings for the logical constants. Once one is involved with logic a choice can be made for one or several of these systems. This is not a choice between "right" and "wrong"; any choice of a formally correct system is "right"."

both support racism or the contrary, although not at the same time. This would be the only irrationality at stake.

In summary, the main point, or one of the main points, is that we need to reconsider our decisions pragmatically speaking. Some of them will be more difficult to reconsider because they are more basic, granted certain natural and cultural features. Generally speaking, the reconsideration of our decisions (apart from the special legal requirements a legal order can settle) is based on intellectual conservatism or the principle of inertia, at least in normal circumstances. I believe that Kuhn's approach about normal and revolutionary changes in mature sciences can be applied here. In any case, we do not want the reconsideration of our decisions to be done in an arbitrary manner. At the same time, this does not mean that we have a formal algorithm that leads us, necessarily, from some premises to a necessary conclusion. This seems a modified version of Dworkin's dream of the "one right answer" thesis.

For example, we know in advance that if a will is made (granted that there is a previous legal rule stating it) violating basic formal requirements, other things being equal, it will be void. Nevertheless, there is not the same certainty when we deal with features that are not formal. Sometimes, legal rules include terms such as "sufficient", "good faith", etcetera, that further interpretations (officials, lawyers and legal scholars) try, *ceteris paribus*, to precise and fit. What we cannot do is know, in advance, when a given set of circumstances will require us to justify a concrete change. This can be done easily in trivial cases, and in these cases a competent jurist is not needed. Hence, we cannot know, *ex ante*, how much evidence will be "sufficient" in order to change, or modify, a decision or a model of decisions. This means, *inter alia*, that the emphasis put on the legislator to completely know what the legal order is, is mistaken. If we also have to know what judges have said, we recognize that the realm of practical reason, evaluations, etcetera, enters into the task of identification of the legal order. The descriptive-neutral approach is not enough.

The above does not mean that when dealing with formal features (or requirements) there is no problem. It means that, normally, formal features will not pose serious problems of interpretation, in the way material features usually do. In this respect, legal formal features (or requirements) could be considered as exclusionary reasons or they can be considered as reasons fostering legal certainty, because of their higher level of preciseness. If we do not consider them as exclusionary reasons we could balance their positive effects (legal certainty) with their negative effects (unjust result) when applied to concrete cases. When this unjust result is considered as more important than the beneficial effects of the formal preciseness, there can be a balance of reasons that can lead to an interpretative change using, for example, a *reductio ad absurdum*.

To rely, excessively, on authority reasons or on material reasons does not work, because of the increasing complexity of our societies, that pushes for an "all things considered" judgement. If the official, who has to decide, is a follower of Alf Ross, he would not have this problem because, for him, justice would be to apply previously settled rules equally. However, these officials (no matter how "scientific" they can be) are a hindrance for the normal development of legal orders, at least legal orders based on the Rule of Law, understood from a relatively "thick" model.

One of the conclusions of the former comments is the following: Relevant legal features, either must-sources, should-sources or may-sources, are the points of reference, when members of the legal community reconsider a given legal decision.

Considerations of relevancy will be needed, and these call for judgement, not for algorithms. It is in the tradition of legal positivism (or at least some tendencies) to give strong support to scientific methods in legal fields, which are basically understood as logical and empirical ones. It has also been an outstanding feature, to consider evaluations as pseudo-sentences, pertaining to the domain of irrationality, and practical reason as a kind of pseudo-rationality. With these saddlebags, their hope for algorithms and their distrust towards "relevant considerations" and other similar expressions is not surprising.

I believe that we cannot avoid the outstanding importance of certain aspects, which differentiate our task from that of "mature sciences". I would say that "authoritativeness", "legal tradition", "legislative purposiveness" and "committed interpretation" are central aspects that, together, help us to understand the task of jurists. The first concept refers to the relative weight that content-independent rules have, because they arise from authority; the third concept refers to the idea that, for a legal order to have sense, it will have purposes to fulfil; the fourth concept refers to the idea that we cannot dispense with interpretation from an internal point of view, at least in part; the second concept refers to the idea that we cannot start from scratch, and that the former tasks are fulfilled with an eye on the legal tradition, which is not separate and autonomous from the present global community.

In spite of the possible existence of partial similarities between the so-called normative sciences and the so-called mature sciences, the above cited features are proper for legal normative fields. To try to fit everything in a Procrustean bed has been another outstanding feature of the heirs of logical positivism. One of the magic instruments is logic. In this view, it is allowed to choose the premises anyone prefers, because this is not a rational task. The only rational side is whether the conclusions follow on necessarily from the premises chosen. Nevertheless, as G. Harman says, not even logic will have the last word in this task because not all inconsistencies are equally "relevant" for certain purposes. I am not criticising logic, but only the overemphasis of those who exclusively identify rationality with logic. In this respect J. Ziman says,

> "... any person who would try to refute the relativity theory would not succeed through, for example, a demonstration that there is a logic fallacy in Einstein's original writing."[70]

To fulfil the above mentioned normative tasks, we need competent jurists. This is a normal pragmatical consequence of having certain features: *inter alia*, human beings with limited information, limited time and disputable decisions. If we are dealing with practical reason and it is a parody of rationality, why not toss up a coin or support the strongest will? The infallibility of methods is a type of transposition of the old belief in God's infallibility. It has also been a feature both of Natural Law doctrines in general and legal positivists' trends in general, to neglect or water down

[70] Ziman, John. *Introducción al estudio de las ciencias*, Ariel, Barcelona, 1986, page 67.

complex balances that include, *inter alia*, evaluations. The reason is, in both cases, the strong emphasis on authority. In the former case, divine authority, in the latter case, human political authority whose statements are seen as exclusionary reasons.

I would insist that the range of application of class words is not (at least always) clear and, hence, the existence of borderline cases. These cases call for meta-legal standards. Granted this situation, as a constitutive feature of legal orders, it seems unsound to claim, from a pragmatical point of view, that we can have a complete description of a given legal order. Although we cannot completely identify a given legal order, at a given time, this is not necessary for proper identification. That is, we do not need to know everything in order to have a proper identification. When I enter into a room I can identify two men sitting, although I do not know whether they are able to talk, reason or laugh. What I perceive is enough to claim that they are human beings, although perhaps somebody made two very perfect copies in order to cheat me. However, be that as it may, what I perceive is a strong *prima facie* reason to identify them as human beings. Of course, human beings are not like legal orders.

However, I can identify a given legal order, although I do not have a complete description (if this is possible) of its meaning contents at a given time. For claiming this I take for granted certain basic formal legal features and certain basic substantial features. I think we should distinguish between a first level identification of a legal order and a second level identification. The first one refers both to basic formal and substantial features. This can be sufficient to identify a given legal order from another, where for example, judges appeal to different institutional coercive apparatuses.[71]

I agree with this solution to the individualization problem. Nevertheless, when we are not trying to distinguish between legal order A and legal order B, and we are placed, let us say, within a given legal order, the former identification is not enough. We need another level of identification that refers to the specific meanings of the units (legal rules) of this specific legal order, at a given time. This is a membership problem at another level of identification. At least at this level, a constructive task is needed, or in other words, a descriptive approach is not sufficient.

3.4 Identification and Rational Agents

I assume that the "best" legal positivist trend goes through the basic idea of legal rules as reasons for action. Granted that legal justificatory reasoning is a type of moral reasoning, it is doubtful that legal positivism can clearly differentiate, in all cases, between legal "is" and legal "ought". Supposing that a "judgement of

---

[71] Nino, C.S. *Introducción al análisis del Derecho*, editorial Astrea, 2ª edición, B. Aires, 1980. Especially chapter III. Nino distinguishes, *inter alia*, between "membership criterion" and "individualization criterion". For the first we can know when a normative text is a member of a given legal order. For this we must pay attention to certain formal and substantive features. However, this chain of validity will end in rules that do not depend on other rules. Nino scrutinises five criteria to individuate legal orders. He believes that two non-derived rules are members of the same legal order when they are recognised by legal organs appealing to the same institutional coercive apparatus.

adherence" is needed for the cited legal justificatory reasoning, as Nino claims, this judgement also supposes an acceptation of a descriptive statement, saying that a certain normative text prescribes (X). It is not only an act of theoretical cognition. Granted that there is a judgement of "normative adherence" we have to pass from the existence of a given legal "ought" to the fulfilment of this legal "ought". This is not a logical conclusion but a pragmatical one. If this is correct, it is hard to see how legal positivism can clearly differentiate, in all cases, "is" from "ought". I mean *ex ante*, not *ex post*, when legal interpretation has been fulfilled.

In other words, if legal positivists can differentiate (as anybody else) law and morals, they can do it at the end of the legal justificatory process, because the legal ought cannot always be known before a constructive task has been carried out. Then, a descriptive approach can take place. Once this task is done, legal positivists can claim that they can differentiate between law and morals. However, they can do so once the legal justificatory process has finished. Given the dynamic character of the legal order, a time will come, once again, when we will not know which is the acceptable legal "is". Again, a constructive process will take place. At the end of this process we shall know which is the new legally justified "is". Nevertheless, this is not necessarily so, because the legal community can reject or neglect a given legal decision.

This is very different from the dream of infallible methods that infallibly identifies "is" and "ought". A related question is that, at least sometimes, to identify what a concrete given law "is", is useless because its legal solution is no more acceptable by the legal community. In these conflictive situations the legal community wants a new "is", not the old "is" that does not deserve this title any more for a variety of reasons. However, this new "is", is what "ought to be" accord to the justified opinion of the legal community or part of it. Once again, this is usually a conflictive task. It is not like the following: we know that this green brick is the old "is", and we choose this yellow brick as the new "is". In legal normative fields we are not just replacing an old "is" for a new "is", we are replacing an old way of directing and justifying certain human conduct for another.

Nevertheless, it is convenient to distinguish between "routine" and "hard" cases. In the former cases, a description of the legal "is" can easily be done. In these cases there is no constructive task, normally because it has already been done. In other words, either the legal community accepts the plain meaning of a given normative text, or accepts a new interpretation of this normative text. In the first case, a constructive task is not needed, because the plain meaning is accepted. In the second case, a constructive task is needed, because the former plain meaning is considered as "not adequate", or "not sufficiently adequate", given the purposes of the normative text, or the legal institution in which the normative text stands.

Once this interpretative task has been fulfilled, and once this legal solution has not been rejected, we can claim that we are able to describe a given legal "is". That is why I believe that this basic tenet of legal positivism (conceptual separation between law and morals) cannot be done, at least always, *ex ante* but *ex post*. Once the constructive normative task has been done, the "legal describers" can do their job, although only for a certain length of time, because they do not all serve forever. To talk of "description" should not deceive us. There are fundamental differences between "description" in empirical sciences and "description" in, let us say, "normative sciences". The description of a rock, by a geologist, has nothing to do with the description of the meaning content of normative texts of a given legal order, by a jurist.

It is not the case though that geologists, for example, never disagree. What happens, *inter alia,* is that the test for proving the results of their work are much more objective. It is usual that left and right wing geologists agree about rocks, because of this reason. However, it is not the same in normative legal fields. At least in hard cases, competent and sincere jurists, even jurists pertaining to the same ideological tendency, can disagree. Hence, legal reasoning cannot only be based on neutral description and deductive logic. In my view, to understand law and identification of law properly requires an understanding of the legal justificatory process. I will try to show that this process cannot stand if there is a conceptual separation between law and morals. I will briefly explain C. Nino's viewpoint because I basically agree with his approach to justificatory legal reasoning. Then, I will develop some critical comments, in order to shape my own view of the matter better.

C. Nino says,[72] before entering into the legal justificatory process, that there are some preconditions, which are a Constitution based on democratic, free and participating consensus on the one hand, and a sufficient respect for the fundamental rights of individuals, on the other. "Sufficient", because there can be no better real alternatives. Once an acceptable level of legitimacy is reached on the former basis, it is possible to move to a second level, whose justificatory reasoning is limited by the starting preconditions of legitimacy mentioned above.

Nevertheless, this does not mean that the morally valid principles and procedures do not have relevance in the legal discourse, nor that this discourse has moral autonomy. First, this would be so because these principles and procedures are the last court of appeal in the first level of the justificatory legal reasoning, and given the priority of the first level over the second, this hierarchy determines the results of the reasoning as a whole. Second, these principles and procedures have a decisive relevance in the second level of justificatory reasoning, granted that they are not incompatible with the conclusions reached in the first level.

Although I basically agree with his approach, I have some critical comments to make. However, I will not criticize a certain vagueness in his approach because some indeterminacies are fertile and some are inevitable. Nevertheless, some others should be precised. First, when Nino talks of "sufficient legitimacy" it is clear (and he knows it perfectly well) that this is vague. I will not try to avoid this, because I believe it is not possible to undertake an arithmetical calculus. Nevertheless, I believe that the problem lies in the realist alternatives. We know very little about the future, but, in this respect, one can say, recalling Popper, that the future is indeterminate or open. The acceptability of a certain alternative depends, basically, on the ideological tendencies of the individuals, more than on objective features. Only in extreme cases (for example "basic" needs) is there an agreement about the probable "realistic" aspects. There is, in between, a fringe where it makes little sense

[72] Nino, C.S. *Fundamentos de Derecho Constitucional*, Astrea, Buenos Aires, 1992, pages 66-77.

to talk of "realistic alternatives". When Nino talks of an "optimum point of legitimacy", he seems to believe in it as something independent of the different ideologies since each has their own "optimum point".

Another aspect refers to what he calls an "acceptable level of legitimacy". However, I will not criticize it for being vague, as is usual in certain analyses, because there is no (or better, I do not know of) more sound concept for this situation. In my view, the problem lies in the possibility for "limitation" of the justificatory reasoning (at the second level) because of the preconditions of legitimacy (of the first level). Nevertheless, it can be accepted that there is some limitation. For example, the justificatory reasoning of the second level cannot accept basic violations of fundamental rights. Moreover, it is hard to see which are the limitations imposed by the above mentioned consensus, except by an acceptable degree of respect for fundamental rights. In summary, Nino claims that there will be no accepted justificatory reasons (in the second level) that are incompatible with the preservation of the Constitution (that has sufficient legitimacy). It is difficult to see how this problem can be solved without interpretation, but which interpretation?

Someone (judges?) will have to interpret whether certain justificatory reasons put the preservation of the Constitution in danger. This borders dangerously on freedom of speech, because Nino talks of justificatory reasons, not of violent actions. Moreover, is the exclusion of certain justificatory reasons an important way to preserve a Constitution? Even more surprising seems the possibility that a moral principle can be exempt, in order to preserve the Constitution. I do not see how a Constitution based on a democratic, free and participating consensus, plus an acceptable respect for the fundamental rights of individuals, needs (and is justified to) to censor in that way. Censorship is suited to authoritarian regimes, not to regimes with legitimate Constitutions. Nevertheless, if the concept of moral principles includes racist ones, for example, Nino would be right.

The last comment refers to the claim that the principles and procedures of the first level (given the priority of this level over the second) will determine the results of the reasoning process as a whole. This seems unsound though, and goes against what Nino himself has written, by explaining the difficulties of the application of norms, given the semantic, syntactic and pragmatic indeterminacies.[73] My conclusion is that Nino's approach is basically correct, but he unduly believes that the first level (its principles and procedures) will determine the following justificatory reasoning process. Only in a very wide sense of "limitation" or "determination" can we give sense to this supposed capacity of the principles and procedures of the first level. Therefore, I will repeat that "the future is open or indeterminate", not only in the sense that it is so, empirically speaking, but it is also so in the justificatory reasoning process, although there are limits. We put them but they call for interpretation.

I will go on briefly explaining the rest of Nino's approach of the structure of practical reasoning, while retaining the basic point of the former brief exposition, that is, the claim that the legal discourse has no autonomy in relation to the moral discourse. Nino claims that the preservation of the Constitution does not mean to

[73] Nino, C.S. *Derecho, Moral y Politica*, op. cit., pages 87 and ff.

freeze this social practice and he emphasizes the existence of tension between preservation and change. He insists that the principles and procedures of the first level will serve to solve the problems of indetermination. He recalls that J. Rawls and M. Singer used this practical reasoning in several levels. Singer especially, claims that there is a gap between institutions and actions, in the sense that a judgement about the justice or injustice of an institution does not allow an inference about whether a concrete action pertaining to that institution ought to be undertaken.

Additional premises are needed. Nino also claims that there is no tension between the moral principles that justify a social practice, and the reasoning that, in order to preserve that practice, ought sometimes to neglect those principles. This happens when this reasoning has to justify specific actions or decisions. Nino's grading of legal reasoning (two levels) claims that the basic evaluative principles determine which social practices have legitimacy but, once this is done, these practices themselves determine which principles will be applied to justify concrete actions and decisions.

My comments are the following: First, Nino insists that the principles and procedures of the first level will allow the solution of the indeterminacies of the second level. As I said, this seems to me an unsound view that Nino himself has criticised in other works. Second, he accepts Singer's claim that there is a gap between the institution level and the concrete action-decision level, and the need for additional premises to fulfil it. On the one hand, if they are so important he should have explained which kind of premises, but, on the other hand, it shows the insufficiency of the principles and procedures of the first level to solve the indeterminacies of the second level. The same can be said in relation to the incompatibilities between the first and second levels.

Third, he claims that, granted that moral principles cannot be accepted for self-interest reasons, there is no tension between the moral principles that justify a social practice and the neglect of these moral principles (sometimes), in order to preserve this social practice. Nevertheless, we do not know when concrete reasoning will preserve this practice or not. The preservation of a social practice does not depend on a specific action or decision. Only a large number of actions and decisions can lead to its preservation or not. How do we know this? That is, how do we know that a concrete action preserves (or will contribute to preserve), or not, a practice? Are there no other elements that help to preserve, or not, this practice? Moreover, it is surprising that a legitimate social practice can accept that its preservation requires the violation (sometimes) of the moral principles that have justified this social practice.

Fourth, it is claimed that certain moral principles determine which social practices have legitimacy but, once this is done, these social practices will determine the principles that justify actions and decisions. To justify this claim, he says that if amusement is the reason to play a game, we cannot decide the moves of the game on the basis of which move produces more amusement. I see a problem here, because it is not the same to have "amusement" as the ultimate reason, as having moral reasons or moral principles. On the contrary to Nino, I believe that the best way to preserve this social practice is to develop reasoning that can be justified on the basis of (or not be contradictory with) these moral principles.

In this respect, we could differentiate between important cases, in which fundamental rights of individuals are in play, and ordinary cases, in which fundamental rights of individuals are not in play. In the former case, it is hard to see how reasoning cannot take into account these moral principles. In the latter case, it is not seriously problematic because if there is a conflict, fundamental rights are not in play. In summary, if these moral principles are ultimate reasons, or the last court of appeal, it is hard to see how they can be neglected in concrete cases when justifying (for prudential reasons?) certain actions or decisions. As I have said, there can be cases in which prudential reasons are enough to justify an action, because they do not conflict with an ultimate reason, but in these cases we cannot say that the moral principles have not been taken into account. Only that they were not required.

In any case, the problem, if I properly understand it, is how can we violate our basic moral principles, in specific reasoning, because, supposedly, it preserves -or helps to preserve- our social practice? I retained from the first brief exposition of Nino's approach that legal discourse is not autonomous from moral discourse. In the second part of Nino's discourse, there is an idea that I will take into account. The idea that we ought to justify our actions and decisions to the perfection of the Constitution, although this means working for the perfection of the foundations of legitimacy at the first level. I agree with this complex idea[74] that will be a part of the criticism towards a conceptual separation between law and morals.

Now let us move towards the structure of legal justificatory reasoning,[75] according to Nino's view. In summary, there is (One) a major premise, that is a general moral reason (it cannot be a prudential reason because the interests of others are compulsively affected) and it is usually called an operative reason; (Two) Minor premise(s), that is, a descriptive judgement of the existence of a legal rule, not settled against the requirements made in (1), is usually called an auxiliary reason; (Three) Minor premise(s), describing a fact that is justifiably included in (2); (Four) Minor premises(s) trying to solve the syntactic, semantic and pragmatic indeterminacies, solutions which are, at least in part, evaluative; (Five) A conclusion, that is a consequence of the former premises.

From this structure of legal justificatory reasoning a conceptual separation between law and morals does not follow, for the following reasons: First, the major premise is a moral reason (an operative reason). Second, the conclusion is a practical legal decision, that is, a concretion of a moral general reason plus other minor premises. Third, the intermediate premises imply, *inter alia*, moral evaluations. Fourth, we cannot know, *ex ante*, which will be the concretion of the major and minor premises, in all cases, because it is (at least in some cases) a reconstructive and disputable process. Fifth, this reconstructive process supposes a tension between what the law "is", at a given time, and what the law "ought to be", namely, it supposes a moral compromise of improvement (not only in a technical sense but also in a moral sense) of the social practice in play.

---

[74] Urbina, Sebastián. *Reason, Democracy, Society*, Kluwer, Dordrecht, 1996. Especially chapters I, III and IV.

[75] Nino, C.S. *La validez del Derecho*, Astrea, Buenos Aires, 1985, especially pages 52 and ff., and 137 and ff.

Sixth, this is a feasible task for the participants in this social practice. It is not possible, at least pragmatically speaking, to be engaged in a moral and legal-technical reconstruction of a legal order without commitment to (at least) some basic moral reasons, that function like operative reasons. A basic one is to believe that a given legal order deserves critical and reflective obedience. This binomial expresses fidelity to law as something different from mere obedience, which is the citizens' behaviour expected by some old trends of legal positivism. This type of behaviour is considered as sufficient by Hart's positivism for the existence of a legal order, in so far as officials adopt an internal point of view, which can, or in my opinion, should be equated to fidelity and law.

3.5 Beliefs, Evidence and Rationality

I will deal with the pragmatical necessity of practical judgement when we want to know, justifiably, what we ought to do, in a given context with competing reasons. It is not necessary that these competing reasons be formulated by different individuals. It is enough that the subject, involved in a problematic practical decision, bears these competing reasons in mind. As I said, one of the mistaken views, when dealing with practical reason, is to identify rationality with logic. Often related with this approach is the idea that "beliefs" are necessarily unconscious.[76] This unconsciousness would condemn practical reasoning to the field of irrationality. It is a mistaken view to suppose that there is, on the one hand, "evidence" as a safe background that leads to

---

[76] An example of this line of thought can be seen in, Redondo, Cristina, *La noción de razón para la acción en el análisis juridico*, Centro de Estudios Constitucionales, Madrid, 1996. She believes that practical reason works not through the exercise of reason but will or passion (page 20); she believes that not everybody accepts that there is a causal link between psychological states and individual behaviour (page 25, note 12); she claims a clear separation between empirical and ethical issues (page 27); she claims that if acceptance of norms is just a matter affecting the believers in the moral correctness of these norms there is no possibility of rational discussion (page 211); she claims that the acceptation of beliefs is, either an attitude not dependent on will, or exclusively based on non-voluntary attitudes (page 210); finally, she believes that the only rational way -in relation to a given proposition- is to dispense with beliefs and rely exclusively on evidence. Nevertheless, she accepts that there can be more than one evidence in relation to the same proposition. In this case, a decision (not based on evidence) is needed to decide what is "adequate" (page 211); she claims that who does not believe in the truth or falseness of a given norm is in a better position to evaluate it than a person affected by a belief in that norm (pages 211-212); she claims that accepting a standard as a justificatory reason does not mean that there is a justification from an objective point of view. It is not clear what "objective point of view" means. A God's Eye view? An intersubjective view? It seems that she cannot accept the latter. Moreover, although it is not my aim in this paper to cope with these important issues I would say, very briefly, that there can be difficult problems in relation to the position of the author towards "belief" because, *inter alia*, it should be distinguished between "justified" and "non-justified" beliefs. Suppose that two policemen find evidence that indicates that a black man is the author of a murder. Both policemen believe that the black man is responsible but policeman (1) believes it on the basis of the evidence, while policeman (2) believes the same because he is racist. Both policemen have the same evidence but only the first has a justified belief. I cannot see why belief is related to bare irrationality. On the other hand, it is also doubtful that a person who does not believe in the truth of falseness of a given norm (by the way, I think that these terms are not adequate) is in a better position for evaluation than a "committed" person. Does it mean that a person who is "neutral" between racist and non-racist doctrines is in a better position?

truth and, on the other hand, "belief" as an unsafe (and -at least sometimes-involuntary) background that leads to bare irrationality. The former would be the proper baseline of theoretical reason, while the latter would be the proper baseline of practical reason.

"Evidence" is a controversial term. Consequently, I will not try to scrutinize it but just say that we should, at least, distinguish between "evidence" in common sense contexts and "evidence" in a mature-sciences context. In the former case we have no conclusive evidence. For example, "I saw you this morning crossing this square", is probably true because I have known you for many years. However, I could have been mistaken because of the distance, because I do not see very well at this distance, or because the square was crowded, etcetera. Nevertheless, the users of a given language accept that this is, normally, sufficient evidence. In mature-sciences the requirements of "evidence" are stronger. Nevertheless, in empirical sciences it is usual to rely on the inductive method. As is known, this method has been criticised because there is no logical step from particular sentences derived from particular experiences and universal laws.

That is, we cannot logically infer "all X are Y" from finite particular experiences where X are Y. Empirical mature-sciences are based, *inter alia*, on inductive methods, although they are not logically conclusive. Nevertheless, the level of conclusiveness is much stronger than in common sense contexts. In any case, "evidence" in legal normative realms is closer to the common sense conception of "evidence". However, in criminal trials (or even in private), although it is possible to request the help of scientists for particular purposes, the last word is the judge's word. This is so because the legal order does not try to describe the reality as it is (as empirical sciences do) but to ascribe reality. Nevertheless, in some cases it is possible that laws give a strong or even definitive weight to scientific proof.[77]

It is often said that "belief" is a mental state or a subjective condition of knowing. However, if so, could we claim that the result of an inductive inference of an empirical scientist (let us say with 95% probability) is a high degree of belief? We should distinguish between justified beliefs and non-justified beliefs. The former, not the latter, would be based on sufficient evidence. In legal normative realms, what is "sufficient evidence" is usually stated by the legislator and, when doubts arise, by judges. Otherwise, although it can be claimed that all beliefs are unconscious, it could also be claimed that intentionality (which is basic for a purposive agent) is linked to consciousness. Nevertheless, our beliefs (in a psychological sense) can be unconscious because it seems obvious that we are not conscious of most of our beliefs at any time. Going back to justification, if we admit that it implies truth, then, we could claim that knowledge is justified belief. However, in legal realms we usually believe that legal justification implies something weaker than truth.

---

[77] Jackson, J. and Doran, S. "Evidence". In: *A Companion to Philosophy of Law and Legal Theory*, edited by D. Patterson, Blackwell, Oxford, 1996, pages 172-183. They say, "Whatever view we may form on such questions, the foregoing discussion suggests that far from shrinking into nothingness, the law of evidence has a vital role to play in the preparation, presentation and evaluation of evidence."

For example, in a hard case, to accept the above would imply support of the Dworkinian single right answer. I do not think this is a correct approach though. In any case, it is extremely stringent and also useless to claim that, for a belief to be rational, it must be the result of a formal inference. In normative legal contexts we need another conception of rational belief linked to a conception of justification, which is not exclusively logically formal. On the other hand, in order to have a "justified true belief" it is not sufficient to reach truth, because we can reach it by chance. For a belief to be sufficient for knowledge, good justification is needed. Nevertheless, in legal realms we do not expect truth, at least that understood as correspondence. In some cases we can have a logical truth, in the sense that we have accepted a certain chain of deductive valid inferences from given normative premises.

This situation will remain as long as this interpretation, its logical consequences and its legal consequences, are accepted by the legal community. If not, the logical chain will continue being logically valid (if properly inferred) but the legal community can decide that a shorter or longer chain of logical consequences should be accepted, because they lead to "better" legal results. Otherwise, the above mentioned interpretation of a given legal text can be modified. If we claim that only infallible justified true beliefs lead to knowledge, and we require legal knowledge, this will be useless for legal reasoning. Someone could say, "the worst for legal reasoning", but this is to have one's back to the legal community. To enhance rationality out of context and to neglect contextual rationality is a good way to be useless, for the expected social functions of the so-called legal science.

Let us see, for example, the belief that there is an external world. This is, as B. Russell says, an "instinctive belief", and all knowledge is based on our "instinctive beliefs".[78] Unfortunately for the critics, Russell was not a kind of over-credulous monk. Should we reject the whole of our belief-web because we are not dealing with "evidence" but with belief? Moreover, "evidence" is not a yes-no issue. On the contrary, "evidence" can be graded, and we cannot decide its hierarchy on the basis (at least exclusively) of evidence itself. Furthermore, we have certain evidences in so far as we have accepted certain theories, but the theories themselves cannot be built (at least exclusively) on the basis of evidence. Newton's theory is a famous and repeated example.

The search for knowledge, if it has sense in legal realms, (except for the pure and neutral description of the legal normative texts, which is otherwise a poor task if understood as the only one) can be, at least sometimes, rather unsound, granted that economic cost (not only related to economic resources but to time too) is another basic aspect to be taken into account. Suppose I want to know whether the students of a crowded University will attend the lectures of visiting Professors on Friday evenings or not. In order to know, I should ask everyone (granted that their answers were considered reliable) but, usually and soundly, people rely on reasonable beliefs, deciding that they have "enough" information at a certain point in order to

---

[78] Russell, Bertrand. *Los problemas de la filosofía*, Biblioteca de Iniciación Cultural, segunda edición, Barcelona, 1953, page 30. Schmitt, Frederick F. *Knowledge and Belief*, Routledge, London, 1992, can also be seen, especially chapter seven.

provide sufficient evidence to reach an answer. Pragmatical aspects such as disposal of time, money, concrete purposes, the importance given to certain mistakes, etcetera, play a basic role.

Moreover, several senses of "belief" should be distinguished. This would be similar to "knowledge", but it is not my aim in this paper to scrutinize this too. First, "belief-in", as when someone believes in ideas or persons. A typical example is to believe in God, but also to believe in Democracy. Second, what is usually called "object-belief". For example, a judge believes a witness. People can believe politicians or not. Third, "propositional-belief". In this case, beliefs refer to propositions that can be true or false. As the reader will have noted, the "object-belief" has close relationships with "propositional-belief" because the judge of our example believes the witness. He believes the witness because he supposes that this witness has stated the truth.

Even more, it can also be seen that "belief-in" is not sharply separate from "propositional-belief". In which sense? In so far as we are talking about legal normative realms, we should bear in mind a classical distinction (although not pacific) concerned with "internal and external point of view". Therefore, to "believe-in" Democracy, Human Rights, or in the basic values of a given legal order (I mean legal order based on the Rule of Law) is very important, not only for the existence of Democracy, legal order, etcetera, but also for their efficient running.

As I said, when a judge believes a witness, he believes the statements uttered because he believes the truthfulness of what has been said, although there can be, in some cases, certain legal restraints in order to know the material truth. This is one of the reasons that makes it unsound to talk of knowledge in legal normative realms. As far as the judge's belief is concerned, it is important to see that a belief should not be understood in isolation. The justification for believing a concrete statement from a specific witness is related, directly and/or indirectly, to other beliefs. For example, when a judge believes a given statement, he also believes many other related beliefs, such as legal rules, principles, duties, social expectations, etcetera, providing he shares an internal point of view. Here we can see the importance of coherence and systematisation.

Hence, if we are going to understand a belief properly, we should fit it into a "belief-web". This is similar to claiming that one of the features of beliefs is that they are holistic. This is important, at least in legal normative realms, because it is both a restraint and a help for the judge, for the legal scholar or the jurist in general. It is a help, because one can see (granted special training) whether this belief fits into the "belief-web" or not. It is also a restraint, because there is no justification, at least *prima facie*, to accept a belief that does not fulfil the former requirement. This also means that beliefs are contextual. In the case of the legal order, with a more delimited and precise contextuality, this is especially so in certain branches such as criminal law.

Then, beliefs should cohere if we are going to place them, justifiably, within our "belief-web". Nevertheless, our beliefs, as in the case of the above mentioned judge, are not always determined. It is wrong to claim that, for example, "all contracting parties ought to behave in good faith" is determined. This is, let us say, an "empty determination". To accept the latter does not imply the acceptation of judicial arbitrariness, although much more should be said about the issues of indeterminacy and underdeterminacy. The latter can be understood as the view that there will always be more than one theory consistent with any body of empirical data. The same can be said in relation to legal theories that try to say what the law (the object) is.

Moreover, we cannot avoid a certain level of semantic indeterminacy in legal orders. One reason is that we identify and understand legal rules granted that they are elements of wider sets, like branches of a legal order or the legal order itself. At the same time, different legal theories (and their acceptation) condition the understanding of the legal order. Another reason for this relative indeterminacy is that legal orders use class names and we do not know clearly in advance the specific members that will fit in. There will always be borderline cases. In any case, there is an interaction of beliefs and preferences (desires, interests or values) with states of affairs that may, and usually do, lead to action. The above should not be understood as a causal relationship like that of gravity.

In this respect P.F. Strawson says, referring to beliefs which relate to parts of the world which are not (so to speak) in view,

> "what is it to hold such a belief? Is it to entertain a thought or an image with a peculiar vividness, as Hume seems sometimes to suggest? Certainly not. One might thus conceive or imagine something which one strongly desired or greatly feared -without, however, believing in its reality. Or one might simply entertain oneself with vivid images."[79]

Before finishing this epigraph I just want to mention some further distinctions about the concept of "belief" that should be taken into account for a proper understanding of the term.[80]

3.6 Reasons for Action and Practical Judgement

It is known that people generally try to mould living together with their individual behaviour, on the basis (*inter alia*) of certain values. Taking this for granted, it is not surprising that "reasons for action" is a matter of special concern, because both law and morals are not, at least primarily, objects of contemplation. First, let us have a brief look at two known distinctions, those of Internalism and Externalism. Let us

---

[79] Strawson, P.F. *Analysis and Metaphysics*, Oxford University Press, Oxford, 1992, pages 79-80.

[80] As Harman G. says: "I assume one believes something explicitly if one's belief in that thing involves an explicit mental representation whose content is the content of that belief. On the other hand, something is believed only implicitly if it is not explicitly believed but, for example, is easily inferable from one's explicit beliefs" ... "the distinction between explicit and implicit beliefs is not the same as either the distinction between belief that is available to consciousness and unconsciousness belief or that between "ocurrent" and "dispositional" beliefs. We normally consider a belief "unconscious" if one is not aware one has it and one cannot easily become aware of it simply by considering whether one has it. Otherwise, the belief is available to consciousness. Now, clearly, implicit beliefs can be available to consciousness. The belief that the earth does not have two suns is normally only implicit in one's implicit beliefs and it is not itself explicitly represented, even though it is immediately available to consciousness" ... "So the distinction between implicit and explicit beliefs is not the same as that between unconscious beliefs and those available to consciousness." Harman, G. *Change in view*, op. cit., pages 13-14.

state, schematically, that Internalism claims once a person has, for example, a certain moral belief he has a reason for action, and this represents enough motivation to do it. On the other hand, Externalism claims that a person may have a certain moral belief (or a belief that he is under the obligation to do X) but it does not give a reason for him to do it.

At least in legal normative fields, it seems more sound to support Internalism, even accepting that the above claim of Externalism is true. Let us take an example from H. Kelsen. For Kelsen, a sanction is an unpleasant consequence even though there may be some people who enjoy to be in prison. I will come back to the social dimension of this idea later. In a similar sense, we can say it is possible that a person claims racism is morally unacceptable but, from time to time, gives a black man a beating because he is a black man. However, although this is possible it is not normal, probably because it is not coherent. Generally speaking, legal orders are made firm, *inter alia*, on the supposition that, if people believe freedom of speech, pluralism, tolerance, etcetera, are morally good, they will behave accordingly. That is, in general, a coherent behaviour is expected. In addition, to believe so, is to believe that there is a reason (at least a *prima facie* reason) to behave in a certain way (*ceteris paribus*). Legal orders would not work properly if it were equally probable that people behaved either in a coherent way or not.

All of this is related to the important issue of "social practice". We cannot constitute and maintain social practices, such as law, in general, or promise, in particular, if people do not have a coherent behaviour. At least in many cases, there is a former commitment, *inter alia*, to certain moral beliefs. In this respect, an internal point of view is (although not exclusively) a moral point of view, that is, a recognition that certain behaviour is morally good, because of certain accepted moral premises, at least *prima facie*. It does not mean that at all times, all people have to accept the same moral beliefs. Practical reason is contextual and it does not have a God's eye view. Apart from participants, there are outsiders but I will not scrutinize the possibilities of an outsider, in order to "survive" better within participants of a given social practice. I will just say that, if the participants realise that this is so, they will probably not use a normative language with the outsider, and it is probable that his conduct would have certain negative social consequences.

I believe that this shows the paramount importance of the normative language, and its concepts such as "justifying", "guiding", "acting purposively", "criticising", etcetera. Even when we are able to explain or to recognize legal behaviour, this is done by a central reference to normativity, not to causal aspects. Even more, a legal order can settle legal fictions to ascribe reality, given certain purposes. Moreover, when hard legal conflicts appear, sound people do not necessarily call on physicists or chemists to solve them or take them to be the last word. When these experts are called by a judge, in order to solve a technical aspect of a legal conflict, it is not necessary that what they state is accepted by the judge, because it is usual, at least in Rule of Law legal systems, to know that the legal truth is a task undertaken by judges. This task is undertaken according to the legal settled procedures that, usually, impose certain limits to enable material truth to be reached. For example, legal fictions or legal presumptions.

Now, it is time to scrutinize the concept of "practical judgement" because it is central in legal orders. Practical judgement is here understood, not as a human faculty (although it is presupposed) but as the act or the process of judging and the result of it, that is, normally, a proper action. First, I will quote some basic features of practical judgement and some situations where we run out of rules. In spite of this, we do not decide to act in an irrational manner. Second, I will scrutinize hard cases and practical judgement, taking as a reference N. MacCormick's legal approach. Before hand though, it is worth emphasizing how practical judgement has been, and is, neglected by legal positivist tendencies in general as something irrational, something that would spoil any scientific inquiry.

This is a mistaken view that has some backing, especially within the supposedly most scientific legal trends. As W.H. Newton-Smith says,

> "Many predicates assigned by us to objects are predicates whose ascription we cannot justify ... . Hence, there is something radically wrong in the dominant image of a scientist as somebody who refrains from entrusting in judgements that he cannot explicitly found on ... This capacity of judgement, of adopting decisions without having, at the same time, an explicit justification, it is not only practised in the lower levels we have been considering until now."

Similar considerations can be seen in some of M. Bunge's works.[81]

I think it is time to move, without embarrassment on our part, to practical judgement and hard cases. The features of practical judgement according to H. Brown are,

> "A) judgements are not made by following rules, B) judgements are fallible, C) judgements must be made by individuals who are in command of an appropriate body of information that is relevant to the judgement in question."[82]

These features are very important for our concern, especially for hard cases, and I will briefly comment on them. If we do not have faith in the omnipotence of deductive logic, we shall have no problems in accepting that not everything can be soundly solved by this procedure and, hence, we are led to fallibility, as the second feature tells us. This requires an exercise of humbleness though, because it means that we can be mistaken.[83]

---

[81] Newton-Smith, W.H. *La racionalidad de la ciencia*, Paidos Studio, Barcelona, 1981, pages 252-253. In a similar vein it is worth considering the opinions of Mario Bunge, *Intuición y razón*, Tecnos, Madrid, 1986. "Not few philosophers are responsible for the spread myth according to which scientists use two clear cut and standardized methods through which any problem of knowledge can be tackled. Those methods would be the deductive and inductive procedures that, it is supposed, allow scientists to dispense with guesswork, hunch and, perhaps, also talent (as Bacon believed, just adopting his rules)." He also adds, "Contrarily to the common opinion among semantics, I believe that the interpretative capability cannot be mechanized or trivialized formulating explicitly all designation rules and interpretative postulates that give meaning to the symbols at stake. A reason for this is that these rules and postulates do not *exhaust* the meaning." Pages 92 and 98. (The underlining is mine).

[82] Brown, Harold. *Rationality*, Routledge, London, 1990, page 139. Among a wide literature, von Wright, George, *Explicación y Comprensión*, Madrid, Alianza, 1981; Aarnio, Aulis, "Remarks on the Theory of Legal Actions", University of Tampere, forthcoming publication.

[83] According to K. Popper, the principle of fallibility is an ethical principle, which is on the basis of any rational discussion. *Sociedad abierta, Universo abierto. Conversación con Franz Kreuzer*, Tecnos, Madrid, 1983, page 153. (The underlining is mine).

The third feature refers to "experts", who are needed to cope with practical judgements. It is not the case that citizens lack this practical capacity of judgement but, soundly, they rely on experts. We usually rely on doctors when we are ill, because we believe that they are experts, or more expert than us. It is even possible, in legal fields, to compel certain people to be protected by legal experts because, it is supposed, certain basic material and formal safeguards will be better fulfilled in this way, as in the case of a legal aid lawyer. I believe that the first feature is mistaken, in so far as legal normative fields are concerned. We shall expand on this point in the following.

Now, let us see what happens when we deal with situations where we have run out of rules but, nevertheless, we want to act in a reflective way. H. Brown says that we have the following three cases,

> "... cases in which we are attempting to develop new rules, cases in which we have to choose between a number of competing rules, and cases in which familiar rules fail us."[84]

Let us examine the first case. It is supposed that the experts, in our case the legal experts, do not find the rules that would solve the legal conflict in the legal order. Let us suppose that this is what happens with the "problem of relevancy", as Neil MacCormick puts it.

> "Is there any relevant norm if p then q?"[85]

Then, what is needed is a norm to solve the legal conflict at stake. If I properly understand N. MacCormick, we are trying to see whether this norm is or is not in the legal order. Here, a basic problem relates to the meaning of "there is". When we claim that "there is a green chair in the garden" and when we claim "there is rule X in the legal order" we are not claiming the same, in spite of the structural similarity. The first claim calls for a yes-no answer and no proof is demanded, at least for sane people, in the sense that everyone (or nearly everyone) agrees with "chair", "green" or "garden", etcetera.

The second claim can allow for a yes-no answer, or not. I believe that it is easier, generally speaking, to state a yes-no answer when we are dealing with formal features.[86] When material features are at stake (and/or when formal features are seen as a continuum, as in R. Summers' case) it is doubtful that a yes-no answer can be justified easily. This would be so because of the importance of substantive reasons, especially when dealing with a problem of relevancy. That is, we have to decide,

---

84 Brown, H. *Rationality*, op. cit., page 139.

85 MacCormick, Neil. *Legal Reasoning and Legal Theory*, Clarendon Law Series, Oxford, 1978, page 72.

86 In this respect it can be seen what Atiyah, P.S. and Summers, Robert, say, "... a formal reason typically continues to exclude, or override, or assign diminished weight to (at least) some countervailing considerations arising at the point of application. The extent to which otherwise relevant substantive considerations are thus overridden, excluded, or diminished in weight -either *prima facie* or at the point of application- determines the ultimate degree of mandatory formality of the reason. Clearly, not all formal reasons are of maximal mandatory formality; in fact they distribute themselves at various points along a continuum." *Form and Substance in Anglo-American Law*, Clarendon Press, Oxford, 1987, page 17. "The Juristic Study of Law's Formal Character", by Robert Summers, *Ratio Iuris*, Volume 8, Number 3, December 1995, pages 237-247 can also be seen.

justifiably, whether there is, or not, a relevant norm to solve a concrete legal conflict. In relation to the so-called "problem of relevancy", we can have a yes-no answer *ex post* (that is, we can reconstruct the process that already took place) but not an *ex ante* one, because we have a problem of relevancy and this problem does not correspond with an *ex ante* yes-no answer, at least not in all cases.

This problem can have different perspectives depending on whether we adopt a legal positivist approach, (including the separation thesis, legality based on previous competence and procedures, and general effectiveness of the legal order)[87] or a non-positivist approach, that rejects the separation thesis. However, I will not deal, at least directly, with this important issue but I will try to show that attempting to develop new rules for solving legal conflicts, is a constructive task typical of hard cases. When there is no legal rule to solve a specific conflict, officials can justifiably decide on a new interpretation of a given legal rule, or decide that there is an axiological gap, in order to fill it with a "better" new content, that coheres better (or has better consequences) with the legal order, or with the legal institution at stake, or both. Although undertaking this task requires practical judgement, legal practical judgement does not lack rules as I have already said, because there is a more or less formalized legal tradition in written texts.

This means that rules, principles or modes of reasoning, can be found in this legal tradition as "guiding and justifying juridical devices". Granted an internal point of view, that is, a critical engagement in a given legal tradition, it is not necessary to deal with practical judgement from scratch. In this respect, there is neither an empty space under our feet nor a strict following-rules procedure. There are, certainly, problems with legal tradition, both Civilian and Common Law tradition, because they can be seen, *inter alia*, either as a watchtower to glimpse the future or as an escape road towards the past, where our authentic self supposedly rests. Nevertheless, things are not so sharply divided in day-to-day work. In my view, the claim that practical judgements are not made by following rules, should be understood in the sense that there is no algorithm. For example, if there is a legal rule stating that vehicles travelling faster than 100 km per hour on the road (Y) will be fined by (X) and there is a vehicle running at 120 km per hour on that road, there is no need for complex and competing legal practical judgements. I will not though deal with the possible complications that even this simple case may have.

Typically, cases such as Riggs v. Palmer (commented on by Dworkin) require legal practical judgement because there is no algorithm that can solve the legal conflict, stating a necessary conclusion. Competent legal experts can reasonably disagree, although it has no sense to disagree in the former case, granted that the term "vehicle" does not pose problems of interpretation, although it is always a possibility. One way of attempting to "find" a legal rule that will solve a specific

[87] Alexy, Robert. *El concepto y la validez del Derecho*, Gedisa, Barcelona, 1994, pages 13 and ff. According to R. Alexy there are many legal positivists' concepts of law depending on whether they are primarily oriented towards effectiveness or primarily oriented towards formal validity. I suppose here that there are several legal positivist concepts but remaining as an underlying feature, the tenet of conceptual separation between the law that "is" and the law that "ought to be", which is related to the other basic distinction between description and prescription.

legal conflict, can be made through "distinguishing" former precedents.[88] What matters, again, is that this is done through legal practical judgements, undertaken by experts and combining, in different ways, must sources (binding), should sources (guiding) and may sources (permitted). A hard case, in so far as a legal practical judgement is needed, relies more strongly on should and may sources than routine cases. Nevertheless, when a legal practical judgement (including the conclusion) has been accepted by the legal community, it may become (in time) a routine case, and therefore it will not be, in the future, a complex legal practical judgement but a legal deduction (if A, then B).

Let us consider, now, the second case in which we have to choose between a number of competing rules. In our case, a legal case, we may have to choose between competing rules or between competing interpretations of a given rule. The latter is the "problem of interpretation", in MacCormick's approach.[89] Again, we have no algorithm that safely leads us to a necessary conclusion, through clear and settled rules. If we elaborate meta-rules they can lead to different, but sound, solutions. The third case is similar to the first one, because when familiar rules fail us, we are led to develop new rules that try to solve the practical problem at stake. It should be emphasized that, when familiar rules fail us, this is not something that we know as we can know, for example, "the green chair is in the garden". Granted that there are no settled and precise rules, determining when familiar rules fail us, a legal practical judgement is also needed. Namely, we do not always know, *ex ante*, when a routine case (that is, the specific interpretation of a given rule that leads to an accepted conclusion) will fail to solve a given legal problem properly for us. The expression "will fail" does not mean an "objective" failure.

The legal experts will have to decide, justifiably, whether legal certainty or justice of the case, *ceteris paribus*, weigh more. How can we know, *ex ante*, whether the underlying principle of a given *ratio decidendi* will be considered too restrictive or not? We do not know. A later judge will make a legal practical judgement and will justifiably decide, although this will probably not be the last time. This is so because the solution is open to a new reconsideration. At the same time, it should be accepted that we cannot reconsider the rule every time it is applied because, in that case, it would not be a rule. However, we do not know, in advance, when this reconsideration will happen again. We know that it will happen when relevant reasons are at stake, but we do not have algorithms that allow us to know when it will happen, or which reasons we shall consider relevant in future concrete cases, given certain circumstances. Once again, disagreement is possible, even among legal experts. The problems, commented on above, have relationships, as has been

---

[88] Simmonds, N.E. *The decline of juridical reason*, Manchester University Press, London, 1984, pages 112-118. I agree with Simmonds' view of the problem and his criticism of Raz's approach based on a rather weak distinction between "tame" and "strong" views of distinguishing.

[89] MacCormick, N. *Legal Reasoning and Legal Theory*, op. cit., page 68. "But a complete justification of that decision must hinge then on how the choice between the competing versions of the rule is justified: evidently a deductive justification as analysed in Chapter II is impossible. Our problem then is how such a choice is justified -and that problem, for obvious enough reasons I shall call the "problem of interpretation"."

claimed, with the problem of relevancy and the problem of interpretation, as can be read in MacCormick's approach.

The former also has relationships with the "problem of classification" and the "problem of proof". In this respect, N. MacCormick says,

> "But there may be special legal reasons for treating the "problem of classification" (to give it a name) as being different from, albeit closely related to, the problem of interpretation. So we shall treat the question "Is r, t, s an instance of p for the purposes of applying "if p then q" as the standard form of the problem ...?"[90]

The distinction between these latter problems (classification and proof) and the former ones (relevancy and interpretation) is hard to settle. MacCormick himself recognizes that there is no logical distinction between the problem of interpretation and the problem of classification[91] and this can occur because, in legal normative fields, law ascribes, rather than describes, reality. In this respect, what facts exist (or at least certain facts) depend on legal rules.

Another problem is the "problem of proof". MacCormick says,

> "People who do not dispute that there is a law *if p then q* nor what is its proper interpretation may well dispute over whether or not p has happened ... Not even many of the most hotly contested murder trials have cast doubt on the rule defining murder or its meaning: the more common dispute is centred on the prosecution's assertion and the accused's denial that it was he who killed the victim, and that (if he did) he did so with malice aforethought."

Therefore, the problem of proof refers to "proving", which depends on "evidence". "Proving depends on the adduction of evidence.

> "Evidence is something which enables us (a) to hold as true propositions about the present; and (b) to infer from these, propositions about the past."[92]

There are also, according to MacCormick, "secondary facts" that can be seen as an issue of interpretation or as an issue of facts. However, what matters most here, is not MacCormick's legal theory (I have had the pleasure to write, at length, about it in my book Reason, Democracy, Society) but how some legal problems have no clear cut rules, allowing for a mechanical application. If this is a non-contingent feature of legal orders, then, practical judgement is a necessary feature of legal orders. At least, as we know them.

"Evidence" is related to "relevancy". We cannot find "evidences" for a murder in nature. What we can find in the world are "evidences" that we have previously decided to be "relevant facts", given certain purposes. Then, two things should be emphasized, <u>first</u>, that there is, in legal orders, a complex and endless intertwinement between normative and factual problems and, <u>second</u>, that we have to deal with certain situations in which there is no clear cut following-rules

---

[90] Ibidem, page 95.

[91] Ibidem, page 95. In this respect MacCormick says, "For example, when there is an appeal from one tribunal to another and the appeal is restricted to questions of law, it may be held that "questions of classification" (as characterized here) are questions of fact, not law ... On the other hand, just because there is not any genuine logical distinction between the two types of problems, the Court can decide to treat a problem of classification in the form of a problem of interpretation ..."

[92] Ibidem, page 88.

procedure to solve some legal conflicts. In cases like the one commented on above, (1) we do not find authoritatively settled rules that mechanically lead us to the proper solution; (2) we do find these rules, but they fail to solve "properly" the legal conflicts we have to solve; (3) we do find these rules, but they lead us to contradictory solutions and the legal order does not state, or does not state "with sufficient preciseness", the concrete solution. In these and, probably, other cases we have to appeal to a complex, and probably disputable, legal practical judgement.

The conclusion of a legal practical judgement does not lead, logically, to action. Nevertheless, at least for the participants (those who share an internal point of view), a justified decision, as the normal result of a legal practical judgement, undertaken by officials of a given legal community, is "action-guiding", that is, a *prima facie* reason for action. Legal decisions, given by legal experts or by participants (or by good simulator-participants), can also be "action-guiding", although even they usually have a different strength or intensity. It is logically possible that a legal order works but lacks justified legal decisions and, hence, without "action-guiding-justificatory" legal devices. However, it is of little importance, for our practical legal purposes, to recognize this logical possibility. At least in our legal normative fields, participants usually believe that they ought to behave, *prima facie*, according to the legal decisions given by the officials and experts.

In addition, they believe so for a group of reasons based on desires, interests, moral values, certain states of affairs and legal rules, although it is not necessary to bear them all in mind in order to act. In order to behave soundly (in a given context), human agents have to use a given scheme of concepts, which leads to interpretation and to action in a social dimension. In other words, social practices mediate between the individual and society. At least for participants, this conceptual scheme includes, *inter alia*, several key concepts such as: "justification", "fidelity to law", "the best, here and now", "*ceteris paribus*", etcetera. They form part of the justificatory background of the participants. We rely on a certain belief because it coheres sufficiently with the rest of our beliefs, or coheres better than other beliefs, that altogether form our Welstanschauung, our global view of the world around us.

3.7 Presuppositions, Purposes and Values

One of the basic points, when dealing with practical judgement or practical reason, is that the soundness of a given argument cannot be properly seen in isolation, that is, out of context. The other basic point is that analysis of form is not enough. In relation to the first point, it should be emphasized that our conceptual scheme, that allows us to deal with the world around us, is holistic. This means that we value our beliefs with an eye on the background of the rest of our beliefs, relevant to the point at stake. Furthermore, the valuation of a given belief is related to public criteria. In normative legal fields, this means that both law and legal interpretation are social practices. A consequence of this is the paramount importance of the legal experts, in particular, and the citizens, in general, when we are dealing with these normative matters.

In this respect, justified acceptation of legal decisions is an equivalent to truth, in natural sciences, based on the correspondence theory. Another central point is the rejection, in part of the legal task (either Adjudication or Legal Science), of answers of the yes-no type, because any legal order has a certain "core of meaning" for a certain time, although there are also borderline cases. These clear answers represent, in quantitative terms, the majoritarian part because legal certainty is a central tenet of this social practice. The other part, the most interesting one for legal scholars or legal philosophers in general, is not properly grasped in terms of a yes-no answer, because a complex and disputable practical judgement is needed. It does not mean that everything is defensible in law because certain formal requirements and certain basic values and expectations are very much entrenched.

This is a kind of endless feedback that influences the evolution of both the more dynamic and the more calculable part of law. Each part, in spite of stressing different basic values (basically the legal certainty and justice of the case), influences each other, because they are like two sides of the same coin. This latter part is the more constructive one, although any legal order (at least one like ours) requires both parts, dynamically understood. This would be so because human beings require certain stability and certain change, as well as also requiring positive and critical morality. The relatively static side of the legal order is better represented by the bigger part of it. If it is seen from a syntactical point of view, nothing seems to change and straight lines can be drawn from one side of a legal order to the other, with geometrical perfection and safe calculability. The other part is, *servata distantia*, like the critical morality and is the more dynamic side of the legal order.

Nevertheless, the line that separates one side from another is not a line that can be drawn simply by observing the object. It is the result of an interpretative task. A second important point refers to form. It is known that at least some legal positivist tendencies claim law is form and not content. In this respect, the idea that law may be a matter of degree is usually criticised. Lon Fuller, for example, was criticised for this view.[93] Let us look at some examples in which, if we just rely on form, we shall have a yes-no answer, but if we do not just rely on form, we shall have a different understanding of the matter at issue.

> First example: "If Peter spends all day sun bathing at the beach he will be ill. He is ill. Then, he spent all day sun bathing at the beach". Second example: "If Peter strangles John he will be charged with murder. He has been charged with murder. Then, he strangled John". Third example: "If a fire is burning in this room now, then oxygen is present in this room now. Oxygen is present in this room now. Then, a fire is burning in this room now".[94]

If we just rely on form, we can see that if the structure of the three examples is the same, then the answer has to be the same. Are they correct inferences? No, because they are examples of the fallacy of affirming the consequence. Nevertheless,

[93] Fuller, Lon. *The Morality of Law*, revised edition, Yale University, 1969, pages 122-123. "To speak of a legal system as an "enterprise" implies that it may be carried on with varying degrees of success. This would mean that the existence of a legal system is a matter of degree."

[94] Copi, Irving. *Introducción a la lógica*, editorial Universitaria de Buenos Aires, 1972, page 265; Naylor, Stephen. *Practical reasoning in natural language*, Prentice Hall, 1986, page 212.

if we take into account our background knowledge, we will be able to state differences between them.

However, not all these examples are equally sound or unsound. We know that it is not usual to strangle people. Granted this, the second argument is stronger than the first one, and much more than the third. What we are claiming here, is that arguments can have different weight, depending also on our background information. Unfortunately, these two terms, "weight" and "background information", produce annoyance in certain scientific legal minds.

From a Platonic theory of forms, we can support the idea that concepts have "the one correct understanding". Moreover, in a Quinean vein, we can say that strength is not something that arguments have in "themselves", but their relative strength depends on many factors. For this reason, when we are carrying out a practical legal judgement, we can emphasize some of the relevant aspects of a given situation. More properly speaking, legal experts justifiably decide to give relevance to some aspects and not to others, because, *inter alia*, of their awareness of the background where the legal conflict arises, and because of their skilful legal abilities.

However, "background information" or "background knowledge" should not be confused with "tacit knowledge". According to some linguists, there is a "tacit knowledge" of the rules of language. In other words, language users would have these rules "in their minds". That is, it is supposed that language users have a disposition to know when a given proposition has fulfilled the proper truth-conditions. Hence, it is supposed that there is a "tacit knowledge" of a given theory of meaning, probably the true one, although this is not a clear point.

Moreover, "background information" does not have the causal-neurophysiological explanation that "tacit knowledge" has. A practical judgement is required to evaluate a certain practical problem within a given information background. Of course, we can be mistaken and there can be disagreement between experts (or citizens), or between alternative "relevant" interpretations of a given information background, for a given specific practical problem. Nevertheless, we cannot avoid presuppositions in order to deal with our practical problems, although we have seen that natural sciences have presuppositions too. These presuppositions, which are required to solve practical problems and are taken from our background information, will be tested according to the relative fulfilment of the purposes of the practical conflicts at stake.

If legal orders are seen as dynamic orders, action is a basic aspect, because a practical legal judgement is of little use if it does not lead to action. I suppose that action is closely related to will and purpose. I want something and, in so far as I behave as a rational agent, I have a purpose for this want, and a justification for this purpose. It is not necessary that I am conscious all the time of any action I undertake. For example, I can buy a newspaper as a routine or mechanical action. Nevertheless, if somebody asks me, "why do you buy a newspaper?" I will be able to give a reason. In this respect, it is a basic tenet of our culture that "a citizen is only responsible for his acts". Of course, there is also non-intentional tort but it does not deny the importance of the above tenet.

Does it mean that there can be legal responsibility without action? Yes, in some cases legal responsibility is assigned because a given fact has taken place (for example, a car's breaks failed, the car hit a person and somebody died because of it). Probably, the former tenet ("a citizen is only responsible for his acts") has a moral dimension and, in this case, it would be true that there is no responsibility without a certain control over the action at stake. In any case, if all legal consequences were like the car's example, the paramount importance that "purposive" action has in legal order, would disappear, and we would have to look for a new concept of legal order. Law would be applied without will, without actions in the purposive sense.

Nevertheless, this is not the case, since many legal consequences depend on intentional action. The example of the car's accident is different from a wedding or from a purchase, etcetera. This means that will goes hand-in-hand with purpose, at least from a pragmatical point of view. However, "purpose" should not be understood in isolation, in the sense that each citizen has a different purpose. This is not so because law is a social practice and a social practice cannot work without a certain level of normative confluence. The "paste" that unifies thousands of individual purposes in a generic purpose is not only a given rule(s) and human needs but also a share of normative fidelity with the basic values and some purposes of the community that the legal order partially represents. (I will not deal here with the nazi legal order case but I suppose that there is no "fidelity" to law but fear, or mere obedience, when basic human rights are systematically violated. It can be a matter of degree of injustice to claim whether there is a legal order or not, as R. Alexy claims).

Currently, very few believe that the only desires we can fulfil are the rational ones. However, the main point, here, is that legal orders are put in motion by individuals' behaviour, and this is based on the intertwinement between desires, interests, moral values and legal rules. We may have a desire (based on instrumental reason), an interest (based on prudential reason) and a moral duty (based on moral reason), although to have these reasons is not enough for action. I may have a desire to do something but no will to fulfil my desire.

Nevertheless, generally speaking, society and legal order are based on the supposition that there is an ordinary fulfilment of certain desires, interests and moral duties. If not, our societies and legal orders would be very different from their present appearance. Once we have a justification for a "why" question (why are you behaving that way?) we have a reason for action, but to have a reason for action is to have a purpose(s) or, at least, to be able to "see" it, although this is not a logical necessity. As is known, the problem of the "will" is an old and difficult problem that, *inter alia*, opposes two tendencies.

On the one hand, that of Descartes and Leibniz, who emphasized intellect, because to know something as true or false does not depend on will. On the other hand, Hobbes and Hume, who emphasized voluntariness, linked both with the starting point of action and of fulfilment of action. I will not deal though with the difficult issue of voluntariness or freedom. I will suppose that, being at least a basic tenet of our form of life, we cannot dispense with it, at least from a pragmatical point of view.[95]

---

[95] Meyer, Philippe. *La ilusión necesaria*, Ariel, Barcelona, 1996, page 13. "Freedom, scientifically speaking, can be an illusion, but the polymorphism of the interactions between heredity and milieu,

This is an important point, because if we do not know, in general, why we are doing something, we are watering down the rational and ethical dimension of our behaviour and our social practices. Here, we have a type of middle ground between, not knowing why we are doing X, and knowing from an impartial and universal view. We are placed in this middle ground, because we have an imperfect understanding of our purposes, our beliefs, our practical judgements, our social practices, etcetera, although we have had sufficient to survive (to say the least) until now. As N. Rescher puts it,

> "Some philosophers (Peirce included) see fallibilism as having ethical implications. They project an ethics of belief according to which we have no right to claim definitive truth for our current scientific claims, a view which they co-ordinate with a purported duty for the community of inquirers to pursue inquiry to the greatest extent possible in the circumstances."[96]

Then, we have a reason that motivates our action (for example, I desire X) and a reason that justifies our action (I desire X because of Y, in a justificatory sense). All this is linked to the concept of "commitment", that can be understood as an "internal point of view" when applied to a legal order.[97] The justification can be prudential and moral and, at least in our culture, moral reasons are considered as ultimate reasons. However, how does it all affect legal order? First, if there are no desires, no interests, no moral duties, how can there be will? If this were the ordinary situation, legal orders would be unrecognisable. I have posed the car's accident example to see how a legal order would be, if legal responsibility without will were the normal situation. There would not only be a modification of the legal order but a new concept of it.

Although some have claimed (like Nagel) that reason can determine the will, it is supposed here that, generally speaking, desires, interests and moral duties, put or can put will in motion. However, our will should not be understood in isolation, as something autonomous that can be explained in itself because, if so, the social dimension of wants is lacking. In this case, the desire would only be the expression of an isolated individual. I may desire to drink a certain type of beverage but this desire has a strong social dimension. If I watch a certain beverage (B) many times on TV, it is probable that, when I desire "a beverage" I will also desire to drink "B's beverage". It has to be understood that I do not create my desire of drinking. I simply have it. What I can create is the desire to drink "this specific beverage". Here, the "why question" (why do you drink?) has a different meaning from the

---

the extraordinary human diversity as a result of it and the transcendental illusion of the Jewish-Christian culture, make it necessary."

[96] Rescher, N. *Satisfying reason*, op. cit., page 86.

[97] Moya, Carlos. *The Philosophy of Action*, Polity Press, Cambridge, 1990, page 46. "Meaningful actions imply, then, the existence of subjects able to *commit* themselves to do things *in the future*. I shall contend that this notion of commitment is essential to our notion of agency and to the important sense of the distinction between actions and happenings. It constitutes an essential part of our idea of ourselves as agents, as beings who are able to change the world and not mere victims of its evolution. And the reason why it cannot be accounted for in terms of basic actions is that it is a *normative* notion."

"why question" related to the specific beverage, (why do you drink this specific beverage?).

The first question relates to biology, the second relates to culture and personal preferences. Our cultural-normative realm is dependent both on nature and on culture. Hence, only the second calls for justifying reasons and choices. I could have preferred (although this is not a pacific question) a different beverage, but I could not have preferred not to drink or not to breath, because most human beings do these for at least most of the time. That is, survival is a basic presupposition for most people, most of the time. The structure is the same if my desire or my interest is to read a book, although the objects of my desires are not equally interchangeable, given certain individual preferences and a certain cultural context.

My desire may end in the proper action, to drink the beer or to read a book or a specific book, or I may fail to perform the action because of weakness of the will, or because of error, or because my desire or my interest has been beaten by a moral duty, in so far as moral reasons are ultimate reasons. Hence, the first point is based on will (given certain desires, interests and moral duties) as the normal motivating reason. However, it is not only based on the authorities' will, but also on the will of citizens, because of the mentioned reason of treating them as rational agents and because the legal enterprise (to use a known expression of Fuller) cannot work properly if just based on obedient donkeys. However, why not?

Here comes the second point. A living social practice supposes that the participants of this practice try to reach the "best" possible results, given certain purposes and certain circumstances. It does not mean though that all citizens do this all the time, for all actions. Practical purpose(s), social practice and "striving for the best, here and now", are interconnected elements. I want to point out that the above comments do not mean that all social practices are equal and I will therefore recall here Wittgenstein's "family resemblance" concept. For example, the usually cited social practice of men taking their hats off when entering church. Although any social practice can change or disappear, the concept of "striving for the best, here and now" is radically more complex when applied to the legal order rather than to the church case.

Nevertheless, some basic aspects remain: participants share several purposes and criticize deviations of the correct behaviour. These "wrongs" that ought to be avoided by the participants, have similarities with the utilitarian concept of "pain". "Pains" in the utilitarian sense, and "wrongs" are what ought to be avoided. In the latter case, it is not a bodily pain but a "pain" that negatively affects the social practice. At this point I will make a brief comment in relation to the concept of "striving for the best, here and now". It can be thought that, if an internal point of view supposes that the participants commit themselves to do certain things in the future, this concept is not able to explain this behaviour. However, this would be a wrong interpretation.

"Fidelity to law" and "internal point of view" are aspects of a dynamic object. Participants cannot just say, once and for all, that they will strive for the best. Like the oarsman, condemned to carry people across from one side of the river to the other, participants have never completely fulfilled their task. An endless feedback of legal sources, wants, purposes, facts, consequences, expectations, etcetera, make a social practice (especially if a practice is as important as the legal order) an endless task. As N. Rescher says,

> "We are rational animals and must feed our minds even as we must feed our bodies. In pursuing information, as in pursuing food, we have to settle for the best we can get at the time."[98]

The last point refers to "values". In order to make it rather concrete, because this issue is very wide and complex, I will just refer to some precise aspects. First, values should not be understood as something existing out there because, as E.J. Bond says,

> "Could anything be more absurd than that? Is it not apparent that value is nothing but a reflection of desires, emotions, "pro-attitudes", and other subjective states? Is it not absurd to suppose that value might exist in the universe without persons (or other animals) and their appetites, inclinations and purposes? And if so, are they not dependent on these things?"[99]

Once we have brought values down from the Popperian third world, where ideas, etcetera, can exist by themselves, we can differentiate, as we have already done, between "motivating reasons" and "justifying reasons". "Motivating reasons" would be based on desires (instrumental reasons) while "justifying reasons" would be based on interests (prudential reasons) and moral duties (moral reasons).

As has been said, will is also needed to put desires, interests and moral duties in motion. Nevertheless, when a participant recognizes that he has a prudential reason or a moral reason for doing something, there is a reason for action. Once this point is reached a moral relativist can complain angrily. Quickly, however, we can answer him with the known distinctions between "descriptive relativism", "normative relativism" and "metaethic relativism". As is known, the first states the fact that things are different in different places, the second states that what is good for some persons or communities is not necessarily good for others, and the third states that any comparison between different moral rules is unsound because they are not commensurable. I would argue for the second kind of relativism but with the proviso that there is no conceptual or empirical impossibility of agreement, at least on basic moral rules, which are usually needed for a peaceful survival. Of course, this is a point that deserves more scrutiny.

Legal orders, (at least ours), are based on the supposition that, generally speaking, participants will be sufficiently motivated by the benefits, interests and moral duties underlying legal rules. Some of the former ones are: fostering freedom and power of different kinds, supply of certain basic needs, payment of taxes, solution of certain co-ordination problems, a certain level of peace and order and, in general, respect for Human Rights. If all this is recognised by the participants, as something valuable, it has, generally speaking, a motivation capacity for action, although not, or not primarily, in the causal sense but in the justifying sense. It is appropriate here, to recall the importance some have given to the "authority reasons", which are understood as "exclusionary reasons".

---

[98] Rescher, N. *Satisfying reason*, op. cit., pages 198-199.
[99] Bond, E.J. *Reason and Value*, Cambridge University Press, Cambridge, 1983, page 85.

In so far as the legal order is not only the result of the authorities' will, but also the citizens' will, the emphasis on the former becomes somewhat weakened, because when this democratic result happens, the authority reasons are reasons already accepted by the citizens or, at least, not rejected by them. From this point of view, they are privileged reasons and not to obey them would mean that citizens behaved in an incoherent way. Only in authoritarian political regimes would it be ideologically rejectable (from a democratic point of view) to support the idea that citizens have exclusionary reasons to obey the authority reasons. Or slaves in the Roman Empire, for example. Should we expect them "to strive for the best"?

Hence, at least in democratic political regimes, citizens have *prima facie* reasons to follow, *ceteris paribus*, what they have already backed, (explicitly or implicitly), or are coherent with. In these cases, authority reasons are kinds of formal reasons, in the sense that the formal origin stems from political authority, but not from its own autonomous will. I shall not deal here with the problems of collective will, although it is not necessary to believe in it for solving this problem. What matters is that authority reasons are privileged (from a normative point of view) when citizens have participated in their contents, that is, in so far as they have justifiably accepted the purposes that these authority reasons convey, and the efforts (if not benefits) needed for reaching them. Here we have a basic requirement of any rationality, whether theoretical or practical, the requirement of justification. Rational justification is probably not equal in all fields, except for Procrustean minds, because we cannot sensibly reduce normative justification to the language of physics, as the heirs of physicalism would dream.

As R. Alexy says, there are three conceptions of practical reason, Aristotelic, Hobbesian and Kantian.[100] I basically agree with his approach but although argumentation and impartiality, based on the two kinds of rules he is claiming, try to show the universalistic feature of practical rationality, I believe that a contextual stance should be added, when we deal with legal practical reasoning. It not only tries to fulfil universalistic requirements but to solve certain practical problems in the "best way here and now". These practical problems are based on concrete purposes and are backed by justifications. This contextual aspect allows some of the basic goals of legal practical reasoning to be reached. In addition, it justifies legal decisions properly and also their reconsideration, before the legislative power has formally enacted or derogated laws, granted the existence of a permanent practical need for adaptation of the legal order to changing circumstances.

This can be considered, either as a violation of the principle of separation of powers, or as a weighting between two important requirements. These are: the due respect for the cited constitutional principle and the requirement of solving, in the "best way here and now", the practical problems we have to deal with. It can be problematic, at least sometimes, to respect both at the same time. Moreover, participants expect justified "guidance", not geometrical perfection. I will try to show where we should place these Alexian rules, granted that "justified guidance" and motivation to act are two basic issues. In order to deal with this problem I

---

[100] Alexy, Robert. *El Concepto y la Validez del Derecho*, Gedisa, Barcelona, 1994, pages 131 and ff.

propose the following terminology: 1) Technical-desire rules; 2) Technical-interest rules; 3) Social-moral rules; 4) Ultimate moral rules.

1). For example, to drink is a means to fulfil my desire for drinking. Having this desire I will use, normally, the proper means, although I can fail. We have to distinguish between (1A) Natural-technical desire (natural needs), for example, to drink *tout court*, and (1B) non natural-technical desire, for example, to drink a specific beverage. Although it is always problematic to distinguish which desires are natural and which are not (because of the intertwinement between natural and cultural) it is useful to make this distinction, because of the important difference between them. The former does not call for justifying reasons because drinking, *tout court*, is a natural need. However, drinking a specific beverage is not a natural need.[101]

2). For example, to study and to practice, in a certain way, is a means to fulfil my interest to be a violinist. The main difference between (2) and (1A) is that the latter is natural while (2) is not. What is the difference between (2) and (1B)? The former has more relevant preferences for my life plan than the latter. I can drink a different beer than I expected without damage to my self-respect and my life plan. On the contrary, if I want to be a violinist, and if I have to change my decision, not because of my own will but because of the decision of others, this will probably affect my self-respect and my life plan more seriously. On the contrary, it is not normal that changing the trademark of beer, or even spending my holidays in a different place than I expected, results in serious damage to my personal identity and self-esteem. Therefore, although the formal structure of (1) and (2) are the same, there are material differences. Another important difference is the following: if I am coherent, and if my desire for drinking beer seriously damages my interest in being a violinist, the latter preference will defeat the former, other things being equal.

3). We can place, here, Alexian rules. These rules help us to reach fair agreements, enhancing individual autonomy and dignity, in so far as instrumental rationality is not the dominant one. Hence, these rules are means to reach something. In (1) the goal was to fulfil my desire (to drink a beer); in (2) the goal was to fulfil my interest (to be a violinist), but what is the goal of these rules? The goal is not, or is not primarily, to fulfil an individual goal but a social one. Not only a social goal but also a moral one. It can be said that (1) and (2) are also, in some sense, social. It can be accepted that to drink beer is not only an isolated behaviour but also a social behaviour that is related to production and distribution, and the latter are important social aspects affecting many individuals.

---

[101] Bayón, J.C. *La normatividad del Derecho*, Centro de Estudios Constitucionales, Madrid, 1991. The author distinguishes, *inter alia*, two senses of desire which are of interest here, "As Hare recognizes, the distinction between these two senses of "desire" is, with broad strokes, the same as the notions of *órexis* and *epithymía* in Aristotelian ethics: *órekton* is what is wanted as a result of deliberation while *ephiesthai* -usually translated to Latin as *appetere*- is "to want" in the sense of feeling a spontaneous propensity." In our example, we cannot deliberate a natural desire such as drinking, we just have it. Another distinction of the author is between "what one desires" and "what one believes he ought to do". He also claims that it is easy, from an *ex post* perspective, to believe that the action performed is the conclusion of practical reasoning. This paper supports the view that the conclusion of a practical reasoning is a judgement, normally followed by a proper action.

Furthermore, the consequences of drinking have (or can have) more than individual consequences. Nevertheless, it is me that drinks the beer, and it is me that is the violinist. In (3) there is no individual goal in the same sense. This means that in (3) the social dimension of my individual behaviour is fundamental. I fulfil some technical-moral rules because I want to participate in a social practice, because I am interested not only in myself but in others and because efficacy is not the only point. Nevertheless, these rules are validated in so far as they serve, for example, to reach some fair agreements. We cannot expect to fulfil Alexian rules completely and we cannot expect to reach complete success in their application. Nevertheless, they guide us in the right direction. Therefore, their goal is not (or not basically) mine as it is in (1) and (2).

We could say that these technical rules can be seen as hypothetical imperatives. For example, (1A) would be a means for survival; (1B) would be a means for my happiness and could be called "pragmatic hypothetical imperative". The example of the violinist in (2) could be seen as a mixture of "pragmatic hypothetical imperative" and "technical hypothetical imperative". The cases of (3) and (4) relate to morality either stressing sociality or individuality. Although there is some technical dimension too they should not be seen as hypothetical imperatives because it is difficult to state that they are true or false depending on whether they have reached or not the proposed end. It would be easier in (4) than in (3) because, at least in principle, it is easier to confirm whether an individual end has been fulfilled or not. Nevertheless, once our behaviour affects other interests (in a wide sense) we are dealing with a moral behaviour and a moral responsibility. A judge's decision is an example. Then, (3) and (4) would be moral imperatives.

4). Differently from the previous three cases, we are now not using means to reach a certain goal, but are dealing with ultimate reasons, moral reasons. I suppose that desires, interests and moral values have motivational force (although not always) and that moral reasons can (and ought to) defeat my interests and desires, and my interests should defeat my desires, if I am a coherent agent, with all other things being equal. While desires and interests are subjected (with the cited proviso) to moral reasons, Alexian rules are not subjected to them, but are a kind of procedure for their proper fulfilment. Levels (1) and (2) are the contingent human substratum (except 1A) over which it is possible to build (3) and (4), which are less contingent or more entrenched. A short word is needed here on the important relationships (sometimes called "private") of mother-children and friendship. It is usually said that these are not relationships based on duties because they are "true" relationships (for example, Gilligan's morality of care), although I will not deal here with this important problem. However, I will just say that, at least in societies based on individual rights, we cannot dispense with legal duties, although I believe that a theory of rights needs the help of widespread social virtues to work well.

Another important point is whether there is a conceptual connection between legal-duty-based societies, the capitalist market and the Rule of Law. Although this question deserves deeper scrutiny, I believe that the burden of proof relies on those that claim a "better" society can be reached without respect for individual rights and individual preferences. A different thing, although related, is the claim that we should limit individual freedom for reaching a certain level of distributive justice and survival of the planet, if aggregate individual preferences would lead to serious environmental damage. In any case, the burden of the justification will rest on those that try to make radical changes from an "enlightened-holistic" view, leaving out the "mediocre citizen alienated by the industries of conscience manipulation, belonging to the capitalist market". There is not only a potential danger in selfish individual freedom but also in the perfectionist and paternalist voices of the Illuminati. Once again this is the problem of Scilla and Caribdis.

In any case, I have tried to show that there is a continuous intertwinement between legal rules and (at least part of) desires, interests and moral values. This intertwinement is stronger and more frequent in some parts of the legal order than others, depending on variables that are also legal and meta-legal. This dynamic character of the legal order makes it impossible from a pragmatical point of view to have a whole fixed picture of the legal order, at a specific given time. While we are trying to fix the social practice in question, legal and social reality have moved again. However, this does not lead to chaos for the reasons already mentioned.

3.8 Actions, Events and Internal Points of View

It is supposed here that "action" is a theoretical construction, which means that it is not only an observable phenomenon. Therefore, "values" play an important role in the qualification of actions and omissions. Values can also play a role in the qualification of non-intentional actions or, in a von Wright vein, in the changes of the world. A legal order can value, in different ways, either action-omission or a change in the world. For example, to harm a person or not to help a person, in certain circumstances, may lead to legal consequences that are evaluations of these actions-omissions. That is, the unintentional failure of a car's brake, knocking down a pedestrian and as a result killing him, can have legal consequences for the car's driver.

In relation to the nature of causal connections, von Wright rejects the view of causality as accidental regularity and of logical necessity. Thus, supporting the view that between cause and effect there is a "nomic connection", a natural need whose characteristic allows the formulation of a counterfactual causal proposition such as,

> "If (A) had occurred in a different moment in which it did, (B) would have occurred also".[102]

It seems that, in this view, something occurred because of my intervention. Therefore, we are facing the problem of determinism, although I will not deal with this here. Nevertheless, it is supposed here that I could have made a different choice. For example, I choose to walk but I could have chosen to ride a bicycle.

If I was determined to walk, then it cannot be true that I could have chosen to ride a bicycle. In this view, the complex set of circumstances, personal and non-personal, determine my choice or, in general terms, the laws of nature determine the

---

[102] González, Daniel. *Acción y Norma en von Wright*, Centro de Estudios Constitucionales, Madrid, 1995, pages 528-529. In relation to these issues, Mosterín, Jesús, *Racionalidad y Acción Humana*, Alianza Universidad, Madrid, 1978, especially chapter 5, is also worth reading.

events. If this is correct, I could not have chosen to ride a bicycle instead of walking. Therefore, it seems that if determinism is true (at least understood in this sense) we have no real alternatives. However, which role, if any, do my desires, interests and moral values play? Is all this a dream, like believing in unicorns? If my desires, interests and moral values do not lead to action, what does?

One of the counter-intuitive possibilities is that everything is determined by the laws of nature, whereas another is that nothing is determined in this way. In the former case, we would have no responsibility. I could murder another person but this would happen according to a previously determined line of events, completely out of my control. The latter case concerns events that have no explanation, because they have no determination at all. Granted that determinism and anti-determinism have no decisive proofs (what could they be, and uttered by whom?), I will suppose that intentional human actions are partly removed from determinism, that is, the idea that any event is a necessary consequence of a given set of previous events. Another question is to accept that events arise, not from nothing, but from previous circumstances. As a result, it is not accepted, here, that everything is causally and previously determined. Namely, having seen the participants as "insiders" I do not see them as the causal result of outer forces.

This is a way that can lead to options such as the "naturalized epistemology" of Quine. Nevertheless, if we reject notions such as "justification", "rational acceptability", etcetera, then, as Putnam puts it, we are led to an incoherent view,

> "... for the notions the naturalistic metaphysician uses to explain truth and reference, for example the notion of causality (explanation), and the notion of *appropriate type* of causal chain depend on notions which presuppose the notion of reasonableness. However, if *all* notions of rightness, both epistemic and (metaphysically) realists are eliminated, then what are our statements but noise makings?"[103]

Therefore, our technical rules should be seen as a kind of institutional practical requirement, once the practical syllogism (ending in a proposition) has concluded. If an atomistic view of the rational agent is neglected, the importance of the institutional dimension arises. That is, we properly understand practical syllogisms and intentional actions in given socio-historical contexts.

The secondary character of physical events can be seen if we consider that the same observable physical events can be equally carried out by different persons, in the same circumstances, although they have different legal consequences. This is the case, for example, when a person under age is doing the same observable physical facts as an adult. They are doing the same in physical observable terms but they are not doing the same in legal normative terms. Namely, the latter is performing a valid mortgage, while the former is not. Legal orders have "coercion" as one of the most important defining features (or the defining feature, according to others), but it does not mean that all legal rules are coercive. In a similar way, "intentional action" is a basic defining feature of legal orders, although not all legal actions are intentional actions. For example, it is not only possible but also usual to include liability for non-intentional civil wrongs.

---

[103] Putnam, Hilary. *Realism and Reason*, Cambridge University Press, Cambridge, 1983, page 246.

Nevertheless, if this were normal in legal orders, our conception of them would have to change radically. A basic feature of the Rule of Law is intentional action, because it is based on a given conception of human beings that includes freedom, dignity and autonomy, *inter alia*. Granted these features, there can be cases of non-intentional actions (such as the liability for damages because of the accidental failure of a car's brakes), and cases of different levels of intentionality. For example, to marry has a stronger intentionality than buying a beer. It is supposed, at least usually, that beer is more interchangeable than the person with whom I am going to marry. When persons or goods are more interchangeable (for example, a waiter or a beer) the stronger intentionality is put on the genus and the weaker one on the particular.

Especially in the citizen-administration relationship, one can accept different levels (with some limits) of legal answers because expediency is at stake. This usually happens with perishable or interchangeable goods or benefits of any kind. There can be fuzzy boundaries, but the primacy is on intentional action, at least in our legal orders, because of the conception of human beings (*inter alia*) that underlies them. This would be so, in spite of the growing importance of some administrative relationships, where the citizen is an almost passive receptacle of certain benefits or burdens. This also means that there are several forms or instantiations of the "following a rule" concept.

What has already been said has a close relationship with the so-called "internal point of view". To adopt, or to realise that one is within a given internal point of view (and accepting it, in the way of consciously conforming -in a reflective and critical way- ones conduct to certain patterns) means a rational compromise with certain ways of social behaviour and certain kinds of justifications. It is not necessary to have a full wise understanding of it, because there are many levels of understanding. Participants in a given IPV expect certain regularities of behaviour and certain kinds of justifications. The interplay between them and the institutions, give life and shape to purposive social practices, such as law. Rights, duties and powers (understood in the Rule of Law sense) are probably some of the most important legal devices for fulfilling our individual and social purposes.

To be a conscious participant of a given IPV we require, not only rights, duties and powers, but also desires, interests and moral values. I know that, from a communitarist point of view, a discourse based on rights and duties is, at least, insufficient. Share feelings, commitments and virtues would be more important. Nevertheless, I will not try to deal here with this important issue. Be that as it may, the above cited complexity makes the balance of several considerations and the *prima facie* character of part of our decisions practically inevitable. Although this would occur only in part, because our social practices (and probably any social practice) need, practically speaking, an interplay between stability-predictability and innovation. What changes are the intensity and features of this interplay.

This is closely related to the so-called legal routine cases and legal hard cases. The former, represent the stable and predictable side of our social practice, shaping a special way of fulfilling the concept of "following a rule". On this side, the basic concept of "striving for the best, here and now" is not demanded as a constructive task. "Following a rule", on this side, fulfils what is previously expected by the other participants. The mentioned basic concept takes relevancy on the hard-case side of the social practice. In this case, it is not enough to obey, because either it is a disputable matter that should be obeyed or what has been obeyed until now ought to be reconsidered. On this side, "following a rule" is a creative fulfilment of the mentioned basic concept.

However, while it is practically necessary that participants share the concept of "striving for the best, here and now", (at different levels) it is neither necessary nor convenient that all participants share the same interpretation of it. This is relatively similar to what happens in "mature sciences", where dynamic and purposive social practices have, in reasoned disagreement, a source of intellectual fecundity, because we are not in the imperial road of logically necessary steps. Consequently, in so far as "striving for the best, here and now" supposes the existence of intentions of human beings and that intentions are purposive, rational agents have a practical need for justification of these purposes. Hence, there is a complex interplay between intentions, purposes and justifications that gives a deliberating feature to the mentioned basic concept. The participants can change the current interpretation of this concept but they cannot change the concept itself, unless they give up being a participant or there are exceptional social circumstances.

It is logically possible, for the participants, to change a given interpretation of this basic concept but, from a practical point of view, stability and calculability make frequent changes difficult, although this desirable frequency cannot be stated in *a priori* way. We can see, here, the importance of the "inertia principle". It is also logically possible, that nobody shares an IPV because the members of a given social practice believe that the other members are not participants and they just simulate it for convenience. However, these logical possibilities are of little importance from a pragmatical point of view. What matters is the interplay between the routine side and the deliberative-creative sides of "following a rule". They show the dynamic aspect of social practices, especially for the legal order at stake.

Natural sciences cannot give us a full account of rational practical human behaviour. If this is correct, reasons for action have sense, partly outside the deterministic chain of cause-effect. Rational agents form their intentions with an eye on the physical limits and practical possibilities. All this is always imperfect but it is not a tragedy for imperfect rationality. What matters most is that, if I have no real alternatives or courses of action, "reasons for action" play no role in human acting, spoiling, in a kind of ripple effect, all our institutions and traditions. In other words, ourselves as persons. Intentional actions, if they exist, are closely related to our common expectations as participants in a given IPV.

In behaving as participants we do not only reproduce but also create social expectations, related to predictability and coherence. These are both linked to the future, although an uncertain one, because of the interplay with the other side of social practice and because of societal changes. All this means that, in this context, predictability and coherence represent a compromise of future behaviour, both in the routine sense and in the hard-case sense. However, how can a participant have a compromise to behave in a way that is still not created? Because it is both a formal duty to "reach the best" and a material *prima facie* duty, that call for a balance of types of reasons and consequences.

Although it is difficult to understand the concept of "human being" without desires, interests and moral values, the role they play in human life is different. The fulfilment of desires, both natural and unnatural, form the substratum over which it is sound to have interests and moral values. Of course, the level of fulfilment, and to what extent it is considered sufficient for sound claims about interests and moral values, is a socio-historical matter. It is difficult to create a complex web of concepts and expectations related to interests and moral values, without a certain fulfilment of desires. Nevertheless, life plans are not made only of interests, but of desires, interests and moral values, because I cannot "see myself", either now or in the future, lacking any of them. Moreover, human beings expect each other to have life plans. However, as is known, there are both provisional (children) and definitive (certain types of handicap) exceptions.

We can say that there is an interplay, let us say an "inside" interplay, of the individual, between desires, interests and moral values. This interplay can be complex because, there is, at least in principle, a greater weight of moral values over interests, and both of them occur over desires. Of course, this is not always so for the reasons already stated. There is not only a "global inside" interplay, when there is a conflict among desires, interests and moral values, since there can also be conflictive interplays, let us say "particular inside" interplays, within the same level, for example, when the agent faces a variety of conflicting desires. The same may happen in relation to interest and moral values. There is also an "outside particular interplay" between parts of this whole set of desires, interests and moral values of a person and parts of other persons. A global interplay between one person and another is more difficult, although not impossible.

The levels already cited can conflict because, although there is an ideal hierarchy among them, made more or less explicit by the subject, it is not always respected. In summary, there is an interplay "inside" the agent -his or her stratified set of preferences- and there is an interplay between him-her and "outside" that includes other agents, material things and intellectual constructs. These interplays have, in a similar vein as happens in legal orders, a routine side and a hard side related (although not exclusively) to positive and critical morality. It should be also emphasized that there is a feedback in both levels. Their importance does not only depend on the subject but also on the society in which the subject lives. In societies where the interplay between positive and critical morality is more accepted (or less repressed) there will be more possibilities for the working of the cited feedback.

In relation to legal orders we could say that, granted that legal orders are not autonomous, there is also an "inner" interplay between parts of the legal order, on the one hand, and an "outer" interplay with society in which the legal order works. The term "society" is certainly a complex and disputable one. It is supposed here that our human relations with the society where we live are different from other animals because ours are more open and theirs are more determined. At the same time, we cannot deal with "society" but only with certain persons who represent certain roles, institutional or not, having certain status, etcetera. However, "society" is not something outside us. We are part of the society. We are moulded by it but not completely.

We are not living in a close and determined world as if we were worms. In any case, participants behave as if they were not worms but persons with dignity, relative autonomy, life plans, etcetera. All this shows, *inter alia*, the dynamic basic feature, both of legal orders and the individuals, that put them in motion but that are also affected by them and by society. Moreover, not even revolutionary changes produce a radical change of legal orders and society, because legal orders are not (although it is logically possible) absolutely conventional. Some important features remain for a long time in spite of revolutionary declarations.

4. LEGAL DOGMATICS, IDEALS AND SCIENTIFIC PURENESS

A final comment will be concerned with something that is important for any social practice and for any society. I mean "ideals". What is an "ideal"? According to N. Rescher,

> "The "reality" of an ideal lies not in its substantive realisation in some separate domain but in its formative impetus upon human thought and action in this imperfect world."[104]

It is worth emphasizing that ideals are not something to be completely fulfilled and that they are validated pragmatically, because they are not ends in themselves. It is interesting to recall some of the important ideals of our culture;

> "The perfectly just man of Plato; the perfectly wise man of the Stoics; the ideal community of utopian political theorizing; the social contract between ideally rational agents; the perfection of inquiry in "ideal science" (Kant, Peirce); the "perfectly rational agent" of economic theorizing."[105]

It should be clear, then, that ideals are not like "chairs". They are products of our thought, of our imagination. Nevertheless, unlike unicorns, they have an important pragmatic function, they guide us and stimulate us towards certain directions, directions that can be geographical or not. For the attainment of some value or values, ideals have, according to Rescher, another limit.

> "An ideal functions as simply one component within a system, which makes it possible to strike a reasonable balance between the different and potentially discordant values."[106]

This seems familiar to the requirement of balance between principles of a given legal order. Consequently, we can distinguish between concrete ideals that have to be in balance, because they form a set of ideals, and the set of ideals itself.

We can suppose that a "good" balance, here and now, of different ideals of a given set will foster, in the best possible way, our whole set of, let us say, the Rule of Law. Hence, supererogatory acts have no place within the legal order (at least in ours), because supererogatory acts (heroes and saints) are not subjected to balance and because they cannot be demanded to citizens. For example, some mother-

---

[104] Rescher, N. *Ethical Idealism. An Inquiry into the Nature and Function of Ideals*, University of California Press, 1992, page 118.

[105] Ibidem, page 120.

[106] Ibidem, page 125.

children relationships, some friendship relations, the behaviour of Mother Teresa of Calcutta and her nuns, etcetera. They are neither subjected to duty-right nor to balance. It is supposed here that while we have, as human beings, a natural dualistic dimension of our language (descriptive and normative), we have also a natural tendency towards a realistic view of our world and, at the same time, an ideal view of it. This is not a logical necessity, but I do not know any society relying, exclusively, on the "is" level, which is understood as something that has a correspondence in the world out there.

Let us consider, finally, the basic tenets of legal positivism, according to U. Schmill who says,

> "The objects of Legal Science are legal posited norms (empirical legal tenet one); the function of Legal Science is the description of the relations between legal posited norms (empirical legal tenet two); we must reject any theory claiming the existence of non posited norms (empirical legal tenet three)."[107]

Therefore, legal positivism deals with special facts, legal facts. In so far as ideals are not legal posited norms, they must be rejected. The legal positivist scientist "qua" scientist will reject these idealisations because they are not part of a legal system and, hence, they cannot describe them. Nevertheless, the legal positivist scientist "qua" citizen can believe in these idealisations.

I accept that there can be a minority of people that are not participants. They believe that the central features of our societies are rejectable and they do not want to participate in this tragicomedy. However, no society can survive if the majority believes so. Hence I suppose that the majority are participants on different levels, although there are many possible combinations, levels and intensities. Is legal dogmatics going to be useful for the majority of citizens who share, to a certain extent, the basic tenets of the Rule of Law? It is difficult to see how one can understand the Rule of Law while rejecting ideals, in the sense already commented on. Legal dogmatics is not something undertaken from outside, although some could believe in the ideal of a "perfectly rational agent". On the contrary, it is a social practice that tries to understand and foster certain social practices.

Moreover, it is doubtful to see how a "legal positivist scientist" can leave his body and purely observe. If he cannot, it is hard to claim that he works completely uncommitted and is able, in consequence, to claim that his utterances are exclusively uncommitted descriptions of a purposive object, such as a legal order. I believe that this is an ideal, although, in my view, a mistaken one. As I have said, the basic task of legal dogmatics is not only descriptive but also constructive, and it has been undertaken by participants, as history of legal dogmatics shows. This explains that, while assuming rules, ideals and traditions of a given practice, they "strive for the best, here and now". This complex and constructive task develops in a tension between, *inter alia*, efficiency, coherence and deontological values. This complex task of legal dogmatics is, to a certain extent, like a school of morality.

As M. Bunge says,

---

[107] Schmill, Ulises. *El Derecho y la Justicia*, editorial Trotta, Madrid, 1996, page 68.

> "The scientific activity is a school of morality because it demands the acquisition or the strengthening of the following habits or normal attitudes: 1) intellectual honesty ... 2) independent judgement ... 3) intellectual courage ... 4) love for intellectual freedom and for individual and social liberties that make it possible ... 5) sense of justice ..."[108]

Therefore, the legal practical reasoning of participants of a given legal order take a moral ought as a major premise. For example, "we ought to obey the rules enacted by the legislator". This major premise is a moral premise, because the rules enacted by the legislator will be imposed on the citizens, and an instrumental or a prudential reason will not have enough justificatory force. As a minor premise, we check that the legislator has enacted a rule (R) and as a conclusion, we may have a practical judgement stating that "we ought to obey (R)". However, we shall not obey all legal rules enacted by the legislator (irrespective of their content) unless we see them as exclusionary reasons, or we adopt an ideological positivist stance.

As I have said, legal orders can survive, *inter alia*, because coherent behaviour is expected of the citizens (at large) and, if they agree with the major legal premise they will accept, *prima facie*, the conclusion that is, not only a practical judgement but, a reason for action. Legal orders (at least ours) are complex social practices where a controlled continuous tension runs between what is accepted as the "is" of the legal order (here and now), and what tries to occupy its place, that is, a new and more justified interpretation, which is, *ex ante*, an "ought" that can become a legal "is", or not. This is so because reality changes and social practice tries to solve, "in the best possible way", these changing conflicts. If we were able to stop a whole legal order for a while, perhaps we would be able to describe the "is" of this legal order (at a given point in time) but it is not practically possible.

According to a certain level of analysis, I can claim that my skin, hair, nails, etcetera, are the same as they were last month or year, but at another level of analysis we can claim that they are not the same. Therefore, a decision is required. We have to decide which is the better level of analysis, given our main purposes. In relation to the legal order (at least in the Rule of Law sense), we cannot dispense with calculability, and its related legal certainty. However, in so far as a legal practice is a living social construction, there are dynamics inside it. I have already commented that efficiency, coherence and deontological values are elements of a continuous controlled (because of procedures, *inter alia*) tension because, stressing one aspect or another, a different solution could be reached.

Besides this internal tension within the legal order (to talk metaphorically, because there is not a strict "within"), there is an external tension, that is, the feedback between the legal order (or parts of it) and the society (or some groups) that calls for a legal linguistic understanding and concretion. Interests and values will push legal understanding and concretion in one or another direction and, in so far as justification is a basic feature of our legal culture, new justified interpretations will try to occupy a place in this living and conflicting social practice. However, it is not necessary to see this last comment as a strict translation of a Darwinian niche competition, because legal orders have a primary, although not exclusive, normative dimension.

---

[108] Bunge, Mario. *Etica y Ciencia*, ed. Siglo Veinte, Buenos Aires, 1976, page 35.

CHAPTER 4

MODELS OF THE RULE OF LAW

In this chapter, I try to expose some features of the Rule of Law Model. I take for granted that there are two main tendencies, which are on the one hand, a more or less thin model of the Rule of Law, and on the other hand, a more or less robust theory of the Rule of Law. I will, finally, support a kind of robust model of the Rule of Law, claiming that this is not only a legal option but also an ideological one.

1. RULE OF LAW AND PERSONAL AUTONOMY

I believe that, at least in our times, it is a mistake to set aside both some kinds of universalism and some kinds of particularism, in the following sense. Different cultures, that we could call "neighbour cultures", should be morally respected in so far as they have both democratic support and they do not violate basic human rights. However, it is disputable what "basic human rights" can be and this problem goes further than my present concerns. Nevertheless, it is usually distinguished among first, second and third generation rights. The first would refer, at least basically, to life, freedom (as no arbitrary interference) and property. The second would try to compensate or regulate (to a certain extent) the results of the market economy to warrant certain basic social rights that the market itself does not guarantee, fostering a certain State intervention. The third would refer, *inter alia*, to steady development and a balanced environment.

Getting back to "neighbour cultures", I do not see how a minority could impose itself over a majority and expect to receive some moral backing from either inside or outside. By "universalism" I mean that there are certain features that do not pertain to concrete "neighbour cultures" but to human beings as such. This is not a descriptive claim but a normative one. In saying that some kinds of universalism and particularism are required I claim that some disputable common basic features should be respected, not because they pertain to a specific culture, but to human beings, as understood in a certain sense. Moreover, a certain kind of particularism means that there are some features that, being particularist, have enough importance to be respected, at least in principle.

Namely, when they do not conflict with universal claims of justice. This though is a disputable matter because, although many can share a given concept, such as freedom of speech, they do not necessarily share the same conception.[1] The

[1] Hollis, Martin. *The Philosophy of Social Science*, Cambridge University Press, 1994, pages 215-216. Even accepting a certain concept, for example, "poverty" we have several conceptions at hand and no algorithm will decide the problem because it is, mainly, a moral problem. In relation to the concept of "poverty" Hollis shows how this concept was understood in Britain, in different times, in terms of "subsistence", "basic needs" and "relative deprivation". Furthermore, any of these conceptions may have different and competing interpretations. In relation to the variety of conceptions and the possibility of reaching universal agreements: Stevenson, Leslie, *Siete Teorias de la Naturaleza Humana*, ed. Catedra, Madrid, 1983; Campbell, Tom, *Siete Teorías de la Sociedad*, ed. Catedra,

expression, "basic features" is also disputable but one thing is to accept their existence (no matter how disputable the features can be) and another is to deny them. I take for granted that we, human beings, have some basic common features that make peace, co-ordination and human rights possible, *inter alia*, although they cannot be "discovered" because they should be the result of argumentation and agreement. Given certain circumstances, like food, shelter, education, freedom, respect, etcetera, human beings are better placed for reaching certain basic universal claims on the basis of common basic features.

When we claim, for example, that "only those rules that may reach the approval of all participants in a practical discourse can aspire to validity", we have (*inter alia*) to deal with the problem of the content of these rules. In this respect, my claim is that the Rule of Law is, as a matter of fact, a legal-ethical model of certain cultures, and that it is not particularist but universalist, at least from a normative point of view. That is, if a basic premise is to consider human beings as ends in themselves, this shows a universalistic vocation. This would be so because the Rule of Law, understood as a relatively robust one, supports the basic moral requirement of human beings as ends in themselves better than any other model. It does not imply that there is only one rationality or that we can dispense with a constructive task, in so far as rationality is concerned. This constructive moment is required because the universal requirements of justice cannot be put in motion alone or by imposition of the representatives of the "true" rationality. Dialogue is also required.

I also take for granted that formal moral requirements, understood as unconditional and universal, cannot determine whether a concrete action is needed. At the same time, categorical imperatives would be duties expressing the objective need for action. I disagree not only with the former view (if understood as sufficient for guiding human action) but also with communities of love and friendship or compassion. While in the former model the individual is artificially seen as a rational-impartial universal being, with no particular contaminations, in the latter model, his personal autonomy is impoverished in so far as it is embedded in a particular flock. However, it is not the case that we can have synthetic *a priori* judgements in relation to normative moral realms. These types of judgements would give us information and, at the same time, would be universal and necessary. This is not the case though, since these basic moral requirements originate in our western culture and try to transcend a concrete given community, fostering (*inter alia*) an ideal of fair and friendly co-operation among human beings. Nevertheless, we are able to perceive the moral world differently and also to create different moral points of view.

It is probably correct to claim that certain moral agreements, on certain matters, form a basic paste that joins a given society together to a certain extent. However, even if this is so, a problem remains in relation to the extent of this agreement. It is also important to know at which level of abstraction we reach this agreement. It is not the same, as I said, to agree on the concept of equality or on a given conception

---

Madrid, 1985; Marina, J.A. and de la Válgoma, M., *La lucha por la dignidad*. Anagrama, Barcelona, 2000.

of equality. With the first we will probably have a wider moral agreement, although with less preciseness and, probably, intensity. With the second we will probably have a less wider agreement, although a more intensive and precise one. What is required to have a working Rule of Law? And what do we mean by a "working" Rule of Law? However, although these are interesting matters, I will just focus here on certain restricted items.

Going back to the problem of universalization, I would say that the exceptions to basic moral requirements that call for justification, are not those referring to music, dance, literature, philosophy, cooking, etcetera, but those exceptions referring to basic rights. A person is unjustly treated if he/she is not allowed to wear the traditional clothing of his community (to take an easy example) but he is not unjustly treated if he has to pay the same taxes as others, given the same relevant circumstances and granted a reasonably just redistribution of welfare. Nevertheless, this implies a certain conception of person and society. It is supposed here that if we take personal autonomy seriously we cannot dispense with a certain interference with freedom. In this respect, in so far as a Rule of Law model takes personal autonomy seriously it will have to be a relatively thick model.

The satisfaction of certain social rights (that make the exercise of freedom more probable and rich) implies a certain restriction of freedom (basically economic). If this is correct, we have to deal with a justified level of restriction for economic freedom, to enhance a higher level of equality which allows, in its turn, a higher level of positive freedom. Not only is an acceptable level of equality of opportunities required but an acceptable level of equality in the results is also required. However, we should bear in mind two dangers. On the one hand, it is dangerous for individual freedom to impose on a population certain social ends that have to be fulfilled, apart from the higher or lower efficiency that these commands may have. Nevertheless, it is also dangerous to rest exclusively on opportunities, because of the inevitable inequalities that exist in any hypothetical social starting point, where all individuals run a hypothetical race. We should not rely exclusively on opportunities (which are never practically equal) and completely overlook the results, when these results negatively affect the basic rights or basic needs of individuals. On the other hand, we cannot rely exclusively on results because, in this case, a too strong and long lasting interference with individual freedom would be required. This is also a dangerous road to follow because history shows how much we have to be mistrustful of those "Illuminati" who claim to know (better than ourselves) our "true" freedom and "true" happiness.

Unless we accept a dogmatic and linear point of view, we are condemned to deal with competing basic requirements that call for a provisional and unstable balance, although they are able to reach sufficient stability to give us a certain level of legal certainty and legal predictability. These are, *inter alia*, inescapable challenges to any Rule of Law that tries to promote fidelity, rather than mere obedience. This results in one of the weaknesses of the "thin" models of the Rule of Law, because there is no content to be committed to. Consequently, how can we have fidelity in a void mechanism that gives us predictability about any content? If participants are needed for a good working of a legal order, if only participants can sincerely utter committed legal claims and if principled legal decision making is expected (*inter alia*), then, because of the piecemeal legislation typical of pluralistic societies, some flesh has to be offered up.

This flesh is the moral and social content of the Rule of Law. It does not mean though that there is any neglectful attitude towards procedures, because they can serve values such as impartiality and coherence. At the same time, I also value the importance of Fuller's "internal morality of law", that is, the eight procedural requirements that should be met to a sufficient degree before a legal system can be said to exist. Be that as it may, in a Rawlsian vein, we could only reach "imperfect procedural justice" that cannot guarantee only results in all cases. We cannot reach true solutions or the one right answer. We can only reach justified decisions within a fair procedure. Nevertheless, we look for fair procedures because we expect them to tend or foster certain material results.

A neutral liberal conception of the Rule of Law should not be defended if this means an inert mechanism serving any master and any value. One basic difference between liberal and communitarian conceptions is not that the former lack a conception of the good life (only procedures and abstract rules of any content) but the latter are based on concrete conceptions of a good life. In my view, one of the main differences is that the former (or a certain conception of it) is able to support a concept of the good life that allows more pluralistic interpretations, more tolerance and a more self-critical attitude. To condemn somebody as a "traitor", for example, is easier in communitarian conceptions (at least radical ones) than in liberal conceptions, because there is a tendency to overstate the importance of the community itself, shared sensibilities and virtues. When this happens, some dissenting individuals tend to be diminished in their intrinsic importance (as ends in themselves) or they are mainly (or only) seen as members of a given flock.

Nevertheless, a human being in a liberal society must have some values to defend, rather than only procedures and effective means. I cannot deal here though with the important issue, presented by MacIntyre among others, of whether it is possible to have a common good in our liberal societies. Be that as it may, I believe that "thin" models of the ideal Rule of Law are a necessary condition for the model of the ideal Rule of Law I support, but it is not a sufficient one. How should we understand a "thin" model of the Rule of Law? Although there are several opinions, I will not scrutinize all of them. I will only expose, very briefly, what could be the main features of a "thin" model of the Rule of Law, accepting that this is a disputable matter. If we pay attention to what Robert Summers says, legal predictability and freedom from arbitrariness are basic features of this model.[2] He

---

[2] Summers, Robert. "The Ideal Socio-Legal Order. Its Rule of Law Dimension", *Ratio Iuris*, Volume 1, Number 2, July 1988, pages 154-161. Aleksander Peczenik also emphasizes "legal certainty" but it has a different meaning. He says, "I thus interpret "legal certainty" in the material sense, as the optimal compromise between predictability of legal decisions and their acceptability in view of other moral considerations. *On Law and Reason*, Kluwer Academic Publishers, Dordrecht, 1989, page 32. George P. Fletcher says that there are two conceptions of the Rule of Law; one, "simply means that the government is bound by rules fixed and announced before hand". In relation to the other, he says, "Those who think that the Rule of Law is an ideal for good government stress the dimension of Right

also believes that if we adopt this model we shall reach more conceptual unity, that is, more simplicity and systemacity.

At the same time, it would be a far more politically neutral model than a "robust" one. Friedrich Hayek supports a similar, but unequal, view because while Summers believes that the Rule of Law is mainly a technique, able to be filled up with different material contents, Hayek sees the Rule of Law as a conception of human beings and society. However, it is not the same to internalize a certain technique or a form of life. Hayek supposes that individuals share practices that enhance freedom, in a context of order, that makes it possible to exercise this very freedom. This would call both for a market economy and a conception of a citizen as a moral agent, able to make choices freely. Summing up, the basic values of the "thin" model of the Rule of Law, would be the following: generality, legal predictability, and freedom from arbitrariness or control of the state.

I believe that for a more effective exercise of personal autonomy, a more "robust" model is needed. If we accept this step, we have moved from being the "isolated individual" to a "committed participant". If a rational human being has, in a Rawlsian vein, a sense of justice and the capability to make life plans, at least two considerations arise. First, it seems difficult to have a sense of justice only towards formal justice, towards a more or less effective mechanism. The second is that this capability of making life plans will be practically enhanced in a more or less "robust" model but not in a "thin" one. On the other hand, I accept that "collectivistic approaches" or "social engineering" are dangerous devices for individual freedom and also fertile producers of unhappy side effects.

Even if we take this for granted, we have to face the problem that it is possible to agree with beliefs but not with attitudes. In other words, we may agree with the factual side effects but not necessarily with their evaluation. Hence, it seems that certain normative premises have to be accepted as a starting point, unless we want to plunge into an infinite regression. In this respect, I would say that we cannot prove that a "robust" model is better than a "thin" model but, if we believe in human beings as ends in themselves, a certain type of "robust" model should be adopted. In this respect, I agree with Neil MacCormick's criticism of "thin" models when he claims that they fail to show that there cannot be positive duties of justice.[3]

If you take "individual autonomy" seriously, you cannot rely exclusively on Pareto optimality. However, I will not plunge into this complex question. For our present purposes, it would be enough to say that this means "an increase in total welfare as occurs in those conditions in which some people are better off as a result of the change, without at the same time anybody being worse off".[4] Even if

---

in the Rule of Law. The vision of a state based on ideal law is captured in the German notion of Rechtsstaat". In: *Basic Concepts of Legal Thought*, Oxford University Press, Oxford, 1996, page 12.

[3] MacCormick, Neil. "Spontaneous Order and the Rule of Law", *Ratio Iuris*, Volume 2, Number 1, March 1989, pages 41-54.

[4] Bannock, G., Baxter, R. and Davis, E. *Dictionary of Economics*, The Penguin, 1987, pages 308-309. It is also interesting to see Peter Benson's opinion about this, "The Paretian and compensation dilemmas make clear the need for normative principles to supplement the efficacy criteria." In: *A Companion to Philosophy of Law and Legal Theory*, edited by D. Patterson, Blackwell, Cambridge, 1996, page 49.

economic efficiency was possible[5] the problem would be whether to accept market competition as the only referee of our welfare. Therefore, the problem is not only if there is a situation where nobody can improve without someone else being worse off. Individual autonomy is also related to social justice and to the socio-economic starting point, that is, what the distribution of resources was when the hypothetical social run started. In addition, autonomy is not only related to opportunity but also to the real possibility of fulfilling the expected life plans of individuals that should be evaluated within a concrete social context.

Autonomy not only refers to fulfilling life plans but also to being able to think deeply about them. This is related to a previous capability that the market alone cannot give, that is, the capability to reflect deeply about oneself, other human

---

In this respect, Richard Posner says, "The Pareto approach may seem to offer a solution to the problem of measuring satisfaction. A change is said to be Pareto superior if it makes at least one person better off and no one worse off. Such a change by definition increases the total amount of (human) happiness in the world. The advantage of the Pareto approach it that it requires information only about marginal and not about total utilities. And there seems ready at hand an operational device for achieving Pareto superiority, the voluntary transaction, which by definition makes both parties better off than they were before. However, the condition that no one else be affected by a "voluntary" transaction can only rarely be fulfilled. Moreover, the voluntary-transaction or free-market solution to the problem of measuring utility begs two critical questions: whether the goods exchanged were initially distributed so as to maximize happiness (were the people with money those who derive the most happiness from the things money can buy?) and whether a system of free markets creates more happiness than alternative systems of resource allocation would." In: *The Economics of Justice*, Harvard University Press, Cambridge, 1983, pages 54-55.

Tom Campbell, in *Justice*, MacMillan Education, London, 1988, says, "This approach is exemplified by the use of the idea of "Pareto optimality", according to which one situation is superior to another if at least one person is better of (or prefers that situation) and all other persons are equally well off (or think that the situations are equally acceptable) ... This uncontroversial concept is not only of very limited application in practice but has the disadvantage of giving a veto over any proposed changes to every member of a community, thus giving unjustified weight to the *status quo* ...", page 128.

Jules L. Coleman, "Efficiency, Utility and Wealth Maximization", in *Justice*, edited by Thomas Morawetz, pages 203-245, says: "Resources are allocated in a Pareto-optimal fashion if and only if any further reallocation of them can enhance the welfare of one person only at the expense of another. An allocation of resources is Pareto superior to an alternative allocation if and only if no one is made worse off by the distribution and the welfare of at least one person is improved ... Like Pareto superiority, Kaldor-Hicks efficiency is a relational property of state of affairs. One state of affairs (E') is Kaldor-Hicks efficient to another (E) if and only if those whose welfare increases in the move from (E) to (E') could fully compensate those whose welfare diminishes with a net gain in welfare. Under Kaldor-Hicks, compensation to losers is not in fact paid." He also says that, "Even were we to agree that pursuing efficiency would be morally defensible, we would argue that it is a further question whether judges have the authority to do so. In addition, we argue that adjudication primarily -or always- concerns rights rather than the promotion of some useful social policy while at the same time it provides a substantial and meaningful role for economic argument."

[5] Economic efficiency can be understood as follows: "The state of an economy in which no one can be made better off without someone being made worse off. For this to be the case, three types of efficiency must hold. The first is *productive efficiency*, in which the output of the economy is being produced at the lowest cost. The second is *allocative efficiency*, in which resources are being allocated to the production of the goods and services the society requires. The third is *distributional efficiency*, in which output is distributed in such a way that consumers would not wish, given their disposable income and market prices, to spend these incomes in any different way." Bannock, G., Baxter, R. and Davis, E., *Dictionary of Economics*, Penguin, fourth edition, 1987, page 125.

beings and the world around us. This will affect the concrete life plans a human being is able to plan. The "thin" models of the ideal Rule of Law seem to be close to this restricted view of freedom. They seem to rely very much on the market as the unique device that will lead us to the best possible result. However, the best possible result is seen exclusively in economic terms and neglects redistributive issues. That is, they have a restricted concept of freedom that does not seriously face the problem of social justice, or in other words, the problem of real autonomy of individuals. Nevertheless, as I said, we also have to take care of "social engineering" as another permanent danger. I have tried very briefly to expose the main features of the two models (the "thin" and the "robust" ones), and also some of the problems involved in this choice.

2. CONCEPTIONS OF PERSON AND MODELS OF RULE OF LAW

The "thin" ideal model of the Rule of Law cannot cope adequately with a concept of "person" that is understood as a committed participant. Therefore, we need a relatively "robust" model based, *inter alia*, on a different conception of "person" that will not see human beings as irrepressible maximizers of any desire that is not incompatible with either the legal rules in force or the market. On the contrary, the ideal type of rational agent underlying this relatively robust model that I support, should accept the rules of discoursive-rationality[6] plus the Kantian imperative that human beings are ends and not only means in themselves. If not, rational behaviour should only be understood in an economic sense, that is, rational behaviour would be to fulfil our own preferences, whatever they are. It can be argued though that in a given structure of personal stratified preferences for a given human being, it is not necessary that all preferences be self-interested because the agent may also have altruist preferences. These latter preferences open us to other human beings emphasizing our moral relational dimension because we see others not only as means but also as ends. This would make solid and reliable social co-ordination possible.

These self-interested and altruist preferences would be seen more clearly in competitive situations. In this respect, a given agent could decide, in certain circumstances, to give priority to the preferences of other agents in detriment to his

---

[6] Aarnio, Aulis. *The Rational as Reasonable*, Reidel Publishing Company, Dordrecht, 1987, pages 196 and ff. I will summarize them. "Consistency-rules ... the principles of logical consistency covers, for example, the demand that there is no internal conflict, the third excluded law, and the transitiveness rule ... Efficiency-rules. In order to be rational, practical discourse presupposes effectiveness: the discourse must result in a conclusion ... This means, for instance, that people using language use expressions in the same way ... Sincerity-rules. Everyone who speaks the language in question has a right to participate ... The demand of honesty means that a discussant may not refer to justification that he knows is nonvalid ... In other words, he must follow the principle of *audiatur et altera pars*. Generalization-rules ... violation of the rule of generalizability leads to the use of grounds that are only connected to the situation in question. They are, so to speak, *ad hoc* arguments ... Support-rules. The rule of the necessity of justification states that when so demanded, every proposition must be justified ... As far as the substantial support is concerned, the key concept is coherency.

own interests. However, it is difficult to see how he would behave in this way unless he adopted a moral point of view that, by definition, requires both impartiality and that the interests of others are taken into account. If you do not accept that human beings are ends in themselves, why should you damage your own interests to favour the interests of others? The answer could be that a rational agent can do this for prudential reasons. Nevertheless, it is not clear, at least from a pragmatical point of view, how a legal order can survive when an important part of the population behaves as an irrepressible maximizer, or just pretends not to be an irrepressible maximizer. It is hard to believe that the normative structure of a society would not be seriously damaged if citizens, in general, behaved in this way. Granted that we live in a market society, to rely exclusively on procedural rationality would imply, practically speaking, to foster the "logic" and the "justice" of the market.

I will recall here that H. Hart claimed a "minimum content", based on survival, that legal systems must have if they are to be feasible. According to him, certain necessary features of reality and of human beings must lead to the acceptance of certain rules. In a way, Hart tries to supersede the supposed irrationality or arbitrariness of normative premises. He realized the need for a respected normative structure if legal orders were to be feasible, although he supported these premises because they were (or at least he thought so) empirical features of human nature. In this respect, I have commented[7] that Hart's discourse (based on the modest goal of survival) implies more than what he explicitly accepts because survival is not sufficient to explain and justify the five well known obvious truths: human vulnerability, approximate equality, limited altruism, limited resources and limited comprehension and will power.

The highest point of the personal stratified structure of preferences (that any normal person would have, even unconsciously) would be occupied by moral reasons, which are understood as ultimate reasons. In a "thin" model of the Rule of Law, moral reasons as ultimate reasons have no place, or are not required, because, at most, we have formal justice, which is the procedural requirement of "treat like cases alike". If there are moral reasons, they only exist within the personal hierarchy of the preferences of each individual. The only possible incoherence would be inside this personal hierarchy. There would be nothing outside this personal hierarchy of preferences that could make a claim of incoherence. In other words, there are no objective moral reasons, hence any moral reason is as good as any other. Then, how do we convince people that we have some overriding duties for social justice?

In this respect, it seems that we should accept the requirements of discoursive rationality rules plus the cited Kantian imperative of human beings as ends in themselves, if we are going to rely on overriding moral reasons that are able to put moral limits on our behaviour. This is especially important in our societies where God is not, as he was in the Middle Ages, the inevitable objective reference. The only limits would be what is most beneficial for me. It is a problem for the supporters of "thin" models of the Rule of Law to claim a model with no moral

---

[7] Urbina, Sebastián. *Reason, Democracy, Society*, Kluwer Academic Publishers, Dordrecht, 1996, pages 172 and ff.

premises and expect, at the same time, that we shall meet morality, trust, social co-ordination and the rest. Another problem is whether a legal order can expect "fidelity" without a moral dimension and committed participants.

Finally, if objective morality (in the intersubjective sense) comes, at least in part, from "outside" the individual, which moral contents should we accept? Should we accept anything? A person may internalize something coming from "outside" but it would be heteronomous, not autonomous. Two basic dangers we have to deal with are: on the one hand, the search for a practical reason based on unconditional and universal features, and, on the other hand, the search for a practical reason only based on our own history and institutions. As is already known, the first Kantian option emphasizes subjectivity and morality while the second Aristotelian-Hegelian option emphasizes community.

I accept Hegelian criticism that Kantian formal principles require content but I reject that this content should be exclusively filled by the community itself. It is emphasized here that the best option is a tension between the requirements of the positive and critical morality. This proper tension is more probable in a community where freedom, plurality and personal autonomy are fostered. It also means that we cannot be completely autonomous because we cannot see our society or our form of life, from outside.

3. RULE OF LAW AND INTERPRETATION

One of the main reasons for backing a relatively "robust" conception of the Rule of Law is that legal orders require official interpretation and application, as a pragmatical necessity. If this is correct, the next claim is that interpretation-application by judges cannot dispense with moral evaluations. That is, our legal systems have a theory of justice (explicit or implicit) that supports and justifies them. At least in hard cases, moral evaluations usually enter into the process of reasoning, together with (at least) a must source, such as an authoritative enacted rule. Hard cases are not only those that face a conflictive interpretation of the meaning of a legal text, but also (*inter alia*), when given a certain accepted meaning, we are not sure whether this is the most coherent and just option, here and now.

Therefore, I will try to show that a "thin" model of the Rule of Law does not properly face this necessary task of our legal orders, at least from a pragmatical point of view. It is not an acceptable view that we must leave this matter to what "society believes", because judges should not assent, *tout court*, to any majoritarian demand. Why not? Because, at least in our legal contexts the set of constitutionally recognized individual rights require, *inter alia*, that individuals ought to be treated with equal concern. This is, obviously, a very abstract claim though. From it, several interpretations can be proposed, although these interpretations will be moral proposals about how we ought to understand the claim. A first moral requirement would be to give equal weight to a person's preferences if they did not conflict with the basic requirements of justice. Nevertheless, I would distinguish between preferences related to basic human needs and basic individual rights, on the one hand, and preferences not related to them, on the other.

I agree that it can be difficult to separate them clearly in all cases. Be that as it may, the former are too important to leave completely to personal preferences. Only in the latter case, would respecting personal preferences be a proper respect or an equal concern for everyone. A clear example would be not to respect those personal preferences that deny preferences should count equally, bearing in mind the condition cited above. However, we should except, as I said, those preferences related to basic needs and basic rights. We only have a moral duty to put ourselves in other people's shoes (and try to imagine how our behaviour could affect their interests) in relation to these basic aspects that are political and moral constructions. To do more would mean undertaking supererogatory actions.

Nevertheless, we do not have a moral duty to perform supererogatory actions because we have no duty to behave as saints or heroes, although it does not always have clear boundaries. What matters, here, is that the Rule of Law should incorporate a welfare net in order to compensate, to a certain extent, certain unequal circumstances. However, legal rules are necessary in order to reach certain levels of predictability because predictability is a necessary condition, although not a sufficient one, for personal autonomy. A welfare net is also needed for compensating, to a certain extent, social or natural inequalities that should be seen as irrelevant from a moral point of view. I say, "to a certain extent" because a full dedication to compensate for these inequalities could spoil the "ambition-sensitive" requirements of the rest of the individuals. This tension calls for a provisional and justified balance that has no *a priori* answer.

This fundamental moral requirement for treating individuals with equal respect is closely related to the Kantian categorical imperatives. I will briefly recall what is well known, that the three formulations of the categorical imperative state central aspects of our legal systems. They are necessary but not sufficient conditions for democracy. We have freedom, in so far as we are autonomous; we have dignity in so far as we are treated as ends and not only as means in ourselves; we have equality in so far as there is universalization. Nevertheless, all these basic moral requirements are not completely formal.

This is not only because racist doctrines would not fit into them, for example, but also because it implies a bet for human freedom, dignity and autonomy. Perhaps it does not prescribe specific material contents but it makes some of them incoherent with these moral requirements. Inevitably, at least pragmatically speaking, these moral requirements will have to be concreted, in the sense that any society, "here and now", has some concrete special features that call for specific ways of fulfilling these basic requirements. All this will require, *inter alia*, decisions and these decisions, judgements.

However, these legal requirements will call for the "best" interpretation, at least in hard cases. Clearly, it does not mean that in "routine cases" there is not the "best" interpretation. Granted that the jurists (generally speaking) share an internal point of view (and surely most of the citizens), they try to "optimise" the legal order. Then, the "best" interpretation is always conceptually required. In "routine cases" it is considered, at least by the legal community, that this "best" interpretation has already been reached, whereas not in "hard cases" (at least before interpretation).

When searching for this interpretation, jurists are not trying to state their own personal judgement but the "best" interpretation of the legal order itself. This is a fiction but a working one. Jurists, granted that they are participants, try to foster the values of the legal order because they have "fidelity to law". Inevitably, individual human beings undertake these interpretations but they make them, let us say, "in the name" of the legal order. That is, they accept and try to "optimise" the basic values of the legal order at stake.

As is known, the main difference between routine and hard cases is that in the latter there is not the usual agreement found in the former. This means, *inter alia*, that hard cases foster legal and moral reasoning, to fulfil the expectations of our basic constitutional principles better. What has been said implies that the Rule of Law cannot only be a procedural requirement because, even if we accept that what judges ought to do is to guarantee a fair trial, it will not only be a formal requirement, at least in all cases.

The preceding comments should not be understood as if the substantive requirements had to search for a "higher law" than the positive one. Irrespective of the empirical possibility of some judges to do this, coherence and justice are ideals that should guide, *inter alia*, the judges' task, although they should rest on some interpretation of the theory of justice that underlies the legal system, except in cases of extreme injustice, where a non-technical dilemma arises. I do not claim that, in fact, all legal orders of the Western world work as I have commented. This is a normative proposal that has an inevitable level of tension that should avoid either-or solutions.

In this respect, I would not accept only one of the two possibilities proposed by M. Oakeshott, in other words, either "civil association" (without purpose, only oriented towards universal, abstract, formal rules) or "enterprise association" (with its own goals and expecting the citizens to fight for themselves). I believe that neither is acceptable, taken exclusively, because we either need both of them or some dimensions of both. This leads us to the moral basement of our legal orders. I believe that, with broad strokes, two main lines of thought push for two different basic moral justifications.

On the one hand, we have communitarian approaches that enhance certain goods within certain social practices as something prior to rights. At least in case of conflict, the latter would be subordinate to the former. This means, *inter alia*, that individual autonomy is subordinated to communitarian traditions or to some communitarian traditions, at least when there is a conflict between them. On the other hand, we have liberal Kantian approaches. I maintain that these approaches, mainly based on individual rights, are the best support for a relatively robust model of the Rule of Law, as I understand it. Although different from the former approaches we are dealing here with relatively formal ones. Only relatively though, because we cannot expect "fidelity to law" and "internal point of view" to be based only on a formal approach. I believe that both have to deal, *inter alia*, with a concept of person and with some moral principles like treating persons as ends and not means, as well as other values cited above.

I have defended that the rules of discoursive rationality, the Kantian principle that persons are ends and not means in themselves, freedom, dignity, equality, and certain moral practices making it more specific, can lead to a better moral justification of the Rule of Law. These comments justify the requirement of autonomy, understood as real autonomy and not only formal autonomy, which is closer to the concept of negative freedom. We cannot dispense with the societal dimension of personal autonomy because I cannot reach autonomy exclusively by myself. This implies the interaction of my autonomy with another human being (or other human beings) and with goods, that also have a societal dimension. The latter can allow me to survive as a biological entity, whereas the former can allow me to reach self-respect although it cannot only be an individual matter.

In this way, we can eliminate the historical and abstract view of a lonely human being reaching autonomy by himself. However, we can also eliminate the view that the individual is "embedded" in (in the best case) or "sucked" into (in the worst case) the community. This latter view tends to make a critical stance towards social practices and traditions more difficult, fostering a tendency to see what is real as rational. Nevertheless, the Kantian idea of the autonomy of reason is not supported here. The idea of "pureness" is not supported either, neither in law (Kelsenian pure theory) nor in ethics (Kantian unconditional and universal requirements). On the contrary, what is supported are the ideas of "tension" and "contamination".

4. RULE OF LAW AND RIGHTS

Joel Feinberg distinguishes between, "(i) making claim to ....(ii) claiming that ...and (iii) having a claim."[8] He seems to believe that the first is to demand something as due. The second differs from the first, since it is only a linguistic claim. Someone could claim that he has a right that ought to be recognized. The third is in a position to claim the first or the second. Feinberg believes that a right is a valid claim. In this sense, it is an "all or nothing" question. He stresses that a claim can be "more or less" but it cannot be a right. Hence, you have a right or you do not have a right.

I think that Feinberg supports the correct view in so far as he believes in rights from an *ex post* point of view, since, because of legal certainty, *inter alia*, a claim right has to be concluded in one sense or another. In this respect, rights are not "*prima facie* rights", as he says, although he is only in a correct position in so far as we are supposing an *ex post* view. In other words, from this *ex post* view (that is, after interpretation) it has no sense to talk of "*prima facie* rights" but it has sense to talk of "*prima facie* rights" from an *ex ante* point of view. In this case, we could not be sure (at least always) whether a concrete claim right will finish in its legal acceptance. Likewise, once the judicial acceptance has been made, we can say that the plaintiff had a right to something concrete. However, when a right has to be recognized in a concrete case, and for a concrete person, it is not always so clear. I want to stress that if we see rights *ex post* we see them in an "all-nothing" vein, in the sense that a concrete person in a specific situation had, or not, a concrete right.

---

[8] Feinberg, Joel. "The Nature and Value of Rights". In: *Rights*, edited by Carlos Nino, Dartmouth, Aldershot, 1992, page 193.

Nevertheless, if we see rights *ex ante*, we can suppose (or even believe) that a concrete person will have his claim recognized or not, but we can be mistaken. It is true that in routine-cases we have more probabilities to know *ex ante* what the result will be, but not in hard-cases. However, a routine-case is not so forever. Formally speaking, we know that this is an "all-nothing" element, but we do not necessarily know who will have the right, or we do not know whether a concrete person will have his claim recognized in a concrete case. Probably Feinberger wants to stress the difference between legal rights, on the one hand, and moral claims, on the other hand. The latter would not be a valid claim against any individual.

This is correct in so far as we accept the old legal positivist distinction between "justice of norms" and "justice in the application of norms". As regards justice in the application of norms, Feinberg's analysis seems clear. A concrete person, in a specific situation, may have a right to (X), granted that there is a normative premise that states that certain persons in certain situations have a right to (X) and a judicial decision stating that this concrete case applies. It is also clear that a person not included in the realm of the cited normative premise cannot expect a judicial decision stating that he has a right to (X).

Therefore, I agree with Feinberg that moral claims are not valid claims against any particular individual if we accept the above mentioned distinction. That is, the justice of the normative premises is not the realm of reason but of will. If the will of somebody (the legislator) has not stated a premise saying that "all persons with feature (A) will have a right to (B) in circumstances (C)", then they do not have a valid claim at all. If legislation is the realm of will, we cannot expect that reasons decide because it would be a waste of time to argue about the justice or the reasonableness of stating certain rights to all (A).

Perhaps the "objective conditions" (whatever they are) will determine, in the final analysis, the change of will. However, it is not necessary that we agree with this deterministic view. In this case, we would have to explain how the will changes and, granted that reason has nothing to do with justice (or does not have the last word) -as a premise-, what should we do? We can say, as A. Ross and others have said, that the only rational justice is the justice in the application of law. In this respect, it would be unjust for a judge to state that a person, not included in the realm of a given normative premise, has a right to (X). I do not agree with some positivist claims stating that legislation is the realm of will and adjudication the realm of reason, at least in a democratic legal order. While in the former, anything, within physical limits, can be stated as a premise, whereas, in the latter, anything coherent with the premises would be just.

Even a defender of human rights as legal valid claims for all human beings, such as L. Ferrajoli, supports a view of legislation as the world of will and adjudication as the world of reason,

> "Summing up, jurisdictional cognitivism (*veritas, non auctoritas facit iudicium*) implies necessarily legislative voluntarism (*auctoritas, non veritas facit legem*), while the intended normative cognitivism (*veritas, non auctoritas facit legem*) factually implies the most complete jurisdictional voluntarism (*auctoritas, non veritas facit iudicium*) ...

> The truth to which substantialist models of criminal law aspirate is the so called *substantial or material truth*, that is, an absolute and all-comprehensive truth ...".[9]

Be that as it may, Feinberg sees Human Rights as basic human needs that ought to be recognized as valid legal claims. Nevertheless, as a matter of fact, it is clear that the moral claim, made by persons with these basic human needs uncovered, is not a valid legal claim. Therefore, we should accept that no one has a legal duty to fulfil these moral claims. In my view, the main problem (seen from a normative point of view) is whether we accept these valid legal claims are higher than valid moral claims or not, since the latter are ultimate reasons. As Feinberg puts it,

> "The manifesto writers on the other side who seem to identify needs, or at least basic needs, with what they call "human rights", are more properly described, I think, as urging upon the world community the moral principle that all basic human needs ought to be recognized as claims (in the customary *prima facie* sense) worthy of sympathy and serious consideration right now, even though, in many cases, they cannot yet plausibly be treated as valid claims, that is, as grounds for any other people's duties."[10]

One thing is that moral claims cannot be treated "plausibly" as valid legal claims for more or less justified empirical reasons and another thing is to deny, from a normative point of view, that valid moral claims, based on basic human needs, ought to be considered as valid legal claims. In this respect, I would repeat something similar to what I said above about the moderate robust models of the Rule of Law. They are similar arguments, because our duties towards basic human needs are stronger than other "needs", no matter, here, how difficult it can be to draw a sharp delimitation between them. Therefore, one thing is the empirical success (or not) in having these moral claims recognized as valid legal claims, and another is to recognize (or not) that these moral claims are ultimate reasons. That is, if they have enough importance for being the proper ground for people's duties. If it is true that moral reasons are ultimate reasons, and we accept that there is a moral reason for any human being (principle of universalization) to demand the satisfaction of these basic human needs, then this should be a valid legal claim. Let us look at some possible criticisms though.

First, this view falls into the old flaw of confusing law and morals. One thing is what the law is and another what the law ought to be.

Second, we cannot fulfil these world demands about basic human needs.

In relation to the first criticism, I would say that, here, we are not trying to claim that these demands, backed by moral reasons, are law. The problem is whether moral reasons are ultimate reasons or not. If they are, it is strange to claim that an addressee of a given legal system has certain basic needs and a valid legal claim to fulfil it, whereas another human being (not an addressee of this legal system) having the same basic needs in similar relevant circumstances does not have a valid legal claim. If we accept that moral reasons are ultimate reasons, once we have accepted the validity of a concrete moral reason for a particular type of situation, the principle

---

[9] Ferrajoli, Luigi. *Derecho y razón*, editorial Trotta, Madrid, 1995, page 44.

[10] Feinberg, Joel. "The Nature and Value of Rights". op. cit., page 197.

of universalization demands that it be applied to the other human beings, in similar circumstances.

The burden of proof would be on the shoulder of those who deny it. Then, it would not be valid as a legal reason but valid as a moral reason. Nevertheless, we have accepted that moral reasons are ultimate reasons. I do not claim that we ought to be converted into Calcutta mothers but only that the acceptance of the former argumentation implies certain consequences that we cannot easily disdain. It should be clear that the point, as I see it, only refers to the fulfilment of basic human needs, granted that there are valid moral reasons for any human being to have a right to have these basic needs fulfilled. It seems that to take "personal autonomy seriously" faces serious problems.

One of which is to reach an agreement about what "basic human needs" are, although, probably, the most important thing is actually to undertake the task. Nevertheless, some accepted interpretation and delimitation of this concept is needed in order to undertake this task soundly. Although I will not deal with this important question, I believe that, both too strong a feeling of exclusiveness to a given land (which would not only be a geographical feature but a kind of holy place) and strong economic-technological groups submitted to the logic of the global market, are important aspects that make a gradual move towards world-citizenship difficult.

The second element would seem to work in the proper direction because it would help globalization, although this is not so. The tendency towards world-citizenship (probably an empirical tendency and also a moral demand) should not mean that the richness of the diversity is spoilt. I would recall, again, my view that this world-citizenship should be understood in relation to basic human needs. I do not see that there is any higher demand than this, irrespective of the empirical difficulties, both material and psychological. Globalization is not understood here as a complex process of economic decisions of very influential groups, liberalization of capitals, weaker political control over these influential groups, etcetera. The main idea is that while markets and capital should not stop at legal frontiers, it should also happen with basic human rights and personal autonomy.

In relation to the second criticism, we could say that one thing is the moral duty we may have and another, the present empirical possibilities of its fulfilment. However, in order to avoid a strong utopian scheme we would have to take into account the maxim "ought implies can". If this "can" refers to the circumstances that limit the capability of certain individuals to fulfil a given duty, we can claim that, at present, developed countries can do more in order to fulfil the basic human needs of many human beings all over the world. Then, it is not the case that we are claiming strong utopias but weak utopias, because their requirements can be fulfilled currently at a higher level, without the individuals of Western countries loosing any basic element needed for reaching real personal autonomy. In so far as we move in this direction, the relatively thick model of Rule of Law can be an appealing model with universal vocation and not a parochial one.

5. AUTONOMY AS A LEGAL AND A MORAL CONCEPT

Rule of Law seems to be based, *inter alia*, on a theory of rights. Claims of "thin" theories basically stress generality, legal predictability and freedom from arbitrariness. It does not seem that the issue of personal autonomy is an issue of special concern, because its supporters believe that autonomy is only a matter for the individuals themselves, their private lives, legal rules and the market. It is also a matter of no due interference from the political authorities. I believe that "thin" theories are more unable to cope with the question of personal autonomy than "robust" models, both in national terms and international ones. "Thin" models have to leave the issue of personal autonomy to individual benevolence (when a person is unable by himself to satisfy his basic needs) but they cannot face the problem from an institutional point of view.

It is doubtful though that this problem should be faced only from an individual benevolent view. I would say, provisionally, that "thin" models of the Rule of Law do not take "personal autonomy seriously". Although leftist doctrines, generally speaking, claim that autonomy (in our real world) is a form of egoism or a false market equality or something similar, I believe that we should differentiate between autonomy, according to the thinner models of the Rule of Law, and autonomy according to the robust models of the Rule of Law. As I have said, I do not defend extreme robust models because they imply, more or less explicitly, the idea of a Procrustean bed of perfection.

All members of the flock, group, nation or world, must be designed according to a previous idea of perfection designed by the Illuminati. Any minor level of fulfilment is seen either as a treachery or a weakness of the will, which can be appropriately modified by intensification of the "true" doctrine. Hence, I will leave aside extreme robust models of the Rule of Law because of their nearness to perfectionist doctrines. I think it is possible to see, according to what has been said so far, that adopting one type of Rule of Law model (a relatively thin one or a relatively robust one) has different consequences, *inter alia*, for personal autonomy and also different starting conceptions of "person".

Extreme doctrines, let us say, would ignore Hart's "obvious truth" that we are neither angels nor devils. We have genetic information codified in our DNA not by chance but as a result of a long process of natural selection. However, it is important to recognize also that we have certain natural features such as egoism, envy, desire of domination, aggressiveness, etcetera, that cannot be eliminated, although we can soften and guide them to a certain extent. We also have some natural features, such as altruism, that cannot be eliminated, at least from the human species. The possible objection that Pol Pot, for example, did not show any altruism, can be answered in the following manner. Although legal orders are coercive, not all of their rules are, and in the same way, the human species has altruism as one of its features but not all of its members necessarily do. Therefore, perfectionist doctrines build a Procrustean bed and lengthen or shorten individuals until they reach the ideal moral measurement they have designed. In this respect, supporters of perfectionist views would not take personal autonomy seriously.

Also in this respect, D. Richards says:

> "My aim in this essay is to clarify the human rights perspective (i.e., the underlying structure of the language and thought of human rights) ... I characterize and explicate this structure in terms of the autonomy-based interpretation of treating persons as equals."[11]

Hence, the problem is to scrutinize what "treating persons as equals" means. Although he shows four interpretations of autonomy (Psychological Theory and Autonomy-Autonomy not Causal Indeterminism, but consistent with Social Theory-Autonomy not Wilfulness-Autonomy not Egoism), I will focus on rights as trumps (deontological view) and maximum strategy (consequentialist view).

I believe it is an important point of departure to claim that,

> "No animal other than man, however, appears to have the capacity for reflective self-evaluation that is manifested in the formation of second-order desires."[12]

If this is correct, we can claim that the fulfilment of first order-desires (I would say, basic human needs) are a necessary condition for the formation of second-order desires. If these second-order desires are a manifestation of the personal autonomy of human beings, then, if we take autonomy seriously, we ought to do something in order to make these second order desires possible. It is clear that the fulfilment of these desires would pose difficult problems that I will not deal with here. For example, should we pay for some expensive ones? What does "expensive" mean? An important point is that without these basic human needs fulfilled there is no pragmatical possibility of exercising practical rationality.

How should we understand human basic needs? A famous specialist on human needs such as A. Heller says:

> "Each form of life has to be linked to their own distributive justice. Only the members of each community are qualified to decide which form of distribution is just or unjust."[13]

If we accept this conclusion we could face puzzling situations such as the following: members of a given community state that women will not have the right to vote in the assembly and that they will receive a third of the recourses men receive with the consequence, *inter alia*, that women have higher death rates and illnesses. We cannot decide whether this is just or not. It is not clear, then, why Heller has also written,

> "Recognition is due to the person *for being* a person -due to her specific being, her human self. Respect is due to the humanity and, consequently, to each person as a member of human species."[14]

---

[11] Richards, David. "Rights and Autonomy". In: *Rights*, edited by Carlos Nino, Dartmouth, Aldershot, 1992, page 202. It is worth emphasizing the conception of person Nicholas Rescher has. According to him it implies seven conditions: Intelligence, Affectivity, Agency, Rationality, Self-understanding, Self-esteem and Mutual recognizance. *Human Interests. Reflection on Philosophical Anthropology*, Standford Series in Philosophy, California, 1990, pages 6-21.

[12] Ibidem, page 204.

[13] Heller, Agnes. *Mas allá de la Justicia*, editorial Critica, Barcelona, 1990, page 261.

We can reconcile these two quotations, that seem to be contradictory, if we accept that, in relation to human basic needs and individual rights, the human community (universalism) should decide what is just or not, while the members of a given community (particularism) should decide what is just, or not, in the other matters. From a nation-state view we would say something similar: the most important values are not at the free disposal of individuals (universalism from a nation-state view) while the individuals can freely decide the rest (particularism). In my view, a proper theory of justice requires a balance (an unstable one) between individual and community but, at the same time, also a balance between a particular community and the global human community, in so far as we are something more than members of a particular flock.

As I have already said, two basic concepts, *inter alia,* should be taken seriously into account: human beings as ends and not only means, and personal autonomy. In relation to the first concept I believe that it should not be understood as something we can describe purely because it is not an external empirical reality. It is a created moral requirement that calls for a permanent moral compromise. Just as it was created at some time in History (although it has to be understood as a process) it can gradually weaken until it disappears. In so far as personal autonomy is concerned, I understand it not as producing preferences of any kind but as a responsible and solidary process of choice.

We should not be constrained (as much as possible) either by the state or by the citizens but, at the same time, we construct ourselves not as a Robinson Crusoe but as a social individual. In so far as freedom exists within a causal universe, personal autonomy ought to exist in relation to other societal human beings, not in a kind of glass bell jar. We should exercise our personal autonomy with an eye on the basic interests of other human beings, if we are going to reject personal autonomy from the *homo economicus* point of view. However, we cannot completely reject it because we should be, and to some extent are, both *homo economicus* and *homo sociologicus*. This shows, once again, that we cannot avoid tension, adaptation, balance, judgement, etcetera, in an endless process.

There is also a problem related to the concept of "needs". We, human beings, probably have a common ground for stating our physical needs. Although we can meet exceptions, the identification of our physical needs is rather general. Nevertheless, more problems appear when we face cultural and psychological needs. The problem though does not change if we call them "psychological desires" to emphasize that they are not "really" needs.

One of the main problems of this inescapable problem is the individual or social perspective. If we face the problem of the satisfaction of psychological needs from an individualistic point of view, we are condemned to failure, because they cannot be completely satisfied. Here we should recall what we commented on above about

[14] Ibidem, page 250. It is interesting to note that the School of Budapest, either during Gyorgy Lukacs' times or later on, has understood the foundations of Human Rights as a permanent task and not as a definite metaphysical definition, as can be seen in, *Los Derechos Humanos desde la Escuela de Budapest*, Tecnos, Madrid, 1989, written by Joaquin Herrera.

human rights of the third generation. They, *inter alia*, deal with environment and steady development. It means that one way to limit, *inter alia*, the irrepressible maximizer is the respect for these third generation rights. Nevertheless, why should any rational agent limit himself? I believe that we could reach a get out if we rely on moral agents able to go beyond themselves and, for this reason, be able to build and participate in a common moral background.

This common moral background would be able to justify the limits of the psychological needs and desires. I cannot see though how it can be justified unless human beings share, at least to a certain extent, an ideal of human flourishing which is a formal aspiration that can be fulfilled in different ways. Nevertheless, it is hard to see how human flourishing can be fostered without personal autonomy. Once again we are dealing with the problem of individual and society. It is accepted here that our human needs should be understood, not as something natural or essential, but as expressing (basically, but not exclusively, in a symbolic way) the interests, values, traditions and material possibilities of a given society, at a given time.

However, this is not a passive process. Individuals are not passive receptacles that reflect (in a certain historical way) a given society in which they are members. On the contrary, there is always a complex feedback between individual-society. But this feedback is not exclusively a natural one. We are not biologically determined as other animals are. We can build our future relatively although we cannot choose our starting conditions. The Rule of Law is a model for shaping ourselves and our societies and also a model shaped and modified by ourselves. In this respect, I would like to emphasize that we should not expect "fidelity to law" on the exclusive basis of formal models of Rule of Law. If "fidelity to law" is a good thing to strive for, we should rely on relatively thick models of Rule of Law able to include, not only procedures, but some substantive moral principles for enhancing seriously personal autonomy.

Law and Philosophy Library

1. E. Bulygin, J.-L. Gardies and I. Niiniluoto (eds.): *Man, Law and Modern Forms of Life.* With an Introduction by M.D. Bayles. 1985 ISBN 90-277-1869-5
2. W. Sadurski: *Giving Desert Its Due.* Social Justice and Legal Theory. 1985 ISBN 90-277-1941-1
3. N. MacCormick and O. Weinberger: *An Institutional Theory of Law.* New Approaches to Legal Positivism. 1986 ISBN 90-277-2079-7
4. A. Aarnio: *The Rational as Reasonable.* A Treatise on Legal Justification. 1987 ISBN 90-277-2276-5
5. M.D. Bayles: *Principles of Law.* A Normative Analysis. 1987 ISBN 90-277-2412-1; Pb: 90-277-2413-X
6. A. Soeteman: *Logic in Law.* Remarks on Logic and Rationality in Normative Reasoning, Especially in Law. 1989 ISBN 0-7923-0042-4
7. C.T. Sistare: *Responsibility and Criminal Liability.* 1989 ISBN 0-7923-0396-2
8. A. Peczenik: *On Law and Reason.* 1989 ISBN 0-7923-0444-6
9. W. Sadurski: *Moral Pluralism and Legal Neutrality.* 1990 ISBN 0-7923-0565-5
10. M.D. Bayles: *Procedural Justice.* Allocating to Individuals. 1990 ISBN 0-7923-0567-1
11. P. Nerhot (ed.): *Law, Interpretation and Reality.* Essays in Epistemology, Hermeneutics and Jurisprudence. 1990 ISBN 0-7923-0593-0
12. A.W. Norrie: *Law, Ideology and Punishment.* Retrieval and Critique of the Liberal Ideal of Criminal Justice. 1991 ISBN 0-7923-1013-6
13. P. Nerhot (ed.): *Legal Knowledge and Analogy.* Fragments of Legal Epistemology, Hermeneutics and Linguistics. 1991 ISBN 0-7923-1065-9
14. O. Weinberger: *Law, Institution and Legal Politics.* Fundamental Problems of Legal Theory and Social Philosophy. 1991 ISBN 0-7923-1143-4
15. J. Wróblewski: *The Judicial Application of Law.* Edited by Z. Bańkowski and N. MacCormick. 1992 ISBN 0-7923-1569-3
16. T. Wilhelmsson: *Critical Studies in Private Law.* A Treatise on Need-Rational Principles in Modern Law. 1992 ISBN 0-7923-1659-2
17. M.D. Bayles: *Hart's Legal Philosophy.* An Examination. 1992 ISBN 0-7923-1981-8
18. D.W.P. Ruiter: *Institutional Legal Facts.* Legal Powers and their Effects. 1993 ISBN 0-7923-2441-2
19. J. Schonsheck: *On Criminalization.* An Essay in the Philosophy of the Criminal Law. 1994 ISBN 0-7923-2663-6
20. R.P. Malloy and J. Evensky (eds.): *Adam Smith and the Philosophy of Law and Economics.* 1994 ISBN 0-7923-2796-9
21. Z. Bańkowski, I. White and U. Hahn (eds.): *Informatics and the Foundations of Legal Reasoning.* 1995 ISBN 0-7923-3455-8

Law and Philosophy Library

22. E. Lagerspetz: *The Opposite Mirrors*. An Essay on the Conventionalist Theory of Institutions. 1995 ISBN 0-7923-3325-X

23. M. van Hees: *Rights and Decisions*. Formal Models of Law and Liberalism. 1995 ISBN 0-7923-3754-9

24. B. Anderson: *"Discovery" in Legal Decision-Making*. 1996 ISBN 0-7923-3981-9

25. S. Urbina: *Reason, Democracy, Society*. A Study on the Basis of Legal Thinking. 1996 ISBN 0-7923-4262-3

26. E. Attwooll: *The Tapestry of the Law*. Scotland, Legal Culture and Legal Theory. 1997 ISBN 0-7923-4310-7

27. J.C. Hage: *Reasoning with Rules*. An Essay on Legal Reasoning and Its Underlying Logic. 1997 ISBN 0-7923-4325-5

28. R.A. Hillman: *The Richness of Contract Law*. An Analysis and Critique of Contemporary Theories of Contract Law. 1997 ISBN 0-7923-4336-0; 0-7923-5063-4 (Pb)

29. C. Wellman: *An Approach to Rights*. Studies in the Philosophy of Law and Morals. 1997 ISBN 0-7923-4467-7

30. B. van Roermund: *Law, Narrative and Reality*. An Essay in Intercepting Politics. 1997 ISBN 0-7923-4621-1

31. I. Ward: *Kantianism, Postmodernism and Critical Legal Thought*. 1997 ISBN 0-7923-4745-5

32. H. Prakken: *Logical Tools for Modelling Legal Argument*. A Study of Defeasible Reasoning in Law. 1997 ISBN 0-7923-4776-5

33. T. May: *Autonomy, Authority and Moral Responsibility*. 1998 ISBN 0-7923-4851-6

34. M. Atienza and J.R. Manero: *A Theory of Legal Sentences*. 1998 ISBN 0-7923-4856-7

35. E.A. Christodoulidis: *Law and Reflexive Politics*. 1998 ISBN 0-7923-4954-7

36. L.M.M. Royakkers: *Extending Deontic Logic for the Formalisation of Legal Rules*. 1998 ISBN 0-7923-4982-2

37. J.J. Moreso: *Legal Indeterminacy and Constitutional Interpretation*. 1998 ISBN 0-7923-5156-8

38. W. Sadurski: *Freedom of Speech and Its Limits*. 1999 ISBN 0-7923-5523-7

39. J. Wolenski (ed.): *Kazimierz Opalek Selected Papers in Legal Philosophy*. 1999 ISBN 0-7923-5732-9

40. H.P. Visser 't Hooft: *Justice to Future Generations and the Environment*. 1999 ISBN 0-7923-5756-6

41. L.J. Wintgens (ed.): *The Law in Philosophical Perspectives*. My Philosophy of Law. 1999 ISBN 0-7923-5796-5

42. A.R. Lodder: *DiaLaw*. On Legal Justification and Dialogical Models of Argumentation. 1999 ISBN 0-7923-5830-9

43. C. Redondo: *Reasons for Action and the Law*. 1999 ISBN 0-7923-5912-7

Law and Philosophy Library

Volumes 1–55 were published by Kluwer Academic Publishers.

KLUWER LAW INTERNATIONAL – THE HAGUE / LONDON / NEW YORK

Lightning Source UK Ltd.
Milton Keynes UK
14 June 2010

155578UK00004B/115/A

9 789041 118707